MYP by Concept
4 & 5

Individuals & Societies

Andy Dailey
Danielle Farmer
Emily Giles
Robbie Woodburn

MYP by Concept
4 & 5

Individuals & Societies

Andy Dailey
Danielle Farmer
Emily Giles
Robbie Woodburn

Author acknowledgements

Andy Dailey: In remembrance of my parents Shirley Angela Burress Dailey (1948–2017) and Charles Kenneth Dailey (1942–2018). A special thank you to Kareem Almusharaf for indispensable assistance.

Danielle Farmer: Many thanks to my husband Rob for all his support in looking after our children while I wrote this! I would also like to thank the publishing team at Hodder and project manager, Estelle, for all of their continued efforts in getting this book published.

Emily Giles: This book is dedicated in loving memory of my mother, Aagje Giles Creutzberg.

Robbie Woodburn: I would like to thank my father and mother for their love and unwavering support through this process. I hope that this text serves to inspire students to conduct further inquiry-based learning into the topics introduced through these chapters.

Although every effort has been made to ensure that website addresses are correct at time of going to press, Hodder Education cannot be held responsible for the content of any website mentioned in this book. It is sometimes possible to find a relocated web page by typing in the address of the home page for a website in the URL window of your browser.

Hachette UK's policy is to use papers that are natural, renewable and recyclable products and made from wood grown in well-managed forests and other controlled sources. The logging and manufacturing processes are expected to conform to the environmental regulations of the country of origin.

Orders: please contact Hachette UK Distribution, Hely Hutchinson Centre, Milton Road, Didcot, Oxfordshire, OX11 7HH. Telephone: +44 (0)1235 827827. Email education@hachette.co.uk. Lines are open from 9 a.m. to 5 p.m., Monday to Friday. You can also order through our website: www.hoddereducation.com

© Andy Dailey, Danielle Farmer, Emily Giles, Robbie Woodburn 2020

Published by Hodder Education
An Hachette UK Company
Carmelite House, 50 Victoria Embankment, London EC4Y 0DZ

Impression number   7
Year   2024

All rights reserved. Apart from any use permitted under UK copyright law, no part of this publication may be reproduced or transmitted in any form or by any means, electronic or mechanical, including photocopying and recording, or held within any information storage and retrieval system, without permission in writing from the publisher or under licence from the Copyright Licensing Agency Limited. Further details of such licences (for reprographic reproduction) may be obtained from the Copyright Licensing Agency Limited, www.cla.co.uk.

Cover photo © Shutterstock / AndreAnita
Illustrations by DC Graphic Design Limited, Hextable, Kent
Typeset in Frutiger LT Std 45 Light 10/14pt by DC Graphic Design Limited, Hextable, Kent
Printed in Dubai

A catalogue record for this title is available from the British Library

ISBN 9781510425798

Contents

1. Why do individuals form social groups? ... 2
2. Why are empires formed? ... 26
3. How do empires work? ... 46
4. How do empires fall? ... 80
5. What impact do humans have on natural environments? ... 110
6. How does population change affect individuals and societies? ... 144
7. Can urban systems and environments be managed sustainably? ... 168
8. How do we decide what to produce? ... 188
9. Can we make a fairer world through trade? ... 218
10. How can developing countries successfully increase standards of living? ... 244
11. Is our exploitation of the Earth sustainable? ... 264
12. How has our perspective changed now? ... 294

Glossary ... 310

Acknowledgements ... 314

Index ... 316

How to use this book

Welcome to Hodder Education's *MYP by Concept* series! Each chapter is designed to lead you through an *inquiry* into the concepts of Individuals and Societies, and how they interact in real-life global contexts.

The *Statement of Inquiry* provides the framework for this inquiry, and the *Inquiry* questions then lead us through the exploration as they are developed through each chapter.

Each chapter is framed with a *Key concept*, *Related concept* and set in a *Global context*.

KEY WORDS

Key words are included to give you access to vocabulary for the topic. **Glossary terms** are highlighted and, where applicable, search terms are given to encourage independent learning and research skills.

As you explore, activities suggest ways to learn through *action*.

■ ATL

Activities are designed to develop your *Approaches to Learning* (ATL) skills.

Key *Approaches to Learning* skills for MYP Individuals and Societies are highlighted whenever we encounter them.

◆ Assessment opportunities in this chapter:

Some activities are *formative* as they allow you to practise certain parts of the MYP Individuals and Societies *Assessment Objectives*. Other activities can be used by you or your teachers to assess your achievement *summatively* against all parts of an assessment objective.

Hint

In some of the activities, we provide hints to help you work on the assignment. This also introduces you to the new Hint feature in the on-screen assessment.

Definitions are included for important terms and information boxes are included to give background information, more detail and explanation.

EXTENSION

Extension activities allow you to explore a topic further.

▼ Links to:
Like any other subject, Individuals and Societies is just one part of our bigger picture of the world. Links to other subjects are discussed.

We will reflect on this learner profile attribute …
- Each chapter has an *IB learner profile* attribute as its theme, and you are encouraged to reflect on these too.

Finally, at the end of the chapter you are asked to reflect back on what you have learned with our *Reflection table*, maybe to think of new questions brought to light by your learning.

Use this table to reflect on your own learning in this chapter.					
Questions we asked	Answers we found	Any further questions now?			
Factual					
Conceptual					
Debatable					
Approaches to learning you used in this chapter	Description – what new skills did you learn?	How well did you master the skills?			
		Novice	Learner	Practitioner	Expert
Communication skills					
Critical-thinking skills					
Transfer skills					
Learner profile attribute(s)	Reflect on the importance of the attribute for your learning in this chapter.				
Knowledgeable					

You are prompted to consider your conceptual understanding in a variety of activities throughout each chapter.

We have incorporated Visible Thinking – ideas, framework, protocol and thinking routines – from Project Zero at the Harvard Graduate School of Education into many of our activities.

! Take action

! While the book provides opportunities for action and plenty of content to enrich the conceptual relationships, you must be an active part of this process. Guidance is given to help you with your own research, including how to carry out research, guidance on forming your own research questions, as well as linking and developing your study of Individuals and Societies to the global issues in our twenty-first century world.

Time, place and space | Culture; Identity; Perspective | Orientation in space and time

1 Why do individuals form social groups?

Individuals can change the **world they inherit**, but to do so they must understand how **human societies and environments depend on each other.**

CONSIDER THESE QUESTIONS:

Factual: What is equality?

Conceptual: Why do people form social groups? How does the structure of social groups promote the participation of individuals? How and why do social groups behave in a similar way? What impact do social groups have on the sustainability of resources? How does culture shape individuals and their societies? What role has social media played in shaping society? How do we study Individuals and Societies?

Debatable: Why is it important to explore different cultures?

Now **share and compare** your thoughts and ideas with your partner, or with the whole class.

■ **Figure 1.1 (a)** Chad's ancient Ennedi cave paintings; **(b)** Pieter Breugel's *Netherlandish Proverbs*, 1559; **(c)** N. Tomoya's painting, *Toronto*

IN THIS CHAPTER WE WILL ...

- **Find out** about the ways we study Individuals and Societies.
- **Explore** concepts that help explain the relationships between individuals and societies.
- **Take action** by discussing how our society has changed in positive and negative ways.

Individuals & Societies for the IB MYP 4&5: by Concept

These Approaches to Learning (ATL) skills will be useful …

- Communication skills
- Information literacy skills
- Critical-thinking skills
- Creative-thinking skills

We will reflect on this learner profile attribute …

- Thinkers – thinking critically and creatively about the role of individuals in social groups.

Assessment opportunities in this chapter:

- **Criterion A**: Knowing and understanding
- **Criterion B**: Investigating
- **Criterion C**: Communicating
- **Criterion D**: Thinking critically

KEY WORDS

culture
judicial system
penal system
society

THINK–PAIR–SHARE

Look at the images in Figure 1.1a, b and c.

Can you **identify** similarities and differences between the types of societies depicted here?

Discuss the differences you have identified with your learning partner. What has changed in the world since these pictures were created? What has stayed the same?

Share your ideas as a class and **summarize** your ideas.

1 Why do individuals form social groups?

Why do individuals form social groups?

Archaeological evidence suggests that our species – *Homo sapiens* – has been a 'social animal' ever since it appeared, as long as 300,000 years ago, according to recent evidence. It seems that this was also true of our earlier ancestors, known as the **hominids** or **hominins**. The study of evolutionary biology suggests that some kinds of behaviour might be **inherited** because they provide some kind of advantage. So, what might be the advantages of living in a group?

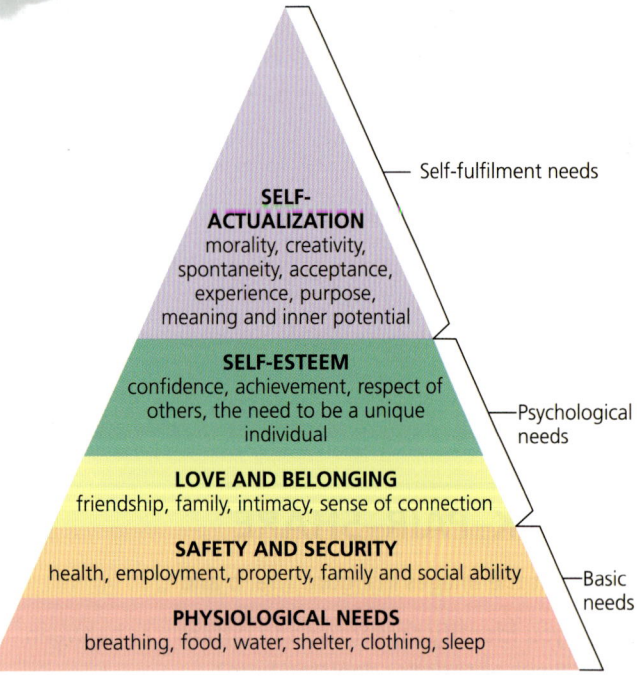

■ **Figure 1.2** Maslow's hierarchy of needs

Abraham Maslow was a psychologist who developed the hierarchy of needs during the 1940s and 1950s as a psychological model to understand what motivates us. Maslow suggested that our most basic need is to survive and feel safe, and this requires that our food, water, warmth and rest needs are met. Our early ancestors would have struggled to meet these needs all the time. Once these needs are met, the rest are to do with our psychological makeup, and are what make us different from most other animal species. Our desire to receive acknowledgement from others, and to gain a sense of fulfilment throughout our lives motivates the way we interact with others. You will know this to be true from your own behaviour and the way you interact with your friends at school.

One problem with Maslow's choice of a hierarchical model is that it suggests that we cannot meet some needs without other needs being met first. It is certainly true that we can do very little if we are not fed, watered or have some form of shelter, but it is worth considering how far our social interactions with each other and our social group are necessary for our basic survival.

Being part of a social group allows us to achieve the needs laid out in Maslow's hierarchy. Working together enables us to find or make food, keep each other safe from harm, give each other the sense of belonging, but also allows us to feel that we each play an important role in shaping our own future and that of the group.

While social groups might confer benefits on individuals, they may also limit the behaviour of individuals in certain ways in order that the social group remains stable and functional. This means that some social groups develop ways to 'manage' or control the behaviour of their members. Various theories exist to explain how this happens.

How does the structure of social groups promote the participation of individuals?

DURKHEIM AND THE SIZE AND COMPLEXITY OF SOCIAL UNITS

Émile Durkheim was an early **sociologist** who studied the way social groups form, how they change and what drives interaction between individuals.

The main causes for change to social groups are, according to Durkheim in his book *Division*, changing **population density** and technology. Changing population density (more on this can be found in Chapter 5) brings people physically closer together and technology changes the way that people communicate with each other. The way in which people interact with each other, and how often they do this, was referred to as **moral density**. Durkheim's exploration of changing social units, as a result of increased moral density, led him to try to explain the changing roles that individuals play in the social group that they belong to.

Small groups, such as ancient nomadic communities, are made up of a closely knit group of individuals, who together form close bonds with each other. They resemble each other in many ways, practise the same cultural behaviours and share the same views. Durkheim termed the nature of the relationship between individuals in this type of group **mechanical solidarity**. Individuals in the group work closely together to ensure basic needs are met, hunting for and gathering food, repairing shelters and defending their shared interests. Individuals perform multiple functions in the group and can share the workload between them.

In larger groups that live together in towns and cities, the bonds that keep people working together change. As the population increases, each individual has to find a way to keep playing an important role so that they can continue to be part of the community. Competition for resources is more fierce, and the amount of resources available starts to decrease. Thus the tasks that individuals perform must become more specialized. In today's society, we train and become educated in order to get jobs that are all very different from each other, and don't much resemble the jobs that were needed in hunter-gatherer societies. This reduces competition between individuals, and allows for harmonious

■ **Figure 1.3** Women from the Karen tribes of north Thailand

interaction within a much larger population because everyone relies on each other to complete the particular, specialized kind of work that each individual does. Without this specialization, it would become more difficult to distribute resources within the group. This process of specialization leads to what Durkheim described as **organic solidarity**.

As societies grow in size, the role of the individual changes dramatically. In groups with mechanical solidarity, individuals share similar behavioural characteristics. Their attitudes are similar, and these likely derive from a shared set of beliefs or religious system. Groups characterized by mechanical solidarity are often organized around strong **kinship** ties. In groups with organic solidarity, individuals are much less similar. They don't perform the same tasks as each other, and live more separately. Religious systems and kinship become less important drivers of behaviour, and individuals exert more free will over their own choices. Formal structures, such as judicial and penal systems, need to exist to ensure that communities can continue to live harmoniously.

MEET A SIGNIFICANT INDIVIDUAL: ÉMILE DURKHEIM (1858–1917)

Along with Karl Marx and Max Weber, Émile Durkheim was one of the fathers of sociology. Born in the Lorraine region, France, in 1858, Durkheim was an excellent student at school and developed a strong work ethic that enabled him to gain entrance at the École Normale Supérieure in Paris. Eventually he taught at the University of Bordeaux and the Sorbonne. His efforts were concentrated on developing the study of society as a single discipline, rather than rooted in philosophy or history. He saw the study of what is now known as sociology as an easily defined subject in its own right. Durkheim lived during a time when France was undergoing significant social upheaval. As a result of the increasing prominence of the natural sciences at that time, there was a fast-developing **trend** to study society's problems in a scientific way in order to find their solutions, and this was encouraged through national government policy. In addition, there was a breakdown in national unity in the country, and a rise of the role of the individual.

The Dreyfus Affair of 1894 was an incident of anti-semitism and miscarriage of justice against a captain of the French army, Alfred Dreyfus, who was falsely accused of communicating military secrets to the Germans. The Dreyfus Affair was extremely fractious and exposed many differences in opinion that had, until that point, remained relatively underreported. It led to an intense focus on the rights of an individual and their priority ahead of the needs of the state. The press played a pivotal role in shaping the debate and questioned the actions of the government in response to the affair. Durkheim saw this as a clear indication that the rise of the individual takes place at the expense of social cohesion.

ECONOMIC SYSTEMS FOR ALLOCATING SCARCE RESOURCES

Our planet only has a finite number of resources. These also exist in finite quantities. The wants and needs of human beings are potentially limitless, however, and we must find ways of allocating resources between competing uses. In small, simple social groups, this is relatively easy in the sense that there is less competition for resources between individuals. As we have seen, small groups organize themselves in a communal way, working together to meet the needs of the group. In complex societies, where people are more individualistic, and don't work together to meet the needs of the entire group, different systems of allocating resources are needed. The following four broad categories can be useful in thinking about the differences between economic systems:

- **slavery**
- **feudalism**
- **capitalism**
- **communism**.

Slavery

Many societies have made use of slavery to accomplish their objectives. This is the most violent of the four systems listed above. Individuals are deprived of their right to freedom, and are forced into work by a person to whom society has granted the power. Often, enslaved people belonged to particular groups of people (e.g. Jewish people in Ancient Egypt, or enslaved African people in the British empire). Enslaved people have been used as servants in the home, in the production of crops and for construction of buildings and monuments.

Figure 1.4 An ancient Roman fresco found in Pompeii, Italy, of a conversation between a family and their slave

Figure 1.5 A Union soldier stands with black Americans on the plantation Thomas F. Drayton, Hilton Head Island, South Carolina, 1862. Photo by Henry P. Moore, May 1862

Feudalism

Feudalism was a system predominantly in place in Medieval Europe, but also in other places such as Russia until Tsar Alexander II emancipated the serfs in 1861, and in Japan until the start of the Meiji period in 1868. Broadly, this is a system of organizing production based on hereditary rule and land ownership. There was usually a monarch, who had either inherited the title or acquired it by some claim of right to it, and a group of landowners who managed production in the society. Production was mostly agricultural, together with some manufacturing of tools, weapons, textiles and carpentry items. The landowners also had hereditary titles which they could pass on to their descendants.

The rest of the population were peasants, or serfs, who had few rights, and were tied to the land where they lived. They were essentially enslaved to the landowner, without being property of the landowner. Without the freedom to move to places offering better situations, and without the education to build better circumstances for themselves, these people were left with little choice but to work the land and produce food and other goods for the landowners.

Capitalism

Capitalism is an economic system of production that is employed throughout most of the world today. In this system, ownership is of capital, rather than land as in the feudal system. Owners of capital, or capitalists, use the capital and employ workers to help turn raw materials into something of use or exchange value that can be sold. Most people work for businesses, which at some point were started by entrepreneurs and are still being invested in by owners of capital.

Although it is common around the world, there are detractors of capitalism. Moral philosopher Adam Smith said:

> 'It is not from the benevolence of the butcher, the brewer, or the baker, that we expect our dinner, but from their regard to their own interest. We address ourselves, not to their humanity but to their self-love, and never talk to them of our necessities but of their advantages.'

Communism

For some individuals alive during the Industrial Revolution in Europe, the changes they witnessed were not positive. European writers such as Pierre-Joseph Proudhon, Pyotr Kropotkin, Karl Marx and Friedrich Engels all wrote critically of the capitalist Industrial Revolution and explored the historical development of the capitalist system. Their revelations about the system led them to see it as no less oppressive of the average individual than slavery or feudalism.

What is equality?

> **DISCUSS**
>
> To what extent are today's differences in income inequality still a legacy of the systems of slavery and feudalism?

> **THINK–PAIR–SHARE**
>
> Read Source A from *Utopia for Realists* by Rutger Bregman. Today, there are many people, organizations and governments working to improve the lives of people who experience daily hardship. Do you think we will ever be able to eradicate poverty? What barriers currently prevent people from escaping poverty? Write some of your thoughts down, share them with a partner and **discuss** with the rest of the class.

They argued that because production's purpose is not for consumption straight away, but for trade and exchange, the worker has no choice but to enter into a relationship with the owner of the means of production. In other words, workers are no longer producing their own food, equipment, etc. needed for daily survival, but they must instead work to earn a wage to buy those items.

Marx viewed this relationship between the worker and his production in an extremely negative way:

> 'First, the fact that labour is external to the worker, i.e. it does not belong to his essential being; that in his work, therefore, he does not affirm himself but denies himself, does not feel content but unhappy, does not develop freely his physical and mental energy but mortifies his body and ruins his mind. The worker only feels outside himself. He is at home when he is not working, and when he is working he is not at home. His labour is therefore not voluntary, but coerced: it is forced labour.' – *Marx*, The Economic and Philosophic Manuscripts

Given that labourers are the sole owners of their own labour power, and that capitalists have no means of turning resources into things with value without labourers, Marx and others thought that power should be in the hands of the workers. As capitalists competed increasingly strongly with each other for profits, which would eventually cause them to lower workers' wages, it was predicted that workers would rise up against the capitalists and overthrow the capitalist system. Where private property rights protected capitalists' ability to generate profit from what they owned, under communism there would be no private property, so that any surplus value generated by economic activity would be shared and owned by all citizens.

SOURCE A

'Let's start with a little history lesson:

In the past, everything was worse.

For roughly 99% of the world's history, 99% of humanity was poor, hungry, dirty, afraid, stupid, sick and ugly. As recently as the seventeenth century, the French philosopher Blaise Pascal (1623–62) described life as one giant vale of tears. "Humanity is great," he wrote, "because it knows itself to be wretched." In Britain, fellow philosopher Thomas Hobbes (1588–1679) concurred that human life was basically "solitary, poor, nasty, brutish and short."

But in the last 200 years, all of that has changed. In just a fraction of the time that our species has clocked on this planet, billions of us are suddenly rich, well nourished, clean, safe, smart, healthy and occasionally even beautiful. Where 84% of the world's population still lived in extreme poverty in 1820, by 1981 that percentage has dropped to 44% and now, just a few decades later, it is under 10%.

If this trend holds, the extreme poverty that has been an abiding feature of life will soon be eradicated for good.'

The opening paragraphs of Utopia for Realists: And how can we get there *(2017), by Rutger Bregman*

EQUALITY VERSUS EQUITY

The terms 'equality' and 'equity' may sound similar, but they do not have the same meaning. **Equality** would be achieved if everyone earned the same in society. We also talk about gender equality, which means no discrimination in pay or treatment based on gender. **Equity**, on the other hand, means fairness.

ACTIVITY: How equal do we want the world to be?

ATL

- Communication skills: Take effective notes in class

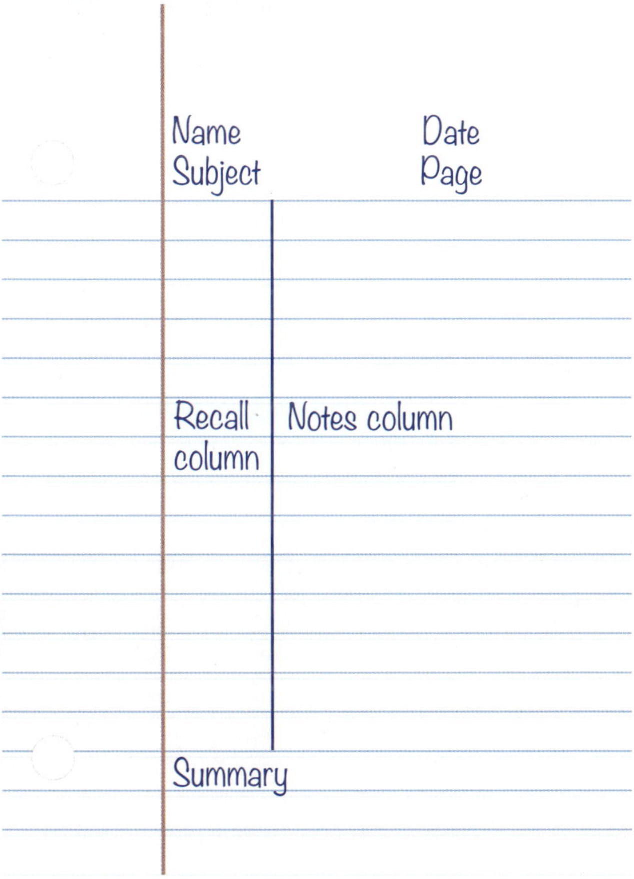

Divide your page as shown in Figure 1.6. On the left-hand side, you write headings or questions, and on the right-hand side you write your notes or answers to the questions. When you have finished taking notes, you write a short summary of what you have read or watched.

Search for **How equal do we want the world to be?** by Dan Ariely at www.ted.com/talks/ Watch the talk.

Take notes on the following questions as you watch:
- **What role do our 'preconceived notions and expectations' play in shaping our perspectives?**
- **How do we use percentage shares of the population to measure wealth inequality?**
- **What is a 'knowledge gap'?**
- **What is John Rawls known for saying?**
- **What is the 'desirability gap'?**
- **Do the results differ if the same questions are asked of different groups?**
- **What lessons can we learn from conducting this research?**

Summarize the video in the box at the bottom of your notes.

Read the accompanying blog post called 'The data shows we want to end inequality. Here's how to start ...'.

With a different colour pen, can you add anything to your notes that would improve them?

■ Figure 1.6 Cornell note-taking

Assessment opportunities

◆ In this activity you have practised skills that are assessed using Criterion A: Knowing and understanding.

Using different note-taking techniques

Note-taking is an important skill to acquire, and students often think it is just a question of copying information down. The Cornell method forces you to think about how the notes are organized, and to become more active in the note-taking process.

This means that note-taking is not just about creating a resource to study from, but becomes part of the learning process itself. You can use the page to test yourself on key material by covering up the right-hand side of the page.

MEET A SIGNIFICANT INDIVIDUAL: DAN ARIELY (1967–PRESENT)

Dan Ariely is an Israeli economist who teaches behavioural economics at Duke University in the USA. Born in New York but returning to Israel at age 3, Ariely suffered from third-degree burns over 70 per cent of his body after flammable materials he was using for a night-time ceremony called *ktovet esh* exploded. His difficult recovery, which included the extremely painful daily removal of bandages and bathing of wounds, led him to ask questions about how to help patients deal with the unavoidable pain associated with some medical procedures. As he continued his studies in this area, he was 'learning more and more about decision making and behavioral economics, [and] realized that this knowledge is relevant to many aspects of our life, from financial decision-making, to health, to better habits, and even to better personal life' (danariely.com). He is the author of the tremendously successful books *Dollars and Sense*, *Predictably Irrational*, *The Upside of Irrationality*, and *The Honest Truth about Dishonesty* (which has been made into a documentary available on Netflix).

Links to: Mathematics

The role of income taxes

Most countries tax people on their incomes. This system of direct taxation is designed to redistribute incomes and raise tax revenue for governments to use to fund essential services. The system of charging those on higher incomes at a higher rate is called a **progressive tax system**. How much these tax rates should be is a heavily contested but also often misunderstood topic. This is because of the difference between a **marginal rate of tax** and an **average rate of tax**.

Take a look at the Australian tax rates in Table 1.1 below.

■ **Table 1.1** Tax rates for Australia for the tax year 2018/19

Income	Marginal tax rate (%)	Tax payable
$0–$18,200	0	Nil
$18,201–$37,000	19	19 cents for each $1 over $18,200
$37,001–$90,000	32.5	$3,572 plus 32.5 cents for each dollar over $37,000
$90,001–$180,000	37	$20,797 plus 37 cents for each dollar over $90,000
$180,001 and above	45	$54,097 plus 45 cents for each dollar over $180,000

The *marginal tax rate* refers to the tax rate paid on the income earned in a particular tax bracket. For example, a person earning $30,000 will pay nothing on the first $18,200 but will pay 19 per cent of every dollar earned within the bracket $18,201–$37,000.

To work out how much this person must pay as a share of their income, we must perform the following calculation:

(0 x $18,200) + (0.19 x $11,800) = $2,242

($2,242 / $30,000) x 100 = 7.47%

Therefore, the *average tax rate* that this person pays is 7.47 per cent while they are paying the 19 per cent marginal tax rate. This means that the amount people pay as a share of their income is always much lower than the quoted marginal rate.

This also means that a person getting a pay rise from $30,000 to $38,000 will not suddenly start paying 32.5 per cent on all their income, but will only pay that percentage on each dollar between $37,001 and $38,000.

ACTIVITY: Calculating income tax rates

■ **ATL**

■ Information literacy skills: Process data and report results

Using the marginal tax rates for Australia in Table 1.1, calculate the amount of tax paid and the average rates of tax for people earning the following incomes:

1 $38,000   2 $85,000   3 $120,000   4 $190,000

◆ **Assessment opportunities**

◆ In this activity you have practised skills that are assessed using Criterion A: Knowing and understanding.

THE FUTURE OF THE WORKFORCE AND AUTOMATION

Since the Industrial Revolution, people have been able to increasingly mechanize production and improve **productivity**. This happened with the development of the coal-fired engine, the use of steel in construction, telecommunications and the internet. While the gains in productivity and **economic growth** have been significant, each time an **investment** boom was followed by an economic bust and increased **unemployment** caused by the resulting obsolescence of jobs (some jobs no longer existed).

Great surge		Installation period 'Gilded Age' bubbles	Turning point Recessions	Deployment period 'Golden Ages'
1st	**1771** Industrial Revolution Britain	Canal mania	1793–97	Great British leap
2nd	**1829** Age of steam and railways Britain (Europe and USA)	Railway mania	1848–50	Victorian boom
3rd	**1875** Age of electricity, steel and heavy engineering USA, Germany (Britain)	Global market infrastructure build-up	1890–95	Belle Époque (Europe) 'Progressive Era' (USA)
4th	**1908** Age of cars, oil and mass production USA (Germany/Europe)	The roaring twenties: housing, cars, radio, aviation, electricity	Europe 1929–33 USA 1929–43	Post-war Golden Age
5th	**1971** Information, telecommunications, biotechnology, nanotechnology USA (Europe and Asia)	Emerging markets, dotcom and internet mania, financial casino	2001–???	Sustainable global knowledge society 'golden age'?

■ Figure 1.7 Technology surges create bubbles and lead to busts

MEET A SIGNIFICANT INDIVIDUAL: CARLOTA PEREZ (1939–PRESENT)

Carlota Perez is a British Venezuelan economist who studies the role of technology in economics and development. She teaches at the London School of Economics and the Tallinn University of Technology. Her work is based on the ideas of Nikolai Kondratieff and Joseph Schumpeter. Economic growth follows patterns of rise and fall, both in the short and longer term. These longer waves of economic activity, lasting approximately 50 years, follow the development and installation of new technology or institutional frameworks. Perez argues that we are in the middle of the installation period and turning points of a tech wave that has burst (and may even burst again before the wave is finished). She also argues that the positive outlook for this wave can only be achieved if there is significant global investment in sustainable technology. Listen to her discuss these issues in a talk called 'Tackling Global Challenges Through Mission Oriented Innovation' with Mariana Mazzucato and Jeffrey Sachs at the Royal Society of Arts on 7th February 2017 https://soundcloud.com/the_rsa/tackling-global-challenges-through-mission-oriented-innovation

1 Why do individuals form social groups?

ACTIVITY: The case for a universal basic income

ATL

- Critical-thinking skills: Evaluate evidence and arguments

There are some who argue that the safest way to protect workers from unemployment as a result of advances in robotics and automation in the workplace is to provide everyone with a universal basic income. This is a guaranteed minimum payment that is paid to everyone. The thinking behind this idea is that it will allow low-income earners to earn a fair amount, and allow recently unemployed workers to take their time to find work again rather than rushing for fear of losing benefits.

- **Use** Source A to **describe** what Keynes envisaged for working lives.
- **Interpret** the message of Source B.
- **Compare and contrast** the similarities and differences between Sources B and C.
- In groups of three, each pick a source and then **summarize** that source by copying and completing Table 1.2.

■ Table 1.2 Origin, purpose, values and limitations of sources

Origin	
Who wrote the source?	
What is their nationality?	
What is the author's social background, e.g. rich / poor, level of education?	
What is the author's job?	
What is the author's political leaning, e.g. capitalist, communist, socialist, conservative, liberal etc.?	
Is it a primary or secondary source? How can you tell?	
Purpose	
Why was the source written?	
Who is the target audience for the source?	
What is the author trying to get the reader to think / believe?	
Values	
Why might the *origin* help make the source useful to historians studying universal basic income?	
Why might the *purpose* help make the source useful to historians studying universal basic income?	
Why might the *content* help make the source useful to historians studying universal basic income?	
Limitations	
Why might the *origin* of the source be a limitation to historians studying universal basic income?	
Why might the *purpose* of the source be a limitation to historians studying universal basic income?	
Why might the *content* of the source be a limitation to historians studying universal basic income?	

◆ Assessment opportunities

- In this activity you have practised skills that are assessed using Criterion D: Thinking critically.

SOURCE A

'I see us free, therefore, to return to some of the most sure and certain principles of religion and traditional virtue – that avarice is a vice, that the exaction of usury is a misdemeanour, and the love of money is detestable, that those walk most truly in the paths of virtue and sane wisdom who take least thought for the morrow. We shall once more value ends above means and prefer the good to the useful. We shall honour those who can teach us how to pluck the hour and the day virtuously and well, the delightful people who are capable of taking direct enjoyment in things, the lilies of the field who toil not, neither do they spin.

But beware! The time for all this is not yet. For at least another hundred years we must pretend to ourselves and to every one that fair is foul and foul is fair; for foul is useful and fair is not. Avarice and usury and precaution must be our gods for a little longer still. For only they can lead us out of the tunnel of economic necessity into daylight.

I look forward, therefore, in days not so very remote, to the greatest change which has ever occurred in the material environment of life for human beings in the aggregate. But, of course, it will all happen gradually, not as a catastrophe. Indeed, it has already begun. The course of affairs will simply be that there will be ever larger and larger classes and groups of people from whom problems of economic necessity have been practically removed. The critical difference will be realised when this condition has become so general that the nature of one's duty to one's neighbour is changed. For it will remain reasonable to be economically purposive for others after it has ceased to be reasonable for oneself.

The pace at which we can reach our destination of economic bliss will be governed by four things – our power to control population, our determination to avoid wars and civil dissensions, our willingness to entrust to science the direction of those matters which are properly the concern of science, and the rate of accumulation as fixed by the margin between our production and our consumption; of which the last will easily look after itself, given the first three.'

An excerpt from The Economic Possibilities for our Grandchildren *by John Maynard Keynes, 1930*

SOURCE B

'Dana Bowman, 56, expresses gratitude for fresh produce at least 10 times in the hour and a half we're having coffee on a frigid spring day in Lindsay, Ontario. Over the many years she scraped by on government disability payments, she tended to stick to frozen vegetables. She'd also save by visiting a food bank or buying marked-down items near or past their sell-by date.

But since December, Bowman has felt secure enough to buy fresh fruit and vegetables. She's freer, she says, to "do what nanas do" for her grandchildren, like having all four of them over for turkey on Easter. Now that she can afford the transportation, she might start taking classes in social work in a nearby city. She feels happier and healthier – and, she says, so do many other people in her subsidized apartment building and around town. "I'm seeing people smiling and seeing people friendlier, saying hi more," she says.

What changed? Lindsay, a compact rectangle amid the lakes northeast of Toronto, is at the heart of one of the world's biggest tests of a guaranteed basic income. In a three-year pilot funded by the provincial government, about 4,000 people in Ontario are getting monthly stipends to boost them to at least 75 percent of the poverty line. That translates to a minimum annual income of $17,000 in Canadian dollars (about $13,000 US) for single people, $24,000 for married couples. Lindsay has about half the people in the pilot – some 10 percent of the town's population.'

Excerpt from 'Basic income could work – if you do it Canada-style' in MIT Technology Review, *20 June 2018*

SOURCE C

A budget-neutral universal basic income would reduce poverty marginally but not provide greater guarantees that work pays, finds a study commissioned by the Finnish Ministry of Finance.

Heikki Viitamäki, a senior expert at the Ministry of Finance, on Friday revealed that although a universal basic income worth roughly 700 euros a month would boost the earnings of low-income earners and business owners, the positive impact would be negated by the tax hikes needed to fund the scheme. The scheme assessed in the study would guarantee pensioners a monthly basic income of 784.52 euros, students one of 220 euros and others one of 696.69 euros.

The scheme is comparable to the universal basic income proposals made in recent years to replace the existing minimum-level social security benefits in a way that if the previous benefits of a recipient exceeded the basic income, the exceeding amount would be paid to the recipient as an earnings-related benefit.

The basic income would cost a total of 37.5 billion euros a year and replace 18 billion euros worth of existing taxable social security benefits.

The beneficiaries of the scheme would be low-income earners and business owners, people without any income and people living on income derived from capital, whereas those hurt by the scheme would be earners and business owners in middle and high-income groups.

Advocates of universal basic income often argue that a basic income scheme would provide greater guarantees that work pays because the basic income would be unaffected by earnings. The study, however, found that the argument is unfounded as the profitability of work would not increase due to the tax hikes necessitated by the scheme.

Viitamäki added that basic income could have positive indirect effects, such as alleviating bureaucratic traps.

Excerpt from `Universal basic income wouldn't guarantee that work pays, finds study' from the Helsinki Times, *12 August 2019*

How and why do social groups behave in a similar way?

NORMS AND VALUES

What happens when a person acts against the needs of the social group? What happens when a person takes something away from the group, or commits an act of violence against the group, or threatens the source of their livelihood? All social groups have systems for sharing the expectations of people's behaviour, and some have a formalized set of consequences for when people step out of line.

For many societies today – and most societies in the past – religion plays an active part in determining the way in which people interact with each other. In ancient China, Confucius's teachings formed the basis of Chinese expectations for conduct from each other, in particular family members, and the treatment of elders. The Christian faith became the dominant faith in Europe after Emperor Constantine converted in 313 CE and later it was declared the main faith of the Roman empire in 380 CE. In the Middle East, Islam has been the dominant religion since the prophet Muhammad lived in the sixth century. There are of course many other religions that have shaped societies.

For centuries, religions have also been intrinsically linked with the governing of countries. Many countries today still have state religions, and use the laws of the faith to influence and determine the laws of the country. Other countries have secular legal systems that evolved from religious values but are not determined by any religious group or organization.

Legal systems, whether these are based on religion or not, are used by social groups to set standards for behaviour. Given that the survival and prosperity of the group relies on the decent participation of all individuals, laws make it unquestionably clear what kind of conduct will and will not be tolerated. They set the 'norms' for the social group, and influence the shared values in the community. The field of philosophy that studies our values is called normative ethics.

> **THINK–PAIR–SHARE**
>
> Consider the following situations:
> - You see someone committing an act of vandalism on the street.
> - During rush hour in the morning, someone barges past you so that you lose your balance.
> - A friend reacts in a negative way when you have been successful in school.
>
> How would you respond in each situation? What values do you have that make you act in this way?
>
> Share your values with a partner. Can you add to your list? **Discuss** with each other where you think your values come from (your family, your religion, your country's laws, etc.).
>
> Be ready to share your ideas with the class.

1 Why do individuals form social groups?

CULTURE

In our analysis of social groups so far, we have touched upon a very important concept: the role of culture in fostering those intangible connections between people. You may have studied culture in *Individuals and Societies for the IB MYP 3*. In Chapter 5 of that book, we came across E.B. Tylor's definition of culture:

> 'that complex whole which includes knowledge, belief, art, law, morals, custom, and any other capabilities and habits acquired by man as a member of society.'

Émile Durkheim (see page 5) described individuals in social groups that exhibit mechanical solidarity as resembling each other. Today, we strongly believe in our own individuality and right to express our differing views. This is something that we have only been able to enjoy relatively recently in human history.

EXTENSION

Listen to the **BBC Reith Lecture called 'Culture'** given in 2016 by Kwame Anthony Appiah, and watch the **TED Talk called 'Don't ask where I'm from, ask where I'm a local'**.

Have people always only belonged to one country, culture or creed? How relevant are national borders today? If you have more than one passport, does that mean you must choose your national identity or can you belong to many places?

CULTURAL DIFFUSION

As we have mentioned above, culture is a set of shared ideas, actions, principles, beliefs and values.

THINK–PAIR–SHARE

What elements of other cultures have you adopted? Think especially about foods, sports, music, dance and customs. For example, St Patrick's Day is an example of a custom that has grown and been adopted by many. There are now Irish bars around the world and the day is celebrated in many places, with New York having a St Patrick's Day parade.

Share your thoughts with a partner. Did you have any examples in common? Can you add to your list?

Be ready to share your ideas with the class.

In an increasingly globalized world, culture has become fluid and may adapt and change because of new influences. This is known as **cultural diffusion**: the spread of cultural ideas from their place of origin to other regions, groups or nations. Some might say culture has become more **homogenized** because of this, while others may say that culture has diversified because of the increased choice and variety.

Examples of cultural homogenization can be seen in Figure 1.8 where global transnational companies can be found in even the most remote of places, often adapted to suit the culture and architectural style of the country they inhabit. Clothing and music are also areas where it is often said that there is one globalized or americanized culture with people all around the world choosing to follow particular styles of fashion and listen to the same types of music. This is sometimes referred to as **glocalization**.

■ **Figure 1.8** Examples of glocalization

DISCUSS

Is it necessary for minority groups to protect their culture and identity in the face of increasing **globalization**?

ACTIVITY: Are we heading towards one global culture?

ATL

- Critical-thinking skills: Gather and organize relevant information to formulate an argument; Consider ideas from multiple perspectives

Construct a written response to the following question: 'Are we approaching a single, dominant homogenized global culture? Is such a thing desirable?'

Your answer should be balanced, consider both sides of the argument and use examples to support your points.

◆ Assessment opportunities

◆ In this activity you have practised skills that are assessed using Criterion A: Knowing and understanding and Criterion D: Thinking critically.

DISCUSS

While there are undoubtedly benefits to cultural diffusion in that it can enrich our experiences and broaden our horizons, it is important to consider the potential downsides that it may bring. An example of an element of culture that is often said to be threatened by cultural diffusion is language. Read this article published in the *Guardian* newspaper (https://bit.ly/2IVo8bD) about Icelandic language battling the threat of 'digital extinction'. **Discuss** with a partner what you have read. What is causing 'an ocean of English'? What do you think? Do you think there is a real threat?

EXTENSION

Explore the notion of **diasporas**, the spread of people from their original country to other countries. Diasporas are found all around the world; for example, in New York City's Chinatown there is the largest concentration of Chinese people in the western hemisphere.

Identify one global diaspora and suggest reasons why this group of people can be found in this particular location. Consider historical, geographical, economic and political reasons.

1 Why do individuals form social groups?

What role has social media played in shaping society?

Globalization means that the social and cultural influences on which services and goods are bought and sold is gradually becoming similar across the world.

In the twenty-first century, social media have become increasingly important to the PR (public relations) of almost all businesses. The surge in public accessibility to this technology across the globe has resulted in a rapid increase in the potential market for businesses, creating new opportunities as well as challenges in PR practices.

Through social media platforms, companies are able to display their profile and advertise products, events and services to potential customers on a scale that was previously impossible. These organizations and companies use social media platforms like Facebook, Twitter and Instagram not only to inform their public about events, but also to ask them for feedback about the organization, its events and products. They may also ask people to refer friends or to start following the organization on social media.

Type of social media	Corporate function					
	R&D	Marketing	Customer service	Sales	HR	Organization
Blogs	low	medium	low			
Business networks					very high	low
Collaborative projects	very high					
Enterprise social networks	medium				medium	very high
Forums	low	low	very high			
Microblogs		medium	low		low	
Photo sharing		low				
Products/services review	low	medium		very high		
Social bookmarking		low				
Social gaming		low				
Social networks	low	very high	medium		low	low
Video sharing		very high	low			
Virtual worlds	low	medium		low		

Importance: (empty) none or almost none; low; medium; high; very high

Figure 1.9 The importance of social media for a company's operational functions (Aichner & Jacob, 2015) (R&D = Research and Development)

ACTIVITY: Using social media to do business

■ ATL

- Information literacy skills: Process data and report results

- In a paragraph, **describe** the key features of the table in Figure 1.9.
- In two sentences **describe** and **explain** how you think this table would have looked in 1990 (before widespread use of the internet).

◆ Assessment opportunities

◆ In this activity you have practised skills that are assessed using Criterion A: Knowing and understanding.

THINK–PAIR–SHARE

Think of your favourite clothing company. **List** the different ways in which you find out about their latest fashion lines.

In pairs, **describe** the different ways in which your chosen company uses celebrities to advertize their latest brands. **Explain** their use of celebrities.

Share your thoughts with the rest of the class and **investigate** why these celebrities have become popular.

Companies use **social media influencers** in their marketing in order to build relationships with such people who can then, through their social media following, build relationships for the company. Whether an influencer's audience is small or large, they can reach consumers via their blogs and social media posts that a company may not otherwise be able to reach.

According to the 2018 Instagram Rich List compiled by Hopper HQ, entrepreneur Kylie Jenner makes an estimated US$ 1 million per sponsored post on her Instagram. She is followed by singer Selena Gomez, who gets US$ 800,000 and footballer Cristiano Ronaldo, who earns US$ 750,000.

DISCUSS

Why do celebrities get paid for posting on social media platforms?

ACTIVITY: Is social media a force for good?

■ ATL

- Communication skills: Negotiate ideas and knowledge with peers and teachers

Divide the class into two groups in preparation for a debate **discussing** the question: Is social media a force for good?

Using Table 1.3 below and any other ideas you can think of, prepare arguments for your side of the debate. Each student should participate, presenting main arguments, rebuttals or asking questions.

■ Table 1.3 Arguments for and against social media

To argue that social media is good	To argue that social media is bad
• Improved democracy through improved transparency and access to information • New opportunities for economic growth	• Rise of fake news and **echo chambers** • Increased pressure on people and lost self-confidence as a result of perceived fear of missing out and body-image issues

◆ Assessment opportunities

◆ In this activity you have practised skills that are assessed using Criterion C: Communicating and Criterion D: Thinking critically.

What impact do social groups have on the sustainability of resources?

It took all of human history until approximately the year 1800 for the world population to reach 1 billion. Since then, the world population has grown to more than 8 billion. This puts huge pressure on our natural resources, as people work to ensure all their needs are met.

Sustainability is a word we hear often, especially in the study of Individuals and Societies. But what does it mean and why is it so important?

In 1987, the Brundtland Report introduced the term 'sustainability'. It was defined as sustainable development: 'development that meets the needs of the present without compromising the ability of future generations to meet their own needs'. Since then, this term has become widely used as we struggle to balance meeting our needs now with ensuring that future generations are also able to meet theirs. This is a concept that you will see runs throughout all of the chapters in this book and is a vital consideration in the study of Individuals and Societies.

There are commonly thought to be three elements to sustainability – sometimes known as the three pillars of sustainability – and these are social, environmental and economic sustainability.

ACTIVITY: Sustainable ideas

ATL

- Creative-thinking skills: Use brainstorming and mind mapping to generate new ideas and inquiries

Individually, write down on sticky notes or in a shared online workspace the first three words that come to mind when you look at this word: SUSTAINABILITY.

As a class, collect your words together and enter them into a word cloud generator such as Wordle www.wordle.net or Word it out https://worditout.com/

Discuss the result. What does this suggest about your class ideas on sustainability?

Print out your class word cloud and display it in a space reserved for this chapter, and save it in any shared online workspace.

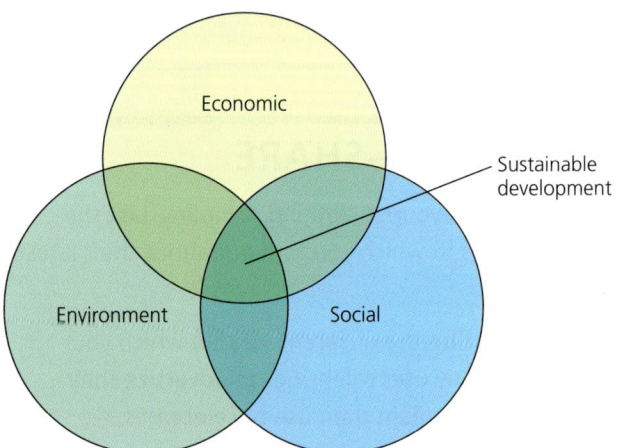

■ **Figure 1.10** Venn diagram showing sustainable development

SEE–THINK–WONDER

Figure 1.10 shows the considerations that need to be balanced when contemplating sustainable city design or making improvements to existing cities. What does it make you think? What does it make you wonder?

Consider the three components of sustainable development in more detail in Table 1.4.

■ **Table 1.4** The three components of sustainable development

Environmental sustainability	Economic sustainability	Social sustainability
Definition: Improvements in the standard of living that do not cause long-term damage to the environment that impacts future generations	**Definition:** Development that includes everyone, where everyone has the right to economic improvement. The development should be long term, non corrupt and avoid increasing or creating debt.	**Definition:** Development that is inclusive and ensures an improvement in the standard of living for all. It should incorporate everyone and ensure equal access to health care, education and resources, while respecting individual cultures.
Examples: • Protecting biodiversity • Stopping human-caused climate change • Elimination of damage to the ozone layer • Reduction of pollution (air, water, noise, etc.)	**Examples:** • Access to finance • No corruption • No **absolute poverty**	**Examples:** • Freedom of speech • Health and safety at work • Access to clean water and sanitation • Access to needs, i.e. water, food, shelter, clothing • Access to education • Access to health care • Equality between the sexes, religions, etc. • Right to vote • Access to justice • Safety – no threat from crime • Respect for cultures

In Chapter 7 we will build on this introduction to sustainability and examine the UN's Sustainable Development Goals, exploring whether urban systems and environments can be managed sustainably. The Sustainable Development Goals will also be explored in Chapter 10 about economic development.

■ **Figure 1.11** Pollution: an oil spill

How do we study Individuals and Societies?

THINK–PAIR–SHARE

List as many skills/techniques you have used or are familiar with in your studies of Individuals and Societies so far.

DISCUSS: Disciplines within a faculty

All subject disciplines within Individuals and Societies (or humanities or social sciences, as they are sometimes called) study the way in which social groups are formed and the way they interact, but do so with different lenses. For the subjects listed below, **discuss** the lens through which they study social groups:
- business management
- economics
- geography
- history
- law
- politics
- psychology
- sociology.

Whether you have studied separate Individuals and Societies subjects, or studied them together, you will have explored the ways in which human beings organize themselves into groups, how they interact with each other and with their environment. Each separate subject approaches this from a different angle.

When we are exploring individuals and their relationships with societies we use a wide range of skills and techniques to help us. These skills and techniques are vital to the successful study of Individuals and Societies subjects. If you can master these, then you will be able to analyse and write with confidence.

USING SOURCES

Primary sources are those that are put together at the same time as the period being studied. In historical investigations, these give us a direct link to that period of time and the people alive then. In other Individuals and Societies subjects, we might not necessarily use historical primary sources, but might compile our own. In business or economics, we might conduct surveys or interviews of people when investigating the impact of a particular marketing tool or government policy. It is always important to bear in mind the limitations of primary sources – they can never tell the whole story, and you must try to find as many sources as possible when answering any research question.

Secondary sources are those put together after the period in question or by people who did not experience first hand the events in question. Historical secondary sources tend to be books written by historians. The use of secondary sources in a historical investigation provides different perspectives of historical analysis. The causes and effects of historical events are often disputed, and therefore introducing the views of significant historians in an essay that you write brings balance and credibility to your own analysis. Secondary sources also include any dataset constructed by private or public organizations (such as the IMF's World Economic Outlook database released in April and October every year).

OBSERVATIONS

In business and geography, a lot can be gained by observing the interactions of people in particular areas, for example in shops or along roads. You might have been, or will at some stage be taken, on a field trip to a river to conduct field work with your geography teacher. Measurements of water speed, **silt** and sediment qualities, or rock size and type will be taken and compiled in an organized manner.

GRAPHICAL SKILLS

Presenting gathered data in work is best done using graphs. Graphs allow us to present numerical data in a way that makes patterns and trends easier to see. It is important to put effort and care into developing this skill. When drawing graphs by hand you should always use a pencil and a ruler. Scatter plots should include a line of best fit, so that the trend can be established. Time series data can be plotted by connecting the dots. Any images or charts included in work should have a figure number and title, just as we have modelled in this textbook.

INTERPRETING DATA

Interpreting data is a more difficult skill to master than gathering and presenting it. How far data goes to give us the answers we are looking for is dependent on a number of things. First, it is dependent on the quality of the gathering process. For example, economic data such as growth, **inflation** and unemployment require extensive procedures

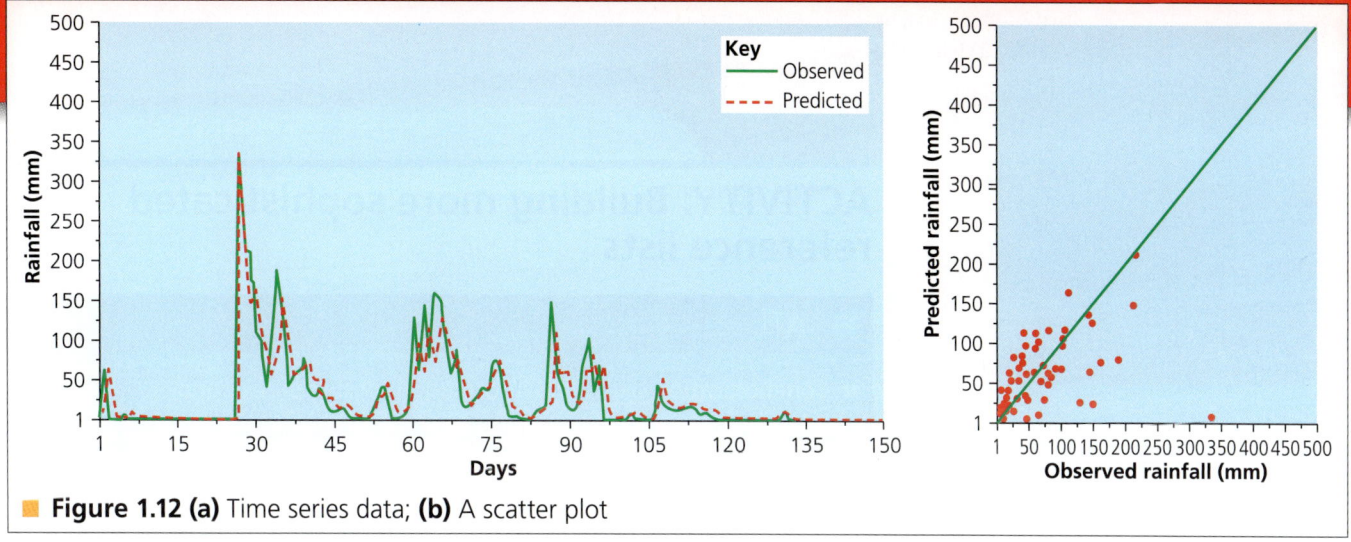

Figure 1.12 (a) Time series data; (b) A scatter plot

and rigour in order to be able to gather the necessary information about an entire country and population. Inflation (a measure of price changes each month) is usually measured by looking at a basket of typical things bought by a typical household. What is typically bought will vary regionally, by socioeconomic status, gender, size of household, and over time. This makes comparison over time and across different groups more difficult. Second, a set of data that suggests a correlated relationship does not necessarily imply that the variables have a causal relationship. This is what the field of econometrics (something you might study at university one day) tries to establish with complex statistical techniques and great difficulty. Take a look at Figure 1.13 below to help you understand that two variables that move together may not necessarily cause each other.

CRITICAL THINKING

Enormously important in all subjects, critical thinking is needed in the study of Individuals and Societies because of the limitations of the methods outlined above. When we study the past, we only have access to the writing and artifacts left behind by people (whether deliberate or not). These do not always provide a complete picture, and information can be interpreted in different ways. In geographical, psychological, management or economic studies about people, it is difficult to gather all the information needed to fully know what we want to know. We can gather survey evidence, we can look at data, we can build mathematical models, but people are complicated and our world changes fast. We must always be aware of the limitations of our methods of investigation.

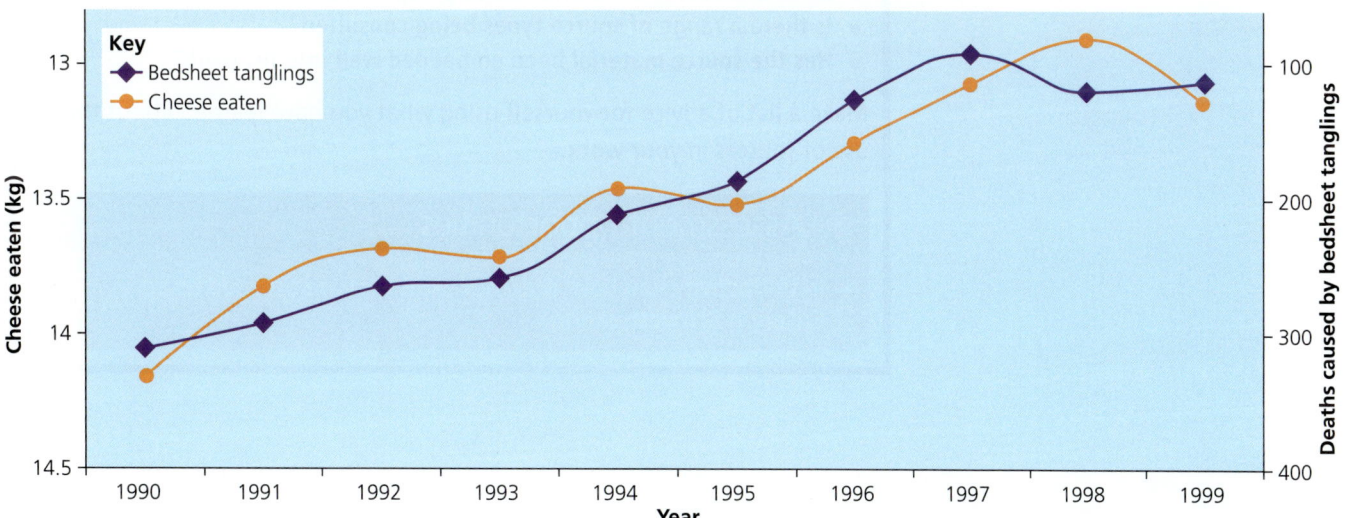

Figure 1.13 Amount of cheese consumed per person correlates with number of people who died by becoming caught in their bedsheets. Correlation in data does not mean one of the variables causes the other

1 Why do individuals form social groups?

When you write anything in Individuals and Societies, but especially when you are being assessed with criterion D (Thinking critically), essentially you are being asked to be clear about the extent to which you know the answer to the question being asked. The best work is balanced and demonstrates an awareness of different perspectives and limitations of the research methods employed.

ACTIVITY: Building more sophisticated reference lists

■ ATL

- Communication skills: Find information for disciplinary and interdisciplinary inquiries, using a variety of media

As you progress to the final stage of your Middle Years Programme, you will need to start recognizing what a more sophisticated reference list looks like.

Choose an essay that you have written in the past, in which you consulted and cited sources. (If you don't have one, your teacher should have one for you to look at.)

Construct a table like the one below with columns for the name of the source, the weblink (if relevant) and the source's strengths and weaknesses.

Source	Weblink	Strengths	Weaknesses

When assessing a source's strengths and weaknesses, consider the following questions:
- Will the reader of my source think this information is credible?
- How do we know the source is credible?
- Does this source offer alternative perspectives?
- Is there a range of source types being consulted?
- Has the source material been embedded well into my work?

Make a **list** of advice for yourself using what you have learned about the use of sources in your work.

◆ Assessment opportunities

- In this activity you have practised skills that are assessed using Criterion B: Investigating.

Reflection

In this chapter, we have **explained** the reasons why individuals form social groups, and **described** what happens to relationships between people when populations grow. We have defined the concepts of equality and equity, **explained** how governments might use taxation to redistribute income, and calculated marginal and average tax rates. We have **discussed** the role that systems of law, globalization and social media play in shaping our societies.

Use this table to reflect on your own learning in this chapter.					
Questions we asked	Answers we found	Any further questions now?			
Factual: What is equality?					
Conceptual: Why do people form social groups? How does the structure of social groups promote the participation of individuals? How and why do social groups behave in a similar way? What impact do social groups have on the sustainability of resources? How does culture shape individuals and their societies? What role has social media played in shaping society? How do we study Individuals and Societies?					
Debatable: Why is it important to explore different cultures?					
Approaches to learning you used in this chapter	Description – what new skills did you learn?	How well did you master the skills?			
		Novice	Learner	Practitioner	Expert
Communication skills					
Information literacy skills					
Critical-thinking skills					
Creative-thinking skills					
Learner profile attribute(s)	Reflect on the importance of being a thinker for your learning in this chapter.				
Thinker					

Systems | Conflict; Power; Resources | Identities and relationships

2 Why are empires formed?

○ Empires are **systems** of **power** arising from **conflict** over **resources**, creating new **identities and relationships**.

CONSIDER THESE QUESTIONS:

Factual: What are common characteristics of empires?

Conceptual: What role does the military play in the development of empires? What role can innovation and technology play in the development of empires? What role can economics play in the development of empires? What role can climate play in the development of empires?

Debatable: Is empire formation an inevitable part of human history? To what extent can we consider empires a thing of the past?

Now, **share** and **compare** your thoughts and ideas with your partner or the rest of the class.

IN THIS CHAPTER WE WILL ...

- **Find out:**
  - some definitions of empire
  - why empires form
  - the factors that led to the formation of empires.
- **Explore:**
  - the importance of military conquest in empire formation
  - the role of technology and innovation in creating empires
  - economic reasons why empires expand
  - the effects of climate change on the formation of empires.
- **Take action** by researching two modern multi-ethnic states and comparing their formation to historical empires.

These Approaches to Learning (ATL) skills will be useful ...

- Communication skills
- Collaboration skills
- Information literacy skills
- Critical-thinking skills
- Creative-thinking skills
- Transfer skills

We will reflect on this learner profile attribute ...

- Inquirers – using thinking and research skills to address natural curiosity, developing further knowledge, opportunities for collaboration and love of learning.

Individuals & Societies for the IB MYP 4&5: by Concept

(a)

(b)

■ **Figure 2.1** Narmer Palette: **(a)** front and **(b)** back

◆ **Assessment opportunities in this chapter:**

- ◆ **Criterion A**: Knowing and understanding
- ◆ **Criterion B**: Investigating
- ◆ **Criterion C**: Communicating
- ◆ **Criterion D**: Thinking critically

KEY WORDS

conquest	technology
empire	war
innovation	

SEE–THINK–WONDER

Look at Figure 2.1. In pairs, **describe** what you see. What does the imagery communicate to you?

In pairs, **identify** and **discuss**:
- the imagery used to communicate how the unification was achieved
- the role of the ruler in the unification according to the evidence presented
- other images and their possible meanings with relation to the king, the unification, religion, technology, and more.

Based on this image, what assumptions can we make about Egypt 5,000 years ago? What can be implied about this culture's views on the unification?

Look at the photos in Figure 2.1. These images show two sides of the same stone palette which was used to mix ink or cosmetics. Discovered in 1897, this ceremonial item was placed in an ancient Egyptian temple around 5,000 years ago. Called the Narmer Palette, it is interpreted as evidence of the unification of northern and southern Egypt into one large state, perhaps the world's first empire.

Historians use artifacts as evidence in order to understand the past.

What are common characteristics of empires?

Figure 2.2 Famous empires in history: the Mongol empire at its greatest geographic size

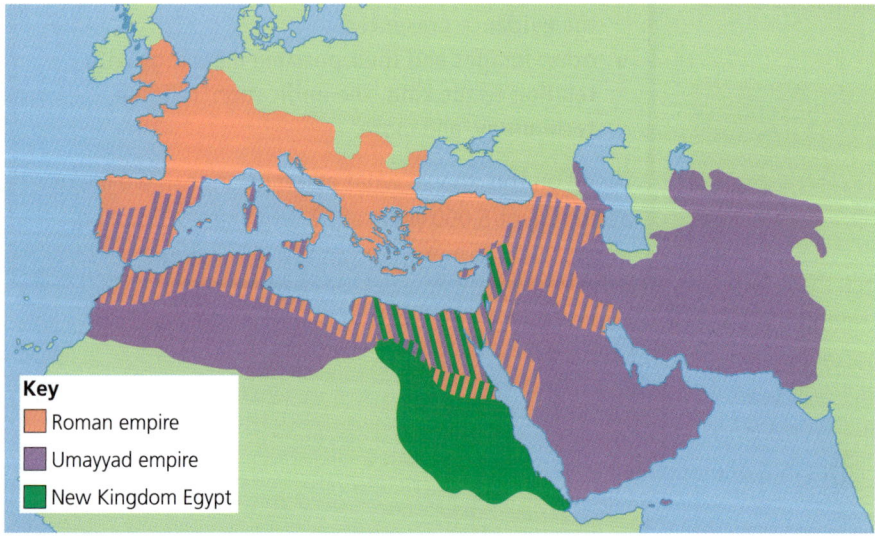

Figure 2.3 Famous empires in history: New Kingdom Egypt, and the Roman and Umayyad Caliphates at their greatest geographic sizes

WHAT IS AN EMPIRE?

Empires have formed throughout human history, from the earliest civilizations until today. There were empires in ancient Mesopotamia, today's Iraq, ancient Egypt and China, and more. Some of these existed for hundreds or even thousands of years. Famous empires have included:
- the New Kingdom Egypt (1570–1070 BCE)
- the Roman empire (27 BCE–476 CE)
- the Umayyad **Caliphate** (661–750 CE)
- the Mongol empire (1206–1368 CE)
- the Republic of Venice (810–1797 CE).

Empires may form when states or countries are ruled by an outside power, whether this is another country, a small group or an individual. The ruler of an empire usually has a title; traditional titles of empires include king, emperor, **sultan**, padishah, tennō, doge and many more, depending on language, empire and translations of terms into English. Empires are usually formed through military conquest and can exist for the purpose of military glory, financial gain, defence, or cultural and religious reasons to the benefit of the empire's rulers.

Some historians indicate that empires may also form when one country economically dominates another state or group of states. In cases such as this, the states dominated may be politically independent, but are economically tied to and dependent upon another state for trade or for specific products or necessities. An example of this type of empire includes the **city-state** of Venice, now part of Italy, which economically dominated trade routes between the Middle East and Europe for centuries.

Imperialism is the modern term for the creation and expansion of empire. You will study aspects of empire formation, including practical examples from the historical empires above, in this chapter.

ACTIVITY: Timeline and evaluation

ATL

- Information literacy skills: Access information to be informed and inform others; Make connections between various sources of information; Identify primary and secondary sources
- Critical-thinking skills: Gather and organize relevant information to formulate an argument; Evaluate evidence and arguments; Draw reasonable conclusions and generalizations; Consider ideas from multiple perspectives

Research: As a class, **identify** 10 to 12 empires from world history (perhaps you can use prior knowledge from previous study). Place each empire on a large timeline, indicating the beginning and end (if applicable) for each empire. Each empire will be assigned a team to **investigate** the size and other important details of the empire.

Analysis: Each group will create a **list** of ten important facts about the empire and then rank these facts in order of importance, practising the skill of analysis. This information should be used to complete the detailed timeline. Consider using this timeline and its information to make a presentation to other students.

Reflection: As a class, **discuss** what these empires had in common and how each was unique.

◆ Assessment opportunities

◆ In this activity you have practised skills that are assessed using Criterion A: Knowing and understanding, Criterion B: Investigating, Criterion C: Communicating and Criterion D: Thinking critically.

While not all empires are the same, the ones studied in this chapter share common attributes that differentiate them from states, **federations**, **allied states** or city-states. Some of these common attributes are that all:
- recognize a central authority
- exist as a result of military conquest or economic domination.

CENTRAL AUTHORITY

The empires explored in this chapter all had a central authority, or power, in the form of an individual or small group of people. All had a capital city, from where the central government would manage the empire as a whole. The importance of the capital city derived from its position as the home of the ruler or from the government institutions there. These capitals were:
- New Kingdom of Egypt: Inbu-Hedj (Memphis), Waset (today's Luxor), Pi-Ramesses
- Roman empire: Rome
- Umayyad Caliphate: Damascus
- Mongol empire: Karakorum, Khanbaliq (today's Beijing).

As part of their authority, the governments of these empires controlled law, the military, large parts of (if not all) the **economy**, distribution of resources both within and without the empire's borders, and sometimes religion.

New Kingdom Egypt (1570–1070 BCE)

Egypt's ruler was the **pharaoh**, who was considered to be the deity, or god, Horus who ruled the earth and owned everyone and everything in it. Religion and politics were one and the same. The pharaoh was the government and therefore controlled all resources, including people, animals, plants, minerals and land. This also meant that the entire economy was dominated by the state which decided what

■ **Figure 2.4** Statue of Genghis Khan, founder of the Mongol empire, at a government building in the capital of Mongolia, Ulaanbaatar

ACTIVITY: Imperial capitals

ATL
- Creative-thinking skills: Use brainstorming and visual diagrams to generate new ideas and inquiries
- Communication skills: Organize and depict information logically

Empires had capitals. These were located in specific places for various reasons and were the centre of government.

As a class, **discuss** the economic, geographical and political considerations that are made when founding a capital city.

As individuals, **identify** and **list** the requirements of a capital city, including government buildings, housing, sources of water, entertainment, markets and more. Using tools of your choice, create a map or plan of your ideal capital city. Make sure to include any geographic features. Don't forget to include a key or legend for clarity.

Present this either in a display or in a presentation.

Assessment opportunities
- In this activity you have practised skills that are assessed using Criterion A: Knowing and understanding, Criterion B: Investigating and Criterion C: Communicating.

was made, planted, consumed and distributed. It was in the pharaoh's interest to ensure that enough food was grown and distributed, as well as having people's needs met for cloth, building materials and daily life, as these were his worshippers, his property, and their labour led to his personal prosperity and glory.

Egypt was a prosperous state with great resources due to the fertility of the Nile Valley, but also due to mineral resources such as gold and copper. Neighbouring states could be a threat and therefore, in order to protect his territory and wealth, the pharaoh was necessarily the head of the military.

SOURCE A

'Confucian scholars … argued that rulers [in China] were established by Heaven for the benefit of the people. The people, in turn, could rightfully hold their rulers to account. They had the right to banish [get rid of] a bad ruler and even to kill a **tyrant**. Moreover, a benevolent ruler was justified in waging '**punitive war**' against the tyrannical ruler of another state, in order to punish him and to comfort the people.'

Luke Glanville, quoted in 'Retaining the Mandate of Heaven: Sovereign Accountability in Ancient China,' *Millennium Journal of International Studies, 8 November 2010*

Imperial Rome (27 BCE–476 CE)

The ruler of the Roman empire was the emperor, who was sometimes called **The Augustus**, **The Caesar**, among other titles. Unlike Egypt, where the pharaoh held all the power, in the Roman empire, power was often shared between various individuals and bodies or organizations, including the Roman Senate, the governors of Rome's provinces, the military and the wealthy elite.

The first five emperors were from the same family, but later emperors were usually military leaders who rose to power with the army's support. The authority of the emperor varied through time, with some having almost complete control and others being forced to share power with other groups or individuals. This meant that although Rome was the capital, the central authority might be wherever the emperor, who frequently travelled for military purposes, was located at the time. Similarly, shifts in the geographic location of Rome's many armies could affect where power was located.

As central authority was not always invested completely in one individual or group, the state could not control the entire economy. At various times, the state did control large areas of production, such as that of salt, grain crops and purple dye, as well as marble mining and the construction of public buildings. The military built all roads and bridges and therefore had a considerable effect on the economic systems of the state. This said, there was private ownership of businesses and farms, and the majority of the empire's economy was operated by private individuals.

ACTIVITY: Politics and religion in China

ATL

- Critical-thinking skills: Interpret data; Evaluate evidence and arguments
- Transfer skills: Inquire in different contexts to gain a different perspective

Look at Source A. What does it tell us about the relationship between politics and religion in China?

Why do you think this approach to religion and politics began? Can you think of any other approaches to the relationship between religion and politics in the empires you have studied?

How do governments today view the relationship between politics and religions? To what extent is this similar to or different from ancient China?

◆ **Assessment opportunities**

◆ In this activity you have practised skills that are assessed using Criterion A: Knowing and understanding and Criterion D: Thinking critically.

What role does the military play in the development of empires?

UMAYYAD CALIPHATE (661–750 CE)

The Umayyad Caliphate began in 661 CE with the **Caliph** Mu'awiya I, who had previously been a governor for the early Islamic empire, or Caliphate. The Umayyads expanded the territories under their control so that within a few years, they dominated not only the Middle East from Damascus, their capital that is in today's Syria, but also all north Africa, today's Spain and Portugal, parts of today's France, Cyprus, Rhodes, Persia and much of central Asia. The sheer size of this empire meant that the Umayyads dominated world trade.

The expansion of the Umayyads was the result of military conquest. While the rulers and military elite were Muslim, the majority of the empire's population was not Muslim. The Umayyads allowed the majority Christian population to join the military, greatly expanding the army. Additionally, a navy was created, almost completely dominated by Christian sailors.

Military alliances with nomadic Bedouin tribes allowed rapid movement which surprised and defeated enemy soldiers across north Africa. The Umayyad Caliphate engaged in warfare almost constantly. Their empire was one of the largest ever created through military conquest.

■ **Figure 2.5** The Umayyad Mosque, or the Great Mosque, is located in Damascus, the capital of the Umayyad Caliphate. Construction was completed in 715 CE. It is one of the oldest mosques in the world

MONGOL EMPIRE (1206–1368 CE)

The Mongol empire was established by a nomadic chieftain named Temujin, who was later titled Genghis Khan. Through a series of military conquests, Genghis Khan and his descendants conquered a large portion of Asia, the Middle East, Africa and parts of Europe to form the largest land-based empire in history.

The strength of the Mongol military was their reliance on horses, which allowed rapid movement, as well as use of the **composite bow**. Horses, travelling up to 160 km per day, meant that enemies were often taken by surprise; no other military in history before the Mongols was capable of such rapid movement on land. Horses provided transport and were the main means of war since the Mongol military fought from the back of their horses as much as possible, whether using bows and arrows, swords or lances. Mongol horses did not require grain for food and instead ate grass and twigs from trees and bushes. This meant that Mongol armies were not slowed down by supply wagons carrying grain for horses.

Another strength of the Mongol armies was their organization. The command structure for the Mongol army was highly flexible, based on a decimal system. Each unit of ten, hundred, thousand and ten-thousand could act independently. As they conquered territory, they discovered new weapons of warfare, and adopted and improved on

Abbasid Caliphate (750–1258 CE)

The Abbasid rulers overthrew the Umayyads in a civil war in 750, establishing a new caliphate. The capital moved from Damascus to the newly constructed city of Baghdad. Baghdad became one of the largest cities in the world, a centre of trade, learning and government. In time, the Abbasid rulers faced revolts, civil war and domination by various governors, tribes and military units. The greatest threat faced by the empire was the Mongol military who eventually destroyed Baghdad and annexed all its territory to the Mongol empire.

these for their own use. Examples of these weapons include fireworks, siege equipment, gunpowder and the cannon. Conquered enemy soldiers were often incorporated into the military structure if useful. They prized translators, engineers and guides when entering a new region. Engineers, none of whom were Mongol, were needed because the army did not carry siege equipment; building needed items from materials found at their destination instead.

Mongol armies also used terror to conquer enemy cities. If a city did not surrender but was eventually captured, it would be destroyed, with the majority of its citizens killed intentionally. Baghdad, capital of the Abbasid Caliphate, or empire, that was the **successor state** to the Umayyads, was completely destroyed after a short siege in 1258. The city was systematically destroyed and hundreds of thousands of people were killed to warn other cities and countries about the consequence of resistance to the Mongol military.

SOURCE A

'The Mongol legions increased at the gates of Baghdad on Thursday night … [January, 1258] when Ibn al-Kor … and other emirs (commanders) were killed in the event [battle] and the battle took place … and spread toward the shore, to the [Tigris] River, and to Bašir stream. Baghdad was besieged on Tuesday … they [Mongols] entered Baghdad, and on Wednesday [22 February 1258] killed all the dwellers of Baghdad, except those whose hour (of death) had not yet come. They also burnt the other streets. Their stay around Baghdad lasted for forty days. Yusof ibn M'aāli ibn Ša'abān al-Mo'addab, a weak servant of [God] Allah, has written this …'

Ali Bahrani Pour, 'A Study of an Unknown Primary Document on the Fall of Abbasid Baghdad to the Mongols,' Acta Via Serica, Vol. 2, No. 2, December 2017

ACTIVITY: The fall of Baghdad

ATL

- Critical-thinking skills: Gather and organize relevant information to formulate an argument; Recognize unstated assumptions and bias; Interpret data

Kitab Al Wara'a is a religious book written in 1150 CE. Recently, it has been discovered that some of its pages were copied into the text at a later date. These pages include a first-hand account of the Mongol attack on Baghdad in 1258. This is known as the Report of Yusof ibn M'aāli.

What can be learned from Source A? What details does the writer give us about the fall of Baghdad? Based on the text, was the writer present during these events? How are you able to determine this?

Assessment opportunities

- In this activity you have practised skills that are assessed using Criterion D: Thinking critically.

What role can innovation and technology play in the development of empires?

Empires often take advantage of new ideas and technology to take over new lands. These technologies often arise through interaction with other states (e.g. conquest, invasion, trade or alliance) or through local innovation.

CHARIOT WARFARE

One of the greatest developments in terms of warfare in human history has been the creation and use of the chariot. The chariot, a type of two-person cart, was used in conjunction with the composite bow to make an effective weapon that revolutionized warfare and ancient society.

The chariot was a sophisticated type of vehicle that was being used in battles by 1750 BCE. A typical chariot by 1500 BCE was a lightweight cart that was pulled by two horses and held one or two warriors. The horses were essentially the engines of the vehicle which would travel as fast as the two horses could gallop. There were two spoked wheels on a chariot. Spoked wheels are stronger and lighter than solid wheels. The sides of the carts were often made of twined vines or small branches like a basket, protecting the legs of the warriors. The warriors themselves stood on a platform of woven leather strips that were also light and which moved up and down as the chariot moved along uneven ground or over stones. A chariot was light enough that a single warrior could pick it up and move it. The lightness meant that chariots could move with great speed.

Composite bow

Chariots were used in conjunction with the composite bow, developed long before the chariot. The bow was made of special woods, horn, animal parts and glues. It may have taken years to assemble one bow. It could shoot arrows much further than a typical bow, with improved accuracy.

SETI I IN BATTLE AGAINST THE LIBYANS

■ Figure 2.6 Seti I in battle against Libyans

ACTIVITY: Ramses the Great

ATL

■ Critical-thinking skills: Interpret data; Draw reasonable conclusions and generalizations

Seti I was the father of Ramses the Great, perhaps the most famous ruler of ancient Egypt. Seti, like his son, was a famous warrior. He fought many battles, including the one depicted against Libyans. Upon his death, Seti I was buried, like most New Kingdom rulers, in the Valley of the Kings in modern-day Luxor, Egypt, in a magnificent tomb.

Look closely at Figure 2.6:
- **Suggest** which of the individuals depicted is Seti I. **Explain** how you know.
- **State** what tools of war are depicted in this image.
- **List** five details about the battle.
- **Analyse** who is victorious, and who is losing the battle.
- Some depictions of people or objects are larger than others. Why?
- **Discuss** whether the images depicted in Figure 2.6 are consistent with what we have learned about chariot warfare.

Assessment opportunities

◆ In this activity you have practised skills that are assessed using Criterion D: Thinking critically.

The Hittite empire

The Hittite empire had its capital at Hattusa, in central Anatolia in the middle of today's Turkey. The Hittite people controlled vast territories in today's Turkey, Syria and Lebanon, and at times extended their control to the Sinai Peninsula in today's Egypt. They were the major source of iron in the ancient world with mines located near their capital city. They were the great rivals and sometime ally of New Kingdom Egypt and the two empires fought a series of major chariot battles that are recorded on tablets found at Hattusa and in inscriptions in Egypt's temples.

Figure 2.7 Stone carving, in Abu Simbel Temple near modern-day Aswan, of Ramses II fighting Hittites

Chariots were used as mobile shooting platforms during battle. A warrior could shoot arrows at the enemy from a distance with his composite bow while standing on the leather floor of the chariot. The distance between the chariot and enemy soldiers meant that the enemy could be engaged without endangering the warrior or the chariot.

If an enemy was close, the warrior could simply drive his chariot to a safe distance and then continue to shoot his arrows. If enemy troops began to leave the battle, the chariot could follow, with the chariot's warrior shooting them from behind. Chariots were used in large numbers in battles during this period. Egyptian Pharaoh Tuthmosis III, for example, fought a battle at the ancient city of Megiddo with about 1,000 chariots, while his enemy, the King of Megiddo, deployed about 1,000 chariots also.

Chariot warfare meant that battles were now fought in fields or open areas. Once an enemy had been beaten in the field, allied soldiers or workers could be brought forward and protected until they reached an enemy **fort** or city. Once a fort or city was reached, workers would be protected from attack by chariot warriors while they dug into or under walls, or simply remained outside while those inside were slowly starved into surrender.

Chariotry

'A **chariotry** was very expensive, the cost of the horses and the chariots being only a beginning. For his vehicles a ruler fielding even a modest number of chariots needed wheelwrights, joiners, tanners and smiths, all with their own workshops, and for his horses he needed trainers, grooms and stable-boys, veterinarians, either traders or breeders, and tracts of pasture and grain fields.

Most important of all, of course, were the skills required of archer and driver. These skills were spectacular enough that several modern scholars have doubted that an archer standing on a rapidly rolling chariot could even draw his bow, to say nothing of hitting a running target. But that is precisely what many men in the second millennium BC, over months of training and practice, learned how to do.'

Robert Drews, *Militarism and the Indo-Europeanizing of Europe*, 2017, p. 109

Chariot warfare in New Kingdom Egypt

Chariot warfare seems to have come to Egypt suddenly around 1675 BCE. A people known to the Egyptians as 'Rulers of Foreign Lands', or Hyksos by later Greek-speaking people, established a royal ruling family or dynasty later called Dynasty 15. Using chariot warfare, they rapidly took control over the entire Nile Valley and ruled from their capital city of Avaris. Their victory can be credited to the fact that they had chariots, while the native Egyptian rulers did not.

After approximately 150 years, southern Egypt (under native Egyptian rulers) fought against Dynasty 15 for several generations, using chariot warfare themselves. Eventually the Hyksos people were defeated and Egypt's Dynasty 18 established the New Kingdom era. New Kingdom pharaohs created an empire that dominated the **Levant**, and much of today's Syria, as well as parts of what is today eastern Libya, and down into today's Sudan. This allowed greater protection of the central Nile Valley in the age of chariot warfare and had the added benefit of supplying Egypt with more resources such as wood, wine, olive oil, gold, ivory and animals.

An empire may have been needed to support chariot warfare. The chariot, its horses and the composite bow were special, expensive tools of war. In addition, specialized, trained warriors were required for using these tools. With large, chariot-based armies, and the equipment makers that supplied them, came a new class, a **warrior class**. In Egypt, this probably numbered several thousand people. The state probably expanded over foreign lands in order to economically support this new warrior class.

ACTIVITY: Innovations and their effect on empire

■ ATL

- Communication skills: Organize and depict information logically
- Collaboration skills: Help others to succeed; Work collaboratively in teams; Listen activity to other perspectives and ideas; Negotiate effectively
- Information literacy skills: Identify primary and secondary sources; Collect and analyse data to identify solutions and make informed decisions
- Critical-thinking skills: Evaluate evidence and arguments

Innovations are closely connected with empires.

In groups of two or three, consider the innovations listed in the table below.

Research each type of innovation, and on a copy of the table, indicate which empire used or was affected by it first.

Of all the innovations in the table, which three had the greatest impact on civilization?

Explain how you arrived at your answer to this final question.

Communicate your completed table and the answer to the question above to the class as a display and/or class presentation.

■ **Table 2.1** Innovations and their effect on empires

Innovation	Empire	Effects on empire(s)
Chariot warfare		
Gunpowder		
Printing press		
Paper currency		
Postal system		
Writing		
Law code		
Astrolabe		
Ceramics		

◆ Assessment opportunities

- In this activity you have practised skills that are assessed using Criterion B: Investigating, Criterion C: Communicating and Criterion D: Thinking critically.

What role can economics play in the development of empires?

As seen with New Kingdom Egypt's expansion, economics plays a key role in the development of empires. A country may wish to secure supplies of grain, water or other resources and this may lead to expansion.

ROMAN EMPIRE (27 BCE–476 CE)

The Roman empire was a large and complex state with vast trading networks, but also economic needs. While some parts of the empire had an abundance of grain, for example, other parts lacked food supplies to support their population. While silver was produced in parts of today's Spain, olive oil was produced in the eastern Mediterranean areas and today's Britain produced tin, a necessary metal for bronze production. Egypt supplied papyrus paper, while certain islands supplied cities all throughout the empire with marble. Rome's economic system allowed the sharing of resources all across its vast territory.

Grain in Egypt

The Roman empire was almost entirely dependent on grain production in Egypt. Before 31 BCE, Egypt was an independent country that supplied the city of Rome with much of its grain. This grain was provided at low cost, or even free, in exchange for Roman support against the enemies of the ruling family of Egypt. These enemies were often other family members, but could be other states.

Rome suffered through several civil wars and internal power struggles. As the supplier of grain, Egypt was critically important in these conflicts as enemies could be starved and allies rewarded with food. The struggle over control of this essential source of food eventually led to a series of great battles between rivals in the eastern Mediterranean. In 31 BCE, Egypt's navy and that of its Roman ally Marcus Antonius, known as Mark Antony in English, were defeated and in 30 BCE Egypt lost its independence. Egypt then became the personal property of the first Roman Emperor, Octavian Caesar, who was referred to as The Augustus.

> ### ACTIVITY: Rome's economic network
>
> #### ATL
>
> - Information literacy skills: Identify primary and secondary sources
> - Critical-thinking skills: Evaluate evidence and arguments; Draw reasonable conclusions and generalizations; Consider ideas from multiple perspectives
>
> Research an archaeological site from the time of the Roman empire. This can be from the list below, or any excavation of your choice:
>
> - **Pompeii**
> - **Vindolanda**
> - **Vindobona**
> - **Caesarea**
> - **Leptis Magna**
> - **Faesulae**
> - **Herculaneum**
> - **Carthage**
> - **Trier**
>
> **Identify** at least ten artifacts that have been found in the excavation of your choice. Locate from where these objects may have come in the empire.
>
> Print out a map of the Roman empire. Plot the location of each of your identified artifacts on the map.
>
> **Suggest** a hypothesis as to how these objects were transported and the possible trade routes, over both land and sea.
>
> #### Assessment opportunities
>
> - In this activity you have practised skills that are assessed using Criterion A: Knowing and understanding and Criterion B: Investigating.

Figure 2.8 The remains of a Roman fort, Vindolanda, near Hadrian's Wall in northern England

Silver and agriculture in Carthage

The Carthaginian empire was a Mediterranean trading power, based in modern-day Tunisia. Carthage was Rome's main economic competitor in the Mediterranean. The competition between them resulted in three separate wars between 264 BCE and 146 BCE known as the Punic Wars.

As Rome's population and strength grew, more sources of grain had to be found. Carthage controlled the island of Sicily, a rich agricultural area. Its **annexation** by Rome in 241 BCE meant that Rome received 1 million bushels of free wheat each year from the island. Additionally, Rome now controlled the islands of Corsica and Sardinia, allowing it to take over trade routes in the western Mediterranean Sea. The second war with Carthage began because Rome wanted to take over the silver mines that were found in today's Spain. When Carthage was defeated in 201 BCE, Rome limited Carthage's territory to north Africa and annexed much of today's Spain.

The third war between Rome and Carthage was arguably the result of Rome's increased reliance on grain grown in north Africa, as well as increasing economic rivalry between Carthage and Rome in the eastern Mediterranean. Rome's victory in the Third Punic War in 146 BCE led to the destruction of Carthage, its annexation as a Roman province, and the enslavement of its population for sale in Rome's markets.

> ### ACTIVITY: The Roman empire
>
> #### ATL
>
> - Collaboration skills: Work collaboratively in teams; Help others to succeed; Listen actively to other perspectives and ideas
> - Information literacy skills: Identify primary and secondary sources
>
> Consider the three maps of the Roman empire in Figure 2.9.
>
> **Investigate** one territorial annexation or loss that occurred in the Roman empire. Determine how that annexation or loss may have affected the empire economically. You may **identify** resources this territory supplied. For example, you are already aware that areas that are in today's Spain were annexed because of their silver mines.
>
> As a class, create a timeline that indicates when areas were annexed or lost to the Roman empire and the effects that may have had on the economy. Be sure to include:
> - **economic resource(s) provided by your chosen region**
> - **the significance of this resource to the Roman empire**
> - **the date this region was acquired or lost by Rome**
> - **any other relevant facts.**
>
> ◆ Assessment opportunities
>
> - In this activity you have practised skills that are assessed using Criterion B: Investigating.

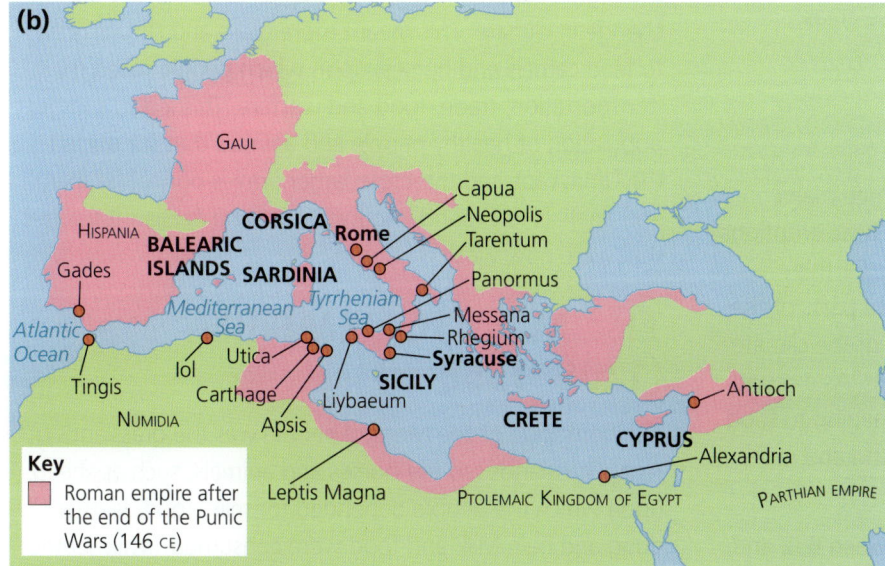
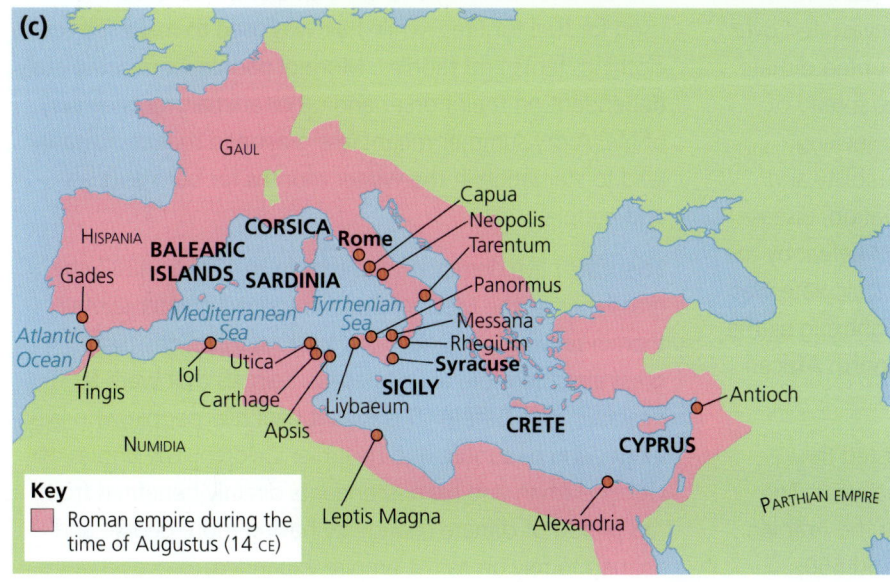

■ **Figure 2.9** The Roman empire during three different periods

2 Why are empires formed?

What role can climate play in the development of empires?

> **Plague of Justinian (541–42 CE)**
>
> The Plague of Justinian was a pandemic that affected the Byzantine empire during the rule of Emperor Justinian. The plague was caused by the bacterium *Yersinia pestis* which originated in Central Asia and lived in fleas. The fleas lived and fed on rats and spread to other animals. The bacterium may have come into the empire with nomadic people who sought new grasslands during this period of climate change, and/or in ships that visited Asian ports. According to Procopius, a historian who witnessed the plague, 10,000 people died daily in the Byzantine capital, Constantinople. Modern historians believe that half the population of the empire died during this plague and later outbreaks. The Plague of Justinian led to the death of millions across the world.

It is now understood that climate change has played a role in the development of empires in history. Climate change can increase rainfall, raise or lower temperatures, and shorten or extend growing seasons over long periods of time. These can have many effects on the populations of these areas.

UMAYYAD CALIPHATE (661–750 CE)

Scientists have discovered that there were three major volcanic eruptions in 536, 540 and 547 CE. These eruptions sent a large amount of dust and ash into the Earth's atmosphere, affecting the amount of sunlight parts of the Earth received. This led to a general cooling of the climate and summers were shorter until about 660 CE. As a result, growing seasons were shorter for farmers, leading to food shortages. People were less healthy due to this and more susceptible to disease.

The early Islamic Caliphate, which ruled between 632 and 661, bordered the Persian and Byzantine, or Eastern Roman, empires. These two large states had been devastated over the previous century as the result of the disrupted climate. Both states had suffered food shortages, the spread of plagues and invasions from nomadic people seeking grasslands. These stresses led to political instability and war between these two states as well. Starvation, disease and war weakened both and assisted in their defeat by the armies of the early Caliphate. The Umayyad Caliphate was able to continue the expansion, eventually annexing all the Persian empire and the Middle Eastern and north African territories of the Byzantines.

This period of climate change may have assisted the Islamic Caliphate and its successors, the Umayyads. The Islamic Caliphate originated in the deserts of the Arabian Peninsula. During the period between 536 and 660, the region experienced greater rainfall as a result of the change in climate. This meant more grass and shrubs grew to feed camels and horses, upon which people relied for transportation, trade, food and warfare. This led to a larger population of healthy people and animals that supported the Umayyads and therefore larger armies of healthy men and animals to expand into Byzantine and Persian territories that were now weak.

THE MONGOL EMPIRE (1206–1368 CE)

The homeland of the Mongol people was the grasslands of Asia. Grasslands fed the horses and animals, such as sheep, upon which the people depended for milk, food, leather, dung and hair. Milk and food were consumed, while leather was used for clothing and armour. Dung was dried and used for fuel for fires, while hair was used to make felt for clothing, tents and saddles. Mongol people were completely dependent on their horses and other animals for their way of life. A dry summer meant less grass and that could easily lead to starvation in the winter months for both animals and people.

Scientists have demonstrated that from 1211 to 1227, the grasslands of the Mongol region received greater rainfall than in previous decades. This led to significantly more grass and therefore an increase in animals that were far healthier than before. This meant healthier people who lived longer and had more and healthier children. The armies of Genghis Khan and his descendants directly benefited from this period of climate change by having more people and animals to rely on as the empire expanded.

■ **Figure 2.10** The Mongol empire, during the time of Kublai Khan, was divided into four distinct **khanates**: the Yuan Dynasty, the Golden Horde, the Ilkhanate and the Chagatai Khanate

ACTIVITY: The importance of economics and climate for empire formation

■ ATL

- Communication skills: Use a variety of speaking techniques to communicate with a variety of audiences
- Critical-thinking skills: Interpret data; Evaluate evidence and arguments; Consider ideas from multiple perspectives

Research either the time period 536–47 CE or 1211–27 CE.

Individually, **identify** another empire that existed during this time period, besides those mentioned in this section.

Brainstorm, in pairs, whether the volcanic eruptions or increased rainfall affected these empires and, if so, how.

Evaluate, in pairs, which is more important for the formation of empire: economics or climate?

Outline, in bullet points, the arguments you would use if you were going to write an essay about this topic. **List** the arguments in order of importance.

◆ Assessment opportunities

◆ In this activity you have practised skills that are assessed using Criterion A: Knowing and understanding, Criterion B: Investigating, Criterion C: Communicating and Criterion D: Thinking critically.

2 Why are empires formed?

Is empire formation an inevitable part of human history?

Empires seem to have existed from the earliest times in human history and still exist today. In some cases, these empires were intentionally created through military conquest and political concerns. In other cases, it seems that empires were formed as a reaction to economic needs.

ACTIVITY: Debate on empire formation

■ ATL

- Communication skills: Use a variety of speaking techniques to communicate with a variety of audiences
- Collaboration skills: Encourage others to contribute; Listen actively to other perspectives and ideas
- Critical-thinking skills: Interpret data; Evaluate evidence and arguments; Consider ideas from multiple perspectives

- **Decide** which factor for empire formation you consider the most important.
- **Divide** into groups or teams based on your choice.
- **Analyse**, as a team:
  o the factors to determine why you consider your chosen factor to be the most important
  o the factors to determine why other factors are less important
  o historical examples that strengthen your argument
  o whether this conclusion is absolute, or whether you can think of exceptions where another factor may be more important.
- Copy and complete Table 2.2 and then hold a class debate on which factor is the most important for empire formation. Use the guidance on debating to help structure and conduct the debate (see page 43).

■ Table 2.2 Factors in the formation of empires

Factor	Ranking (1–4)	Reason(s)
Military		
Technology and innovation		
Economics		
Climate		

◆ Assessment opportunities

- In this activity you have practised skills that are assessed using Criterion A: Knowing and understanding, Criterion B: Investigating, Criterion C: Communicating and Criterion D: Thinking critically.

Debating

Debating an idea with other students is a great way to explore and learn about issues and is a useful skill that can be used in many contexts, both in school and beyond.

One popular format is the Lincoln/Douglas debate format. Table 2.3 gives some guidance on how to carry out a debate in this way. The debate is organized around two groups. The first group makes the 'affirmative' proposition – that something is the case. The second group then critiques this proposition and makes the opposing case – the 'negative' proposition.

■ **Table 2.3** The Lincoln/Douglas debate format

Order of the debate	Tips
First affirmative constructive – 7 minutes	• Start with a good introduction that attracts the audience's attention and interest in the topic. • Clearly state the resolution/proposition. • Clearly state each of your contentions. • Support with reason and evidence. • Conclude effectively.
Cross examination of the affirmative by the negative – 3 minutes	• Ask questions – have a strategy or at the very least a direction to your questioning. • Be courteous. • Face the audience.
First negative constructive – 8 minutes	• Start with a good introduction that attracts the audience's attention and interest in the topic. • Clearly state the negative position on the topic. • Clearly state the negative observations. • Support with reason and evidence. • Attack and question the affirmative contentions/evidence. • Conclude effectively.
Cross examination of the negative by the affirmative – 3 minutes	• Ask questions – have a strategy or at the very least a direction to your questioning. • Be courteous. • Face the audience.
Rebuttal speeches	• No new arguments are allowed – new evidence or analysis is OK.
First affirmative rebuttal – 4 minutes	• Respond to the negative observations – show how they are not as strong/relevant as the affirmative contentions. • Rebuild the affirmative case.
First negative rebuttal – 7 minutes	• Respond to the latest affirmative arguments. • Make your final case to the audience that the negative position is superior to the affirmative. • Try to convince the audience the affirmative has failed to carry the burden of proof. • **Summarize** the debate, conclude effectively and ask the audience to agree with the negative position.
Second affirmative rebuttal – 4 minutes	• Respond to the final negative arguments. • **Summarize** the debate and show the audience how the affirmative position is superior – and the affirmative has carried the burden of proof. • Conclude effectively.

To what extent can we consider empires a thing of the past?

Human history has included many empires. Some of these empires continued for hundreds of years, while others existed for only a short period of time before collapsing. However, whether they existed for a short or long period of time, it is clear that human history has been affected greatly by the existence of empires.

ACTIVITY: Essay on empire formation

ATL

- Information literacy skills: Collect and analyse data to identify solutions and make informed decisions
- Critical-thinking skills: Evaluate evidence and arguments

In this activity, you will create your own research question that focuses on some aspect of why empires form, and write an essay to answer this question.

Some questions to consider may be:
- **Do empires occur naturally, or do they only exist because of the human desire for conquest and expansion?**
- **Did a specific country today form in a way that is consistent with some of the formations of empires we have seen in this chapter?**

Choose one of these questions, or create your own.

Evaluate whether empire formation is a natural part of human history by creating a question that focuses on an aspect of empire formation.

Formulate an argument about empire formation to address the research question you have created.

Use this knowledge to write an essay with an introduction and conclusion and at least two main points, with evidence, and placed in order of importance. You could use the essay frame (right) to help you.

Essay frame

Plan

Organize your sources and ideas to support your question and offer another view. Add details and examples from your knowledge for both sides of the argument.

Introduction

You need to state your argument. What side of the argument do you support? You could briefly state which sources agree and which do not.

Main body

State at least two points that will address the question. Discuss the evidence and sources for each. Have a clear opening sentence that links to the question for each section.

Remember to use linking words: however, on the other hand, conversely, similarly, in addition, etc.

Conclusion

Write a sentence or two that answers the question. This should match the evidence provided.

◆ Assessment opportunities

- ◆ In this activity you have practised skills that are assessed using Criterion A: Knowing and understanding, Criterion B: Investigating, Criterion C: Communicating and Criterion D: Thinking critically.

❗ Take action

- ❗ Although Japan is the only modern country that has an emperor, many countries today used to be empires. Some empires have been responsible for human rights abuses in the last few hundred years.
- ❗ Choose one of the following empires and **identify** a human rights abuse or abuses that occurred towards some of its subjects. Determine if these human rights abuse(s) continue today, and where. Develop a class presentation regarding those abuses and how they have been addressed by the United Nations, other non-governmental organizations or modern governments, or if they have not yet been successfully addressed. Give this presentation in class, or to a wider audience.
  - Abyssinian empire
  - Austro-Hungarian empire
  - British empire
  - Central African empire
  - Chinese empire
  - French empire
  - Italian empire
  - Japanese empire
  - Ottoman empire
  - Portuguese empire
  - Russian empire
  - Spanish empire

EXTENSION

Organize a letter-writing campaign to a relevant government, embassy or non-governmental organization asking that institution about how their organization or government is working to resolve that particular human rights abuse or abuses. Consider creating a petition and involving your peers in protesting human rights abuses in the world.

Reflection

In this chapter, we have **discussed** why and how empires formed throughout history. We have reflected on the characteristics of empires. We have also assessed the relative importance of other factors in empire formation. Through this exploration, we have reflected on the benefits of empires for citizens and their leaders.

Use this table to reflect on your own learning in this chapter.		
Questions we asked	Answers we found	Any further questions now?
Factual: What are common characteristics of empires?		
Conceptual: What role does the military play in the development of empires? What role can innovation and technology play in the development of empires? What role can economics play in the development of empires? What role can climate play in the development of empires?		
Debatable: Is empire formation an inevitable part of human history? To what extent can we consider empires a thing of the past?		
Approaches to learning you used in this chapter	Description – what new skills did you learn?	How well did you master the skills?			
		Novice	Learner	Practitioner	Expert
Communication skills					
Collaboration skills					
Information literacy skills					
Critical-thinking skills					
Creative-thinking skills					
Transfer skills					
Learner profile attribute(s)	Reflect on the importance of being an inquirer for your learning in this chapter.				
Inquirers					

Global interactions | Governance; Interdependence | Personal and cultural expression

3 How do empires work?

○ Empires are **governed** by leaders who must control the **interactions** between **different cultures** both internally and **globally**.

CONSIDER THESE QUESTIONS:

Factual: What systems keep empires in place? What are the effects of an empire's global interaction?

Conceptual: How can empires successfully defend themselves from challenges and threats? What factors might be important for maintaining a successful empire?

Debatable: To what extent is leadership important in the maintenance of empires? To what extent are empires and modern supra-national organizations and superpowers similar? Can empires successfully accommodate the expression of personal and cultural difference?

Now, **share** and **compare** your thoughts and ideas with your partner or the rest of the class.

■ **Figure 3.1 (a)** Statue of the Roman Emperor Augustus (27 BCE–14 CE); **(b)** Statue of the Roman Emperor Marcus Aurelius (161–80 CE); **(c)** Statue of the Emperor Commodus as Hercules (177–92 CE); **(d)** Statue of the Roman Emperor Trajan (98–117 CE)

○ **IN THIS CHAPTER WE WILL …**
- **Find out** the common challenges faced by some of the world's empires.
- **Explore** the reasons why empires are challenged both internally and externally, and how some of the world's empires faced challenges to their rule, both from within the empire and outside it.
- **Take action** by investigating how some states handle internal and external crises today.

■ These Approaches to Learning (ATL) skills will be useful …
- Communication skills
- Collaboration skills
- Information literacy skills
- Critical-thinking skills
- Transfer skills

◆ Assessment opportunities in this chapter:
- **Criterion A**: Knowing and understanding
- **Criterion B**: Investigating
- **Criterion C**: Communicating
- **Criterion D**: Thinking critically

Individuals & Societies for the IB MYP 4&5: *by Concept*

SEE–THINK–WONDER

Look at the images in Figure 3.1.

What do you see?

To **analyse** these images consider the following questions:
- How do these statues seem physically?
  - Consider the colour and size of the statue.
  - What are they wearing?
  - What artifacts or items are they holding?
  - What do they suggest about their subjects?
- What does this make you think?
  - Do you think these statues are true to life?
  - Why were these emperors portrayed in this way?
- What does it make you wonder?
  - How are leaders portrayed now?
  - In what ways is this different?
  - In what ways might it be similar?
  - What does this tell us about the role of leadership in these societies compared to your own?

Why do you think statues and other sculptures are important for the maintenance of empire?

Now share your thoughts with the class.

● We will reflect on this learner profile attribute …

- Reflective – we will thoughtfully consider our own strengths and weaknesses in terms of analytical and debate skills, working to understand our own development as historians, and how our own ideas and experiences are the result of the history of the world around us.

KEY WORDS

alliances	Silk Road
infrastructure	standing armies
military	tax
military infrastructure	

3 How do empires work?

What systems keep empires in place?

Empires develop systems to support the state. These systems are varied, but can be used to aid the government while it engages in trade, communication, law and all other aspects of governance. Examples of these systems include:
- government and **bureaucracy**
- legal systems
- **infrastructure** and communication systems in the form of postal systems, roads and bridges.

GOVERNMENT

Governments are organizations that operate states and therefore empires. These governments come in many forms (see Chapter 2), but generally feature a ruler or rulers, officials who keep things organized and functioning, laws and law enforcement, and the collection of taxes to pay for the government and to be spent on maintaining the state.

Tax collection

Empires have collected taxes for thousands of years. People have been required to give to governments:
- time and labour
- goods, such as farm products or raw materials
- services
- money.

Without taxes, governments would not be able to maintain the systems that allow empires to continue. Empires have used taxes for:
- military expenses such as soldier salaries and food, equipment, ships, fortifications
- construction projects such as roads, buildings and canals
- salaries for government officials in courts and law enforcement and as **scribes**, etc.
- future use in a crisis.

Money

■ **Figure 3.2** Some ancient forms of money

Historians continue to debate the origin of money. We know that in ancient times people traded metals and precious materials such as ivory, silk and shells for other goods. These metals and goods served as a form of money. Manufactured money was first used in China around 1000 BCE when small bronze knives and spades were created specifically to function as money does today. The first coins were minted around 650 BCE by the Kingdom of Lydia, which ruled what is now western Turkey. This innovation spread to Greek-speaking communities throughout the Mediterranean region rapidly thereafter. Paper money was developed by 960 CE by the Song Dynasty. After the Mongol invasion of China, the idea of paper currency spread to much of the rest of the world.

Taxes have been collected in many ways. There have been taxes on:
- people
- families
- services and products
- land
- movement of people and goods.

Hongwu, the first Ming Emperor of China

Figure 3.3 Hongwu, the first Ming Emperor of China

Records were very important throughout China's long history. Government records indicated to Hongwu, the first Emperor of China's Ming Dynasty, that there were not enough people farming for many reasons, including drought, high taxes and soil erosion that meant less could be grown. Hongwu ordered the planting of millions of trees to combat soil erosion, reduced and ended taxes on certain types of farm land, ordered the construction of ponds and lakes to store water for use throughout the year, and had canals excavated for irrigation and transportation. By the end of his rule, more land was farmed in China than at any other time in history up to that point.

In the world today, people pay taxes on their income, their property, the goods and services that they purchase, and licenses. If people travel to another country, they often have to purchase a visa, a form of entry tax. Similarly, in the Roman empire under the Emperor Augustus, citizens of Rome were taxed for a variety of things, including land, homes and real estate, personal wealth, slaves, animals and inheritances. All empires have required the payment of taxes in one form or another.

Neo-Assyrian empire (911–609 BCE)

In 1952, archaeologists discovered part of an **archive** of the Assyrian empire in the ruins of ancient Nimrod, a former Assyrian capital. The archive contained letters written by government officials from other parts of the empire, as well as copies of letters written by the ruler of the city, the future King of Assyria, Shalmaneser the 5th. The letters indicate the importance of the records in running the government and include reports on:
- supplying the army
- building of city walls
- battles (both victories and defeats)
- population and movement of people
- trade with neighbouring countries
- taxes
- political decisions by the Government regarding other countries.

The archive was so important that the reports were kept for over a century, eventually being buried when the city was destroyed in a war that ended the Assyrian empire.

Planning/record keeping

All successful empires have maintained records for successful administration. These have included records of who lived there, soldiers, trade, agriculture, taxes paid and not paid, resources that needed to be imported and resources produced, weather and climate reports, and infrastructure. They also included records concerning diplomacy, the interaction between the empire and other states. These records allowed the government to:
- develop future plans
- keep track of current projects
- meet challenges
- ensure the timely payment of debts, soldiers, servants and other employees
- verify historical information
- ensure that relations with other states were organized and to their benefit.

3 How do empires work?

SOURCE A

'At the age of nineteen, on my own initiative and at my own expense, I raised an army by means of which I restored liberty to the republic, which had been oppressed by the tyranny of a [Roman] faction [of rebels]. For which service the Senate, with complimentary resolutions, enrolled me in its order … giving me at the same time [priority] in voting; it also gave me the imperium [highest military and legal authority]. As propraetor [governor of a province] it ordered me … "to see that the republic suffered no harm." In the same year, moreover, as both consuls [Senate chairmen and military commanders] had fallen in war, the people elected me consul … for settling the **constitution**.'

Funeral Inscription for The Augustus, the first emperor of Rome

ACTIVITY: Source analysis

■ ATL

- Critical-thinking skills: Recognize unstated assumptions and bias; Interpret data; Evaluate evidence and arguments; Revise understanding based on new information and evidence
- Transfer skills: Inquire in different contexts to gain a different perspective

Records are maintained so that an empire can make good decisions based on accurate data. For example, the Neo-Assyrian empire, as mentioned above, kept track of construction, military achievements, trade agreements, taxes and more.

In some cases, however, records, or what appear to be records, may be created and spread to change or influence the opinion of an empire's citizens. This can be known as **propaganda**.

Individually, **analyse** the source on the left, written by the Emperor Augustus and inscribed on his tomb as well as many other temples throughout the Roman empire.

Consider the questions below:
- What factual information can we determine from this source?
- Why did The Augustus discuss those specific events in his funeral inscription?
- Who is the intended audience?
- What image of himself did The Augustus want to portray to the citizens of the empire?

Evaluate the purpose of this source based on your answers to these questions.

> **Hint**
> To find the purpose of a source, think about why the source was written, spoken or drawn, and who it was for – who was the audience?

Formulate an argument about the purpose of this source. Using this source and your own knowledge, write this argument in a short essay.

> **Hint**
> Include an introduction, a conclusion and at least two paragraphs that each deal with a separate issue from the inscription. You may use the essay frame opposite.

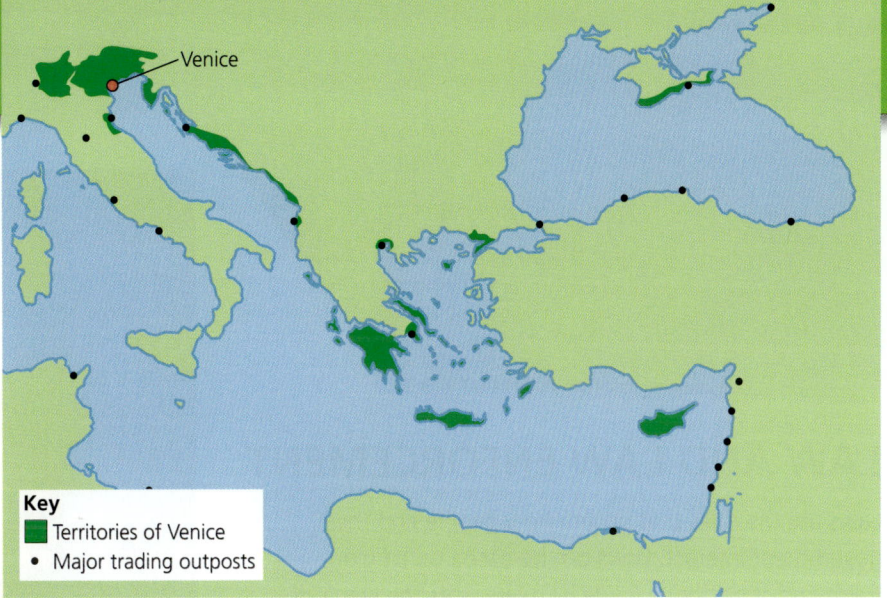

Figure 3.4 Republic of Venice in the fifteenth century

Essay frame

Introduction

Here you set out your line of argument.

First section and Second section

Use these paragraphs to **explain** each point in turn. Don't forget to have a clear opening sentence that links to the question, and remember to refer to examples from the source.

Conclusion

You should write a sentence or two that answers the question and/or supports your argument. For another essay writing frame, see p304.

Assessment opportunities

- In this activity you have practised skills that are assessed using Criterion A: Knowing and understanding, Criterion B: Investigating, Criterion C: Communicating and Criterion D: Thinking critically.

Venice

Venice was a city in today's Italy that operated its own version of empire between the seventh and eighteenth centuries. Although Venice was a form of republic, where eligible voters selected the country's leadership routinely, it ruled over other lands, islands and cities for hundreds of years. The main holdings of Venice were communities on the Adriatic and Aegean Seas, including parts of today's Croatia, Montenegro, Albania, Greece and Turkey. For much of the 1200s, they ruled the city of Constantinople (today's Istanbul) and much of the land around it after defeating the Eastern Roman, or Byzantine, empire. This empire was built on dominating trade between the Middle East and Europe for hundreds of years and this required a very organized government that kept detailed records.

The archives of the Republic of Venice contain hundreds of thousands of documents. The section of the archives that deals with interactions with the Ottoman empire over a 500-year span of time demonstrates the importance Venice placed on records and information. The archive contains:

- 21 peace treaties
- announcements by the ruler of the Ottoman empire regarding battle victories and changes in the law
- reports from Venetian diplomats on the Ottoman government
- reports from Venetian merchants on financial dealings with Ottoman merchants and their government
- letters written by Ottoman officials to Venetian government officers
- accounts of battles between Ottomans and Venetians.

Venetians were able to use comprehensive records in order to understand and manage their relationship with the Ottoman empire. While sometimes allied or working in cooperation with Ottomans, they also fought each other on a regular basis. Without these records, Venice would not have been able to successfully guide their relationship with the Ottoman empire.

LAW AND LAW ENFORCEMENT

Laws are the rules that govern how people and their government interact. Laws can be based on religion, traditions or decisions made by rulers or as the result of people meeting together to create the laws based on common understandings. Law codes generally strengthened empires. In order to ensure that laws were followed, systems of courts and law enforcement were developed.

The Ur-Nammu law code, c. 2100 BCE

The oldest surviving text of laws is the Ur-Nammu law code. It was issued by King of Ur-Nammu, the first king of the Neo-Sumerian empire, which was primarily located in today's Iraq and Syria. The tablet had over 50 written laws, 30 of which we can read today. The laws indicate that people should be executed if they commit murder, robbery, adultery or rape. For other crimes, people were fined, paying specific amounts of silver or grain.

Figure 3.5 First known version of the Ur-Nammu law code inscription, housed in the Istanbul Museum

ACTIVITY: Investigating legal systems

ATL

- Collaboration skills: Help others to succeed; Work collaboratively in teams; Listen actively to other perspectives and ideas; Negotiate effectively
- Transfer skills: Inquire in different contexts to gain a different perspective

Explore, in small groups, the legal systems below:
- The Hammurabi law code
- The Ur-Nammu law code
- The Roman empire's legal system
- The Mongol *Yassa*
- The Republic of Venice's legal system
- The Umayyad Caliphate's legal system

Identify one legal system to study in greater depth per group.

Investigate, as a group, the different ways that your chosen legal system addresses murder, treason and theft.

Discuss, as a group:
- the differences and similarities between these legal systems
- what these differences may say about the societies
- whether the punishments for these crimes are similar to or different from the laws of some modern states.

◆ Assessment opportunities

- In this activity you have practised skills that are assessed using Criterion A: Knowing and understanding, Criterion B: Investigating, Criterion C: Communicating and Criterion D: Thinking critically.

ACTIVITY: Constitutions

ATL

- Communication skills: Organize and depict information logically
- Collaboration skills: Help others to succeed; Listen actively to other perspectives and ideas; Negotiate effectively
- Critical-thinking skills: Evaluate evidence and arguments

Explore two of the following constitutions or forms of constitutions:
- The Twelve Tables
- The Hittite Constitution
- The Ur-Nammu law code
- The Solonian Constitution of Athens
- The Edicts of Ashoka

Use this knowledge to create your own constitution for a city-state or empire.

List, in writing, the rights of your citizens, and the responsibilities of your government towards its citizens. Indicate the type of government and its representative bodies, if there are any.

Discuss and debate the constitutions in class, and merge them to form a single constitution, holding votes on each clause to ensure that it represents the majority view.

◆ Assessment opportunities

- In this activity you have practised skills that are assessed using Criterion A: Knowing and understanding, Criterion B: Investigating, Criterion C: Communicating and Criterion D: Thinking critically.

Roman law

The system of law used during the Roman empire was developed earlier, during the Roman Republic (509–27 BCE). The first written laws were the Twelve Tables which served as a basic constitution for Rome's citizens. The Twelve Tables stated certain rights and responsibilities of citizens, including the right to trial. They also contained laws about religion and crime, and laws that governed the state. Laws made later had to be consistent with the Twelve Tables, including those laws developed during the Roman empire.

The Twelve Tables gave Roman citizens the right to be tried for crimes that they were accused of committing. They also allowed any Roman citizen to bring accusations against others to the appropriate court. For example, accusations of treason were referred to the court that dealt specifically with treason. The right to trial allowed the development of the institution of lawyers who knew the laws and had good speaking skills; it was not reasonable to expect all citizens to know all the laws. **Juries** of citizens, under the guidance of a government-appointed **magistrate**, heard arguments, reviewed evidence and decided whether an individual or group was guilty or innocent. Sentencing was the responsibility of the magistrate in cases of guilt.

The influence of Roman law

The Roman empire lasted for centuries, officially ending in 476 CE with the fall of the Western empire and the sack of Rome by Odoacer, a German military leader, who declared himself ruler of the Italian Peninsula. However, the Eastern Roman empire continued for centuries afterwards (referred to as the Byzantine empire, it eventually fell to the Ottoman empire in 1453). Because of this, Roman law has had a considerable influence on the world.

In the sixth century, the Eastern Roman Emperor, Emperor Justinian I, organized old Roman laws and formulated new ones, forming the *Corpus Juris Civilis*, sometimes referred to as the Justinian law code. This law code, in various forms, was used until the very end of the empire and became the basis of most European legal systems in the nineteenth century. For example, the *Corpus Juris Civilis* was the basis for the legal system of Germany until 1900.

Many ideas that we consider modern, like trials, juries, judges, **precedent** and appeals, are actually from the *Corpus Juris Civilis*. In fact, because of the effect that Roman law has had on the legal field, it is still a compulsory subject for legal degrees in many countries around the world today.

The concept and purpose of empire has largely been replaced by modern superpowers and the supra-national organizations that have established support. Instead of controlling large physical and geographic spaces, these superpowers dominate the world's economy, resources, health care, education, research and diplomacy through these supra-national organizations. Additionally, these supra-national organizations can protect and support smaller countries and bodies to some extent. This system has affected many aspects of modern society, including the nature of conflict, conflict resolution and political change.

ACTIVITY: Comparing supra-national organizations and superpowers

■ **ATL**

- Critical-thinking skills: Recognize unstated assumptions and bias; Interpret data; Revise understanding based on new information and evidence
- Transfer skills: Inquire in different contexts to gain a different perspective

To address the following activity, it is important to understand these terms:

- **Superpower** – a state or empire with a dominant position in world politics, that is characterized by its ability to exert influence or project power through economic, technological, military, cultural and diplomatic strength. Examples include the Soviet Union and the USA during the Cold War.
- **Supra-national organization** – an international group or union where the influence and power of member states exist beyond national boundaries, and decision-making affects all member states of the organization, group, or union. Examples include the European Union (EU) and the World Trade Organization (WTO).

Consider the following historical and modern or contemporary **social movements** (or any others of your choice):

Historical social movements:
- Roman slave revolts
- US civil rights movement (1954–68 CE)
- Chartist movement (1838–57 CE)
- Women's rights movement
- Taiping Rebellion (1850–64 CE)

Modern social movements:
- Arab Spring
- Occupy Wall Street movement
- Environmental Justice Movement
- Anti-Apartheid Movement
- Human rights movement

Compare and contrast one historical social movement with a modern one. Think about the following:
- What rights or benefits were being demanded by the protesters?
- What unique challenges does a historical social movement face that a modern one does not, and vice versa?
- What protections exist, or existed, for social movements?
- How would individuals involved in these protests be treated?
- Who would be opposed to these social movements? Why?
- Did any supra-national organization play a role in mediating this conflict? What effect did this have on the overall outcome?
- Are the answers to these questions dependent on the time period, the geographic region, the local or regional culture, or the politics of the particular state or region? How?

Use these questions to **formulate** an argument on how social movements have changed through time, and the effect of supra-national organizations on the nature of conflict.

Plan an essay, in bullet-point form, addressing your research question. This plan must include your argument, and at least three pieces of significant evidence.

◆ Assessment opportunities

◆ In this activity you have practised skills that are assessed using Criterion A: Knowing and understanding, Criterion B: Investigating and Criterion D: Thinking critically.

Mongol law

The law code of the Mongol empire was known as the *Yassa* and was initially developed by Genghis Khan in order to manage the behaviour and actions of his armies. It was oral in form because most Mongol people, at least at the empire's beginning, could not read and write. While written versions of the *Yassa* existed, these were only available to the royal family.

Since the Mongol empire was managed by the military, and the majority of the Mongol population was soldiers, the *Yassa* focused primarily on:
- the military and its organization
- the requirement of all Mongol people to work together, regardless of former tribal affiliation
- responsibilities of high-ranking members of both the army and the royal family
- forbidding attacks of any kind on members of the royal family
- the banning of retreat in military actions
- the requirement to show courage in war.

Later, the *Yassa* expanded to include laws on:
- marriage and adultery
- treatment of animals and resources like water
- inheritance
- military issues
- crime and punishments
- responsibilities of citizens.

The *Yassa* helped make sure that the strength and unity of the Mongol military was maintained as the empire expanded. Since the Mongol empire included diverse cultures and former states, the *Yassa* acted as a way to ensure the Mongol people did not lose the military strength that had won them the empire in the first place.

INFRASTRUCTURE

Successful empires developed infrastructure. This included roads, bridges, dams, canals and facilities for the public good, such as grain silos. These projects bound the empire together, allowed faster movement of people and goods, and the storage of food to prevent famine.

Roads and bridges

Roads and bridges were very important to many empires. They allowed the movement of people and goods. While some empires maintained paved stone or gravel roads, others, like the Mongol, had systems of roads and paths, like the Silk Road, that functioned in a similar way (see above). Bridges allowed roads to cross bodies of water and ravines.

Roman empire (27 BCE–476 CE)

The Roman empire built many roads in order to connect Rome, the capital, with its vast territory. These roads were built by the military for its use, but also for the transportation of goods, civilians and government officials. In addition to the roads, the military built **way stations** and inns at regular intervals to service the needs of travellers. Distance markers were also installed to help calculate distance and give directions.

It is estimated that 400,000 km of roads and bridges were built by the Roman empire, spread through the empire's 113 provinces. Because of the importance Rome placed on its provinces and the goods they supplied, the building of roads and bridges in the empire was considered the responsibility of the government. In fact, there were specific government officials whose only responsibility was the building and maintenance of roads and bridges to enable the transportation of goods and services. Sections of Rome's roads still exist and some are in use today, having only been modernized. The Via Appia still connects Rome with the southern Italian city of Brindisi, for example, and the Via Egnatia is still basically followed, linking Durres, Albania to Istanbul, Turkey.

Inca empire (1438–1533 CE)

The Inca empire in today's South America was dependent on a vast system of roads that linked its huge territory. Many of the roads were originally built by other states before the Inca expanded these and built additional routes. By the end of the empire, there were approximately 40,000 km of roads in use. Roads were built and used for religious and government purposes (the government owned and controlled all resources). The public had to have permission to use any of the road network. The *Qhapaq Ñan*, the Great Inca road, was the largest road at 6,000 km in length. It linked the north and south of the empire with the capital city of Cusco. Bridges were necessary to cross rivers and swamps, and ravines and were built out of wood, ropes, stone or rafts, depending on local resources and the distance that needed to be crossed.

Roads were primarily used by *chasqui*, human runners, who moved messages and goods, such as fish, cotton, maize and textiles. Pack animals, such as llamas and alpacas, also moved goods along the roads, but were not strong enough to allow human riders. The wheel was not known in South America at this time, so there were no wagons or carts of any sort. The government also used the roads to redistribute supplies, with huge storage facilities built along the roads in case of need (see below).

SOURCE A

'The road you travel from Tana [Azov] to Cathay is perfectly safe, whether by day or by night, according to what the merchants say who have used it. Only if the merchant … should die upon the road, everything belonging to him will become the perquisite [property] of the lord of the country in which he dies … And there is another danger: this is when the lord of the country dies, and before the new lord who is to have the lordship is proclaimed; during such intervals there have sometimes been irregularities practised on the Franks and other foreigners …'

Account of the Silk Road by Florentine merchant [from Florence in today's Italy] *Pegolotti, 1340*

SOURCE B

■ **Figure 3.6** Map of Roman Britain's road system

SOURCE C

'The Romans built over 53,000 miles of main roads from Newcastle in the north west to Damascus in the south east. The way in which roads were built varied according to the level of anticipated traffic, the nature of locally available materials, climate, topography and, particularly in the case of Britain, the disposition of the local people towards the Romans. British Roman roads were unique in being constructed on an embankment or agger, principally as a means of allowing the Roman users greater visibility and in the case of attack, to give them the advantage of height. Lowland British Roman roads were usually built through wooded countryside and a significant clearing was formed each side of the road, again for reasons of security.'

The Romans and their Roads, J. Knapton

ACTIVITY: The benefits of roads

■ ATL

- Critical-thinking skills: Recognize unstated assumptions and bias; Interpret data; Evaluate evidence and arguments; Revise understanding based on new information and evidence
- Transfer skills: Inquire in different contexts to gain a different perspective

Consider Sources A, B and C.

What can these sources tell us about the benefits of road building, and infrastructure in general, for the maintenance of empire?

To what extent do these sources agree on benefits of roads?

According to these sources, how did infrastructure help different segments of society? For example, did merchants receive different benefits from infrastructure than soldiers or tourists?

Now, **discuss** your ideas with the class.

EXTENSION

In groups of no more than four students, **create** an advertisement offering your road-building expertise that will be shown to the Roman Emperor. Consider the benefits of roads to the empire, and be sure to address how road creation will ultimately benefit the emperor. For example, your roads could be specifically designed for faster troop movements, which would increase safety, or they may be extra wide to benefit tourism and trade.

Present this advertisement to the class and **explain** your choices.

◆ Assessment opportunities

- In this activity you have practised skills that are assessed using Criterion A: Knowing and understanding, Criterion C: Communicating and Criterion D: Thinking critically.

DAMS AND CANALS

Management of water has been critical for several empires. Dams not only prevent floods, but also create reservoirs for water storage. This stored water can be used during dry seasons or drought for agriculture and other purposes. Canals have been built throughout history to allow more agriculture and the movement of people and goods on boats.

Middle Kingdom Egypt (2055–1650 BCE)

Egypt was completely dependent on the Nile River. The Nile River provided water for irrigation and served as the main artery of transportation, with boats moving people and goods rapidly. As the Nile was the only source of water in the region, agriculture was limited to its banks. In order to increase the amount of land under cultivation, or to move goods further away from the river, canals had to be constructed. Historians know that canals were important before the Middle Kingdom, having been used over 500 years previously to transport huge blocks of stone in the construction of the Great Pyramids of Giza, for example.

The Great Canal, the Mer-Wer, was one of the greatest projects of the Middle Kingdom. It was a wide, deep channel that linked the Nile to a natural depression called the Faiyum. Dams between the Great Canal and the Nile regulated the water flow.

One significant effect of the Great Canal was the vast expansion of agriculture, as well as the thousands of smaller canals branching off it. This led to a growing population in the region. Furthermore, because of the Great Canal, a lake formed in the Faiyum, which expanded agriculture even more, and allowed for the development of fishing in the area and the creation of new cities. Finally, goods, including stones for the pyramid tombs of Middle Kingdom pharaohs, were transported using the Great Canal. The Great Canal, now called the Bahr Youssef, still connects the Nile River to the Faiyum, where millions of people and vast farms continue to exist today, 4,000 years after its construction.

3 How do empires work?

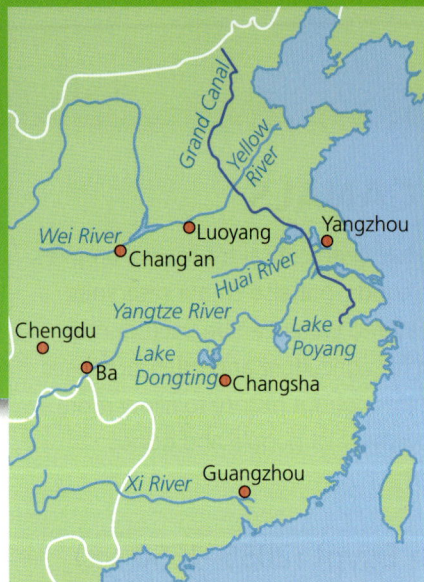

Figure 3.7 China and the Grand Canal

The Grand Canal, China

The Grand Canal in China, also referred to as the Jīng-Háng Dà Yùnhé, is one of the greatest canals in human history. The first sections of the canal were constructed in the 500s BCE, but were linked together about one thousand years later by 618 CE. The Grand Canal connected the two largest rivers in China, the Yangtze and the Yellow, and stretched over 1,790 km in length. Many of China's largest cities were, and are, linked by the Grand Canal which continues to function.

The Grand Canal allowed the transportation of goods, especially grain, between northern and southern China. A thousand years ago, over 8,000 ships travelled through the canal annually, transporting more than 360,000 tons of grain to areas where it was needed. The canal was used by thousands of merchant ships each year and served as the main travel artery between north and south China for government officials, including the Emperor.

FOOD STORAGE

Empires have often developed storage facilities for holding food and other resources in case of need. Famine, caused by inclement weather, such as flooding or drought, war and pestilence occurred regularly and governments often made plans in advance to address the worst effects of these incidents.

Roman empire (27 BCE–476 CE)

The Roman empire relied on the redistribution or movement of certain goods. The most important product for the Romans was grain. This critical food product was produced primarily in Egypt and in north Africa and was needed in order to feed the citizens of the capital city of Rome and nearby cities on the Italian peninsula.

The first Roman Emperor, Octavian Caesar, developed a system known as *annona*, which involved the government contracting private merchants to move grain between the areas of production and the city of Rome. This allowed the movement of 300,000 tons of grain annually into Rome and nearby cities during the first years of the empire. Without this grain, the city of Rome would have starved. The sheer volume of grain meant that there were no grain shortages and prices remained low. Later emperors gave free grain to over 200,000 people living in Rome, while all others received grain at a very low price. The Emperor Tiberius, the second emperor, understood clearly that the government's stability depended on the grain supply, indicating that any disruption in the grain supply would lead to the ruin of the state. Much of Rome's foreign policy centered on gaining access to or protecting food supply for its citizens, including the annexation of north Africa and Egypt.

The grain supply of Rome was critically important, so great facilities were constructed for its storage and safekeeping. These facilities were known as *horrea*, and stored grain, but also other goods such as wine, olive oil and clothing. By the early third century CE, Rome had over 300 *horrea* in the city alone. The most famous of these was the *Horrea Galbae*, a warehouse complex which covered an area of 21,000 m². The *horrea* system in Rome was so great that when Emperor Septimius Severus died in 211 CE, the *horrea* were stocked with enough food to feed the city of Rome for another seven years.

Inca empire (1438–1533 CE)

The Inca empire did not have a **market economy** where goods were bought and sold, but had an economy based on redistribution of goods. Some areas were able to harvest root crops like yams, while others grew grain, produced wool or made blankets. The government required people to give much of their production to the state which then stored it for redistribution to other areas. This was especially important in times when there were food shortages. In this case, the government was able to distribute food that had been stored in years when there were better crops, or it could send food from distant storage facilities where there was no famine.

Qullqa, a type of storage facility, were built all over the empire in great numbers in order to safely store all types of materials that might be needed. In the Mantaro Valley, located in today's Peru, archaeologists have found over 2,500 qullqas with a storage capacity of at least 170,000 m². Near Cochabamba, archaeologists have located over 2,400 *qullqas*, and almost 2,000 have been found near Salta, Argentina. Probably tens of thousands were constructed, always along the Inca road network.

Qullqa were not just important for food distribution during famine, but also in times of war and for government use. *Qullqa* stored vast quantities of weapons, including shields, knives and bows. Soldiers could move rapidly along the road network, not burdened by carrying their supplies, obtaining necessary equipment when they reached their destination from the local *qullqas*.

COMMUNICATION SYSTEMS

Empires required communication networks. We have already seen that the ancient Assyrian empire and Venetian state had networks that regularly submitted reports to a central authority. Those reports allowed planning, but also guidance to officials far from the ruler. All empires had communication systems with reports, information, decisions and questions flowing back and forth. Some of these systems were more innovative, speedy or developed than others. Postal systems were one of the many forms of communication systems.

■ **Figure 3.8** The Mamluk Sultanate (1250–1517 CE)

Mamluk Sultanate (1250–1517 CE)

The Mamluks controlled today's Syria and Egypt and all the territory in between. As they faced attacks by the Crusaders, as well as the Mongol, Byzantine and Ottoman empires at different times, a rapid, efficient system of communication was developed. Sultan Baybars (1260–77 CE) developed a postal system that could carry government messages between its two major cities of Cairo and Damascus in four days, a distance of around 1,000 km. This required new roads, bridges and stations where horse riders and horses could be changed on a regular basis. This allowed a message to move almost non-stop on its journey between the two cities.

ACTIVITY: Communication networks

ATL

- Communication skills: Organize and depict information logically
- Information literacy skills: Access information to be informed and inform others; Make connections between various sources of information
- Critical-thinking skills: Evaluate evidence and arguments

Empires need systems that allow them to communicate. As we have with the Mamluk Sultanate and the Mongol empire, the success of a communication network can be determined by its reliability, its speed and its reach.

Copy and complete Table 3.1 to **identify** the communication network that each of the listed empires developed or used, if any.

Evaluate, using research and your own knowledge, the advantages and disadvantages of these systems.

Finally, determine which one communication network was the most successful.

Explain how you arrived at this answer.

Communicate your completed table and the answer to the question above to the class as a display and/or class presentation.

EXTENSION

Now, choose three empires that are not in the table below.

Explore the communication systems of your three additional empires. Take special note of the advantages and disadvantages of each empire's system.

Formulate an opinion on which empire had the strongest communication system, using evidence to **justify** your choice.

Assessment opportunities

- In this activity you have practised skills that are assessed using Criterion A: Knowing and understanding, Criterion B: Investigating, Criterion C: Communicating and Criterion D: Thinking critically.

Table 3.1 Empires and their communication networks

Empire	Communication network	Advantage(s)	Disadvantage(s)
Mamluk Sultanate			
Mongol empire			
Roman empire			
Song Dynasty			
Inca empire			

Additionally, the sultanate used pigeons to move messages even more rapidly. Stations were built to house and feed pigeons which were outfitted with small carrying cases for messages on their legs. Pigeons with information from Cairo to Damascus, for example, would land at the station in Gaza. Messages would then be transferred to pigeons that would fly to the next station. In addition, pigeons could be kept in places that had no roads, such as distant locations along the Nile. Pigeons ensured that the Mamluk communication system covered every area of their vast empire, far beyond any roads or major cities.

Mongol empire (1206–1368 CE)

The Yam system is one of the most famous pre-modern communication systems. The Mongol empire was the largest empire in world history and as a result had challenges in maintaining communications within their vast territory. It could take years to cross from one end to the other. As a result, Mongol people developed the Yam, or Örtöö, system of messengers.

The Yam system was similar to that of the Mamluks in that relay stations were positioned between 25 and 65 km apart. Each relay station had rested horses and riders, as well as food and accommodation for other horses and riders.

riders. Messages were expected to travel between 200 and 300 km per day. At each relay station, a messenger could change his horse for a rested one or, alternatively, a new messenger could be dispatched. While this system was not new, it was operated on a scale never seen before. Mongol China alone had:

- 1,400 postal stations
- 50,000 horses
- 6,000 boats.

The overall Yam system operated many thousands of stations, riders and boats, as well as hundreds of thousands of horses. Although the primary use of the Yam system was for military and government reports, merchants were also allowed to use the system. At first, usage was free and then later for a fee, helping the overall economy of the empire.

TO WHAT EXTENT ARE EMPIRES AND MODERN SUPRA-NATIONAL ORGANIZATIONS AND SUPERPOWERS SIMILAR?

ACTIVITY: Comparing and contrasting modern superpowers and supra-national organizations with historical empires

ATL

- Critical-thinking skills: Recognize unstated assumptions and bias; Interpret data; Revise understanding based on new information and evidence
- Transfer skills: Inquire in different contexts to gain a different perspective

Remind yourself of what superpowers ad supra-national organizations are (page 54).

Consider the superpowers and supra-national organizations in the list below:
- The USA (1947–91)
- The Soviet Union (1947–91)
- North Atlantic Treaty Organization (NATO)
- World Trade Organization (WTO)
- United Nations

Explore, using independent research and your own knowledge, what systems or institutions supported and maintained two of these superpowers and/or supra-national organizations. (Ideally, you should pick one of each.)

You may wish to consider the systems below (or your own area of interest):
- Bureaucracy
- Voting
- Record-keeping
- Taxation
- Laws
- Communication
- Military systems

Compare and contrast the systems you researched above with those of an empire discussed in this chapter. For example, you may wish to compare the voting, taxation and military systems of the Soviet Union with those of the Roman empire.

List the similarities and differences in a table.

EXTENSION

Discuss, as a class, what these differences tell you about how empires maintained themselves in comparison with modern superpowers and supra-national organizations. How are they similar? How are they different? Why?

◆ Assessment opportunities

- In this activity you have practised skills that are assessed using Criterion A: Knowing and understanding, Criterion B: Investigating, Criterion C: Communicating and Criterion D: Thinking critically.

3 How do empires work?

What are the effects of an empire's global interaction?

Empires are often strengthened through cultural exchange, the borrowing and sharing of ideas, innovations and products. Cultural exchange often strengthens the state through food production, technological innovation and economic development.

CULTURAL EXCHANGE

Empires often allow increased movement of people, which can mean that ideas and goods spread more freely and, possibly, more openly.

Roman empire (27 BCE–476 CE)

The Roman empire stretched roughly from today's Scotland to southern Iraq and from today's Morocco to Romania. The territory was bound economically and socially through a vast network of roads, bridges, **caravans** and ships. Through these, millions of people were brought together and were able to move around this vast network for employment, military service and even tourism. Ideas and goods flowed freely.

Engineering

Romans were successful engineers, building roads, bridges, sewage disposal and water delivery systems, theatres and fortifications in many of the cities within the empire. This brought the Roman way of life into much of the known world, and allowed for local goods and ideas to travel easily back to Rome in the form of individuals, plays, texts and

■ **Figure 3.9** The Roman theatre in modern-day Jordan

medicine. Many of these engineering constructions still exist today, including the Colosseum in Rome, the Via Appia road connecting the city of Rome to the port city of Brindisi, and the 6,000-seat second-century Roman theatre in modern-day Amman, Jordan.

Religion

People throughout the Roman empire had different religious beliefs. As people moved around the empire, they took their religious beliefs with them and sometimes adopted others. For example, archaeologists have discovered temples to gods and goddesses, such as Osiris and Isis, originally worshipped by Egyptians, everywhere in the former Roman empire, and temples to Roman gods in Egypt. Religions that were originally found outside of the Roman empire, such as **Mithraism**, spread through the Roman military and then through civil society. In the later years of this state, Christianity spread from the Middle East areas of the empire into Europe and northern Africa.

Language

The official language of the Roman empire was Latin, although Greek was used as an official language in the eastern parts of the empire. Hundreds of local languages were spoken but merchants, scholars, government officials and soldiers had to speak Latin, or Greek, in order to communicate. This led to Latin-speaking communities throughout the empire. Later, when the empire fell apart, the use of Latin and its local dialects continued. Over hundreds of years, this led to the formation of the languages that are closely related and known today such as Spanish, Portuguese, Catalan, French, Italian, Romanian, Sardinian, **Romansch**, Sicilian and **Aromanian**, but also affected the development of many more, such as Albanian and Arabic, through their use of Latin words.

Mongol empire (1206–1368 CE)

The Mongol empire was vast, stretching from the Baltic Sea to the Mediterranean Sea, to today's Kuwait, and across the Himalayas to what we now know as Vietnam. With hundreds of millions of people living in this vast territory and ruled by one government, there was more sharing of culture, ideas, technology, religion and food during the Mongol empire than had ever occurred in human history up to that point in time.

Religion

From the outset, the Mongol empire was very tolerant of all religious beliefs. The rulers built temples, churches, monasteries and mosques for Buddhist, Christian, Taoist and Muslim people in their capital city of Karakorum, for example. Even in areas with an official state religion, Mongols allowed (and in many cases sponsored) other religions.

Nestorian Christianity spread throughout the empire and many members of the ruling family were Nestorians. During the rule of Mongke, the fourth Great Khan, this type of Christianity was the most influential religion throughout Asia. Other types of Christianity, such as Roman Catholicism, were allowed to send missionaries to China and other locations, as well.

Buddhism, in all its forms, also spread throughout the empire, from east Asia to central Asia and even parts of the Middle East and today's Russia, if briefly. Tibetan Buddhism was adopted as the state religion for the Mongol rulers, the Yuan Dynasty, that ruled China as part of the empire. Kublai Khan in particular, the founder of the Yuan Dynasty and the fifth Great Khan, adopted and encouraged the growth of Buddhism in the region.

Initially, Islam was considered a threat to the Mongol empire as war was waged against the Abbasid Caliphate whose ruler was the religious head of Islam as well. Once the Mongols destroyed the Abbasid Caliphate, they were more tolerant of Islam and in time many Mongol leaders converted to the religion. Eventually Muslim scholars and government officials were of such importance in the empire that they were sent to China to help govern that vast territory. This led to the spread of Islam throughout east Asia.

Technology and ideas

The Mongol empire is known for its impact on the development of technology and ideas, as well as the spread of these ideas to the rest of the world. Gunpowder, originally used for fireworks in China, was adapted for use as a weapon. The Mongol military, discovering this weapon when fighting against China, adopted this technology for use in their wars throughout Asia, the Middle East and into Europe. Through interactions with Mongol people, other states developed gunpowder weapons which changed the way wars were fought, including military architecture, armour and the use of guns, grenades, cannons and more.

Not all technology spread or developed by Mongol people had a military use. In fact, the windmill was developed in Persia, today's Iran, but spread throughout China and the Middle East as a result of these areas being united under Mongol rule. Soon the windmill was in use throughout Asia and appeared in Europe as well.

Similarly, the compass, developed in China, was brought to Europe and the Middle East because of the increased global interactions brought about by the Mongol trade route, the Silk Road. This innovation had several positive effects on society, which included increased navigation capabilities for travel by sea.

Technology and ideas also spread into China from other parts of the Mongol empire. A good example of this was the development of Chinese astronomy and mathematics as the result of increased interaction between Chinese astronomers and mathematicians and their counterparts in Persia. This meant that China adopted the idea of latitudes for mapping, and became more familiar with instruments such as the terrestrial globe and the armillary sphere. The cooperation between multi-ethnic and multi-religious people throughout the empire led to the spread of the use of the decimal and further development of mathematics, especially trigonometry, the use of coordinates and cubic interpolation.

▼ Links to: Mathematics and Science

■ Figure 3.10 An astrolabe

Consider one of the following items or ideas:
- Terrestrial globe
- Armillary sphere
- Astrolabe
- Compass
- Windmill
- Decimals
- Trigonometry
- Coordinates
- Cubic interpolation

Investigate in pairs how the discovery of this item or idea affected the advancement of mathematics and the sciences. What were some of the effects of this idea or item? What exists in the world today because of this discovery?

Discuss the effect of your chosen item or idea with at least one Individuals and Societies teacher and at least one Science and/or Mathematics teacher. Conduct this discussion in an interview format. Prepare at least five questions to determine their views on the relative importance of your chosen item or idea on their field and world society. Share the results with your class and consider making a presentation on your discoveries as well.

> ### ▼ Links to: Literature and Science
>
> Consider one of the following authors:
> - Ibn Khaldun
> - Ibn Battuta
> - Abu Ali Sina (also known as Ibn-Sina, or Avicenna)
> - Omar Khayyam
> - Muhammad ibn Musa al-Khwarizmi
> - Abu al-Hasan ibn 'Ali al-Qalasadi
> - Socrates
> - Plato
> - Aristotle
> - Marco Polo
>
> **Investigate** how the spread of their ideas affected the world today. What did they bring to their respective fields?
>
> **Explore**, through independent research, any other authors who were re-discovered because of 'movable type' or mass printing. What were the effects of this re-discovery on knowledge and understanding? Refer to *Sciences for IB MYP 4&5* Chapter 1 for more on the innovations of these significant individuals.

Some innovations of the Mongol empire have had long-lasting effects on civilizations that followed. An example of this is the use of movable type, an early version of the printing press which meant that letters and words could be arranged permanently on a tray and used to repeatedly stamp paper; this replaced copying by hand. This innovation meant that there were more books produced, reducing their costs and eventually increasing literacy as a result. This also led to the spread of ideas in areas such as philosophy, religion, mathematics, science and literature. Ancient works that were obscure by this time, such as Plato's *The Republic*, were resurrected as the result of mass printing. These spread to Europe, Asia, north Africa and the Middle East affecting law, politics, medicine, literature, architecture, philosophy and more.

Agriculture, travel and commerce

The Mongol empire had a significant effect on the world's commerce and agricultural production, greatly strengthening the empire. The Silk Road, which had existed in prior centuries, expanded and developed greater importance. Before the Mongol empire, merchants along the Silk Road only transported the most expensive luxury items, such as silk, gold and silver. By the time the products reached Persia or the Mediterranean Sea region, they were extremely expensive as a result of taxes charged by each state they had passed through as well as costs for security and animal transport. Products were also sold at a higher price so that merchants could recover from any losses of transport animals or stolen goods.

Once all states along the Silk Road were annexed to the Mongol empire, border taxes were abolished, banditry ended and the Road itself became safer. This greatly reduced travel time, expenses and the need to pay for caravan security so there was easier movement of luxury goods, people, agricultural products like tea and spices, as well as books, textiles and scientific instruments. This also meant that these goods could be moved in greater quantities.

Along the Silk Road, spices such as cardamom and peppercorns spread to the Middle East, becoming part of the local diet for the first time. Noodles, chickpeas and yoghurt spread from Asia into the West, where they were soon consumed in Europe. Tea consumption also spread using the Silk Road, and became a great luxury in much of Asia, the Middle East and north Africa.

Due to the size of the empire and the interdependencies that existed within it, the Mongol empire needed methods to ensure that:

- their officials could travel easily and be recognized as emissaries of the central authority
- trade could be conducted easily, with minimal confusion.

Mongols solved the first of these with the creation of passports, known as *paiza*, *paizi*, or *gerege*. These were tablets of gold or silver (depending on rank) that allowed officials, and certain merchants, to travel freely within the empire. The *paizi* also meant that the official was exempt from taxation, entitled to free use of the horses at the Mongol relay stations and given free food rations.

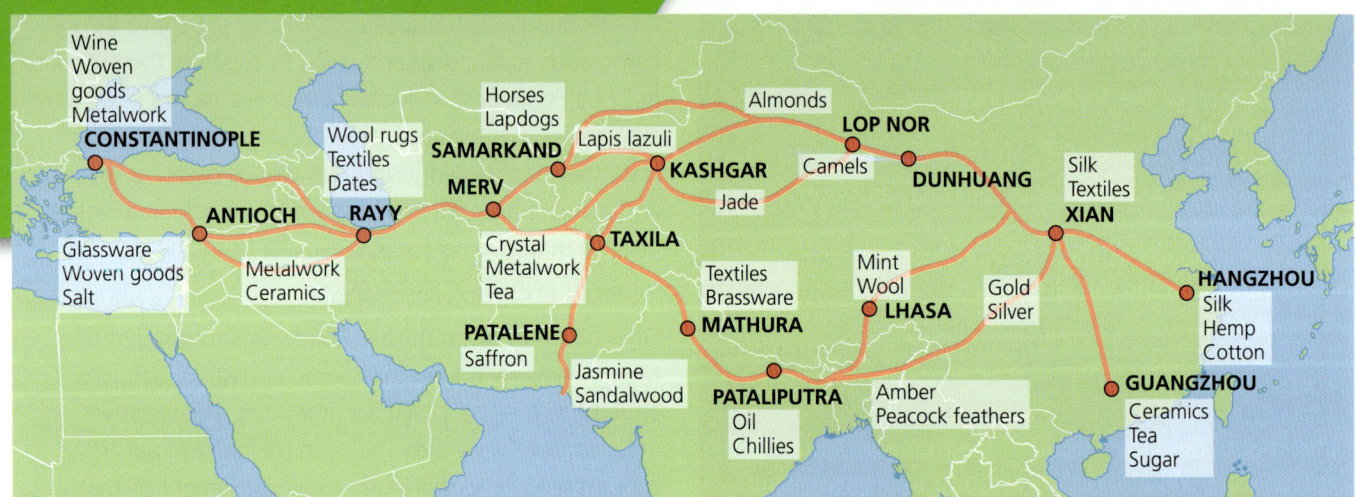

■ **Figure 3.11** The Silk Road during the Mongol empire, showing the primary goods of key regions

ACTIVITY: Modern supra-national entities and cultural exchange

ATL

- Critical-thinking skills: Draw reasonable conclusions and generalizations; Consider ideas from multiple perspectives
- Transfer skills: Inquire in different contexts to gain a different perspective

Consider the following modern supra-national entities and economic agreements:
- Council for Mutual Economic Assistance (COMECON)
- North American Free Trade Agreement (NAFTA)
- Dominican Republic–Central America Free Trade Area (CAFTA–DR)
- Association of Southeast Asian Nations (ASEAN)
- European Union (EU)
- Arab League
- Turkic Council

Analyse whether or not these supra-national entities and/or economic agreements allow for the same exchange of ideas, goods and people as the empires we have discussed. How do they differ? In what areas do they surpass the empires we have discussed in terms of the exchange of ideas, goods and people? In what areas do they fall short?

Discuss, as a class, to what extent supra-national organizations continue to facilitate the continued exchange and movement of ideas, goods and people. Compare and contrast these supra-national organizations with the empires you have studied regarding these issues.

Debate your ideas as a class. At the end of the debate, create a shared Venn diagram that highlights the similarities and differences between empires and supra-national organizations in terms of the exchange and movement of ideas, goods and people.

◆ Assessment opportunities

◆ In this activity you have practised skills that are assessed using Criterion A: Knowing and understanding, Criterion B: Investigating, Criterion C: Communicating and Criterion D: Thinking critically.

ACTIVITY: Columbian Exchange

ATL

- Communication skills: Organize and depict information logically
- Collaboration skills: Help others to succeed; Listen activity to other perspectives and ideas; Negotiate effectively
- Transfer skills: Inquire in different contexts to gain a different perspective

Empires provide opportunities for products and agricultural goods to find new markets, and give people across the world access to new foods and spices. As we have seen, the Silk Road was one means of cultural exchange.

Another example of this is the Columbian Exchange. This term refers to the transfer of goods, plants, people, diseases and ideas that occurred after 1492 when Europeans made contact with and began conquering and settling in what is now the Americas.

Investigate the Columbian Exchange. Make a table of your own design indicating different categories of goods and ideas that were exchanged between Europe and the New World. These should include the goods and ideas shown in Figure 3.12. Be sure to indicate the origins of each and any other details you feel are important, such as the effect of the introduction of that good or idea in its new location.

Debate with your class which items that were exchanged were the most impactful. **Justify** your reasoning with an argument based on evidence.

Assessment opportunities

- In this activity you have practised skills that are assessed using Criterion B: Investigating, Criterion C: Communicating and Criterion D: Thinking critically.

■ Figure 3.12 The Columbian Exchange, showing the primary goods of key regions

3 How do empires work?

How can empires successfully defend themselves from challenges and threats?

Empires must protect themselves from military threats. Protection can be in the form of standing armies, alliances, treaties and constructions.

STANDING ARMIES

Throughout history, empires have used armies to maintain control of provinces or regions that they conquered, defend against armies that are threatening them, or engage in war against rival states. To do this, some empires maintained standing armies that operated as a professional warrior class.

Roman empire (27 BCE–476 CE)

Rome's military was divided into legions of approximately 5,000, which included soldiers and support staff divided into cohorts of 500 and centuries of 100. Each legion was commanded by a general. In most cases, the general answered to a governor of a province or geographic area.

Rome developed the standing army system in 108 BCE. Under this system, all male citizens under the age of 45 were eligible for army service, with equipment provided by the government. Soldiers could serve full time in the army for up to 25 years and were paid a regular wage by the state. Upon completion of this service, soldiers would receive farm land as a reward from the state. This land was often located near the empire's borders so that the soldiers could be called upon in emergencies, but also to make these areas more Roman in culture.

At its peak, the Roman army consisted of 450,000 soldiers in 33 separate legions. These were spread across the empire and acted to defend Rome's provinces and as a police force to ensure order in the geographic region. Rome's large standing army, combined with former soldiers living in newly conquered provinces, ensured that there was stability and security throughout the empire.

Mongols

The Mongol military was organized into armies of 10,000, majority cavalry, known as *tumen*. The command structure, divided into groups of ten, 100 and 1,000, each had a commanding officer. Each army of 10,000 was led by a general, selected by the Great Khan, who could act independently to fight battles against the empire's enemies.

If the Mongol army faced an enemy that was too large for a single *tumen*, the Great Khan could appoint an *orlok* from one of his generals. An *orlok*, a general over other generals, would take charge of several *tumen* for the duration of any conflict.

During the time of Genghis Khan, the Mongol army numbered between 100,000 and 130,000 full-time, professional soldiers. All Mongol males were required to serve in the military, with minor exceptions such as religious leaders and government officials. This number increased through time, as more land was taken over and the Mongol population expanded. The large, full-time standing army meant that the empire was safe from attack and internally stable. This played a large part in the period of peace during the Mongol empire known as the **Pax Mongolica**, The Mongol Peace.

ALLIANCES

It has been common throughout history for states to work together for common interests, including mutual defense and military assistance. Even today, most states are involved in alliances with other countries.

Medes–Babylon Alliance (616–609 BCE)

The Mede people, based in today's Iran, and the Babylonian people, in today's southern Iraq, had been part of the Neo-Assyrian empire for centuries. As the empire weakened, rebellions occurred and Medes and Babylonians created an alliance in 616 BCE to fight against the Assyrian people. In response, the Neo-Assyrian empire formed an alliance with Egypt. Over the next 12 years, both groups of allies conducted all-out war.

The weakened Neo-Assyrian empire was unable to defend itself effectively from the Babylonian–Mede alliance. In 614 BCE, the ancient Assyrian capital of Assur was destroyed by the Mede military. In 612 BCE, the Assyrian city of Nineveh, the largest city in the world at that time with 150,000 people, was captured after a three-month siege. The city was completely destroyed, with its people killed or sent into exile.

In 609 BCE, an Egyptian army moved to help its Neo-Assyrian ally, destroying an army from the Kingdom of Judah, ally of Babylonia at the Battle of Megiddo. In the same year, the new Assyrian capital at Harran was destroyed by the armies of the Medes and Babylonians, ending the Neo-Assyrian empire. The war between Egypt and the allied Medes and Babylonians continued, with Egypt eventually losing control of most of its territories in the Levant. The alliance between the Mede and Babylonian people not only defended each group from Assyrian aggression, but eventually led to their independence, and the destruction of the Neo-Assyrian empire.

3 How do empires work?

Delian League (478–404 BCE)

The Delian League, also known as the Athenian League, was an alliance formed between Athens and approximately 300 other city-states in 478 BCE. The original purpose of this alliance was to minimize, or remove, the influence of Persia on the Greek-speaking city-states and create a system through which they could defend themselves from Persian military power.

The alliance was initially equal with all city-states:
- having a single vote at meetings
- vowing to protect each other from enemies
- creating a common treasury to be used for mutual defence
- contributing to the treasury.

The Delian League was successful against Persia. The League defeated Persian armies and its navy in several engagements. Eventually Persia abandoned the Aegean Sea region, giving the Delian League complete control of the region's political, military and economic systems.

Athens was the largest member of the Delian League and in time came to dominate the alliance, effectively creating an Athenian empire. This was clearly demonstrated when the city-states of Naxos and Thasos attempted to leave the League. Both were attacked by the Athens-dominated League and were defeated, being required to pay vast sums of money to Athens and to give up their own defences, including walls and ships. Although Athens created an empire out of the League, the Aegean people continued to be free of Persian influence. Therefore, it is clear that the Delian League was successful in its aims.

Egyptian–Hittite Treaty

Treaties are agreements between states that govern their relations, including the creation of alliances. These are often related to peace, but can also be for economic and other reasons. Treaties allow states to manage their relationships to prevent conflict.

The Eternal Treaty is the earliest treaty that has been found between two states and in which both sides' versions of the treaty are known. This treaty was created to govern relations between New Kingdom Egypt and the Hittite empire in about 1258 BCE and was agreed to by Ramses II, Pharaoh of Egypt, and Hattušiliš III, King of the Hittite empire. The treaty stated:
- War would end between the two countries.
- Political exiles would be exchanged between the two, including Hattušiliš III's nephew who lived in Egypt and hoped to overthrow his uncle.
- Each country would help the other out against other enemies.
- The leaders of each country would help put down revolts against either of them.

The treaty was to be in effect for all time. Egypt and the Hittite empire remained at peace until the Hittite empire was destroyed approximately 80 years later.

ACTIVITY: Negotiating an alliance

■ **ATL**

- Communication skills: Use a variety of speaking techniques to communicate with a variety of audiences
- Collaboration skills: Help others to succeed; Listen actively to other perspectives and ideas; Negotiate effectively
- Critical-thinking skills: Draw reasonable conclusions and generalizations; Consider ideas from multiple perspectives

Treaties can be agreed on for many different reasons. In some cases, a treaty will be implemented because all the states or empires involved have something to gain from the other state, or empire. In other cases, one state or empire may have something that the other wants, or something that the other state or states fear, such as a larger army. Depending on the situation, the conditions of a treaty may benefit only one side, one side more than another, or all sides of the agreement equally.

Divide into groups of no more than four students each. Half of the groups will represent New Kingdom Egypt and the other half will represent the Hittite empire.

Investigate the political, economic, military and social conditions of your empire during the time period leading up to the Eternal Treaty.

Identify and **list** the advantages that your empire has over the empire you will be negotiating with.

Now, find a group that is representing the opposite empire. Using your knowledge and the findings of your research, attempt to negotiate a treaty that the other empire will accept that still gives you as much of an advantage as possible.

Produce a mutually acceptable treaty. **List** the specific terms of the treaty in order of importance.

Justify the importance of each term in the treaty from the perspective of each empire.

Present the treaty by **discussing** why it was needed, what it resolved and how you reached these specific terms.

In a ceremony, the treaty should be signed by the representatives of the empires. Three witnesses from outside the class and your teacher should also sign that they are in agreement and will work to hold the signatories accountable to the treaty terms. Display your treaty in your classroom or other location in school.

◆ Assessment opportunities

◆ In this activity you have practised skills that are assessed using Criterion A: Knowing and understanding, Criterion B: Investigating, Criterion C: Communicating and Criterion D: Thinking critically.

MILITARY CONSTRUCTIONS FOR DEFENCE

Military constructions aided in defending empires. These defences could be in the form of walls, ditches or fortifications such as castles.

Fortress of Mirgissa

A great fortress was first constructed at Mirgissa on the Nile River in today's Sudan around 2000 BCE by Egypt's Dynasty 12. The purpose of this fortress was to:

- control boat traffic on the Nile River
- be a residential base for government officials
- store grain and other goods for the state
- protect local sources of copper and gold
- house soldiers.

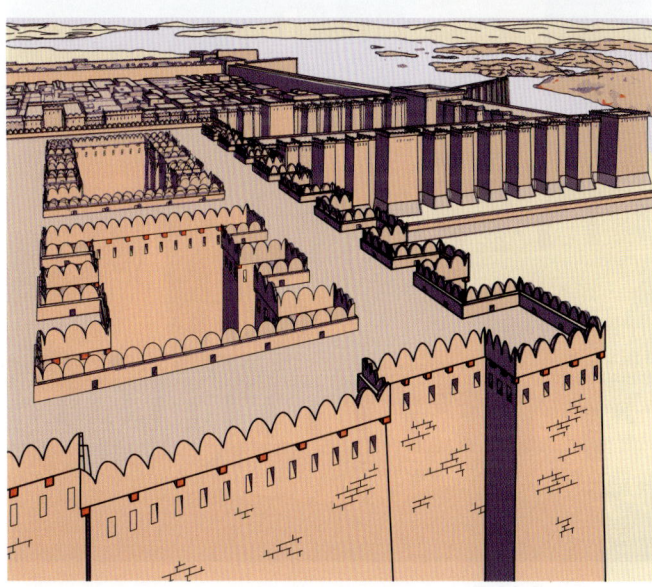

■ **Figure 3.13** Fortress of Mirgissa

Mirgissa was one of a series of fortresses built or reconstructed by Dynasty 12 in order to maintain control of the Kush region. Additionally, the fortresses were meant to deter any invasion of the Egyptian heartland to the north in the event of a rebellion by the people of Kush. Mirgissa covered an area of 40,000 m² with walls 10 metres high and 6 metres thick. The fortress helped defend a large town that was also protected by a wall. At the end of the Middle Kingdom, the fortress was abandoned, only to be re-established during Egypt's New Kingdom a few hundred years later. During the New Kingdom period, Mirgissa and the other fortresses continued to protect Egypt from invasion from the south while serving as administrative centres for the government.

■ **Figure 3.14** Constantinople city walls

Constantinople city walls

The ancient city of Byzantium was located on a peninsula between the Black and Aegean Seas. The Roman Emperor Constantine decided that the city was a better location than Rome for the capital of the Roman empire. In 330 CE, Constantine renamed the city (Constantinople means City of Constantine) and built extensive walls on the city's land side to protect it from attack. By the fifth century, new land walls were built further out on the peninsula, adding more defended space, and sea walls were built to protect the city from any naval attack. As the centre of the Eastern Roman, or Byzantine, empire, it was critical that the city be protected at all costs.

Emperor Theodosius II's land walls consisted of an inner wall that was closest to the city, an outer wall and a low wall. Beyond the low wall, farthest from the city, was a deep moat. The inner wall was the largest and was approximately 12 metres tall and 6 metres thick. This wall was defended by 96 towers. Each tower could be sealed off and function as an independent castle if the wall on either side was captured by an enemy. The outer wall was approximately 2 metres thick and up to 9 metres tall. This wall was also defended by towers that were placed about midway between the towers of the inner wall. The moat in front of the outer wall was approximately 20 metres wide and 10 metres deep, and parts of it could probably be flooded with water from a nearby stream. There was a 1.5-metre low wall along the moat nearest the outer wall.

The city's sea walls consisted of a single wall that created a border between the sea and the city. The sea walls existed in ancient times and were repeatedly improved, enlarged and rebuilt over the centuries. The side that faced the Sea of Marmara was 8.5 km in length and was defended by over 100 towers. The sea wall along the main harbour, the Golden Horn, was just over 5 km in length and had up to 172 towers.

Constantinople's walls protected the city from many attacks over its long history. These included:

- a coordinated attack and siege of allied Avars, Slavs and Persians with 80,000 soldiers and a navy over several months in 626 CE

- a multi-year siege by the Umayyad Caliphate that ended in 678 CE with the destruction of the Caliphate's navy and the loss of 30,000 soldiers
- a one-year siege by the Umayyad Caliphate that ended in 718 CE with the destruction of the Caliphate's navy and army, and the loss of perhaps 100,000 soldiers and over 2,000 ships
- multiple attacks and sieges by rebels during civil wars, and by the Crusaders, the Ottoman empire and other states or factions in the region.

The city was only successfully attacked twice. The first time was in 1204 when Venetians and Crusaders were able to get into the city by climbing over the sea walls along the Golden Horn during the Fourth Crusade. This led to the city being named the new capital of the empire of Romania, also known as the Latin empire, from 1204 to 1261 when it again became the capital of the Byzantine empire. The second time was in 1453 when the city was captured by the Ottoman empire which successfully used cannons to break through the land walls, essentially ending the Byzantine empire. Constantinople, now called Istanbul, became the capital of the Ottoman empire.

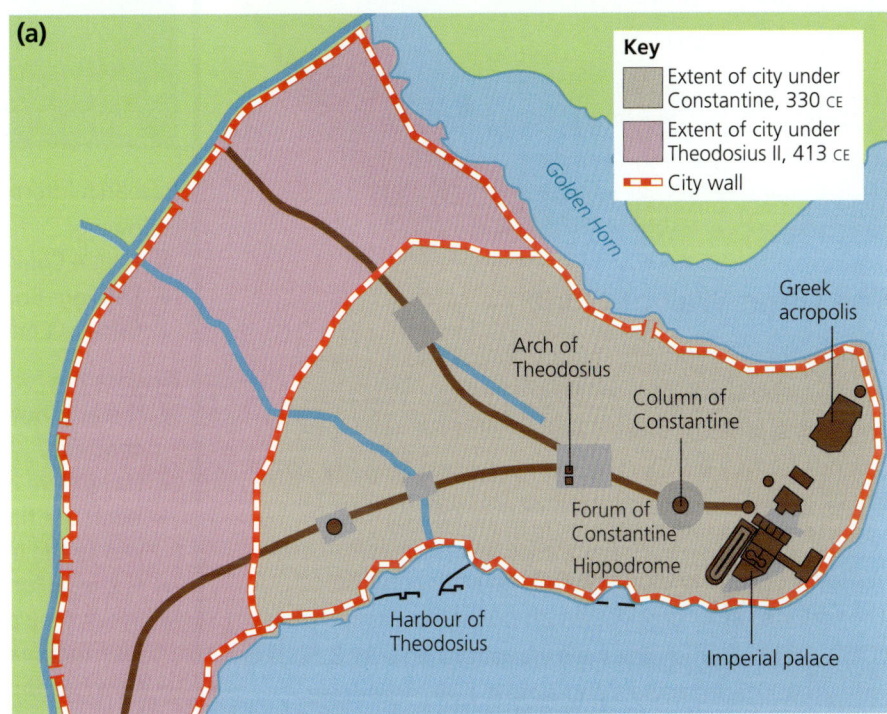

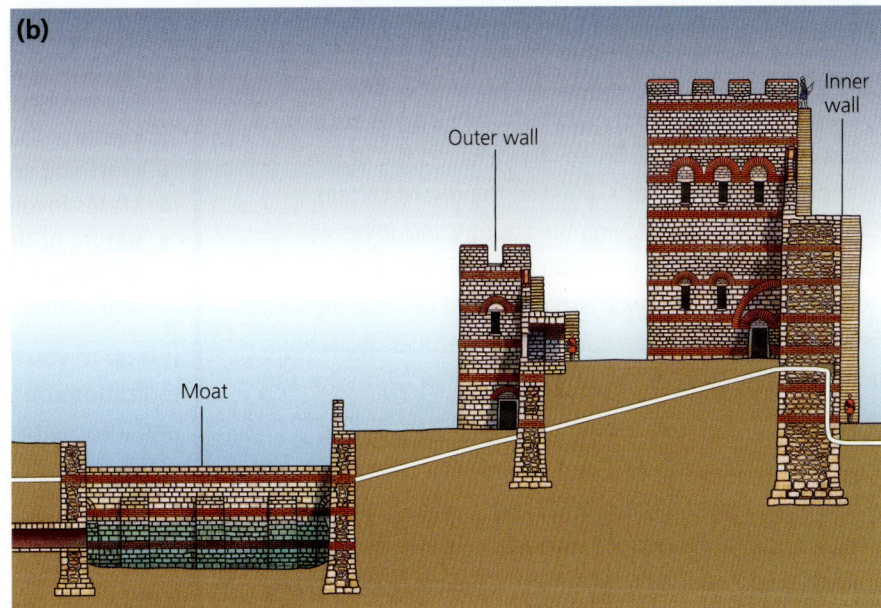

■ **Figure 3.15 (a)** The Constantinople city walls, 330–413 CE; **(b)** side view

The Great Wall of China

Perhaps the most famous military construction in world history is the Great Wall of China. The Great Wall was originally a series of smaller walls, some built as early as the seventh century BCE. Qin Shi Huang, the First Emperor of China, is credited with linking previous walls to create the original Great Wall. Over the next 1,800 years, the Great Wall was enlarged, improved and rebuilt multiple times. The wall was at its greatest length during the Ming Dynasty (1368–1644 CE) when the main wall stretched over 8,500 km with 25,000 watchtowers and almost 1,000 fortresses. Extensions from the main wall protected other areas, bringing the total length to over 21,000 km.

The Great Wall served many purposes. One of these was to control all imports and exports from northern areas of China and along the Silk Road. This allowed the government to impose taxes on goods, but also to prevent certain national secrets from leaving the country, including silk worms that were used to produce one of the most precious export items: silk. The wall also prevented Chinese peasants from leaving China to escape taxation or other obligations from the state such as military duty or other labour for the government.

The main purpose of the Great Wall was to prevent invasion. The people living north and west of the Great Wall, including Mongol people, were primarily nomadic. They relied on their animals for food, shelter, economy and transportation. These groups raided deep into China, taking people, goods and food. The Great Wall prevented these raids, as long as it was manned, as horses and camels could not cross over the walls and could only enter through gates which were usually well defended. The wall protected the greatest strength of China: its agriculture.

ACTIVITY: Peace and conflict in the twentieth century

ATL

- Critical-thinking skills: Interpret data; Evaluate evidence and arguments; Consider ideas from multiple perspectives
- Transfer skills: Inquire in different contexts to gain a different perspective

Research international law and war, including the following:
- Hague Conventions of 1899 and 1907
- Kellogg–Briand Pact (1929)
- Geneva Conventions (1949)

Discuss the following with your class:
- If war is outlawed in the modern era, why does it continue?
- Have there been fewer wars as time has progressed?
- What are the legal and political consequences of war in the modern era?
- Is it legal for countries to annex territory through war?
- When they do, what is the response of the international community?
- How has the nature of peace and conflict changed in the twentieth century?

Using a blank map of the world, indicate the:
- locations where conflicts other than the First and Second World Wars have occurred in the twentieth century
- start and end dates of these conflicts
- states involved in these conflicts
- nature of these conflicts (naval war, civil war, war of independence, revolution, wars between states and more).

It is up to you to determine how you will make these indications on your map so that it is understandable and informative.

Display the maps in the room and **discuss** which areas of the world have seen the most conflict and possible reasons why.

◆ Assessment opportunities

- In this activity you have practised skills that are assessed using Criterion A: Knowing and understanding, Criterion B: Investigating, Criterion C: Communicating and Criterion D: Thinking critically.

What factors might be important for maintaining a successful empire?

ACTIVITY: Comparing the factors that maintain an empire

ATL

- Information literacy skills: Collect and analyse data to identify solutions and make informed decisions
- Critical-thinking skills: Recognize unstated assumptions and bias; Interpret data; Evaluate evidence and arguments; Revise understanding based on new information and evidence
- Transfer skills: Inquire in different contexts to gain a different perspective

Empires, being complex systems, rely on different factors at different times in order to continue to succeed. We have already discussed some of these factors in this chapter. For example, we have seen the role that military strength, military architecture, alliances, treaties and laws play in the maintenance of empire.

Imagine you are now an adviser to the Emperor of China. The Emperor has tasked you with deciding on which factor from the list below the government should spend most of its time, and money, on improving:

- Military strength
- Military infrastructure
- Building alliances
- Negotiating treaties
- Developing a new legal system.

Identify the advantages and disadvantages of each factor using examples from this book, your personal research, rational thinking and analysis.

Evaluate the advantages and disadvantages of each factor based on how important it is to the maintenance of the empire of China. Write a letter to the Emperor addressing these advantages and disadvantages.

Select which of the factors listed above is the most important and **justify** this to the Emperor in your letter.

◆ Assessment opportunities

- In this activity you have practised skills that are assessed using Criterion A: Knowing and understanding, Criterion B: Investigating, Criterion C: Communicating and Criterion D: Thinking critically.

3 How do empires work?

To what extent is leadership important in the maintenance of empires?

> **! Take action**
>
> ! Organize a club that **investigates** the causes of international conflicts. The club will then:
> - propose possible solutions for specific crises
> - decide which supra-national organization is most relevant for resolving these crises
> - invite representatives of supra-national organizations to speak and **discuss** what their organization is doing with regards to the crisis
> - **discuss** possible solutions with these representatives, and how the club could be involved in helping the organization in a meaningful way.

ACTIVITY: Empires under threat

■ ATL

- Information literacy skills: Collect and analyse data to identify solutions and make informed decisions
- Critical-thinking skills: Recognize unstated assumptions and bias; Interpret data; Evaluate evidence and arguments; Revise understanding based on new information and evidence

Empires sometimes face crises or threats. These crises may be political, cultural, economic, military or other types of threats. In these cases, the empire's existence may depend on how well it responds to these threats.

Consider the following crises, or some of your own choosing:
- The End of the Bronze Age and New Kingdom Egypt (around twelfth century BCE)
- The Crisis of the Third Century in the Roman empire (235–84 CE)
- Plague of Justinian in the Byzantine empire (541–42 CE)
- The Second Islamic Civil War in the Umayyad Caliphate (680–92 CE)
- The Jin-Song Wars in the Chinese empire (1125–1234 CE)
- The Toluid Civil War in the Mongol empire (1260–64 CE)
- The Inca Civil War and Spanish Conquest (1532–72 CE)

Create a research question that deals with some aspect of how empires approach, and react to, crises and threats using at least three of the examples mentioned above, or three of your own choosing. Consider whether or not the reaction to these crises or threats was consistent throughout the empire and how local or regional differences may have affected the empire's overall response.

Evaluate the factors that determine the success or failure of the empires you have chosen during threats or crises. Find evidence that supports these factors.

Formulate arguments that address your research question. Use these arguments to create three different introductory paragraphs for an essay that would support your argument, with each introductory paragraph focusing on one of the three examples you have chosen.

EXTENSION

Using your research questions and three introductory paragraphs, write an essay with an introduction and conclusion. Have at least two arguments or main points, supported with evidence, and placed in order of importance in the essay. Be sure to use a different paragraph for each of your main points. You may wish to consider arguments that someone else might make against your argument. In this case, indicate what the counter-argument might be and respond to it. Be sure to **justify** your own beliefs.

◆ Assessment opportunities

- In this activity you have practised skills that are assessed using Criterion A: Knowing and understanding, Criterion B: Investigating, Criterion C: Communicating and Criterion D: Thinking critically.

Reflection

In this chapter, we have assessed the value of systems for maintaining empires. We have also explored how empires facilitate exchange of ideas and allow innovation.

Use this table to reflect on your own learning in this chapter.						
Questions we asked	Answers we found	Any further questions now?				
Factual: What systems keep empires in place? What are the effects of an empire's global interaction?						
Conceptual: How can empires successfully defend themselves from challenges and threats? What factors might be important for maintaining a successful empire?						
Debatable: To what extent is leadership important in the maintenance of empires? To what extent are empires and modern supra-national organizations and superpowers similar? Can empires successfully accommodate the expression of personal and cultural difference?						
Approaches to learning you used in this chapter	Description – what new skills did you learn?	How well did you master the skills?				
		Novice	Learner	Practitioner	Expert	
Communication skills						
Collaboration skills						
Information literacy skills						
Critical-thinking skills						
Transfer skills						
Learner profile attribute(s)	Reflect on the importance of being reflective for your learning in this chapter.					
Reflective						

Change | Conflict; Innovation and revolution | Scientific and technical innovation

4 How do empires fall?

○ Societies **survive, fail or transform** according to their ability to **change** in the face of **innovation**.

CONSIDER THESE QUESTIONS:

Factual: What internal factors have led empires to fail? What external factors have led empires to fail? What is left in the aftermath of an empire's collapse?

Conceptual: Why do empires fail? To what extent can environmental factors affect the stability of an empire? To what extent do empires need to maintain dominance in order to continue to exist?

Debatable: Have empires and superpowers led to a more peaceful world?

Now, **share** and **compare** your thoughts and ideas with your partner or the rest of the class.

■ Figure 4.1 **(a)** City-state of Teotihuacan in the Valley of Mexico; **(b)** Objects found while excavating the ruins of Pompeii, a Roman city destroyed in the 79 CE volcanic eruption of Vesuvius; **(c)** Angkor Wat, capital of the Khmer empire, in modern-day Cambodia

┌─○ IN THIS CHAPTER WE WILL ...

■ **Find out** how and why empires fail.
■ **Explore**:
   ■ the extent to which the natural world, conquest and internal change affect empires
   ■ the consequences of an empire's collapse.
■ **Take action** by:
   ■ investigating one system in our own country that needs improvement
   ■ organizing a letter campaign to local, regional or national government.

Individuals & Societies for the IB MYP 4&5: *by Concept*

KEY WORDS

civil war
innovation
natural disasters
revolt
systems

SEE–THINK–WONDER

Consider the pictures in Figure 4.1a–c.

In a group, **identify** at least two physical details from each picture.

What do these details tell us about the archaeological site or items found? Is this a city, a fortress or something else? What type of items do you think archaeologists may discover when excavating? What different materials can you see? What might be the purpose of the structures that you see in the pictures?

What can you guess or assume about the historical cultures from these figures?

■ **These Approaches to Learning (ATL) skills will be useful …**

- Collaboration skills
- Information literacy skills
- Critical-thinking skills
- Transfer skills

● **We will reflect on this learner profile attribute …**

- Balanced – considering different perspectives and conflicting views in order to reach a balanced opinion, and better understand the interdependence between the world and its citizens.

◆ **Assessment opportunities in this chapter:**

- **Criterion A**: Knowing and understanding
- **Criterion B**: Investigating
- **Criterion C**: Communicating
- **Criterion D**: Thinking critically

4 How do empires fall?

Why do empires fail?

All empires in history have eventually collapsed. This has happened in a variety of ways, and for a number of different reasons. Since empires are complex systems that act interdependently and rely on a number of different conditions, they can collapse when those conditions change.

Some empires collapse due to external issues. For example, climate change can lead to cooler weather which might affect agricultural production. This normally means less food is grown and people are hungry and more susceptible to disease. It can also mean that people move elsewhere to find more food for themselves and their livestock, which usually means invading the territory of other people, including many of the empires you have studied.

Invasion of an empire by a rival state can lead to many outcomes, including:
- expansion of the invading state or, in some cases, the state being attacked
- loss of land
- destruction of cities, people and livestock
- complete destruction of the invaded empire, with the whole or parts of it being taken over by others.

Invasions are made possible by the superior numbers, organization, resources or technology of the rival state or the weaknesses of the state being invaded. It is usually a combination of strengths and weaknesses that determine the duration of any empire's life.

Internal issues can also be a major factor in the collapse of empires. Failure to maintain systems, such as taxation, transportation and economic, can lead to weakening and collapse. Corruption has also been a major issue in the weakening of systems throughout history. When the systems begin to fail, empires often experience civil war, rebellion and independence movements. The collapse or weakening of systems, especially in large states, can lead to dividing of the larger state into smaller, weaker states, or even a collapse of the entire empire.

This chapter will address some of the reasons why empires have collapsed over the millennia.

To what extent can environmental factors affect the stability of an empire?

NATURAL DISASTERS

Natural disasters have occurred throughout human history and include:

- earthquakes
- tsunamis
- volcanic eruptions
- floods
- large storms such as hurricanes, cyclones and typhoons.

Although a single natural disaster has probably never destroyed an entire empire, it may weaken the empire and lead to its eventual collapse.

Earthquakes

A massive earthquake occurred in the centre of the Umayyad Caliphate (661–750 CE) in January 749 CE. This earthquake severely damaged or destroyed most of the cities between today's Egypt and Damascus, Syria. Scholars continue to debate the importance of the earthquake and how it might have affected the decline and collapse of the Umayyads, who were already in the midst of a civil war. What is clear is that large, important cities such as Jerusalem, Gerasa (Jerash today), Gadara (Umm Qais), Pella, Tiberias, Hippos and others were mostly destroyed, reducing the population and trade, and disrupting tax collection in the Umayyad heartland. The Umayyad Caliphate ended the following year, in 750 CE, and was replaced by the Abbasid Caliphate (750–1258 CE).

Tsunamis

Volcanic eruptions and earthquakes can lead to tsunamis. The eruption of the Santorini volcano in the Mediterranean in the 1600s BCE led to a tsunami which destroyed all the settlements on the north coast of Crete and all the ships that were based there. This island was the home to the Minoan civilization that dominated the Aegean region and operated a vast trade network throughout the eastern Mediterranean. The tsunami may not have destroyed the Minoan civilization, but it certainly weakened it. Within a few years of the volcanic eruption of Santorini and the tsunami it generated, the Minoans were conquered by the Mycenaeans, Greek-speaking groups of people from various city-states in what is now today's southern Greece.

Figure 4.2 Remains of the Minoan settlement of Akrotiri, showing ceramic works and ruins of stone constructions

ACTIVITY: Santorini eruption of the 1600s BCE

ATL

- Information literacy skills: Access information to be informed and inform others; Make connections between various sources of information
- Critical-thinking skills: Interpret data; Evaluate evidence and arguments; Revise understanding based on new information and evidence

Investigate the Santorini eruption of the 1600s BCE.

List 10–15 artifacts that have been found in the Minoan settlement discovered on the island that is called Akrotiri today.

Discuss the following questions in groups:
- In what way were the artifacts you discovered significant?
- Did these items seem common or rare? Were they expensive?
- Would these items seem out of place if seen today? How and why?
- What does the absence of skeletons or human remains in the city indicate?
- How have these artifacts expanded our knowledge and understanding of daily life in Minoan settlements?
- What can we learn about Minoan civilization from the frescoes, art and pottery discovered in Akrotiri?
- From the artifacts discovered, what can we infer about the economy of the Minoans?
- With reference to the artifacts, what do we know about the technological abilities of the Minoan civilization?

Now, share your ideas with the rest of the class.

◆ Assessment opportunities

- ◆ In this activity you have practised skills that are assessed using Criterion A: Knowing and understanding, Criterion B: Investigating and Criterion D: Thinking critically.

Volcanic eruptions

Volcanoes release huge amounts of ash and dust into the atmosphere, affecting weather patterns and global temperatures. This affects plant growth and therefore agriculture, which in turn affects people.

One example of a volcanic eruption affecting agriculture and people is the massive eruption that occurred in 536 CE, followed by eruptions in 540 and 547 CE. Scientists know that these happened and when due to:

- constricted tree rings in ancient trees for this and subsequent years as a result of reduced sunlight in North and South America, as well as Europe
- sulfate deposits, which originate from acidic ash from volcanic explosions, being found in ice core samples from Greenland and Antarctica that correspond to these years.

The eruptions ejected enough ash into the atmosphere to cause many years of disrupted weather and crop failures worldwide. Chinese records indicate that there was no summer season and that it snowed in August 536 CE, around the time when crops should have been harvested. Much of the Middle East, Europe and China reported being covered in a dry fog or ash cloud. In Ireland, reports indicate that it was impossible to grow food, which led to mass starvation starting in 536 CE.

The location of the volcano is still not known, but it is likely to have been in Iceland, El Salvador or somewhere else in North America. What is certain is the results of the eruption, which led to the decline and eventual collapse of the:

- Teotihuacan empire in today's Mexico
- Sasanian empire of Persia
- Gupta empire of today's India.

These declines were the result of tremendous stress through rapidly declining populations that had less food and were far less healthy as a result. People from central Asia moved out of their regions, seeking grasslands for their herds, bringing new diseases which devastated the Sasanians and the Eastern Roman empire. As noted in Chapter 2, the Eastern Roman empire, known as the Byzantine empire to many today, lost approximately half its population through starvation and disease in this period.

▼ Links to: Sciences

Historians often rely on scientists to provide evidence. This evidence can come from many sources. Scientists take samples from glaciers and ice deposits on mountains, from **flowstones** in caves, from the ground, ancient rivers, mud and more, and study them for chemicals, geological deposits, and traces of human occupation. **Dendrochronology** is the study of tree rings to determine changes in climate over short and long periods of time. To do this, scientists compare the tree rings from ancient trees all over the world. **Radiocarbon dating** allows scientists to determine the age of organic objects based on the amount of carbon found in them.

All the data gathered by scientists from these and other means is useful to historians. Dendrochronology allows us to understand the amount of sunlight in a particular period of time and how that might have affected agriculture. Radiocarbon dating allows us to **identify** when objects were used, to **evaluate** how they have changed over time and to understand the society from which the objects came. Scientific data is the only data we have about some empires and civilizations that have left no written records. Archaeologists are people who excavate the remains of ancient civilizations. They use science and scientific methods to analyse the evidence found in these remains, which may include bones, tools, grave goods, food, pottery, houses and art. Empires that have left no written records, or only records that cannot be read, include the:
- Indus Valley Civilization
- Minoan Civilization
- Inca empire
- Aksumite empire.

Other civilizations have left some records, but not enough to create a full picture of that society. These include the empires of:
- Xi Xia
- Aztec
- Macedonian
- Achaemenid
- Parthian
- Sasanian
- Khmer.

Innovations and discoveries in science have proven essential for historians to understand ancient cultures and empires and how they changed over time. Find out more about the science of historical dating in *Physics for IB MYP 4&5* Chapter 11.

■ **Figure 4.3** Ancient ruins of Pompeii, destroyed by a volcanic eruption of Mount Vesuvius in 79 CE

ACTIVITY: Accounts of the eruption of Mount Vesuvius (79 CE)

ATL

- Collaboration skills: Help others to succeed; Listen actively to other perspectives and ideas; Negotiate effectively
- Information literacy skills: Access information to be informed and inform others; Make connections between various sources of information
- Critical-thinking skills: Recognize unstated assumptions and bias; Interpret data; Evaluate evidence and arguments; Revise understanding based on new information and evidence

As a class or in a group, **identify** the words or phrases that you find unfamiliar in Sources A and B. Research the definitions of these words or phrases and use this information to help address the questions below.

Analyse Sources A and B about the eruption of Mount Vesuvius in 79 CE.

Consider the following questions:
- What factual information can we determine from these sources?
- Who is the intended audience of each source?
- What is the aim of each source?
- What are the limitations of each of the sources in terms of the information that each conveys?
- What image did Pliny the Younger want to portray about his uncle in Source A? How may this have affected his recounting of the event?
- What information do we get from Source A that we do not from Source B?
- What information do we get from Source B that we do not from Source A?

Now, **discuss** your answers as a class.

◆ Assessment opportunities

◆ In this activity you have practised skills that are assessed using Criterion A: Knowing and understanding, Criterion B: Investigating, Criterion C: Communicating and Criterion D: Thinking critically.

SOURCE A

'At that time [24 August 79 CE] my uncle was at Misenum in command of the fleet. About one in the afternoon, my mother pointed out a cloud with an odd size and appearance that had just formed. From that distance it was not clear from which mountain the cloud was rising, although it was found afterwards to be Vesuvius [...] Like a true scholar, my uncle saw at once that it deserved closer study and ordered a boat to be prepared. He said that I could go with him, but I chose to continue my studies. Just as he was leaving the house, he was handed a message from [a friend] whose home was at the foot of the mountain, and had no way of escape except by boat. She was terrified by the threatening danger and begged him to rescue her. He changed [his plan] at once and what he had started in a spirit of scientific curiosity he ended as a hero. He ordered the large galleys to be launched and set sail. He steered bravely straight for the danger zone that everyone else was leaving in fear and haste, but still kept on noting his observations.'

Letter by Pliny the Younger about the eruption of Mount Vesuvius, written to the historian Tacitus approximately 25 years after the event

SOURCE B

'The process of Pompeii's destruction and burial started with the accumulation of a thick pumice lapilli deposit [...] resulting from the column fallout. The rate of deposition in the city ranged from 15 cm per hour in open areas to 25/30 cm per hour in places accumulating additional pyroclasts rolling from the steeper roofs. Within six hours from the beginning of the eruption the roofs and part of the walls of the buildings had collapsed under the pumice load. By the morning of 25 August most structures were seriously damaged; the pumice fall deposit, generally 3 m thick, totally buried the lower part of the buildings. The percentage of victims (38%) found in this deposit at Pompeii is **anomalously** high with respect to a mean of 4% of deaths caused by tephra fallout in the last four centuries during explosive eruptions (Blong, 1984; Tanguy et al., 1999). This high percentage of deaths is possibly due to the attempt of some people to take shelter into buildings where roofs and walls collapsed under the load of the pyroclastic material. The small percentage of people found dead outdoor within the pumice fall deposit was probably killed by the crumbling roof tiles or by the largest lithic fragments following ballistic paths.'

Excerpt from the article 'The Eruption of Vesuvius of 79 CE and its Impact of Human Environment in Pompeii,' published in September 2003

CLIMATE CHANGE

Climate is weather patterns over long periods of time. The Earth has experienced various climate change events in human history, which have affected empires and their people. One such climate change event is known as the 4.2 Kiloyear Event.

4.2 Kiloyear Event

Historians know that the Old Kingdom of Egypt, one of the earliest empires, which controlled much of the Nile Valley and the Levant into today's Lebanon, collapsed in about 2181 BCE. At approximately the same time, the Akkadian empire, the first empire in Mesopotamia, along the Tigris and Euphrates Rivers, also collapsed, in around 2154 BCE. The Indus Valley civilization, stretching from today's Afghanistan to Pakistan and northwest India, which may have been an empire, began to decline around 2000 BCE and many cities were abandoned as the population moved. Civilizations have collapsed in today's China and Greece, and in many other locations.

Figure 4.4 The Pyramids at Giza, some of the largest buildings constructed by people until the modern era, were built during Egypt's Old Kingdom

Scientists have provided evidence of climate change at this time in the form of ice core samples taken from Mount Kilimanjaro in Africa, Mount Logan in Canada, and the Andes Mountains, as well as flowstone samples from caves in today's India and Italy. These cores have indicated chemically that from 2200 BCE to 2000 BCE, the Earth's climate became much cooler and much drier.

More precipitation, such as rain and snow, was trapped in glaciers on mountains during this time, and did not melt to provide water for rivers such as the Nile, Tigris and Euphrates on which Egypt and Akkad depended as little rain fell in these regions. Additionally, less water for rivers meant less or even no flooding, so that rich silt, which fertilizes the soil, was not deposited. Less water and less silt meant crop failure, starvation, the spread of disease and the movement of people seeking food, water and farmland. This led to the collapse of civilizations and empires.

DISEASE

Diseases have killed millions of people throughout human civilization. Disease could kill so many people that the systems of empire could simply no longer function, leading to collapse.

Antonine Plague of Rome and China

An outbreak of smallpox hit the Roman empire in 165 CE and continued until 180 CE. The disease caused approximately 5 million deaths and killed at least one emperor. Ancient Romans indicated that so many people died that some provinces had no population left. The Roman armies were severely weakened and Germans invaded the northern provinces. It may be that Roman ambassadors and merchants spread the disease to China, ruled by the Han Dynasty (206 BCE–220 CE).

Outbreaks of smallpox devastated China over several years. Chinese officials recorded seven major outbreaks of the virus between 151 CE and 185 CE. It may be that up to 30 per cent of China's population died at this time. This caused millions of farmers and ex-soldiers to move to southern China for work and food. Landlords and government officials exploited them, leading to a revolt, which was called the Yellow Turban Rebellion after the yellow scarves worn by the rebels. The revolt continued until 205 CE, and led to the death of up to 7 million people and the collapse of the Han Emperor's authority, as generals amassed power to fight the rebels and then each other. With the collapse of the government and continual war, officials were unable to respond to crises including disease, drought, famine and floods. While the last Han Emperor abdicated in 220 CE, in reality the state collapsed a few years after the last major outbreak of smallpox in 185 CE.

ACTIVITY: The World Health Organization (WHO)

■ ATL

- Critical-thinking skills: Recognize unstated assumptions and bias; Interpret data; Evaluate evidence and arguments; Revise understanding based on new information and evidence
- Transfer skills: Inquire in different contexts to gain a different perspective

Research how the World Health Organization and world governments deal with modern outbreaks of diseases, including:
- **Ebola hemorrhagic virus**
- **MERS (Middle East Respiratory Syndrome)**
- **West Nile Virus**
- **Covid-19.**

How do world governments and supra-national organizations stop the spread of the virus, educate the public, treat infected people and work towards finding a cure? How do modern systems help them accomplish this?

EXTENSION

Prepare a presentation regarding one specific outbreak that occurred in the twenty-first century, to be shown publicly in your school community. Be sure to address the questions above in terms of that specific outbreak.

◆ Assessment opportunities

◆ In this activity you have practised skills that are assessed using Criterion A: Knowing and understanding, Criterion B: Investigating, Criterion C: Communicating and Criterion D: Thinking critically.

Aztec empire (1428–1521 CE)

North and South America remained isolated from the rest of the world for thousands of years. The only exception to this that has been proven is the settlement of Norse people from today's Scandinavia in Greenland around 980 CE until the fifteenth century, and a few settlements in today's Canada for just a short time around the year 1000 CE. As a result of this isolation, the native peoples of these continents had

had no exposure to various diseases, such as measles, influenza, chicken pox, smallpox, malaria, **typhoid** and perhaps even the common cold virus. These diseases affected humans in the rest of the world for thousands of years and many people inherited some resistance from their ancestors, giving them either some immunity or lessening the severity of the diseases in many cases. North and South Americans had no resistance whatsoever.

■ **Figure 4.5** Monks Mound at Cahokia is the largest Native American construction north of Mexico in North America

MEET A SIGNIFICANT INDIVIDUAL: HERNANDO DE SOTO

Spanish warriors, working on behalf of the Spanish government, sought supplies of gold and silver all over North and South America. This led to contact with hundreds or thousands of different Native American tribes and states. Hernando de Soto was one such exploring warrior and he travelled through what is now the southeastern United States from 1539 to 1543 CE. The following is from the online Encyclopedia of Georgia:

> 'De Soto and his six hundred men trekked diagonally from the southwest corner of the future state [Georgia, USA] to a point on the Savannah River just below modern-day Augusta. De Soto and his men documented villages and towns by the names of the Indian societies and chiefdoms they encountered: Capachequi, Toa, Ichisi, Altamaha, Ocute, Patofa, and Cofitachequi. Reactions to the Spanish varied. Some tribes hid, others offered food and clothing, and some attacked the strangers.
>
> The exchange between the two cultures during the Spanish march was one-sided and destructive. De Soto's path through the Mississippian cultures of what is now the southeast United States spread disease among the local inhabitants, diminished native food supplies, and led to a reduction in native populations. Resisting tribes found themselves under vicious attack by Spanish soldiers. De Soto employed violent tactics to obtain food for his men, while the herd of pigs he brought with him further reduced villages' food sources as they consumed crops such as corn and squash. De Soto's men carried iron collars and chains to physically enslave Indians. They used torture to extract information about gold and silver, ransacked villages, and dug up graves in search of the nearly non-existent precious metals …
>
> The archaeological record confirms the one-sided exchange resulting from de Soto's march through Georgia and much of the Southeast. Skeletal remains of Indians bear the scars of steel weapons. Excavations show a rapid and drastic reduction in the number of natives in once highly populated areas. Records of later European arrivals account for only a fraction of past Native American numbers. Though not all of the Spanish groups were so deliberately violent, the Spanish crown continued to seek new ways to subdue the native population in the New World. Yet even their later tactics proved equally destructive.'

'Early European Encounters' The Source for Georgia History, *Georgia Historical Society*, 31 July 2013

ACTIVITY: Dealing with natural disasters, diseases or environmental events

ATL

- Information literacy skills: Access information to be informed and inform others; Make connections between various sources of information; Identify primary and secondary sources
- Critical-thinking skills: Gather and organize relevant information; Draw reasonable conclusions and generalizations; Consider ideas from multiple perspectives
- Transfer skills: Inquire in different contexts to gain a different perspective

Choose one historical and one modern event or disease from Table 4.1.

Investigate how your chosen events or diseases were handled by the affected state or empire, or relevant supra-national organization.

Compare and contrast the historical and modern methods of dealing with diseases, disasters and environmental events. Consider the following questions:
- Was there advance warning of the events? If so, how did this affect the reaction of the states, empires or relevant supra-national organizations?
- What was the death toll of these events? Is this high or low compared to similar events?
- Are these kinds of events common?
- Which modern supra-national organizations would be involved for these types of situations, diseases or events?
- Did these events or diseases only affect one country, state or empire? If not, how and why did they affect other states or empires?
- If your historical event were to occur today, would the reaction to it be different? How? Why?

Create, using research and your own knowledge, a display comparing and contrasting your modern and historical events. In this display, **evaluate**:
- your chosen historical and modern events or diseases
- the reaction of the state, empire and supra-national organization to these events, environmental shocks or diseases
- the limitations of the state, empire or supra-national organization.

In coordination with your teacher, place your display on an appropriate board or wall to educate others.

◆ Assessment opportunities

- In this activity you have practised skills that are assessed using Criterion A: Knowing and understanding, Criterion B: Investigating, Criterion C: Communicating and Criterion D: Thinking critically.

Table 4.1 Historical and modern events and diseases

Historical event / disease	Modern event / disease
Santorini eruption (seventeenth century BCE)	HIV / AIDs (late twentieth century–present)
Antonine Plague (165–80 CE)	Tuberculosis (ongoing)
Plague of Justinian (541–542 CE)	Deepwater Horizon oil spill (2010)
Black Death (1347–51 CE)	Haiti earthquake (2010)
Shaanxi earthquake (1556 CE)	Indian Ocean earthquake (2004)

Spain invaded the Aztec empire in 1519 CE and had completely destroyed it by 1521 CE. While the Spanish were few in number, they had some advantages in terms of technology (see below). Yet it was disease that ultimately destroyed the Aztec civilization. With no resistance to any of the above-mentioned diseases, perhaps 40 per cent of the Aztec population died from smallpox in 1520 CE, including most of the leadership and military. Such a drastic reduction of population meant that the Spanish colonists had little trouble destroying what remained of the Aztec empire before moving against other states in central and South America who were also devastated by these diseases.

In the coming years, tens of millions of native people in the region died of typhoid and other diseases. It is estimated that 90 per cent of all Native Americans in North and South America were killed by diseases brought by Spanish conquerors in the fifteenth and sixteenth centuries.

What internal factors have led empires to fail?

CIVIL WAR

Civil wars are wars fought between citizens of the same country. They have affected many empires and continue to occur. Examples include the Yellow Turban Rebellion and the Abbasid Revolt against the Umayyad Caliphate.

Civil wars occur for many reasons; for example, someone, or a group, may want to:
- replace the leadership with themselves
- overthrow the governing system and create a new one
- take control of part of the state.

Civil wars almost always weaken a state, at least in the short term, causing destruction of infrastructure and governing systems, loss of lives and reduced military strength. Some civil wars have weakened empires, leading to their end.

Figure 4.6 The remains of the city of Hatra, a fortress city that was important for controlling trade between the Parthian and Roman empires and was attacked repeatedly by the Romans

Parthian empire (247 BCE–224 CE)

The Parthian empire ruled today's Iran, Iraq, Armenia, Azerbaijan, Afghanistan and eastern Turkey, and parts of Syria, Kuwait, Saudi Arabia, Turkmenistan and more. The country was ruled by the Shananshah, or King of Kings, and it was a major rival of Rome for hundreds of years.

Parthia experienced many civil wars over the centuries, often as brothers fought brothers for the throne. Sometimes this allowed the Roman empire to claim some of the western provinces of the Parthians for periods of time. Vologases VI became the Shananshah around 208 CE and by 212 CE his brother, Artabanus IV, rebelled and a civil war erupted across the vast country. Rome took the opportunity to invade the western part of the empire. Artabanus IV defeated his brother by 222 CE, but also fought off the Roman invasion and had defeated them by 218 CE.

Although successful, the government of Parthia was weakened through the destruction of its cities and disrupted economy, with millions of people either dead or living as refugees. The King of Persis, a subject of Artabanus, revolted, causing another civil war, killing Artabanus IV in a battle in 224 CE. The Parthian empire came to an end and the Sasanian empire was established in its place.

Sasanian empire (224–651 CE)

The Sasanian empire continued for hundreds of years and, like its Parthian predecessor, continued wars on and off with the Eastern Roman, or Byzantine, empire. A massive war erupted between these two states in 602 CE and came to an end in 628 CE with the overthrow and execution of the Sasanian ruler Khosrau II by his son, Kavad II. Kavad died within a few months and civil war erupted throughout the Sasanian empire. This war continued until 632 CE, with multiple rulers claiming authority, only to be overthrown and executed by other military factions.

In 632 CE, the grandson of Khosrau II, Yazdegerd III, was put in charge by all major factions in order to end the war that had almost brought the empire to an end. The empire was so weak after the war with the Byzantine and the civil war that now Turks invaded from the east while Khazars attacked the northwest. In 633 CE, Arab armies, united by the establishment of the first Islamic Caliphate, began an invasion of today's Iraq, the economic centre of the Sasanian empire. Within ten years, the majority of the empire had been defeated and annexed to the Islamic Caliphate and, by 654 AD, the conquest was complete, with Yazdegerd III having died in 651 CE.

ACTIVITY: At war with themselves?

ATL

- Collaboration skills: Help others to succeed; Listen actively to other perspectives and ideas; Negotiate effectively
- Information literacy skills: Access information to be informed and inform others; Make connections between various sources of information
- Critical-thinking skills: Recognize unstated assumptions and bias; Interpret data; Evaluate evidence and arguments; Revise understanding based on new information and evidence

Consider this list of wars that were fought between inhabitants of the same state:

- Indo-Pakistan War (1947–48)
- La Violencia War in Colombia (1948–58)
- Sudanese civil wars (1955–1972, 1983–2005)
- Bangladesh Liberation War (1971)
- Angola civil war (1975–2002)
- Iraqi–Kurdish conflict (1981–2003)
- Contra War (1981–88)
- Afghanistan civil wars (1989–present)
- Liberian civil wars (1989–97, 1999–2003)
- Yugoslav wars (1991–2001)
- Libyan civil war (2011–present)
- Syrian civil war (2011–present)

Choose *one* of these conflicts. **Evaluate** the reason why this conflict began, the parties that engaged in this conflict, the aims of each party and the eventual outcome. Present this in the form of a suitable visual organizer (perhaps a table or other chart).

EXTENSION

As a class, vote on *one* conflict that you wish to study further. Each member of the class will be assigned the role of an ambassador of one country in the United Nations, including the five permanent members of the Security Council: France, Russia, United Kingdom, China and the USA.

Each student will **explore** their assigned country's response to the conflict that you have decided to study. Each ambassador will create a **policy statement** which indicates their assigned country's stance on this conflict and will debate from that perspective.

Debate the consequences of this conflict for the country, the region of the conflict, and for the world. What were or are the solutions to this chosen conflict and what steps should be taken to ensure stability in the country and region?

Assessment opportunities

- In this activity you have practised skills that are assessed using Criterion A: Knowing and understanding, Criterion B: Investigating, Criterion C: Communicating and Criterion D: Thinking critically.

Inca civil war (1529–32 CE)

The Inca empire of South America was ruled by the Sapa Inca, or Emperor. Sapa Inca Huayna Capac received reports of foreigners, from Spain, arriving in the empire and moved north to today's Quito in order to investigate and obtain more information. Although he never saw the Spanish colonists, he contracted smallpox, as did his eldest son, the future Sapa Inca, and both died. The empire was probably already weakened by massive population decline as the result of Spanish-introduced diseases (see above). A faction based in the capital of Cuzco named Huascar as Sapa Inca, and he named his brother Atahualpa as governor of the north, based in Quito.

Approximately five years later, Huascar decided to remove his brother by force. A short, brutal civil war ensued. Atahualpa and his armies defeated the Sapa Inca in May 1532 and Huascar was executed. Spanish people had already entered the empire and Atahualpa was curious, inviting them to a meeting in November 1532, just months after becoming the Sapa Inca. He was taken prisoner by the Spanish colonists who demanded an enormous amount of gold, silver and gems such as emeralds for his release. The amount was produced in some months but the colonists killed him anyway in July 1533. The Inca empire was vast and took many years to completely capture, but the Inca civil war weakened the state to a considerable extent, allowing the Spanish colonists to take complete control by 1572.

REBELLIONS

Empires can be weakened when there are attempts to overthrow the government or replace the ruling class. These revolts may weaken the state through military expense, as well as the destruction of the army, property and more.

■ **Figure 4.7** Portrait of Kublai, founder of the Yuan Dynasty of China

■ **Figure 4.8** Portrait of Hongwu, founder of the Ming Dynasty of China

ACTIVITY: Two emperors

ATL

- Critical-thinking skills: Recognize unstated assumptions and bias; Interpret data; Evaluate evidence and arguments; Revise understanding based on new information and evidence

Consider the portraits of Kublai and Hongwu in Figures 4.7 and 4.8.

Compare and contrast the way in which these two emperors are portrayed. What are the similarities? Are there any differences? We know that Kublai was ethnically Mongol. Does this come across in the portrait? Why or why not? What does this tell us about the differences between the Yuan and Ming Dynasties of China?

Now, **discuss** your findings with the rest of the class.

◆ Assessment opportunities

- ◆ In this activity you have practised skills that are assessed using Criterion A: Knowing and understanding, Criterion C: Communicating and Criterion D: Thinking critically.

Ming revolt against the Yuan Dynasty of China

A central belief in China in previous centuries was in the Mandate of Heaven – the belief that an emperor ruled with the blessing and approval of the gods. If the emperor or the imperial family fell out of favour with the gods, then it was acceptable to remove them as they no longer had the Mandate of Heaven. Floods, corruption, plagues, droughts, famine or war could be seen as an indication that the gods had removed their approval.

China was ruled by the ethnic Mongol Yuan Dynasty from 1271 to 1368 CE. In the final decades of the Yuan, the government implemented high taxation to pay for the state's large military. The taxation was so high that farmers abandoned land so that they would not have to pay taxes, fleeing to remote areas. With fewer people farming, food supplies were reduced and food costs rose. Hungry people were more susceptible to disease and in 1333 CE, for example, the **bubonic plague** killed 90 per cent of the population of Hebei province. By 1351, it may have been that almost 70 per cent of China's population had been killed by successive waves of bubonic plague over a 20-year period. Finally, a series of floods further devastated the country.

It was clear to many that the Mandate of Heaven had been taken away from the Yuan. An ethnic Han, or Chinese, anti-Mongol revolt called the Red Turban Rebellion began in 1351 CE.

The rebellion saw the rise of the Red Turbans, a group that wore red scarves and were founded by a Buddhist religious sect, led by Zhu Yuanzhang. His armies had conquered most of China by 1368 when he declared himself emperor, founding the Ming Dynasty. In 1369 CE, his armies took control of the Yuan capital, today's Beijing, driving the Mongol armies and people out of all but the most northern areas of China. War continued against the Mongol people and other groups for many years afterwards, but most of China was now firmly under the rule of the Ming. Ming rule continued until 1644 CE when they too saw their dynasty end at the hands of the ethnic Manchurians from the northeast. Manchurians founded the Qing Dynasty which lasted until 1911.

INDEPENDENCE MOVEMENTS

Rebellions sometimes take place in an attempt to gain independence from an empire. While putting down rebellions can be costly in terms of military expense and the destruction of cities, infrastructure, trade routes and lives, valuable territories may also be lost. These losses may weaken the empire as a whole.

Fatimid Caliphate (909–1171 CE)

The Abbasid Caliphate (750–1258 CE) ruled north Africa to central Asia with its capital in Baghdad, in today's Iraq. The majority of Muslims within the empire were Sunni. The next largest group of Muslims were Shi'a. Shi'a believed that Islam should be ruled by descendants of Prophet Muhammad who established the first caliphate in Medina in today's Saudi Arabia. As the caliphate was not ruled by direct descendants of Prophet Muhammad, Shi'a were considered a real threat to the empire.

The government that Shi'a established is known as the Fatimid Caliphate, named after Fatimah, the daughter of Prophet Muhammad from whom their caliphs descended. In 609 CE, they openly proclaimed their new caliphate from what is today's Algeria, moving soon to Tunisia which they captured from the Abbasid Caliphate. By 969 CE, Fatimids entered Egypt, driving out the Abbasid people, and declared Cairo to be the new Fatimid capital. From Egypt, Fatimids invaded and annexed the Levant, Sicily, Yemen, much of today's Syria, and the cities of Mecca and Medina, which were considered holy to Islam. This brought great prestige.

The Fatimid Caliphate prospered as they controlled all trade between Europe, Africa and the Middle East. Additionally, there was considerable trade between the Fatimid Caliphate and China, as well as with India. The loss of the provinces

■ **Figure 4.9** The Mosque of Al-Azhar in Cairo, the oldest surviving university of any caliphate, was established during the Fatimid Caliphate in 972 CE. Al-Azhar still exists today and continues to function as a university, teaching religion, religious law, science, engineering, business, medicine and more

and their resources negatively affected the Abbasid people. Lucrative trade routes were now dominated by the Fatimid Caliphate and money no longer flowed into the treasury of the Abbasid caliph. As a result, the caliph lost power to his generals and governors who taxed their own provinces and primarily managed their own affairs, often fighting against each other. Religiously, Fatimids challenged the legitimacy and teachings of the Sunni Abbasids, leading to further erosion of the Abbasid caliph's authority.

The independent Fatimid state negatively affected and permanently damaged the Abbasid Caliphate. The Fatimid Caliphate was eventually weakened by infighting between Turks, Berbers and Africans serving in their army. Its decline was hastened by the loss of the Levant to the Western European Crusaders. Sicily was lost to other Crusaders, and north Africa was lost to Berber tribes declaring renewed allegiance to the Abbasid Caliphate. Eventually Egypt was all that remained and it too was taken over by a Sunni dynasty in 1171 CE that created an empire called the Ayyubid Sultanate and pledged religious loyalty to the Abbasid Caliphate.

Saladin

Saladin is known in Arabic as Salah-ad-Din and was the founding sultan of the Ayyubid Sultanate based in Cairo. Before establishing his own rule, he was a soldier and officer for Nur-ad-Din, an independent governor in the Abbasid Caliphate who ruled much of today's Syria, southeastern Turkey and northern Iraq from his capital at Aleppo. Nur-ad-Din had forced the Fatimid Caliphate to appoint Salah-ad-Din as **Vizier**, or head of government. When the last Fatimid caliph died in 1174 CE, Salah-ad-Din abolished the Fatimid Caliphate. He pledged allegiance to the Abbasid caliph in Baghdad and became sultan. After Nur-ad-Din died in 1174, Salah-ad-Din invaded the Levant and Syria, taking over all of Nur-ad-Din's territory by 1182, except for the city of Mosul in today's Iraq.

Salah-ad-Din is most famous in Europe for defeating the Crusader kingdoms in the Levant and annexing them to his sultanate. In July 1187, the main Crusader army was heavily defeated at the Battle of Hattin. Immediately afterwards, Salah-ad-Din's forces captured at least 50 towns and fortifications from the Crusaders. By October, the Crusader capital, Jerusalem, was captured after a siege. The Crusaders now only possessed a few coastal cities and Salah-ad-Din was able to link Egypt and Syria under his control. Crusades by Western European Catholics would continue for decades, capturing and losing control of parts of the Levant, but the Ayyubid Dynasty of Salah-ad-Din defeated all in the end. Salah-ad-Din died in Damascus in 1193. The Ayyubid Dynasty lasted until 1250 CE in Egypt and 1260 CE in Syria.

ACTIVITY: Conflicts

ATL

- Information literacy skills: Access information to be informed and inform others; Make connections between various sources of information
- Critical-thinking skills: Recognize unstated assumptions and bias; Interpret data; Evaluate evidence and arguments; Revise understanding based on new information and evidence
- Transfer skills: Inquire in different contexts to gain a different perspective

Review the list of conflicts below:
- Ionian revolt
- Sertorian revolt
- First Servile revolt
- Zaidi revolt against Umayyad Caliphate
- Kaidu-Kublai War
- Spanish reconquest
- Zenobia's expansion of the Palmyrene empire

Evaluate as a class the nature of each of the above-mentioned conflicts. **Discuss** if these wars were civil wars, rebellions or independence movements, presenting evidence for your answer. Can a conflict be more than one of these?

EXTENSION

Using this research, answer the following question as an essay:

'Some historians believe that there is no real distinction between a rebellion, a civil war and a war for independence. To what extent do you agree with this view?'

Be sure to include an introduction, conclusion and at least three paragraphs that each deal with a separate piece of evidence. Consider using information from this chapter or from your research.

Assessment opportunities

- In this activity you have practised skills that are assessed using Criterion A: Knowing and understanding, Criterion B: Investigating, Criterion C: Communicating and Criterion D: Thinking critically.

BREAKDOWN OF IMPERIAL SYSTEMS

In Chapter 3, we discussed how empires maintain themselves through governing systems. Empires may fall when these systems break down, collapse or become inefficient. For example, bureaucracy, the military and the legal system may not function correctly due to corruption. Similarly, communication systems may become inefficient if the empire becomes too large.

Challenges due to size

Once an empire reaches a certain size, it can become difficult to manage all its systems, concerns and day-to-day realities from a centralized location. As a response to this, some empires have decided to divide into two or more semi-autonomous regions.

Roman empire (27 BCE–476 CE)

By the third century CE, the Roman empire had become very large, leading to some problems. There was war at the borders of the empire almost constantly. Germans and other tribes often attacked in the north, while Parthians and Sasanians attacked in the east. Desert tribes raided Egypt and north Africa. This meant there was a large military at all times which required clothing, food, shelter, fortifications, weapons and oversight.

Armies were led by generals and since communications were slow, they had considerable authority to act on behalf of a distant emperor. This led to many generals being proclaimed as emperor by local troops and government officials, often hoping for promotion and financial award. This caused long periods of instability when generals revolted and fought to become emperor. From 235 to 284 CE, for example, the 'Crisis of the Third Century', there were 24 emperors. This greatly weakened the state due to soldiers not being able to protect the borders, destruction of infrastructure, and severe taxation to pay for all this conflict.

Diocletian was a former Roman general who became emperor in 285 CE. He instituted a reorganization of the Roman empire, splitting it into two major divisions, east and west, with each division having one Augustus and one Caesar, like a vice-emperor. The Caesar would replace the Augustus when the Augustus retired, making the transition between governments peaceful and less destructive. Additionally, these four rulers were able to better administer their part of the empire so that military, economic and political needs were more rapidly addressed.

Over the next century and a half, the empire suffered through several invasions, rebellions and more, but the basic division of Diocletian remained. The Eastern Roman empire continued until 1453 CE, but the Western Roman empire declined slowly until 476 CE when the imperial government was replaced by non-Roman kings and local rulers.

Mongol empire

Before his death in 1227 CE, Genghis Khan had decided that Ogedai Khan, his third son, would be his successor. He gave his other sons territories to rule as **appanages** but still under the ultimate control of Ogedai.

Mongke Khan, the grandson of Genghis Khan and the fourth Great Khan, died in 1259 CE. He was the last Great Khan to rule over the entire Mongol empire. Upon his death, there were several civil wars among the descendants of Genghis Khan. The most important civil war, the Toluid civil war, was between the brothers of Mongke Khan over who would replace him as Great Khan. Both Kublai and Arike-Boke declared that they were the next Great Khan and fought one another, with Kublai winning in 1260 CE. The civil war threatened the unity of the empire.

■ **Figure 4.10** The Mongol empire, following its division in 1259 CE into the Yuan Dynasty, the Golden Horde, the Chagatai Khanate and the Ilkhanate

Great Khan Kublai continued the expansion of the empire by annexing the remaining areas of China under the Song Dynasty. In order to rule in China, Kublai decided to adapt the Mongol governing system by adopting systems from the Song Dynasty. For example, he named himself the founder of a new ruling dynasty, called the Yuan, with the Mandate of Heaven. Additionally, he moved the capital of the Mongol empire from Mongolia to what is today Beijing. This adoption of Chinese ways of doing things alienated some of the other Mongol people.

Due to the size of the empire, and the fact that Kublai was transforming it into something that was similar to previous Chinese dynasties, his relatives that ruled distant territories became more independent. The Mongol empire, over decades, slowly split into four main divisions, each ruled by the descendants of Genghis Khan:

- China and the surrounding regions were ruled by Kublai and his descendants as the Yuan Dynasty.
- Eastern Europe, today's Russia and Turkey, the Black Sea and Caucasus Mountain regions were ruled by the descendants of Jochi, Genghis Khan's first son, known as the Golden Horde.
- Central Asia and the Altai Mountain regions just west of China were ruled by the descendants of Chagatai, Genghis Khan's second son.
- Western Asia, primarily today's Iran, was ruled by the descendants of Hulegu, Kublai's younger brother.

All regions agreed by treaty in 1304 CE that the head of the empire remained the Yuan Dynasty which held the title of Great Khan. In practice, they were separate states.

Corruption

Corruption is both an ancient and modern problem for most states. Corruption in some ancient empires involved such practices as selling government positions to the highest bidder instead of placing qualified individuals in those posts. This allowed those who had bid highest to make money from their offices. This happened, for example, in the Han Dynasty as the state desperately needed funds to fight its civil wars and found that these could be easily raised by selling government positions. Needless to say, corruption weakened ancient states and continues to be a problem in our modern era.

ACTIVITY: What is government corruption?

ATL

- Information literacy skills: Access information to be informed and inform others; Make connections between various sources of information
- Transfer skills: Inquire in different contexts to gain a different perspective

As a class, **investigate** what constitutes government corruption in your own or other countries.

As a class, define government corruption.

Research what laws are in place to address and discourage government corruption in your own or other countries.

Identify, individually, three examples of corruption from the last ten years. **Explain** to your class what that corruption involved and the consequences for the corrupt official(s) and the state in each case. Were the laws that you identified followed in the three cases you found?

Debate the following question as a class: 'To what extent do laws prevent or successfully address corruption?'

◆ Assessment opportunities

- ◆ In this activity you have practised skills that are assessed using Criterion B: Investigating, Criterion C: Communicating and Criterion D: Thinking critically.

What external factors have led empires to fall?

INNOVATION

Advances in technology can radically affect history. These advances often give one group or other some military advantage. We have seen this with the introduction of chariot warfare in Chapter 2.

End of the Bronze Age

The Bronze Age was a period of history that lasted from approximately 3000 to 1200 BCE. It was during this time period that the first writing systems were developed in ancient Mesopotamia and Egypt. It was also the time when people developed enough metal-working knowledge and skills to develop bronze, an alloy of copper and tin. By 1200 BCE, the Egyptian and Hittite empires dominated the eastern Mediterranean, with large populations and cities, highly developed infrastructure and trade, and little conflict.

Almost all cities in the eastern Mediterranean, outside of Egypt, were, however, destroyed within 50 years. By 1150 BCE, the Hittite empire was gone, the population of the region collapsed, and Egypt was confined to the Nile Valley, fending off invasions from previously insignificant groups. The origins of the invaders, referred to in ancient Egyptian sources as the Sea Peoples, and the reasons for the collapse of Bronze Age civilization and empires is still debated. Historians continue to study evidence produced by archaeologists and scientists in order to understand what led to this collapse.

Changes in warfare

Empires and city-states had depended on chariot warfare for centuries. What is clear is that chariot warfare changed at the end of the Bronze Age. Chariots continued to be used, but were limited. Instead, new weapons appeared, as did large, mass infantries or foot soldiers. New weapons were also developed.

End of chariot warfare

In order to defeat a chariot team, one had to kill the horse that pulled the chariot. With one dead horse, a chariot could no longer function and its crew of one or two men, lightly armoured, could be taken prisoner or killed more easily. One historian, Dr Robert Drews, believes that the ancient weapon, the javelin, used to hunt by nomadic people for thousands of years, was deployed in huge numbers for the first time at the end of the Bronze Age. These nomadic or semi-nomadic people, perhaps stressed because of climate change or other unknown factors, invaded the empires and encountered chariot teams. Using their javelins, they were able to inflict defeat on chariot armies. Chariot warfare required specially trained men and expensive, specialized equipment, so chariots and chariot teams would have been hard to replace quickly, leaving the empires and their citizens vulnerable.

■ **Figure 4.11** Egyptian Pharaoh Ramesses III fighting from a chariot, supported by foot soldiers armed with bows, arrows, shields and axes. They are fighting off an invasion of the Sea Peoples on the edge of a sea or river. This huge carving in stone is located in the **mortuary temple** of Ramesses III. Notice that the pharaoh is the only person in a chariot while all the other combatants are foot soldiers

Iron use

Iron, a metal worked in the Bronze Age, now came to greater prominence because it was stronger than bronze. This meant that sword blades could be made much longer, giving warriors a greater reach and therefore advantage in hand-to-hand combat. Soldiers with longer, heavier swords would have dominated in any battle.

New tactics

Dr Robert Drews (see previous page) has also pointed out that for the first time, armies appear to have used lots of foot soldiers, or infantry soldiers, in battle. This may have been made possible through the mass production of arrowheads and spear points in factories. Alternatively, factories may have been needed to arm soldiers out of necessity; the evidence is not clear. What is clear is that instead of elite warriors riding chariots and using compound bows to fight battles, the empires and their adversaries were using thousands of foot soldiers, armed with spears, javelins, and bows and arrows.

Gunpowder

Gunpowder was invented in the 700s CE in China and was used as a form of medicine. By 1000 CE it was being used in warfare. Gunpowder was in use across Asia starting in the thirteenth century, having been spread through the Mongol empire. In 1287 CE, the first gun, the hand cannon, was created and used in China. Soon all types of cannon, hand-held and larger, were in use across Europe, the Middle East and Asia.

Guns allowed for someone of little skill to be an effective soldier. Before this time, archers and other types of warriors, such as cavalry, had to be heavily armed, armoured and trained. Archers needed great upper body strength in order to pull a bowstring back far enough for an arrow to hit a target at high speed. Now someone only had to aim in the general direction of an enemy and pull a lever in order for the gun to function. Gunpowder created a revolution in warfare, making it more destructive, causing more deaths, creating more effective armies and enabling the breaking of sieges through the use of cannon and explosive mines. In some ways, this revolution continues today.

Conquest of the New World

When Europeans landed on ships in North and South America, they encountered people living in the **Neolithic**, or New Stone Age, Period. Native Americans did not generally use metal for making tools and had no forges to melt and shape metal for any purpose. Instead, they shaped various types of stone to make blades, knives, hammers, drills and more. There were no animals that were capable of carrying people, like the horse or camel, in North or South America either.

When it came to military technology, Native Americans throughout the New World used stone points for spears and arrows, and occasionally obsidian (volcanic glass). Aztec and other central American warriors would have carried a type of bat that had edges lined with obsidian blades.

Europeans, on the other hand, had thousands of years of technology and innovations to draw upon, including:
- metal armour for warriors
- horses, also armoured
- iron weapons, such as knives, spears and the **mace**
- guns and gunpowder for hand-held and horse-drawn weapons.

The people that the Spanish, Portuguese, English, French and other colonists encountered were generally no match for the heavily armoured and well-equipped Europeans. This gave a huge advantage to the European invaders, so much so that historians have read accounts of a few hundred Spanish troops defeating armies of thousands. The rapid defeat of the Aztec and Inca empires, along with hundreds of other states within a few decades, stemmed largely from the lack of this technology.

ACTIVITY: Nuclear and biological weapons

ATL

- Information literacy skills: Access information to be informed and inform others; Make connections between various sources of information
- Critical-thinking skills: Revise understanding based on new information and evidence
- Transfer skills: Inquire in different contexts to gain a different perspective

Innovations for military use continue in our modern era. States have developed nuclear and biological weapons in the twentieth and twenty-first centuries. Nuclear weapons and biological warfare have the ability to destroy entire cities. The USA is the only country to have used nuclear weapons on another country, dropping two bombs on Japan in the Second World War, destroying the two cities of Nagasaki and Hiroshima instantly. One notable use of biological weapons was by Japan against China during the Second World War when bubonic plague was intentionally spread.

Consider the following questions:
- **Identify** which supra-national organizations monitor the use of nuclear, biological and chemical weaponry.
- **Determine** what treaties exist to protect against the use of nuclear, biological and chemical weaponry.
- If these types of warfare are outlawed, **explain** how and why they still exist. **Investigate** which countries are allowed to keep these weapons and why.
- **To what extent** do states agree to abide by treaties outlawing military innovation? **Discuss** the benefits of abiding by these treaties, as well as the consequences of violating them.
- **To what extent** has nuclear, biological and chemical warfare affected state relationships in the modern era?

Investigate one of the following events, crises or treaties in order to successfully address the questions above:
- Cuban Missile Crisis (1962)
- Treaty on Non-Proliferation of Nuclear Weapons (1968)
- Use of 'Agent Orange' from 1962 to 1971 during the Vietnam War (1955–75)
- Biological and Toxin Weapons Convention (1972)
- Syrian civil war (2011–present)
- Joint Comprehensive Plan of Action (Iran Nuclear Deal, 2015)

Discuss these questions with your class, using the evidence you have found from an event, war, crisis or treaty above.

EXTENSION

Using research and your own knowledge, address the following question in the form of an essay:

'Supra-national organizations have been extremely successful in preventing the spread of nuclear, biological and chemical weaponry.' To what extent do you agree with this statement?

Assessment opportunities

- In this activity you have practised skills that are assessed using Criterion A: Knowing and Understanding, Criterion B: Investigating, Criterion C: Communicating and Criterion D: Thinking critically.

MILITARY SUPERIORITY

Empires can end when they are defeated by rival empires whose troops are better led, better equipped, larger and/or healthier, or have other advantages.

Mongol empire against Xi Xia and Song Dynasty China

The Mongol conquest of China occurred in several stages. China was divided into three major states: Xi Xia, the Jin empire, and the Song Dynasty. The Mongol empire first defeated Xi Xia, although the Mongol army was outnumbered in terms of soldiers. The Xi Xia had an experienced army as they were often at war against the Jin and Song and had at least twice as many soldiers as the Mongol army. Xi Xia had a number of large, walled cities which the Mongol colonists had not encountered before. To conquer Xi Xia, and then the Jin and Song, the Mongol soldiers would have had to acquire new skills. In time, the Mongol strategy was to defeat the Xi Xia on the battlefield, and then conduct sieges to starve cities into surrender. Xi Xia finally signed a treaty of alliance and provided military support to the Mongol empire when they moved against the Jin. The conquest lasted 22 years, from 1205 CE to 1227 CE.

The Song Dynasty of China also proved difficult to defeat as it too had vast walled cities that required long periods of time to successfully force into surrender or to enter and destroy after months or even years of siege. The Song city of Xiangyang for example, which controlled Song access to the Han River, held out for six years before being taken. The Song deployed innovative weapons, such as **trebuchets** and cannon, in order to fight off the Mongol army, who also used the same weapons. The Song were also protected by vast rivers upon which they had navy ships ready to destroy Mongols who attempted to cross on boats or by swimming. This forced the Mongol empire to develop a navy for the first time. Between 1270 and 1273, the Great Khan Kublai constructed approximately 8,000 ships in order to help defeat the Song. The Mongol empire slowly defeated the Song over a 52-year period, from 1227 to 1279.

The Mongol empire was successful for a variety of reasons. The Mongol army was professional, and had great leadership in the form of generals with decades of experience. Additionally, they adapted their forms of warfare to the conditions that they found. They were not afraid of innovation and change. Although it took decades to defeat the Song, the Mongol leadership believed in long-term aims and remained committed to achieving them.

ECONOMIC WEAKNESS

Trade has been a traditional source of great wealth for kingdoms and empires. When goods crossed into the country, they were taxed, and sometimes when goods were leaving as well. If the state itself brought the goods into a country, then the state could sell them directly and make money.

In many empires throughout history the state had the sole right to trade in certain goods. The government of Han Dynasty China (202 BCE–220 CE), for example, completely controlled the production, sale and distribution of salt, iron, copper and bronze. Control of salt and metals earned the state a vast sum of money.

Empires that lost control of their monopolies or trade routes could face severe economic hardship. This could potentially lead to the collapse of the state.

Spice trade

The trade in goods between Europe and northern Africa with India and neighbouring regions continued for thousands of years. From today's India, Indonesia and Malaysia came many spices, including cinnamon, peppercorns, nutmeg, mace, cloves, cardamom, ginger and turmeric. Additionally, these areas supplied sandalwood and opium. Silk was exported from India as well, having originated in China. From Europe and northern Africa came gold, silver and textiles. The spice trade made the merchant empires of Venice and Genoa very wealthy, with both trading primarily with the Mamluk people. Spices in Europe were worth their weight in gold due to their rarity at the time.

Mamluk Sultanate (1250–1517 CE)

The Silk Road moved goods from China to the west for hundreds of years. Goods moved relatively freely until the Mongol empire began to break into smaller, more manageable states. Many of these states were then overthrown and broke into even more sultanates and kingdoms. As trade along the Silk Road became difficult the price of goods rose, allowing the development of other trade routes.

The transport of goods along the Silk Road was accomplished primarily by camels, donkeys and horses. This meant that at the best of times, the movement of goods was still relatively slow. Travel by sea, however, could be much faster, depending on winds and the seasons of the year. A major link between Asia, especially from what is today India, Malaysia, Indonesia and places further east, was shipping lanes between the Indian Ocean and the Red Sea. Ships from ports in India would sail to today's Oman and Yemen, and then up the Red Sea to the cities of Jeddah and Suez and back. When the goods reached Suez, camel caravans would transport them to Cairo where they were sorted, stored, taxed and sold to local and international merchants and representatives of European states, especially Venice. This made the capital of the Mamluk Sultanate, Cairo, a rich city.

In 1497, ships from Portugal found a direct sea route between Portugal and India having successfully sailed around southern Africa's Cape of Good Hope. Almost immediately, the Portuguese government decided to remove all competing merchant ships in the Indian Ocean and the Red Sea. They destroyed Mamluk and other ships, selling any survivors as slaves. In 1505, the piracy of the Portuguese government erupted into full war with the Mamluk Sultanate, who were supported by Venice. Venice was a city-state that controlled an empire in the Mediterrean Sea and gained much of its wealth by purchasing goods in Cairo's markets and reselling them throughout Europe. They supported the Mamluk people with weapons and ship builders. The Mamluk Sultanate built a fleet of ships to fight off the Portuguese pirates, but by 1509, the fleet had been defeated and the Portuguese pirates increasingly captured and destroyed all competing ships. Instead of going to Cairo, all goods from the east now sailed around Africa to Portugal. The Mamluk Sultanate was no longer the centre of trade with India and the east.

The economy of the Sultanate collapsed as a result of the war. This meant the state was unable to purchase weapons, much less luxury goods. The Sultanate could not afford to build an army and maintain it. The Venetian and other states had supported the Mamluk Sultanate in earlier times as the stability of the Mamluk Sultanate was critical for their own economies. Now, the Sultanate was far less important to their own needs. The economically weakened Mamluk Sultanate could no longer defend itself or rely on allies to assist it.

In 1516, the Ottoman empire invaded Mamluk territory, capturing Diyarbakir in today's eastern Turkey and then defeating and killing the Mamluk sultan at Barj Dabiq in today's northern Syria soon after. A battle near Gaza in late 1516 was another Ottoman victory. In early 1517, Cairo was captured and the last Mamluk sultan executed. The Abbasid Caliphate had transferred to Cairo after the Mongol empire had destroyed Baghdad in 1258 and it ended in 1517 when the last caliph was sent to Istanbul, the Ottoman capital, where he resigned his position and authority, transferring it to the Ottoman sultan. In 1517, both the Mamluk Sultanate and the Abbasid Caliphate came to an end as the result of severe economic weakness.

What is left in the aftermath of an empire's collapse?

When empires collapse, the systems of those empires often collapse also. In the aftermath, there may be an absence of communication and legal systems, lack of security from either absent or competing armies, and a highly disrupted economy. This can lead to further conflict as different groups fight for control and a long period of instability as one group or the other works to establish order and their rule.

ACTIVITY: The aftermath of an empire's collapse

ATL

- Information literacy skills: Access information to be informed and inform others; Make connections between various sources of information
- Critical-thinking skills: Recognize unstated assumptions and bias; Interpret data; Evaluate evidence and arguments; Revise understanding based on new information and evidence

Consider an empire we have studied in the last three chapters, or an empire of your own choice.

Evaluate what was left in the aftermath of that empire's collapse. You may wish to consider the following questions:

- Did any new states form as a result of the empire's collapse? If so, how were they different from the previous state? If not, did anything form in the aftermath of the empire's collapse?
- What unique problems did these new states face?
- What methods did they use to overcome these problems?
- Were they successful in overcoming these problems? If so, how did they succeed? If not, why did they fail?
- What system of government replaced the empire?
- Did the new state use any of the old empire's systems, or did they create their own? Why?
- How long did it take for the period of instability to end? Why did you choose this date?

Based on your knowledge and independent research, develop a research question to **evaluate** one aspect of an empire's aftermath.

Potential research questions include:

- To what extent was the Byzantine *Corpus Juris Civilis* used in Egypt and other areas conquered by the Islamic Caliphate?
- Explain how the collapse of the Bronze Age affected the government of Egypt.
- How did the Gupta empire differ from preceding empires in India?
- Discuss the differences between Umayyad governing systems with those developed by the Abbasids.
- 'Military innovation is the most important factor for the maintenance of empire.' Discuss.
- To what extent was Ottoman rule in Egypt different from Mamluk rule?
- To what extent did the Western and Eastern Roman empires operate as independent entities?
- To what extent was disease responsible for the end of the Han Dynasty?
- Compare and contrast the Yuan and Ming Dynasties in terms of their governing systems.
- Discuss the most significant differences between the Achaemenid and Macedonian empires.
- 'When empires collapse, systems often continue.' With reference to an empire or empires of your choice, to what extent do you agree with this statement?
- To what extent were the systems of the Aztec and Inca empires adopted by the Spanish empire for ruling Central and South America?

◆ Assessment opportunities

- In this activity you have practised skills that are assessed using Criterion A: Knowing and understanding, Criterion B: Investigating, Criterion C: Communicating and Criterion D: Thinking critically.

Have empires and superpowers led to a more peaceful world?

We have studied the importance of empires in creating periods of peace. We know from our studies that the wars between the Hittite and Egyptian empires led to a peace treaty and a long period of peace and relative stability throughout what is today the Middle East. We have also studied the Pax Mongolica and understand that the creation of the Mongol empire led to a long period of peace throughout Asia. The Pax Mongolica allowed increased trade and the spread of ideas and technology.

There have been other periods of peace in more recent times also. There was no major war in Europe between European empires from 1815 until 1853, for example, and no major inter-empire conflicts between 1870 and 1914. The USA and the Soviet Union/Russia were the superpowers that emerged during the Second World War, replacing empires. No major, direct confrontation between the superpowers has occurred.

However, it is also true that empires have been involved in some of the most devastating conflicts in world history. For example, the death toll of the Mongol empire's conflicts between 1211 and 1337 is estimated at 18.3 million, which was a sizable percentage of the world's population at the time. Similarly, the First and Second World Wars of the twentieth century led to the deaths of up to 100 million people in just over ten years of conflict. Besides the death toll, the aftermath of these conflicts includes shortages of food, destruction of vital infrastructure, and other negative economic and socio-political effects. As such, empires may be responsible for periods of instability, devastation and destruction.

> ! **Take action**
>
> ! In this chapter, we have studied how empires fall and what is left in the aftermath. One factor that often determines how empires fare is the failure of key government systems. Modern states and countries also have key systems that they need to maintain in order for the country to remain stable. Like empires, these systems include communications networks, the economy, the military and law enforcement. Modern states also have to account for systems that deal with travel, taxation, health care, diplomacy, information and more.
> ! **Investigate** one system in your own country that needs improvement in your opinion. This could be the currency stability, health care, education, infrastructure or anything else of your choice.
> ! **Take action** by finding the relevant body that deals with this system in your country and organizing a letter-writing campaign. Make sure that your own letter deals with what needs improvement, evidence to **justify** this and recommendations for how improvements can be made.

ACTIVITY: Empires – peace and conflict

ATL

- Critical-thinking skills: Interpret data; Evaluate evidence and arguments; Revise understanding based on new information and evidence
- Information literacy skills: Access information to be informed and inform others; Make connections between various sources of information

Investigate the view of one historian, article, book or other source that addresses whether empires lead to peace or conflict.

Evaluate your chosen source's views on the relationship empires have with peace and conflict. **List** the main arguments of the source, as well as the evidence used to **justify** the analysis. Additionally, **list** arguments that your source has not considered that may support their view.

Identify counter-arguments to your source's view. These may include:
- opinions of historians, articles, books or other sources
- historical evidence
- flaws or inconsistencies in your source's reasoning
- examples of historical events that seem to contradict the source's reasoning.

EXTENSION

Using this research, as well as your own knowledge, plan and write a response to your source that argues the opposing viewpoint. For example, if your chosen source argues that empires cause conflict, create an argument that empires are responsible for peace. Be sure to structure your piece as a response that directly addresses your chosen historian's original piece and opposes it using evidence.

◆ Assessment opportunities

◆ In this activity you have practised skills that are assessed using Criterion A: Knowing and understanding, Criterion B: Investigating and Criterion D: Thinking critically.

Reflection

In this chapter, we have **discussed** how empires may fail and what is left in the aftermath of an empire's collapse. We have assessed the ways in which military and economic superiority, innovation, climate, size and the breakdown of imperial systems may cause the collapse of an empire. We have also **explored** how these factors may interact with one another to create weaknesses in an empire. Finally, we have **evaluated** the different viewpoints historians have on an empire's significance and collapse, and the reasons why they may differ. Through this, we have learned the strengths and weaknesses of empires, and gained a balanced view on how they have affected the modern world.

Use this table to reflect on your own learning in this chapter.						
Questions we asked	Answers we found	Any further questions now?				
Factual: What internal factors have led empires to fail? What external factors have led empires to fail? What is left in the aftermath of an empire's collapse?						
Conceptual: Why do empires fail? To what extent can environmental factors affect the stability of an empire? To what extent do empires need to maintain dominance in order to continue to exist?						
Debatable: Have empires and superpowers led to a more peaceful world?						
Approaches to learning you used in this chapter	Description – what new skills did you learn?	How well did you master the skills?				
		Novice	Learner	Practitioner	Expert	
Collaboration skills						
Information literacy skills						
Critical-thinking skills						
Transfer skills						
Learner profile attribute(s)	Reflect on the importance of being balanced for your learning in this chapter.					
Balanced						

Time, place and space, Change | Perspective; Sustainability | Globalization and sustainability

 5 What impact do humans have on natural environments?

○ Human choices, through **time** and in different **places**, have led to **global** environmental **change** that may make our current way of life **unsustainable**.

CONSIDER THESE QUESTIONS:

Factual: Where are different environments located? What are the characteristics of natural environments? How do humans impact on natural environments?

Conceptual: Can resources ever be exploited sustainably?

Debatable: To what extent is globalization a driver for development, and to what extent a driver for destruction?

Now **share and compare** your thoughts and ideas with your partner, or with the whole class.

■ Figure 5.1 How do we affect our natural environment?

○ IN THIS CHAPTER WE WILL …

- **Find out:** about the characteristics of major natural environments.
- **Explore:**
  - how human actions can threaten natural environments
  - the delicate balance between using Earth's resources and preserving natural environments.
- **Take action** by raising awareness of how humans are using the Earth unsustainably and by promoting sustainable use.

These Approaches to Learning (ATL) skills will be useful …

- Communication skills
- Collaboration skills
- Organization skills
- Reflection skills
- Information literacy skills
- Media literacy skills
- Critical-thinking skills
- Transfer skills

We will reflect on this learner profile attribute …

- Principled – examining how we can sustainably use our Earth's resources with respect for the dignity and rights of people everywhere and reflecting upon the importance of taking responsibility for our actions and their consequences.

Assessment opportunities in this chapter:

- **Criterion A:** Knowing and understanding
- **Criterion B:** Investigating
- **Criterion C:** Communicating
- **Criterion D:** Thinking critically

KEY WORDS

climate
habitat
sustainability

THINK–PUZZLE–EXPLORE

Consider the relationship between humans and the natural environment. Reflect on any prior knowledge you may have gained from *Individuals and Societies for the IB MYP 1* and the images above.

- What do you know about this topic?
- What questions or puzzles do you have?
- How can you **explore** this topic?

Thanks to its unique ability to sustain life, the Earth is home to a vast range of diverse natural environments. These are sometimes known as **ecosystems** or **biomes**. In this chapter, we will be focusing on forest, desert, grassland, tundra and aquatic areas. We will **explore** the characteristics of these natural environments and examine some of the impacts that humans have had on them.

Where are different environments located?

THINK–PAIR–SHARE

Look at the map showing threats to biodiversity (Figure 5.2). In pairs, **list** as many threats to natural environments as you can think of. Be ready to share your ideas with the class.

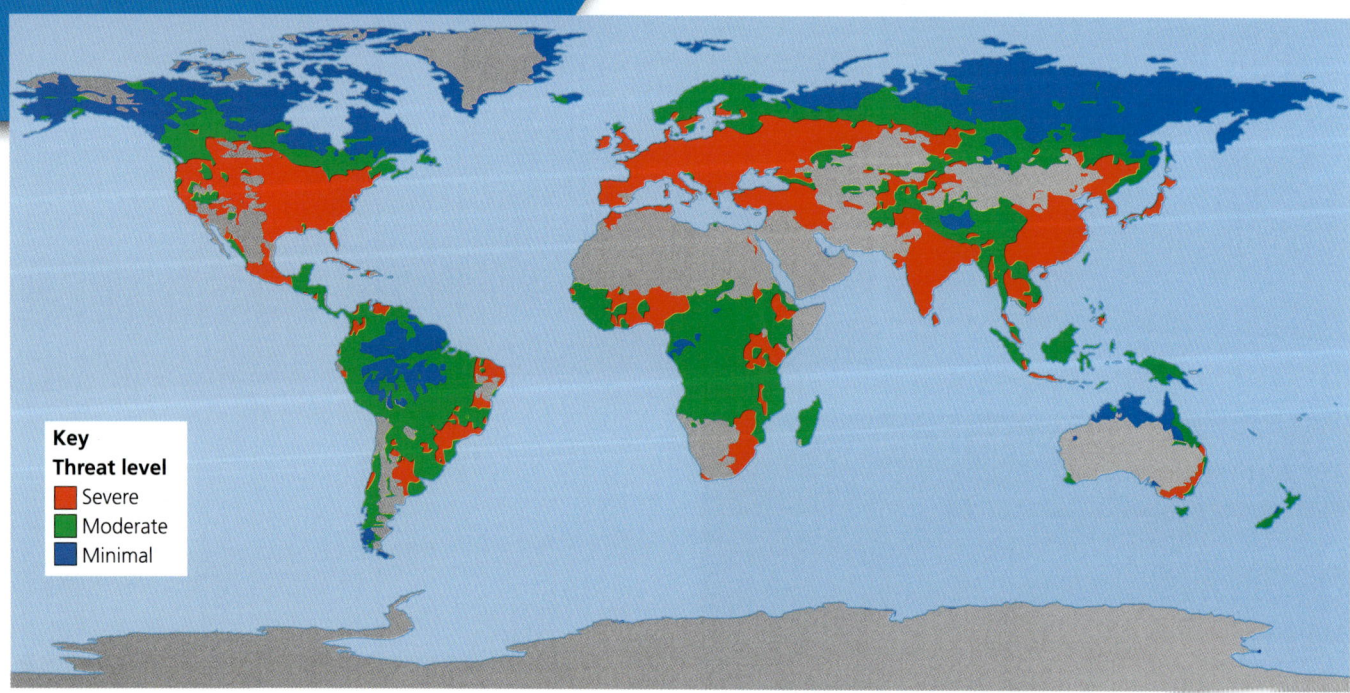

Figure 5.2 Biodiversity threat map

ACTIVITY: Location of natural environments

ATL

- Communication skills: Organize and depict information logically
- Transfer skills: Apply skills and knowledge in unfamiliar situations

In this activity, you will **interpret** information from charts in order to deduce the relationship between environments and their climate features.

Before you begin, you may find it useful to read 'Describing location on a map' and 'Climate graphs' opposite.

- **Describe** the location of the following natural environments: desert, grassland, rainforest and tundra areas. **Identify** the main **climatic** features of desert, grassland, rainforest and tundra areas – think about rainfall and temperature.
- **Construct** a climate graph for one of the natural environments mentioned above.
- **Analyse** the climate you have chosen to display on your climate graph. (Use the prompts in 'Climate graphs' opposite to help you structure your analysis.)
- Select an example of one aquatic environment (either freshwater or ocean-based) and **identify** the climatic features of the area in which it is located.

◆ Assessment opportunities

- In this activity you have practised skills that are assessed using Criterion A: Knowing and understanding and Criterion C: Communicating.

Individuals & Societies for the IB MYP 4&5: by Concept

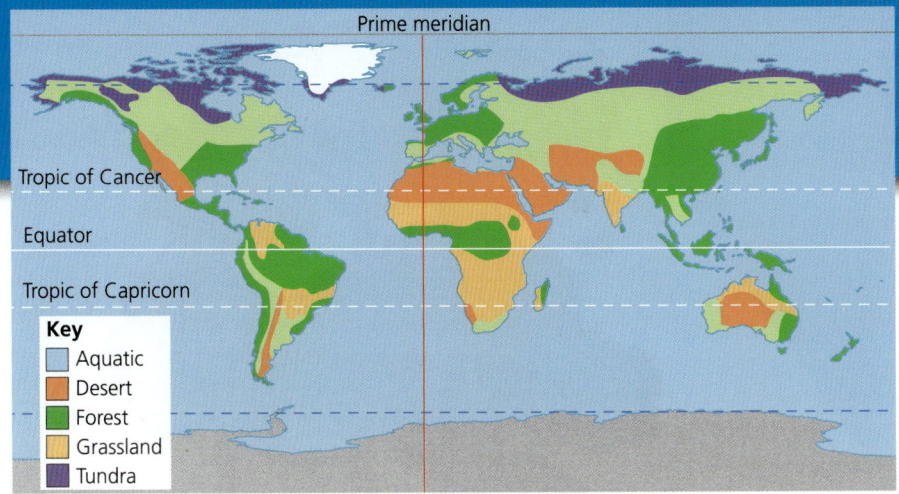

■ **Figure 5.3** A map of the world showing the natural environments to be examined in this chapter

Describing location on a map

When referring to the location of a place on a map, you should consider the following points:
- Whether the place is in the northern or southern hemisphere
- Whether the place is in the eastern or western hemisphere
- Distance from the equator (latitude)
- Distance from the prime meridian (longitude)
- Continent
- Neighbouring countries
- Physical features such as mountain ranges or rivers

Climate graphs

Climate graphs are a combination of a bar graph and a line graph. Temperature is shown on a line graph, with the figures on the right side of the graph. Rainfall is shown by a bar graph, with the figures down the left side of the graph.

When **interpreting** the data, look for patterns in temperature and rainfall, and for relationships between them. It may help to structure your analysis by considering the following guiding questions:
- Is the temperature the same all year round? If it is different, how many seasons does the location experience?
- Which season is the warmest? Is it warm (10–20°C), hot (20–30°C) or very hot (above 30°C)?
- Which season is the coolest? Is it mild (0–10°C), cold (-10–0°C) or very cold (below -10°C)?
- Is there rainfall all year round?
- What is the pattern of the rainfall? Check which season/s is/are drier or wetter than others.
- What is the total annual rainfall? Add each month's total together to get the annual total.

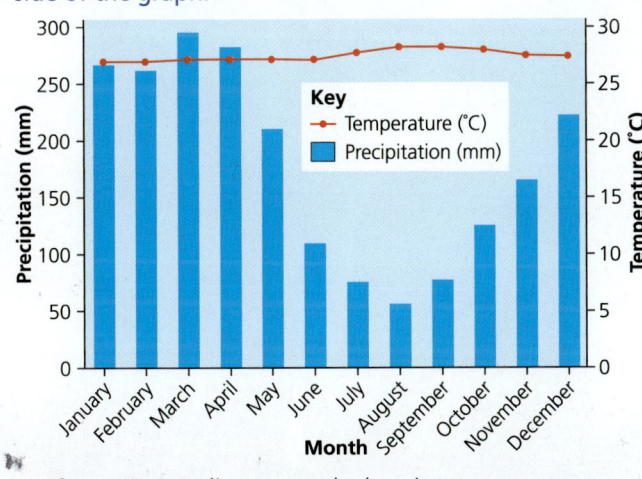

■ **Figure 5.4** A climate graph showing temperature and rainfall

5 What impact do humans have on natural environments? 113

What are the characteristics of natural environments?

■ Figure 5.5 The layers of vegetation in the rainforest

On the previous pages, you explored the climatic features of some of the Earth's natural environments. Now you will focus on other key characteristics of these areas including the plants and animals found in each natural environment.

RAINFORESTS

Rainforests are a unique natural environment in that they cover only a fraction of the Earth's surface – about 6 per cent – but are home to over half the species of plants and animals in the world. Their location close to the equator (see Figure 5.3) ensures a warm and humid climate with plenty of rainfall, which means that vegetation grows in abundance.

Rainforest vegetation

Due to the differing amounts of sunlight received by vegetation in the rainforest, the plants and trees grow in distinct layers, with those that receive the most growing the tallest and those receiving the least remaining at a lower level. You can see the approximate percentages of sunlight received by each layer in Figure 5.5.

The forest floor is dark and gloomy. It has very little vegetation between the trees and is susceptible to flooding during periods of extreme rain due to the lack of plants to absorb the water and protect the ground. The plants and shrubs that do grow in the lower layers have had to adapt over time to the limited light they receive. The under canopy also has limited sunlight and is where woody climbers called lianas are found. These have adapted by growing up the trunks of the trees to reach the sunlight they depend upon for survival. The canopy is where the crowns of the majority of trees are found and this leafy environment is home to insects, birds and some mammals. The emergent layer experiences the most sunlight and is home to the tops of the tallest trees. These trees have straight tree trunks and their lower parts are usually branchless as they concentrate all of their growing efforts in travelling upwards, not outwards.

As well as adapting to limited light, there are a variety of other vegetation adaptations found in the rainforest.

■ Figure 5.6 A drip tip on a leaf

■ **Figure 5.7** A fan palm tree canopy

■ **Figure 5.8** A giant tree with buttress roots

Rainforest wildlife

Rainforests boast a huge variety of wildlife thanks to the near constant supply of water and the diversity of foods for the animals. In addition to large animals such as gorillas, jaguars and tigers, small animals including monkeys, birds, snakes, rodents, frogs and lizards are common in the tropical rainforest. Many never set foot on the ground, favouring the tall trees and under canopy to provide shelter, hiding places from their predators and a source of food.

The vast numbers of animals living in the rainforest produces pressure for food. Adaptation is a way of overcoming this problem, and one of the most common adaptations is to eat a food that is eaten by no other animal. The toucan, for example, has a long bill that allows it to reach fruit on high branches that are too small and weak to support their body weight. The bill is also sharp enough to cut fruit from the trees.

▼ Links to: Biology

The theme of adaptation in ecosystems links to biology. See *Biology for the IB MYP 4&5* Chapter 8 for more on adaptation and ecosystems.

ACTIVITY: Animal inventory

■ ATL

- Communication skills: Write for different purposes

Imagine you are a forest ranger tasked with creating an inventory of rainforest animals for the British Council, which is looking to classify rainforest wildlife.

You should **identify** two rainforest animals (or insects or birds). Create a sketch of each animal and **annotate** the sketches with key features.

Explain how these adaptations have led to the animals being able to survive in the rainforest.

State whether the animals are endangered and if so, why this is the case and what, if any, measures can be put in place to preserve them.

◆ Assessment opportunities

- ◆ In this activity you have practised skills that are assessed using Criterion A: Knowing and understanding and Criterion C: Communicating.

THINK–PAIR–SHARE

Dame Jane Goodall says 'to achieve global peace, we must not only stop fighting each other but also stop destroying the natural world.' How far do you agree with this statement? Is one more important than the other? Take a few minutes of thinking time to consider how you feel about the statement and the question posed before sharing your thoughts with another student. Be prepared to share your ideas with the whole class.

MEET A SIGNIFICANT INDIVIDUAL: DAME JANE GOODALL (1934–PRESENT)

Caring

■ Figure 5.9 Dr Jane Goodall

Jane Goodall is a renowned ecologist and conservationist who has been appointed a United Nations Messenger of Peace, having agreed 'to help focus worldwide attention on the work of the United Nations'. Jane has dedicated her life to the study and protection of chimpanzees and gorillas in rainforest regions. She conducted a 45-year study of chimpanzee social and family life in Tanzania, and the chimp observation, which began in the Gombe in Tanzania in 1960, is the world's longest running continuous wildlife research project. The Jane Goodall Institute had led to her being equally well known as a conservationist and a champion of human rights. She currently travels an average of 300 days per year, speaking in venues around the world about the threats facing chimpanzees, other environmental crises, and her reasons for hope that we will ultimately solve the problems that we have imposed on the earth. 'Every individual counts,' she says. 'Every individual has a role to play. Every individual makes a difference.'

Search the **Jane Goodall Institute** for more information.

ACTIVITY: What other types of forest are there?

■ ATL

- Communication skills: Paraphrase accurately and concisely
- Media literacy skills: Seek a range of perspectives from multiple and varied sources

Rainforests are not the only type of forest area.

Research **coniferous forests** and **deciduous woodlands** and create a poster comparing them with rainforests.

Identify where they are located and **describe** their main characteristics in terms of climate, vegetation and wildlife.

Explore how humans have impacted on these natural environments in both positive and negative ways.

Explore sustainable strategies for management of both areas.

◆ Assessment opportunities

◆ In this activity you have practised skills that are assessed using Criterion B: Investigating.

DESERTS

Deserts are biomes that receive very limited amounts of precipitation each year. To be classed as a desert area, less than 250 mm of rain or other precipitation must fall annually. Deserts are not always the hot and sandy areas we imagine them to be; there are also cold deserts. Antarctica, the coldest, driest continent of all, is in fact the world's largest desert, stretching over 14,000,000 km². Whether deserts are hot or cold, their extreme conditions create challenges in supporting vegetation and wildlife.

Vegetation in hot deserts

The vegetation that grows in hot desert areas has adapted to be able to cope with the extremes in rainfall and temperature, which may reach 50 °C during the day and may fall to below 0 °C at night.

The cactus is a good example of a plant that has adapted to its environment.

Many plants have thick, waxy skins and spiny, needle-like leaves to reduce moisture loss through transpiration and fleshy stems that can store water.

Roots are long and porous in order to absorb moisture from deep underground supplies or are shallow but far reaching so that they can gather water from a wider area during the brief spells of rain.

Some seeds have also adapted so that they have the ability to lie dormant until periods of more heavy rainfall when they are able to germinate quickly and be fully grown and blooming within a period of weeks.

■ Figure 5.10 A cactus

■ Figure 5.11 Desert flowers in bloom

■ Figure 5.12 Vegetation of the desert

Desert wildlife

Many desert animals are nocturnal, only coming out in the cooler night to hunt and eat, and many spend most of their time underground in burrows where it is a lot cooler. Due to the lack of available prey to hunt, most animals in the desert are herbivores, which means that they eat desert plants and seeds. Some animals get all of the water they need from the insects, bulbs and seeds they eat and do not need to drink water even when it is available; for others, the morning dew is enough to maintain their water intake. As well as these adaptations, there are some specific ways in which their bodies have adapted too.

THINK–PAIR–SHARE

Look at Figure 5.12. **Discuss** reasons for the distribution of desert vegetation with your partner and be ready to share your ideas with the class.

ACTIVITY: How has the camel adapted?

The camel is one of the best known of the desert animals.

■ Figure 5.13 A camel in the desert

Identify six ways in which a camel has adapted to its environment.

Search **camel feet** and **camel fur** to get you started.

5 What impact do humans have on natural environments?

In addition to the camel, there are many other forms of desert wildlife that have adapted to the harsh conditions that they face. Although these creatures may look vastly different from one another, they tend to all share the following characteristics: they are usually light in colour, can often provide their own shade and can conserve water.

ACTIVITY: Common desert adaptations

ATL

- Communication skills: Organize and depict information logically

Copy and complete Table 5.1, ensuring that you **explain** fully why each of the adaptations are important for the animal.

Table 5.1 Animals and their adaptations

Adaptation	Why this adaptation is important (use figures and statistics to support your answer)	Example of an animal that illustrates this adaptation
Light coloured		
Can conserve water		
Can provide its own shade		

◆ Assessment opportunities

- ◆ In this activity you have practised skills that are assessed using Criterion A: Knowing and understanding and Criterion B: Investigating.

GRASSLANDS

Grassland areas, sometimes known as tropical savanna grasslands, are different from desert and rainforest regions in that they have a distinct wet and dry season. These areas run in a band along the equator between the Tropics of Capricorn and Cancer, between tropical rainforests and desert regions. They cover much of Africa as well as large areas of Australia, South America and India (see Figure 5.3).

Vegetation in grassland areas

Grasslands are often viewed as transitional zones between tropical rainforests and deserts, with vegetation varying according to the distance between the two distinct zones. Savanna vegetation includes scrub, grasses and occasional trees, which grow near water holes or seasonal rivers. Due to the distinct wet and dry seasons experienced in the grassland regions, the vegetation varies depending on the time of the year.

The wet season

During the wet season, the vegetation does all of its growing and storing of water. Lush green grasses thrive due to the hot and wet conditions and quickly reach heights of 3–4 metres before flowering and producing new seeds. Wooded areas emerge and the baobab tree (Figure 5.14) with its thick trunk stores water for the dry season. Acacia trees (Figure 5.15) flourish and their wide, flat foliage provides shelter and shade for wildlife.

The dry season

As there is very little rain in the dry season (which lasts for approximately five months, depending on the exact location of the grasslands), vegetation has to adapt. Many plants are xerophytic (drought resistant), including the acacia tree, which has small, waxy leaves and thorns to reduce transpiration. Most vegetation has long roots to reach down to the water table and sustain itself when no water is available. The lush grasses of the wet season turn yellow, eventually becoming straw-like before withering and dying.

■ **Figure 5.14** A baobab tree

■ **Figure 5.16** A water hole in Etosha National Park, Namibia

■ **Figure 5.15** An acacia tree and green grasses of the savanna

Wildlife in grasslands

The plentiful food that springs into life in the wet season draws and supports huge herds of grazing animals as water holes appear and vegetation thrives, but animals may migrate great distances in search of food and water during the dry seasons. The grassland regions support both herbivores and carnivores, with tropical grassland animals including lions, leopards, cheetahs, jackals, wild dogs and hyenas. The Serengeti plains of Tanzania are one of the best known of the African grassland regions and are rich in

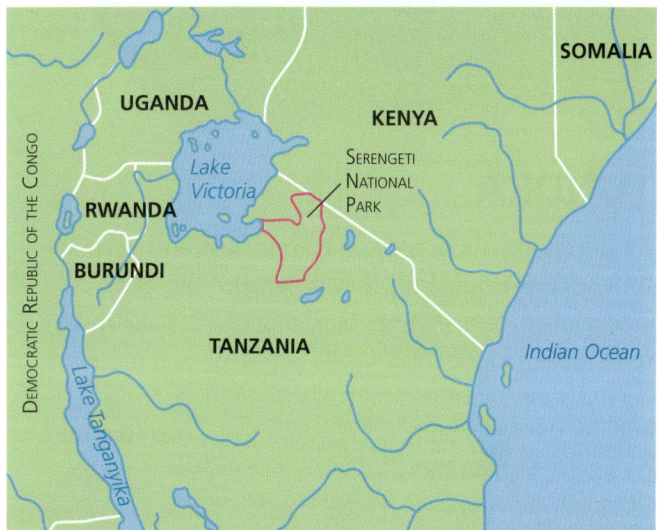

■ **Figure 5.17** Serengeti National Park

wildlife including giraffes, zebras, elephants, lions and over 2 million wildebeest. Many of the animals found on the Serengeti can be found nowhere else in the world and while this is a unique and attractive feature of the area, it has also meant that human choices have led to environmental change which may make life unsustainable here.

ACTIVITY: Scouting for a film location

■ ATL

- Collaboration skills: Exercise leadership and take on a variety of roles within groups

You work for a large film company looking to make a big-budget animated movie set in the savanna. Although the movie will be primarily aimed at children, the company is keen to portray the grassland area accurately and to protect the integrity of the region.

You have been sent, along with two others, to compile a location report on the area.

The report should enable your bosses to understand the key historic, geographic and economic features of the Serengeti region.

Work in your group of three to create a presentation to brief your bosses. You may choose any medium in which to create your presentation and you must be sure to include references for your sources.

◆ Assessment opportunities

- This activity can be assessed using Criterion A: Knowing and understanding and you have practised skills that can be assessed by Criterion B: Investigating and Criterion C: Communicating.

TUNDRA

Tundra are the Arctic areas of Europe, Asia and North America (see Figure 5.3). They experience very little precipitation, temperatures remain below 0 °C for most of the year and the soil is frozen almost all year round. Tundra areas are often at first glance thought to be barren and desolate environments due to the fact that they are covered in ice and snow for much of the year. However, while they are treeless and flat, they are home to a range of vegetation and wildlife which have adapted to survive in the extreme conditions.

Vegetation adaptations

All plants need sunlight and warmth in order to thrive and the tundra vegetation is no exception to this, despite the extreme cold and long dark winters of the tundra.

Vegetation in the tundra has adapted to tolerate the cold by remaining close to the ground to protect itself from frequent high winds and by growing close together in clusters for protection and shelter. Their low height means that in winter months the plants are often covered under a layer of snow, which serves as insulation and further protection. They have adapted to be able to photosynthesize in cold temperatures where there is limited sunlight, many of them having small, dark leaves which conserve moisture by reducing transpiration and absorbing what heat the sun does bring.

Cottongrass is an example of a plant that is well adapted to the tundra environment. It has a short growing season and life cycle, seeds that scatter in the wind and a dense flower head to reduce heat loss. Its roots are also shallow so that they do not need to penetrate the frozen soil.

Other tundra vegetation includes mosses, lichens and low-growing shrubs and grasses.

■ **Figure 5.18** Cottongrass

Wildlife in the tundra

As with the wildlife in the other natural environments you have explored, the wildlife of the tundra has a range of physical and behavioural adaptations which support survival in the extreme conditions. One of the most common behavioural adaptations is migration – most birds and mammals use the tundra as a summer home when the days are long and the sun shines 24 hours a day. Hibernation is a combination of physical and behavioural adaptation, with many animals, such as the brown bear, consuming as much food as possible during the six to ten weeks of summer and then sleeping for the majority of the cold, winter months. The food consumed during the summer forms a layer of fat under the fur and this fat is converted to energy which keeps the bear alive while in deep hibernation. The snowshoe hare also changes between summer and winter – in the winter its fur is white for camouflage and in the summer it turns a reddish brown to match the landscape that is revealed as the snow melts. Polar bears are also well camouflaged during the winter with their thick white fur which covers layers of fat, both of which act as insulation against the cold. Their coats are also greasy, so after they have been hunting for food in the water they shed the water easily and therefore their fur does not freeze in the low temperatures. Many animals, including the polar bear, are rounded in shape with their limbs close to the ground, which provides a small surface area to volume ratio and further serves to minimize heat loss.

■ Figure 5.19 Polar bear

■ Figure 5.20 Snowshoe hare in Winter

■ Figure 5.21 Snowshoe hare in summer

ACTIVITY: Polar exploration journal entry

ATL

- Communication skills: Write for different purposes

You are an explorer who has just arrived in a polar region. You have been **documenting** your travels so far through journal entries on your blog and social media accounts.

Your task is to write an entry that shares your first impressions upon arrival in the polar region.

You should include:
- a description of the landscape, including any vegetation you can see
- any signs of wildlife
- how you are feeling and what you can see, taste and smell
- how *you* are adapting to the harsh climate
- whether there are any signs of human life.

Remember to include accurate, specific details where possible. The website of polar explorer Ben Saunders, **bensaunders.com**, may provide you with some inspiration.

◆ Assessment opportunities

- In this activity you have practised skills that are assessed using Criterion A: Knowing and understanding and Criterion C: Communicating.

AQUATIC ENVIRONMENTS

Aquatic environments are water-based natural environments and can be categorized into freshwater and marine areas. The freshwater biome is defined as having a low salt content whereas the marine biome is predominantly saltwater like the ocean.

Freshwater environments

Freshwater natural environments can be categorized into three groups: lakes and ponds, streams and rivers, and wetlands. They cover approximately 20 per cent of the Earth and are found in various locations all over the world. It is difficult to discuss freshwater environments in general terms as they are all unique, containing a range of animal and plant species, and various amounts of water, and experiencing different climates.

Lakes and ponds

Although found all around the world and essential for many species, including humans, lakes and ponds make up just 3 per cent of the Earth's surface area. Ponds and lakes vary in size from just a few square metres to thousands of square kilometres, with Lake Superior in North America being the largest freshwater lake by area.

The species found in ponds and lakes are usually of limited diversity due to the fact that these bodies of water are usually isolated. Ponds are lakes are, however, divided into different zones, each having its own distinct biodiversity.

ACTIVITY: What are the different zones of a lake?

ATL

- Communication skills: Use a variety of organizers for academic writing tasks; organize and depict information logically

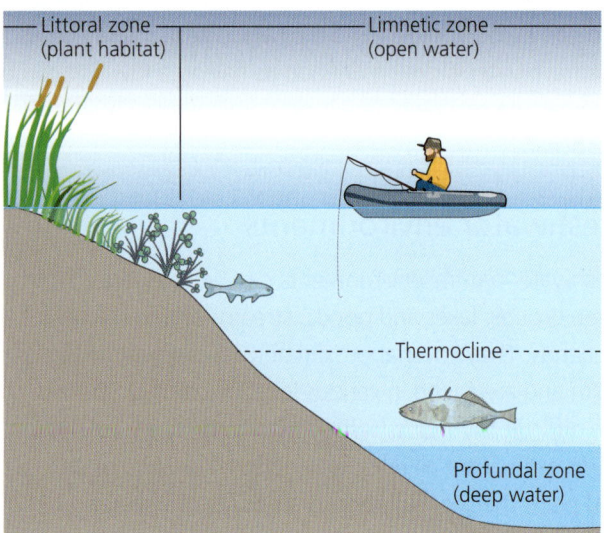

■ **Figure 5.22** Zones of a freshwater lake

The three different zones of a lake are known as the littoral, limnetic and profundal zones.

Create a graphic organizer to present the following information for each zone:
- Main characteristics – What is it like?
- Plant and wildlife found there

Search **graphic organizers**, **mind map**, **brainstorming web**, **Venn diagram** for some ideas to get you started.

◆ Assessment opportunities

- In this activity you have practised skills that are assessed using Criterion C: Communicating.

EXTENSION: HOW DO PLANKTON SUSTAIN HUMAN LIFE?

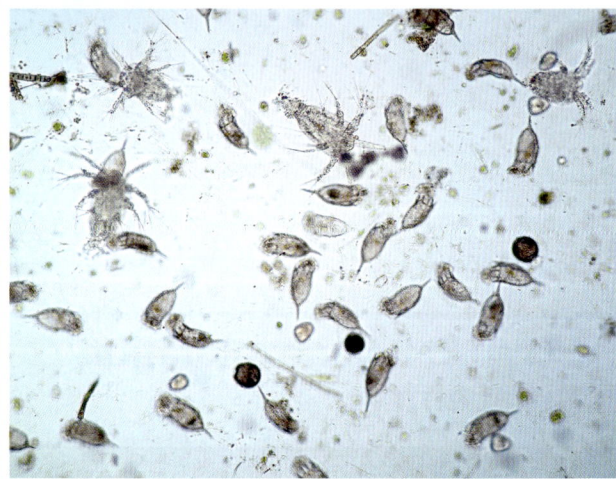

■ **Figure 5.23** Freshwater aquatic plankton under microscope view

Research the ways in which ecosystems depend on plankton.

Search **food chain**, **oxygen** and **carbon pump**.

Streams and rivers

In contrast to lakes and ponds, streams and rivers are bodies of flowing water moving in one direction – travelling from the source to the mouth. The source of the river is found in higher ground and the mouth is where the river or stream meets a larger body of water that it discharges into. The characteristics of a river or stream change during its journey from the source to the mouth, with the most dramatic changes being noted in longer rivers.

Due to rivers rising in higher ground, the temperature at the source of the river is cooler than at its mouth and much of the water may come from snowmelt. At higher altitude the water is generally clearer as it is often less accessible to humans and is home to freshwater fish such as carp. As the river reaches the middle of its journey, the channel widens and as this happens it is able to support a wider diversity of species such as plants and algae. The types of plant and algae differ depending on where the river is located in the world but they all typically live along the edge of the river where the water is moving slower and may include willow trees and river grass.

ACTIVITY: River research

ATL

- Information literacy skills: Present information in a variety of formats and platforms

Research a river of your choice.

State:
- where its source and mouth are
- how the characteristics of the river change as it flows through the upper, middle and lower course
- any notable areas which it passes through, for example the Thames passing through central London.

Use this information to create a long, annotated poster that could be displayed along a corridor or around a classroom.

Ensure that the three stages or courses (upper, middle and lower) of the river are clearly displayed on your poster along with any important landmarks the river passes.

◆ Assessment opportunities

- In this activity you have practised skills that are assessed using Criterion A: Knowing and understanding and Criterion C: Communicating.

When the river nears the end of its journey and moves from its middle to lower course the water becomes murky from all the sediments that it has picked up upstream. This decreases the amount of light that can penetrate the water and therefore there is less diversity of plant life. This in turn produces lower oxygen levels, which means that the river can only support fish that require less oxygen. As with the plants found near rivers, the wildlife also differs depending on the river's location in the world but, in addition to fish, may include snails, crabs, snakes, crocodiles, otters and beavers.

■ Figure 5.26 A beaver works on its dam

Wetlands

Wetlands include bogs, swamps and marshes, and differ from both rivers and streams and ponds and lakes in that they are made up from a combination of water and land. They are lands that are saturated with water; the land may be submerged all year round or just at certain times. Wetlands are often found near other bodies of water, such as lakes and rivers, and can be instrumental in preventing flooding as they provide an overflow area. Wetlands also help to purify and filter water of excess nutrients and dangerous pollutants that may be present in rain and storm water run-off. This takes place before the water reaches the sea, which is vital for marine life and fishermen. Wetlands do this by acting as giant sieves – many of the impurities are trapped as the water works its way slowly through the wetland soil and vegetation.

■ Figure 5.24 Weeping willow

■ Figure 5.25 Grasses on a riverbank

■ **Figure 5.27** A crocodile in wetlands

■ **Figure 5.28** A mangrove tree

■ **Figure 5.29** The Florida Everglades

The wetlands rival rainforests in terms of their biodiversity, supporting a huge variety of plants and animals as their conditions make them ideal for amphibians, birds and reptiles. The largest predators are alligators and crocodiles with other animals including beavers, minks, raccoons and deer. Wetland vegetation has adapted to the moist and humid conditions and is able to grow entirely underwater, float on the top or grow with only its roots in the water. This versatility adds to the biodiversity of plants that the wetlands can support. Vegetation that thrives in wetland areas includes water lilies, cypress trees and mangroves.

Creating a geographical case study

A case study is an in-depth example of an event, place or process. There is no set format of how you should structure your case study but you should always refer to the 5Ws: what, when, where, why and who:
- *What happened?* Can you provide some background on what actually happened, with some facts and figures?
- *When did it happen?* Can you give the date when the case study happened and if possible the time of day?
- *Where did it happen?* The geographical setting is very important, so can you name the location and the country? Could you draw a sketch map to show the location?
- *Why did it happen?* What caused the case study incident to occur? What natural systems were interacting with human activity?
- *Who was affected by it happening?* Which people were affected? How many were affected? Can you say something about the wealth of the people affected?

ACTIVITY: Everglades case study

■ ATL

- Information literacy skills: Present information in a variety of formats and platforms

Using 'Creating a geographical case study' on the left, create a case study of the Florida Everglades. Be sure to apply the 5Ws appropriately.

◆ Assessment opportunities

◆ In this activity you have practised skills that are assessed using Criterion A: Knowing and understanding, Criterion B: Investigating and Criterion C: Communicating.

Figure 5.30 The location of the Great Barrier Reef

Marine environments

Marine environments are made up of oceans (which cover approximately two-thirds of the Earth's surface), estuaries, salt marshes, coral reefs and coastal areas such as lagoons. They are home to fish, aquatic plants, seabirds and smaller, but no less important, organisms such as krill and plankton. The biodiversity in oceans varies, as with freshwater lakes, from closer to the surface to the vast depths of the ocean floor.

The ocean is generally divided into four major ocean basins: the Atlantic, Pacific, Indian and Arctic oceans. Despite their differing locations, they are all believed to be similar below the first 200 metres or so as it is too dark, cold and murky for much life to exist and any that does is the same from ocean to ocean and place to place. However, in the areas where the sunlight is able to reach, the characteristics vary greatly.

The salt content of oceans can vary greatly, depending largely on the amount of freshwater that it receives and the rate of evaporation that is occurring. Oceans tend to experience higher levels of salinity in hotter, sunnier climes as when water evaporates it leaves behind salts and other minerals. Ocean temperature varies with proximity to the equator and poles with temperatures being as high as 27 °C near the equator and as low as –2 °C near the poles.

Biodiversity of marine environments is highest in areas that support coral reefs. These are found in tropical oceans near the equator and between the tropics of Capricorn and Cancer with the largest, and arguably most famous, being the Great Barrier Reef located off the Australian coast.

ACTIVITY: Why are coral reefs important?

■ ATL

- Information literacy skills: Access information to be informed and inform others

Imagine you are a teacher designing a lesson to educate 10- and 11-year-olds about the importance of coral reefs.

You should work with a partner to create an engaging and informative mini lesson that you will present to your peers.

You should include:
- a brief discussion of what coral is
- where coral is found in the world
- the main reasons why coral is so important, giving named examples where possible.

Search **coral reef biodiversity**, **carbon**, **shelter** and **erosion** for some initial ideas.

Your lesson should last approximately ten minutes and you should include a range of activities.

> **Hint**
> Think about the best lessons you have had. What made them good? What did the teachers do? How did they engage their students and keep them motivated?

◆ Assessment opportunities

- In this activity you have practised skills that are assessed using Criterion A: Knowing and understanding and Criterion C: Communicating.

Coral are a type of invertebrate animal. An individual coral is known as a polyp and these are small organisms which are formed primarily of a stomach with a tentacle-bearing mouth on top. They survive by extending their tentacles at night to sting and then eat even smaller organisms such as plankton. Coral live together in huge groups to form colonies and it is their hard skeletons that form coral reefs when they die – they gradually build up over long periods of time and form homes for many other species such as fish, other invertebrates and algae. Reefs occur only in shallow areas that are reached by sunlight as they depend on algae, which needs the sunlight for photosynthesis. Many people confuse coral with plants as they stay in one place and rely on the sun for some of their energy.

How do humans impact on natural environments?

ACTIVITY: Reasons for deforestation

■ **ATL**

- Communication skills: Paraphrase accurately and concisely

Create an infographic to **explain** how the following factors are responsible for deforestation and what the consequences of them are:
- Fuel
- Slash and burn
- Food production
- Commercial farming
- Logging
- Mining
- Hydroelectricity

Give examples of where these are happening in the world and include specific facts to support your points.

It is thought that humans share the planet with as many as 8.7 million different forms of life. According to what we see in the news, it seems that we, as the dominant species on the planet, have had and continue to have a predominantly negative impact on our natural environment. The innovative and technological advances that humans make undoubtedly change many aspects of our planet, but you are now going to question whether the effects of these changes are indeed largely negative.

HUMAN IMPACT ON THE RAINFOREST

■ **Figure 5.31** The location of the Amazon rainforest

Most developed countries grew and prospered in times when society was less environmentally aware, for example the UK during the Industrial Revolution. Is it therefore reasonable to deny less economically developed countries their chance to grow and develop in the same way? Should humans not be allowed to benefit from the wealth of riches that a rainforest environment provides, especially since the majority of them are located in less economically developed countries? Brazil, for example, needs to exploit the Amazon's resources in order to develop, so it could be argued that leaving it untouched is not an option. Rainforests do, however, need to be managed in a sustainable way as human interference can have a potentially far-reaching and devastating environmental impact.

Deforestation is the biggest human threat to the natural environments of the rainforest. The Amazon rainforest has experienced particularly high levels of deforestation, especially in Brazil. Although it is difficult to provide exact rates, according to the World Wide Fund for Nature (WWF), around 17 per cent of the forest has been lost in the last 50 years. This has occurred for a variety of reasons.

HUMAN IMPACT ON DESERT ENVIRONMENTS

The human impact on desert environments can be said to be less severe than that on other natural environments, such as rainforests. This is largely because the impact is more gradual and not immediately visible to the naked eye and opportunities for human development are heavily limited due to the lack of commercial plants, natural resources and inhospitable climate. Nonetheless, the desert remains a

■ Figure 5.32 Chemical pollution

■ Figure 5.33 Indigenous rainforest children

■ Figure 5.34 Carajás Mine

■ Figure 5.35 Slash and burn in the Amazon

◆ Assessment opportunities

♦ In this activity you have practised skills that are assessed using Criterion A: Knowing and understanding.

fragile biome and the impact that humans continue to have on it should not be underestimated. The main threat from humans to deserts and grassland regions is increased desertification.

Desertification

Desertification is the turning of land into desert, and is one of the major issues faced in **arid** and **semi-arid** regions. As such, it is a real issue in both desert and grassland regions. There is a range of complex and varied reasons why desertification occurs, many of which can be related back to humans and how their choices have led to global environmental change.

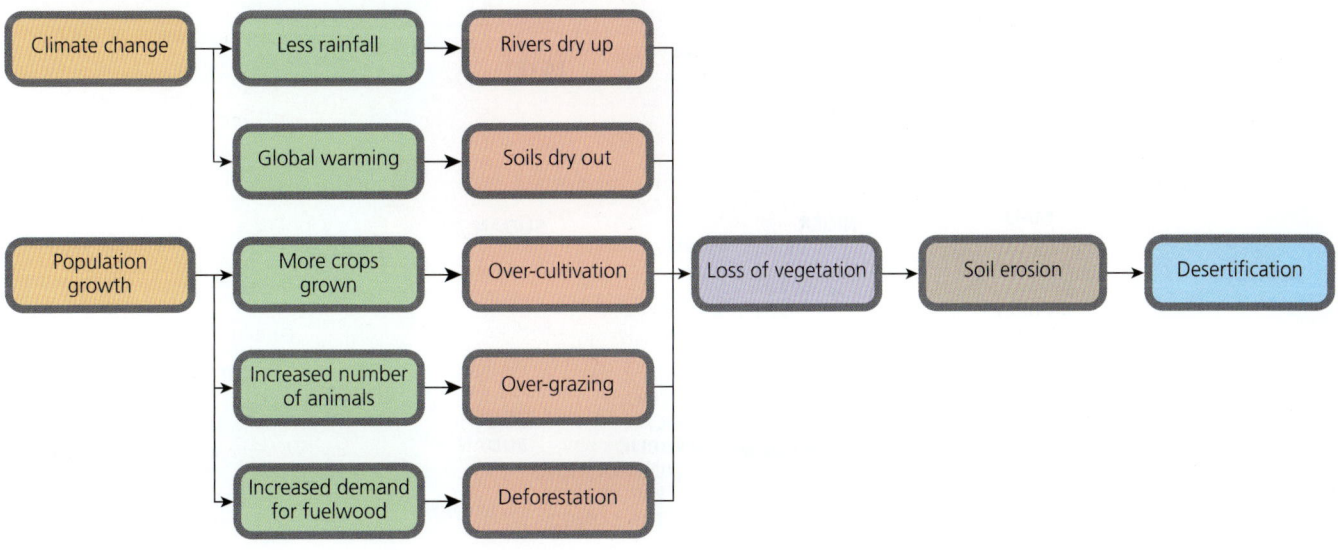
■ Figure 5.36 The causes and effects of desertification

5 What impact do humans have on natural environments?

ACTIVITY: The causes of desertification

■ ATL

- Organization skills: Use appropriate strategies for organizing complex information

Make a copy of Figure 5.36. On your copy, **explain** how the factors listed are contributing to desertification.

◆ Assessment opportunities

◆ In this activity you have practised skills that are assessed using Criterion A: Knowing and understanding and Criterion C: Communicating.

Desertification in the Sahel

The Sahel region is often described as a band of ten countries running across Africa from Mauritania in the west to Eritrea in the east and sits directly south of the Sahara desert. Its position means that it is vulnerable to desertification and all its associated impacts.

■ Figure 5.37 The effects of desertification

Growing population

The primary cause of desertification is a considerable increase in population in the region. Table 5.2 shows high rates of **natural increase** and **total fertility rate** which together lead to a rapidly growing population.

As well as population growth, the region experiences much **migration** due to continued civil conflict in and between its countries. The fluctuating and increasing populations mean that there is an increased need for food in the Sahel region.

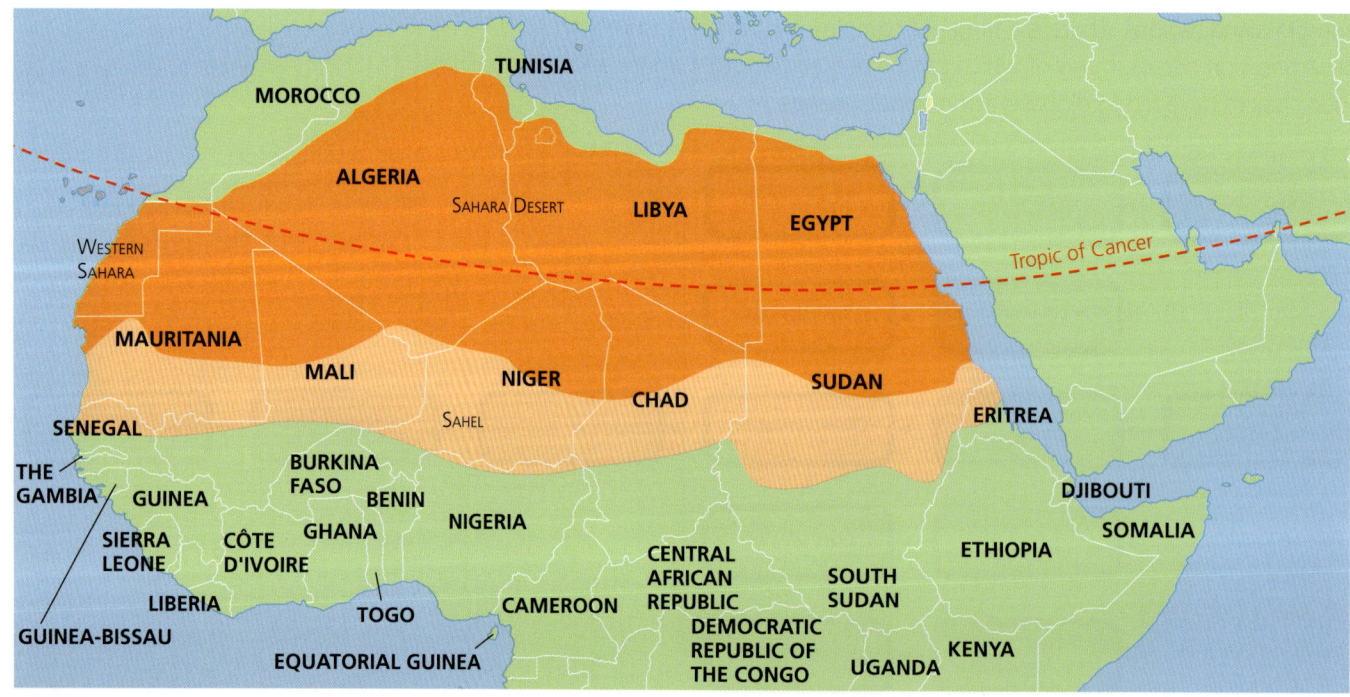

■ Figure 5.38 The Sahara and Sahel region

ACTIVITY: Sahel case study

■ **ATL**

- Information literacy skills: Collect, record and verify data
- Media literacy skills: Locate, organize, analyse, evaluate, synthesize and ethically use information from a variety of sources and media

Select one of the Sahel countries listed in Table 5.2 for which to compile a case study.

- **Describe** the specific location of this country.
- **Interpret** the data in the table and **summarize** how the population has grown over recent years. On the basis of the data, predict how the population might grow further in the future.
- **Identify** civil conflicts this country has experienced or any wars in which it has been involved.
- **Explore** whether this country receives migrants from other countries. Support your answer with figures.
- **Investigate** specific tribes or groups of people who use the land for farming in this country.
- **Outline** evidence of desertification occurring in this country. Include facts and statistics where possible.
- **Evaluate** specific strategies employed by this country to reduce or prevent desertification. Have they been successful or unsuccessful? Provide justification for your evaluation.
- **Summarize** the impact humans have had on this natural environment.

Search the following to begin your investigation: **UNDP Sahel** and **United Nations Population Division**.

◆ Assessment opportunities

♦ In this activity you have practised skills that are assessed using Criterion B: Investigating and Criterion D: Thinking critically.

HUMAN IMPACTS ON GRASSLANDS

The diverse wildlife which the grasslands enjoy has been one of the primary ways in which humans have impacted upon the area with poaching and overgrazing being two specific threats. The grasslands are subject to the same threat of desertification as desert regions with overgrazing from animals being one of the main causes of this.

Poachers are attracted to hunt the 'big ticket' animals that are native to the grasslands, such as lions and elephants, as they can make money from selling their furs, tusks and horns. In 1979, the African elephant population in the wild was estimated to be around 1.3 million but by 1989, only 600,000 remained. Although many ivory traders claimed that the drop in numbers was due to habitat loss, much of the threat was from the ivory trade. Despite attempts to ban the sale of ivory since 1989, it is estimated that between 2010 and 2012, more than 100,000 African elephants were massacred. The death toll continues to rise due to the illegal trade of ivory. In 2012, the black-market price for rhino horn had risen so high that it had become more valuable than gold, with a horn changing hands at £40,000 per kilogram compared with £33,000 for a kilogram of gold. An average horn weighs 7 kg and is worth nearly half a million dollars. Search **Born Free Ivory Trade and Traffic** for more information on charities that are working to combat the illegal trade and poaching of grassland animals.

Safaris, while less immediately damaging than poachers, also create their own problems for the grassland natural environment.

■ **Table 5.2** Key demographic indicators of ten countries of the Sahel, 2014

Country	Population (millions)	Annual rate of natural increase (%)	Population density (persons per km^2)	Total fertility rate (average number of children per woman)
Burkina Faso	17.9	3.1	65	5.9
Chad	13.3	3.3	10	6.6
Eritrea	6.5	2.6	56	4.7
The Gambia	1.9	3.1	169	5.6
Guinea-Bissau	1.7	2.5	48	5.0
Mali	15.9	2.9	13	6.1
Mauritania	4.0	2.6	4	4.1
Niger	18.2	3.9	14	7.6
Senegal	13.9	3.2	71	5.3
Sudan*	38.8	2.5	21	5.2

* Sudan does not include South Sudan.

Source: Carl Haub and Toshiko Kaneda, 2014 World Population Data Sheet (Washington, DC: Population Reference Bureau, 2014)

■ **Figure 5.39** Rhinoceros in the wild

■ **Figure 5.40** The prized ivory tusks that have endangered elephants

Tourism in the Serengeti

The Serengeti is home to many magnificent species of animal and, as a result, the area has become popular for safari holidays on which tourists are given the opportunity to observe animals in their natural environments. As with any interaction between humans and the natural environment, there are both positive and negative impacts associated with safari tourism. These need to be managed carefully to ensure that the natural environment is not damaged for future generations.

> ### THINK–PAIR–SHARE
>
> Take a moment to consider the positives and negatives that tourism can bring to areas, specifically grassland areas.
>
> **List** these effects. **Discuss** them with your partner.
>
> Be prepared to share your thoughts with the class.

■ **Figure 5.41** Trans-Alaska Pipeline

HUMAN IMPACT IN TUNDRA AREAS

Due to the inhospitable conditions the Tundra faces, direct human impact on this natural environment has been limited. However, many Tundra areas are rich in natural minerals and the Trans-Alaska Pipeline is an example of how humans have interacted with this natural environment in order to exploit its wealth of resources.

The Trans-Alaska Pipeline is a 1,287-km-long system for transporting oil from the northern tip of Alaska to the southern port area of Valdez, from where it is transported in huge tankers. The pipeline was built during the 1970s and began its transportation of oil in 1977 (in 2016, an average of 517,868 barrels were transporter per day). Some sections of the pipeline are underground but there are many stretches above ground (see Figure 5.41) where the ground is too frozen to penetrate.

The building, and subsequent operation, of the Trans-Alaska Pipeline have caused significant environmental disruption to the natural environment of the tundra, with much vegetation, wetlands and the habitats of many fish, birds and animals being affected and in some cases irreparably damaged. One of the primary concerns was that traditional migration routes of animals would be disrupted, leaving them stranded in the tundra areas during the cold winter when they would usually have departed to warmer climes. The melting of the snow and permafrost due to the heat produced by the extraction and transportation of the oil is a further threat. To reduce this impact, the pipeline is on raised stilts so that it does not directly touch the ice. There were also social objections to the building of the pipeline, with groups of native people objecting to the use of land they viewed as theirs.

Indirect human impacts on the tundra areas are more noticeable in the form of global warming and the subsequent melting of polar ice which consequently is thought to cause a rise in sea level. Global warming is the rise in the world's temperature. According to the UN, the average global temperature has increased by 0.85°C between 1880 and 2012, and between 1901 and 2010, the global average sea level rose by 19 cm as oceans expanded due to warming and ice melt.

ACTIVITY: News report of an oil spill

■ **ATL**

■ Collaboration skills: Delegate and share responsibility for decision-making

In addition to the environmental and social impact of building the pipeline and extracting the oil, the transportation of the oil is a cause for concern.

Two notable oil spill incidents are the 1989 *Exxon Valdez* oil spill and the 2010 Deep Water Horizon oil spill.

Working in pairs, create a news report outlining the key events in **one** of these two incidents.

You should include:
- the date and time the incident occurred
- a map of the areas affected
- a brief outline of how the spillage occurred
- a summary of the main political, environmental, economic and social impacts
- who, if anyone, was to blame.

You may present your report in one of the following ways:
- A written, newspaper-style report
- A filmed TV news bulletin
- A live TV news bulletin

I USED TO THINK … NOW I THINK …

Oil spill incidents can be analysed in economic terms as examples of **market failure**. You will explore this in Chapter 8. When you have completed that chapter, return to reflect on this activity. To what extent has the economic analysis affected your view?

◆ **Assessment opportunities**

◆ In this activity you have practised skills that are assessed using Criterion A: Knowing and understanding and Criterion C: Communicating.

One of the contributing factors for this is thought to be a rise in greenhouse gases which are emitted by humans through industrialization, deforestation and pollution. These gases have greatly increased atmospheric concentrations of water vapour, carbon dioxide, methane and nitrous oxide, all greenhouse gases that help trap heat near Earth's surface and carbon dioxide is being released into the environment much faster than plants and oceans can absorb it. The UN states that global emissions of carbon dioxide (CO_2) have increased by almost 50 per cent since 1990, with emissions growing more quickly between 2000 and 2010 than in each of the three previous decades.

HUMAN IMPACT IN FRESHWATER AREAS

The human impact on freshwater environments is driven by the growing demand for fresh water. The challenge is whether this demand can be fulfilled without significantly reducing or damaging the supply of this limited resource.

▼ **Links to: Sciences**

Global warming and climate change are discussed extensively in *Sciences for the IB MYP 3* Chapter 2 and *Physics for the IB MYP 4&5* Chapter 8.

Farming and irrigation

The demand for water is increasing as the population rises (see Chapter 6). Not only is water required for drinking but also to irrigate crops and thus help in the production of food. Irrigation (the process of watering plants to achieve optimal growth) affects the quality of rivers, lakes and, arguably most worryingly, groundwater.

The pressure for more food to sustain the population has led to the development of intensive agriculture in both developed and developing countries. In order to meet the demand for high yields, forests have been cleared to accommodate larger ranches and plantations. This lack of tree cover leads to soil erosion, which then means the rivers receive more sediment in the form of run-off. In less developed countries, fields have become waterlogged and therefore useless as inefficient systems have failed. In some cases, increased salinization of water systems has rendered the soil infertile. Both the sediments and increased salt levels in the water systems have damaging consequences. They can result in a lack of usable fresh water, increased expense in purifying the water and, in some cases, health issues for both humans and animals when the water becomes contaminated with harmful chemicals such as low-level arsenic, which can lead to increases in certain types of cancer in humans.

ACTIVITY: Potatoes in the desert

ATL

- Critical-thinking skills: Consider ideas from multiple perspectives

As a way around the problem, crops are being grown in places where the conditions are usually not optimal. For example, potatoes are being grown in desert areas of Egypt.

Use the following search terms to **explore** this idea as a way of providing more food for the growing world population: **agro-industrialization**, **groundwater**, **fertilizers** and **potatoes in the desert**.

Once you have an understanding of the situation, write a paragraph outlining the positives and negatives and ultimately stating your opinion on the matter. Be sure to **justify** your opinion.

Assessment opportunities

- In this activity you have practised skills that are assessed using Criterion D: Thinking critically.

The vast amounts of land and water required for intensive, commercial farming have also led to the draining of freshwater wetlands, lowering of the water table and the reclaiming of land for huge farms. This has meant a reduction in the ecology and biodiversity that wetland environments support, as well as the vital environmental benefits that wetlands offer. These include the reduction in rates of erosion, storing of flood run-off and recycling of agricultural run-off and solid wastes. This in turn causes the quality of freshwater to decline. Growing populations also affect wetland areas as the need for more homes means that rivers are being diverted so that wetlands dry up and the land can be reclaimed for settlements. Wetlands now represent only 6 per cent of the Earth's surface and it is thought that areas of wetland have halved since 1900.

Agro-industrialization requires the use of chemicals, in the form of fertilizers and pesticides, in order to maximize growth and provide protection from insects eating the crop. Fertilizers are added to the soil in order to increase nutrients, such as nitrates and phosphates, which are optimal for plant growth. These fertilizers and pesticides leach through the soil into groundwater supplies and then transfer through modern field drainage into rivers and lakes. The fertilizers then increase the nutrient concentration of the water which enables more algae to grow and their population increases rapidly.

An issue arises when a higher percentage of the river's surface is covered by algae as some fish are unable to survive without this light. A more serious problem arises, however, when the algae begin to die. The breakdown of dead algae by decomposers can greatly reduce the concentration of oxygen dissolved in the water which

■ **Figure 5.42** Algal bloom

can significantly impact on freshwater wildlife and plants, leading to the death of both. This process is known as eutrophication and has been seen, for example, in the River Kissimmee in Florida. Here, the problem of eutrophication is not only an issue for the freshwater environment but due to frequent storms, these stored pollutants rise to the surface of the lake and are transported to the marine environment where they are thought to be contributing to the slow acidification of the coastal environment and the loss of some of Florida's coral reefs and fish-breeding grounds.

Dams and reservoirs

A dam is any barrier that holds back water. They are used to save, manage, and/or prevent the flow of excess water into specific regions. Some dams are known as multi-purpose dams and are used to generate hydropower. A reservoir is an artificial lake that is primarily used for storing water.

■ **Figure 5.43** Three Gorges Dam

■ **Figure 5.44** Three Gorges reservoir

Dams and reservoirs have a wide range of impacts on the conditions of the rivers and surrounding areas that drain into them. The most obvious of these is the amount, and direction, of water that flows throughout a river system. Dams work by holding back the flow of water, which creates a deep reservoir of water upstream, where the water pools in front of the dam. A result of this is that the flow of water downstream becomes more regulated. This means that large-scale floods can be prevented, saving many lives but at the same time, natural wetlands are deprived of essential water and erosion of the river channel can increase due to the variations in the amount of water flowing through. This is problematic as it can cause channel depth to decrease and result in a lowering of the water table.

While reservoirs undeniably have their advantages, they are not as useful as they may initially seem as their water quality can be affected by several factors. Upstream towns and industry, as well as agricultural areas, feed a constant supply of sewage, industrial waste and agricultural run-off into the reservoir. The reservoir also slows down the river's flow upstream and so these pollutants are not broken down by the movement of water. Sediment is also trapped in the reservoir as it cannot flow through the dam. This quickly builds up and can reduce the amount of water the reservoir can store and requires expensive, long-term maintenance.

ACTIVITY: The Three Gorges Dam

■ ATL

- Communication skills: Make inferences and draw conclusions
- Critical-thinking skills: Draw reasonable conclusions and generalizations

The engineering triumph of the Three Gorges Dam is seen as a sign of 'progress', though the project has many negative side effects that may not *seem* like progress to many Chinese citizens.

1 **Explain** how the Three Gorges Dam may potentially create an economic boom in China that could offset the huge costs of the project.
2 As a result of the Three Gorges Dam project, approximately 2 million people are going to have to be re-homed – whether they want to be or not. **Discuss** the challenges you might face if you were to be forcibly re-homed in this way.
3 Another consequence of the project is the loss of 3,000-year-old antiquities, such as artifacts belonging to the Qing and Han dynasties. More than 2,000 known archaeological sites – some dating to the Paleolithic era – have been submerged, along with numerous historic buildings and anthropological sites. Suggest what impact this loss might have on Chinese society.
4 Suggest what justification the Chinese government might give for the impacts of the project. How is 'progress' defined by the government? **Evaluate** this definition.
5 Outline the costs and benefits of replacing coal-produced electricity with alternative forms of energy, for example hydroelectric power, solar power and wind power.

◆ Assessment opportunities

◆ In this activity you have practised skills that are assessed using Criterion C: Communicating and Criterion D: Thinking critically.

Because sediment is being trapped upstream, farmers downstream, who rely on the sediments as nutrients for their crops, suffer. The wildlife of the river also suffers as the water stored in reservoirs is colder than the rest of the river and so when it is released, it changes the temperature of the river and therefore the ecology of the river environment.

HUMAN IMPACT IN MARINE AREAS

As with the other natural environments examined in this chapter, humans are increasingly turning to the oceans as a source of much-needed resources to support and sustain a growing population and unsustainable use is causing damage to marine natural environments.

Overfishing, to provide food for our ever-growing population, is another example of how the decisions humans make are impacting our natural environments. The North Sea is one area that is suffering greatly from a depletion of fish stocks.

■ Figure 5.45 The North Sea

As you can see from Figure 5.45, seven countries have a coastline on the North Sea and this shared boundary has led to many of the problems that this aquatic natural environment has experienced. It is one of the world's most important fishing grounds but because it has been viewed as a common area, open to everyone, the number of fishing vessels operating in many areas has exceeded the amount of fish available. This means there has been a huge decline in the amount of fish, especially cod, living in its water. The constant fishing means that few cod are now able to reach adult size. As a result, more fishing is required to make up for the smaller size of cod now available, which makes the problem worse and allows no time for recovery.

Large-scale industrial fishing is also harming fish stocks due to the ways in which fish are caught. Many fish are injured in the process and are thrown back into the sea because they don't meet standards. Dolphins are also harmed and sometimes killed in the fishing of tuna. Many companies and supermarket own brands now display a dolphin-friendly label on their tins of tuna to indicate that dolphin-safe methods are employed in the catching of the tuna. However, Greenpeace has pointed out that this logo is often misleading as it implies that the catching of tuna is safe for dolphins and does not take into account any environmental impacts that may be caused by the fishing.

In warmer oceans that support coral reefs, the coral is being damaged in a wide variety of ways. Coral bleaching is one of the most prevalent forms of destruction, and happens when the temperature of the ocean increases and is sustained for a period of at least two weeks. The polyps, which make up the coral reef, are vulnerable even to temperature increases as small as 2 °C. The stress of the temperature change affects the nutrient exchange between them and the microscopic algae that live inside them, supplying them with energy. In extreme cases, the algae leave the polyps and, as the algae is responsible for giving the coral its distinctive colour, the coral turns white, hence

■ **Figure 5.46** Dolphin-friendly tuna logo

EXTENSION: EXPLORE FURTHER

How are dolphins harmed in the fishing of tuna? Search **pole-and-line method** and **tuna fishing nets**.

ACTIVITY: The positives and negatives of reef tourism

■ ATL

- Communication skills: Use a variety of organizers for academic writing tasks
- Critical-thinking skills: Consider ideas from multiple perspectives

Create a table to **explain** the costs and benefits of tourism in reef ecosystems.

◆ Assessment opportunities

◆ In this activity you have practised skills that are assessed using Criterion A: Knowing and understanding, Criterion C: Communicating and Criterion D: Thinking critically.

■ **Figure 5.47** Bleached coral

the term coral bleaching. This can lead to the death of the coral as the algae provides it with approximately 70 per cent of its energy. The Great Barrier Reef experienced its worst episodes of coral bleaching in the years 2016 and 2017; the BBC reported that 67 per cent of coral died in some sections of the reef. Being hit so severely two years in a row means that the coral has little chance to recover and the damage is likely to be permanent.

While undoubtedly having huge economic benefits, tourism is also causing damage to the reef. A rapid initial growth meant that tourism was largely unregulated and had a negative impact on the reef ecosystem through anchor damage to reefs, boat collisions with large animals, fin damage to coral from scuba divers, trampling and littering and sewage and pollution from hotels, boats and resorts.

Plastics in the ocean is another pressing issue in relation to humans and the aquatic natural environment. This is explored in *Individuals and Societies for the IB MYP 1* (pages 10–15) with the discussion of the **Great Pacific Garbage Patch**. The impact of plastic debris contaminating the ocean is wide reaching and includes harm to animals, environmental damage and health consequences for humans should plastic enter the food chain through fish.

! Take action

! With a partner, create an outline for a social media campaign to encourage sustainable use of the oceans.
! Develop a mission statement. This should be:
   ◆ short and concise – no more than four sentences
   ◆ memorable
   ◆ realistic
   ◆ easy to understand
   ◆ motivational / inspiring
   ◆ full of high-impact and precise verbs.
! Examine other media campaigns for environmental issues and critique these. **Identify** successful elements and those that you think did not work so well. Search #refusethestraw and #Earthday for inspiration.
! Outline where you will centre your campaign – which form of social media will you use? Will you need to use other methods to support the social media aspect?
! Go for it – put your campaign out there and encourage people to use oceans sustainably!

Can resources ever really be exploited sustainably?

With the impact of human choice weighing heavily, many countries, companies and charities are exploring and promoting sustainable ways of using natural environments.

SUSTAINABILITY IN RAINFORESTS

Many rainforests have been cut down to make way for palm oil plantations. There have therefore been a number of campaigns to raise awareness of the use of palm oil by Oxfam and the RSPO (Roundtable on Sustainable Palm Oil). Green Palm Sustainability logos have been launched which allow consumers to make sustainable choices when it comes to the products that they buy.

Sustainable logging schemes are in place in many countries including Brazil where there are strict laws on the practices of deforestation. Areas of the forest are protected and monitoring has improved with the use of satellite technology and photography to check that any activities taking place are legal and follow guidelines for sustainability. Education for those involved in this practice has helped to ensure that they understand the consequences of their actions. Popular procedures employed include agro-forestry where trees and crops are grown simultaneously which lets farmers take advantage of shelter from the canopy of trees, prevents soil erosion and allows the crops to benefit from the nutrients from the dead organic matter which is produced by the trees. Selective logging, which means that trees are only felled when they reach a certain height and guarantees young trees a specific lifespan, and afforestation, the replacement of trees that are cut down are also popular strategies in using the rainforest sustainably.

The World Wide Fund for Nature (WWF) has established the Global Forest and Trade Network (GFTN), which links many companies, forest-dependent communities, non-governmental organizations and entrepreneurs in more than 30 countries around the world with the overall aim of creating a market for environmentally responsible forest products. It helps its participants benefit from sustainable forest management and reduce demand for products produced from illegal sources. It is also working to raise awareness of bio energy in the forms of oils, fats, sugar and starch crops to reduce the dependence of people on forests for their sources of heating and cooking and it hopes that by 2050, 100 per cent of the world's energy will come from renewable sources.

Advances are also being made in sustainable mining. The company that runs the Carajás Mine has a restoration plan to try to return the forest to its original state by replanting, and replacing and repairing damaged soil. It also supports the monitoring operation in the forest by employing extra rangers, cars, boats and helicopters to help in the fight against illegal logging and poaching.

■ Figure 5.48 RSPO logo

The botanical resources of the rainforest have provided many medical advances. Approximately 7,000 medical compounds prescribed by doctors in developed societies are derived from rainforest plants.

The following ailments can be treated with the use of these plant derivatives:
- Cancer
- Rheumatoid arthritis
- AIDS
- Parkinson's disease
- Kidney stones
- Anxiety
- Fever
- Headaches
- Type 2 diabetes

Many operations are also possible due to the anaesthetic qualities of plants.

Figure 5.49 The UN Sustainable Development Goals

DISCUSS

If we didn't explore and use the rainforest, many medical advances would not have been made. **Discuss** how this can be balanced with sustainable management.

Member States in 2015 contains specific targets for life on land. In particular, target 15.3 specifically refers to halting and reversing land degradation:

SDG 15.3: By 2030, combat desertification, restore degraded land and soil, including land affected by desertification, drought and floods, and strive to achieve a land degradation-neutral world.

Further to this, the UN has declared 17 June as World Day to Combat Desertification and Drought and many awareness-raising activities take place on this day.

SUSTAINABILITY IN DRYLANDS

The need to prevent desertification has been recognized in many regions and there is a range of both small-scale and larger global awareness strategies in place to try to minimize further spread of the desert.

Aid agencies and charities are working with locals to educate farmers on productive farming methods that will protect the soil, such as crop rotation which allows the soil a chance to regenerate and recover, minimizing the chances of soil erosion and preserving vital nutrients. Land restoration and afforestation are favoured in some areas of the Sahel and Sahara where a 'Great Green Wall' is created using drought resistant shrubs and grasses to help bind the soil and protect against further erosion. Once complete, the wall will be the largest living structure on the planet: 8,000 km of natural habitats on fertile land across the entire width of the African continent. Other local strategies include improving small scale-irrigation projects and controlling grazing.

On a larger scale, the UN declared the decade 2010–20 the United Nations Decade for Deserts and Fight Against Desertification in an attempt to raise awareness of the issue facing deserts and drylands. The 2030 Agenda for Sustainable Development, adopted by the United Nations

Figure 5.50 World Day to Combat Desertification and Drought

THINK–PAIR–SHARE

Take a few minutes of thinking time to consider how the need to provide for people now can be balanced with the maintenance of environments for future generations. Is one more important than the other? Share your thoughts with a classmate and then be ready to share with the class.

5 What impact do humans have on natural environments?

> **! Take action**
>
> ! Create and organize a campaign in your school to promote the next World Day to Combat Desertification and Drought. You could focus solely on raising awareness of the issue or you could incorporate some fundraising activities too and donate any proceeds to a charity that helps in areas experiencing desertification. Search UN world day for desertification, Oxfam and wateraid.

SUSTAINABILITY IN GRASSLAND AREAS

Desertification is also one of the pressing issues faced by grassland areas. Sustainable management of the grassland areas, including and especially the Serengeti, is vital if the area is to be preserved for future generations. People working in the local areas are trying to employ sustainable measures and practices, introducing improved conservation education programmes for local communities and farmers and encouraging investors to employ local people and give local communities a percentage of any profits received from tourism.

SUSTAINABILITY IN TUNDRA AREAS

In recent years there have been many efforts put in place by governments, companies and charities to work on the reduction of carbon emissions. The 2015 Paris climate summit was instrumental in the implementation of current policies and commitments to reduce the impact of climate change, with 195 countries adopting the first-ever universal, legally binding global climate deal. In the agreement, all countries agreed to work to limit global temperature rise to well below 2 °C and, given the grave risks, to strive for 1.5 °C. The UN Sustainable Development Goals (see Figure 5.49) build on this agreement, with Goal 13, 'Take urgent action to combat climate change and its impacts', relating specifically to climate change. Many charities, such as Oxfam, work to support this goal and also strive to raise the awareness of individuals through their campaigns and education resources. Search UN Sustainable Development take action to see a list of ways in which you can help.

ACTIVITY: Design a brochure or travel blog for eco-tourism

■ ATL

- Communication skills: Write for different purposes
- Information literacy skills: Present information in a variety of formats and platforms

Design a brochure or travel blog for **ecotourism** in the grassland regions. Think about how your tour can be sustainable and reduce the environmental footprint on the region while simultaneously supporting the locals who depend on tourism to sustain their livelihood.

You should include:

- specific information about the location of the area and the challenges it faces
- visual components, such as maps and photographs, along with descriptive text about the featured location, the endangered species and the ecosystem where they live
- tips on how to travel responsibly and sustainably, in the spirit and practice of ecotourism
- information about volunteer conservation programmes focused on endangered and threatened species that travellers can participate in
- a bibliography detailing where you got your information from. This should be completed using a recognized convention.

◆ Assessment opportunities

- In this activity you have practised skills that are assessed using Criterion A: Knowing and understanding and Criterion C: Communicating.

! Take action: Reducing your carbon footprint

! Look at some of the suggestions in the list below. With your partner, decide which ones you:
  ◊ are already doing
  ◊ could perhaps achieve by the end of the week
  ◊ could achieve by the end of the month
  ◊ could achieve by the end of the year (with the support of adults at home where necessary).

- Reduce electricity consumption – switch off unnecessary lights, computers and TVs, etc., standbys and chargers (at the wall socket).
- Replace bulbs with energy efficient ones.
- Put on more clothes rather than turning on/up heating.
- Only boil as much water as you need.
- Buy food as seasonal and as local as possible – aim to reduce food miles.
- Buy fair trade products whenever available.
- Try not to cook or prepare more food than you can eat.
- Avoid bottled water – ask for tap water in restaurants.
- Grow your own vegetables.
- Eat less meat.
- Recycle.
- Have a compost heap.
- Use new paper rarely.
- Use recycled paper products as much as possible.
- Reuse plastic bags.
- Try to reduce water use (showers rather than baths).
- Turn off the tap when you are cleaning your teeth.
- Use public transport as much as possible.
- Walk to school.
- Buy a bicycle and cycle to school.

ACTIVITY: Climate change role play

ATL

- Communication skills: Negotiate ideas and knowledge with peers and teachers
- Collaboration skills: Listen actively to other perspectives and ideas

'Whose responsibility is it to reduce carbon emissions?'

1. Consider the above question and give your opinion. **Justify** your answer using examples or evidence to support your opinion where possible.
2. Now think about the following groups. Suggest which one/s you think have the biggest responsibility to reduce carbon emissions and why. **Justify** your answer and use examples or evidence to support your opinion where possible.
   - Governments
   - Industries
   - Scientists
   - Individuals
   - Other of your choosing
3. In pairs or groups of three or four, you will be assigned one of the following roles. They represent a broad range of viewpoints from different sectors.
   - A business person from China
   - A scientist
   - A farmer from Bangladesh
   - The UK Environment Secretary
   - A Maasai community leader from Kenya
   - An environmental campaigner
   - The chief executive of carbonoffset.com
   - The CEO of a leading airline

For the person you have been assigned, you need to do the following:
- Consider what stance this person is likely to have on whose responsibility it is to reduce carbon emissions.
- Research and prepare your person's viewpoint. (Use evidence to support your opinions and to make your argument as persuasive as possible.)
- Examine the other characters and try to predict their arguments and who they are likely to think is most responsible for cutting carbon emissions. Then prepare some questions to ask them.
- Try to predict what questions other characters may ask you and plan answers to these questions.

Within your group, elect a spokesperson to play the role.

After hearing all the speeches your teacher may want you to vote as a class to decide whose responsibility it is to reduce carbon emissions.

Reflect on which group had the most persuasive speech and **justify** your choice. What did they do or include that made you want to vote for them? (The Links box on page 140 may give you some ideas about what to look for.)

◆ Assessment opportunities

- In this activity you have practised skills that are assessed using Criterion C: Communicating and Criterion D: Thinking critically.

5 What impact do humans have on natural environments?

▼ **Links to: Language and literature**

The following are the level descriptors from MYP Language and literature. Can you use these to design or **evaluate** effective speeches or other kinds of persuasive writing?

- uses a varied range of appropriate vocabulary, sentence structures and forms of expression competently
- speaks competently in a register and style that serve the context and intention
- uses grammar, syntax and punctuation with a considerable degree of accuracy; errors do not hinder effective communication
- pronounces with a considerable degree of accuracy; errors do not hinder effective communication
- makes sufficient use of appropriate non-verbal communication techniques

SUSTAINABILITY IN MARINE AREAS

Attempts have been made to use the Great Barrier Reef sustainably through the introduction of the Great Barrier Reef Marine Park in 1975 and several subsequent acts to protect and limit damage of the area. The introduction in 2004 of zoned areas including preservation, scientific research, general use and habitat protection zones is part of an attempt to monitor and limit the number and type of activities that happen throughout the Park. Charities such as Greenpeace Australia are encouraging people to sign online petitions and use the social media hashtag **#coalfreeaustralia** to support a reduction in the carbon dioxide pollution that can contribute to warming oceans and coral bleaching.

Pollution in the form of land run-off is also impacting on coral and the formation of coral reefs. Soil sediments, nutrients and chemicals are being washed into oceans at a higher rate. The amount of soil washed into the oceans impacts the coral as it decreases the amount of sunlight received by the coral and the algae they rely on for energy. Sediment that settles at the bottom of the reef can also smother coral and other reef organisms. Other nutrients in the run-off include phosphates and nitrates used as fertilizers. These help to increase algal growth on the reef and lead to eutrophication.

The North Sea

A number of countries have a North Sea coastline (see Figure 5.45) and as a result, laws have been implemented to regulate usage of the sea. Since the 1960s, various regulations have attempted to protect the fish stocks by limiting fishing times and the number of fishing boats. It has proved difficult to systematically enforce these regulations and they therefore did not bring much relief. The EU Common Fisheries Policy has tried to bring North Sea fish stocks back from catastrophically low levels by setting quotas for each type of fish and encouraging various market interventions. This is expensive, however, as it means you have to pay fishermen not to fish!

Measures such as banning catches in nursery areas and using nets with larger holes to allow young cod to escape, have contributed to increased stocks of North Sea cod. The industry decided to enter the Marine Stewardship Council (MSC) ecolabel programme to achieve certification for the fishery and in July 2017 were independently assessed and awarded sustainable status. Unfortunately, since then, stocks have fallen below safe biological levels and in October 2019 the MSC certificates for North Sea cod were suspended. The reason for the decline in stocks is unclear, however the fishing industry is already taking action to rebuild the stock and get the fishery back to a sustainable level, by placing the fishery in a Fishery Improvement Project. These proactive steps will help ensure the fishery is taking the right steps to hopefully regain its MSC certification in the future. In the meantime, there are other sustainable cod options available, including Norwegian and Icelandic sources. MSC certification is the global benchmark for sustainable fishing with the blue MSC label clearly showing consumers which seafood is from sustainable sources.

THINK–PAIR–SHARE

Take a moment to think about the question below:

'To what extent may the North Sea be affected by the UK's decision to leave the European Union?'

When you have some ideas of your own, share them with your partner. Then prepare to share them with the rest of the class.

ACTIVITY: Reflecting on human impacts

■ ATL

- Reflection skills: Consider ethical, cultural and environmental implications

After reading about the different ways in which humans interact with their environments, which do you think is the most damaging and why? Which of the sustainable methods employed do you think has most benefit?

Write a paragraph to answer the questions above, being sure to **justify** your answers.

■ **Figure 5.51** Marine Stewardship Council (MSC) logo

To what extent is globalization a driver for development, and to what extent a driver for destruction?

Globalization and development can be applied to the study of natural environments when we think about whether globalization is a driver for development or destruction. The notion that global trade brings global responsibilities to make a future that is fair for all is explored alongside globalization in Chapter 9. Development is defined and examined in Chapter 10.

ACTIVITY: Globalization: development or destruction?

■ ATL

- Critical-thinking skills: Gather and organize relevant information to formulate an argument

Revisit the examples of human impact on natural environments that you have explored throughout this chapter and consider them through the lens of globalization.

Make notes on the following:
- **Identify** the human impact that you feel is the biggest result of globalization.
- **Explain** why you feel this human impact is a result of globalization.
- **Consider** to what extent this impact results in destruction and then to what extent it results in development. Use examples to support your points.

Be ready to share your ideas with the class and to defend your viewpoint.

◆ Assessment opportunities

- In this activity you have practised skills that are assessed using Criterion D: Thinking critically.

ACTIVITY: Natural environments report

■ ATL

- Communication skills: Make inferences and draw conclusions; Structure information in summaries, essays and reports
- Media literacy skills: Locate, organize, analyse, evaluate, synthesize and ethically use information from a variety of sources and media (including digital social media and online networks)

You are a curator for a museum exhibition on world environments.

Your task is to gather the information required for the exhibition in report form, prior to the exhibit being created.

Select one natural environment that you have studied in this chapter.

- **Explain** why you chose that natural environment (for example, out of personal interest or because you have visited such a place).
- **Formulate** your own research question.
- **Explain** how the question you chose is relevant and important to investigate.
- Locate the environment.
- **Describe** and **explain** the climate. (Include an annotated climate graph.) Think in terms of precipitation, temperature, wind, humidity, light, seasonality, growing season, temperature range, total precipitation, seasonal precipitation, maximum and minimum temperatures.
- **Describe** the vegetation and how it adapts to the climate. Think in terms of competition between plants and between animals. (Draw diagrams of how the plants have adapted and link this with the climate section.)
- Think about how humans have affected/managed the biome. **Describe** how humans have changed the ecosystem. Think in terms of change in species diversity and number, input flow, output, energy transfer, productivity level and sustainability.
- Include a bibliography.

◆ Assessment opportunities

- In this activity you have practised skills that are assessed using Criterion A: Knowing and understanding and Criterion C: Communicating.

Reflection

In this chapter, we have **summarized** the characteristics of some of the variety of Earth's natural environments. We have **explored** the different ways in which human activity is impacting those environments and **examined to what extent** human choices, through time and in different places, have led to global environmental change. We have **considered** how this interaction has made our current way of life unsustainable and **debated** the need to balance the use of resources now and with preserving the environment for the future.

Use this table to reflect on your own learning in this chapter.					
Questions we asked	Answers we found	Any further questions now?			
Factual: Where are different environments located? What are the characteristics of natural environments? How do humans impact on natural environments?					
Conceptual: Can resources ever be exploited sustainably?					
Debatable: To what extent is globalization a driver for development, and to what extent a driver for destruction?					
Approaches to learning you used in this chapter	Description – what new skills did you learn?	How well did you master the skills?			
		Novice	Learner	Practitioner	Expert
Communication skills					
Collaboration skills					
Organization skills					
Reflection skills					
Information literacy skills					
Media literacy skills					
Critical-thinking skills					
Transfer skills					
Learner profile attribute(s)	Reflect on the importance of being principled for your learning in this chapter.				
Principled					

Change | Causality | Orientation in space and time

6 How does population change affect individuals and societies?

Population **change** in certain **places and times drives** social and environmental change, but we must take action to ensure that the benefits are shared by all.

CONSIDER THESE QUESTIONS:

Factual: How and why does population growth differ between different regions of the world? What are the causes and consequences of forced migration and internal displacement? What are the consequences of megacity growth for individuals and societies?

Conceptual: How has population changed over time and how can it be measured? Can population change be managed?

Debatable: Is population growth destructive or can it be viewed as a driver for development?

Now **share and compare** your thoughts and ideas with your partner, or with the whole class.

■ Figure 6.1 Our populated Earth

IN THIS CHAPTER WE WILL …

- **Find out** how population varies within and between countries and what the impacts are on individuals and societies.
- **Explore** contemporary case studies of countries where populations are affected by migration, natural increase and rapid growth.
- **Take action** by looking at issues of internally displaced people and refugees.

These Approaches to Learning (ATL) skills will be useful …

- Communication skills
- Collaboration skills
- Organization skills
- Media literacy skills
- Critical-thinking skills

We will reflect on this learner profile attribute …

- Balanced – understanding the importance of balancing different aspects of our lives – intellectual, physical and emotional – to achieve well-being for ourselves and others; recognizing our interdependence with other people and with the world in which we live.

Assessment opportunities in this chapter:

- **Criterion A:** Knowing and understanding
- **Criterion B:** Investigating
- **Criterion C:** Communicating
- **Criterion D:** Thinking critically

KEY WORDS

migration
natural increase
trends

SEE–THINK–WONDER

Look at Figure 6.1. Write down what you see, what this image makes you think and what it makes you wonder. Be ready to share your ideas with the class.

The population of our Earth is always changing. In this chapter, we will explore areas with contrasting populations and examine reasons why this may be the case. We will look at how and why population has changed over time, what the environmental and social implications of population growth may be and develop our knowledge and understanding of the works of significant individuals in the study of **demography**.

6 How does population change affect individuals and societies?

How and why does population growth differ between different regions of the world?

■ **Figure 6.2** Hong Kong and an isolated dwelling

> **THINK–PAIR–SHARE**
>
> Looking at Figure 6.2 and thinking back to what you may have already learned in Chapter 5 of this book and in *Individuals and Societies for the IB MYP 1*, think about the following question: 'What are some of the reasons for different population densities?'. Share your ideas with your partner and then be ready to **discuss** them with the class.

People are not distributed evenly all over the Earth's surface. As shown in Figure 6.3, some places are home to millions of people and some to just a few. This can be due to physical and/or human factors. Physical factors such as **relief**, soils and climate can encourage settlement in an area. Densely populated areas are common where there is low, flat land, fertile soils and a moderate climate. Where the climate is extreme and there are high mountains or deserts (such as in some of the natural environments explored in Chapter 5), the environment is inhospitable to people and these areas are often only sparsely populated. Social, environmental and political factors also play a role in where people live, as explored in Table 6.1 on page 149.

DISCUSS

With a partner, suggest reasons why the following factors can lead to densely and sparsely populated areas:
- Economic
- Social
- Political

When you have discussed your ideas, **identify** some examples to support them.

ACTIVITY: Interpreting population data

■ ATL

- Critical-thinking skills: Interpret data; Draw reasonable conclusions and generalizations

Figure 6.3 shows global population distribution by country for the year 2015. Use the map and any prior knowledge you may have to do the following:

1 **Define** 'population density'.
2 **Explain** how physical factors can cause variations in population density in different parts of the world.
3 **Suggest** reasons why there may be some densely populated areas in parts that are otherwise sparsely populated. **Identify** and state specific examples from the map to support your ideas.

◆ Assessment opportunities

- In this activity you have practised skills that are assessed using Criterion C: Communicating.

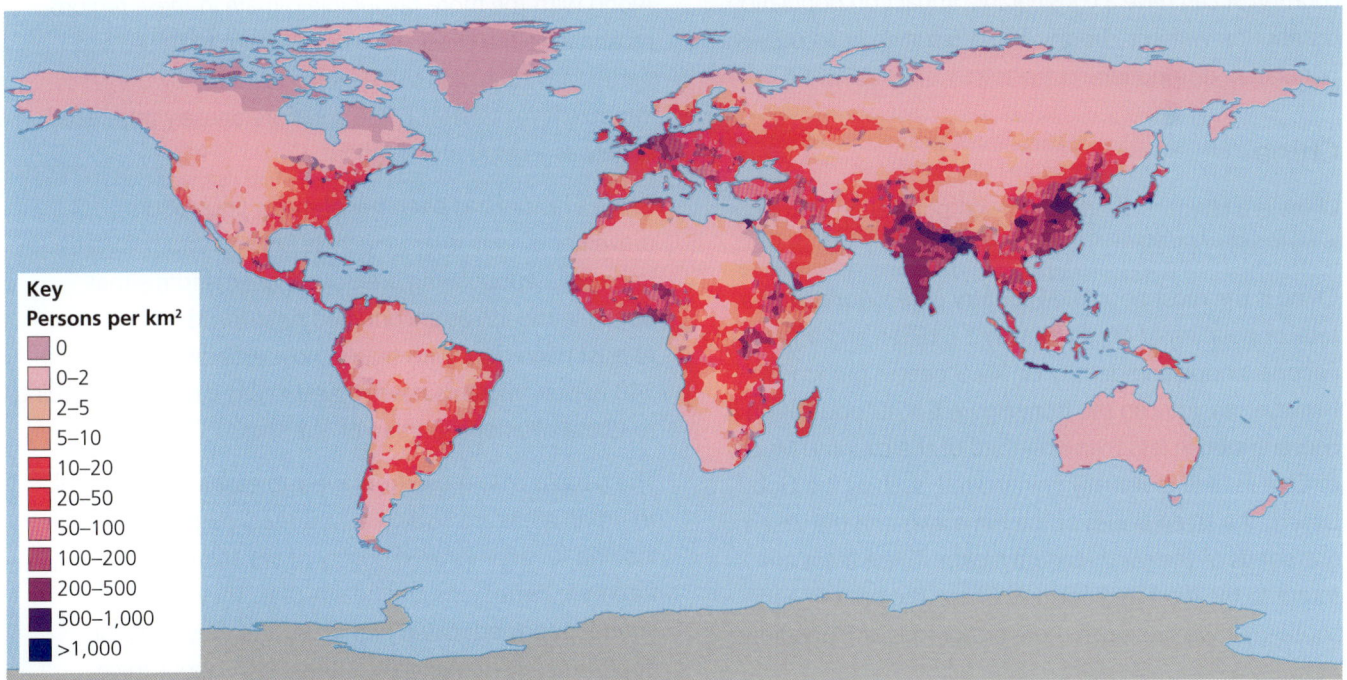

■ **Figure 6.3** World population densities by country, 2015

6 How does population change affect individuals and societies?

How does population vary within countries?

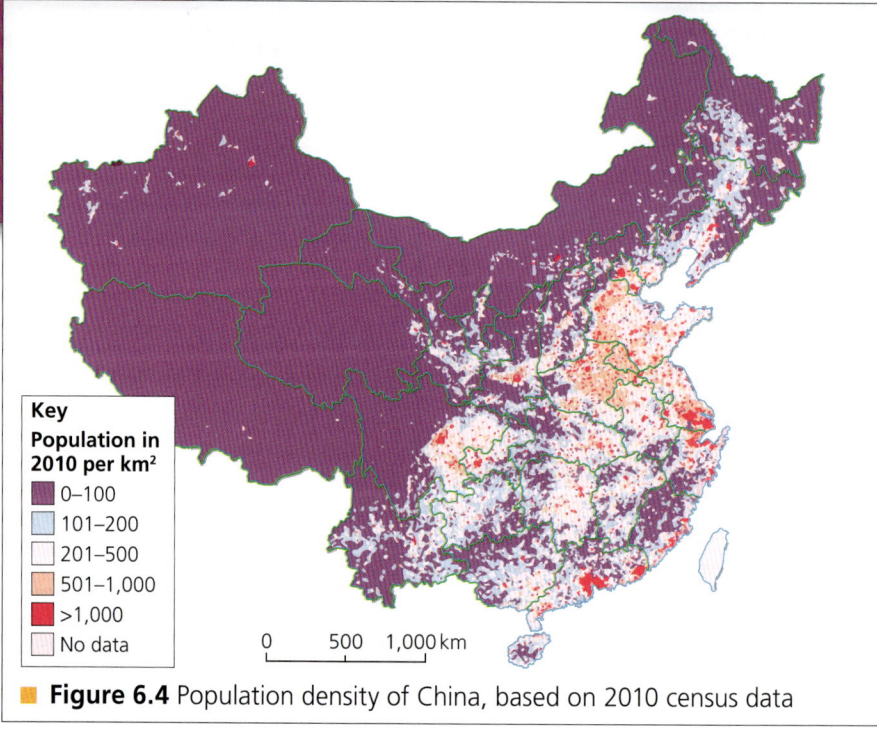

Figure 6.4 Population density of China, based on 2010 census data

Key
Population in 2010 per km²
- 0–100
- 101–200
- 201–500
- 501–1,000
- >1,000
- No data

Chapter 10 discusses growth and development. It explores global patterns of economic development and how we classify countries according to their development levels. These levels and patterns are important when considering why population varies from place to place. While the population density of a country has very little to do with its level of economic development (both Bangladesh and Japan are very densely populated, but Bangladesh is a low-income country and Japan is a high-income country), it can have a considerable impact on population distribution within a country, often resulting in an uneven population distribution.

China

China is a country where an uneven population distribution is especially prevalent.

China is the most populated country in the world with a total population of approximately 1.4 billion and an average national population density of 142.5 people per km². However, as you can see from Figure 6.4, its population is concentrated in less than one-third of the country. Much of China's land is virtually uninhabited, such as the Gobi Desert, the steep slopes of the Himalayas and the vast dry grasslands of the north-central region. These areas are found to the west and north of China; the eastern and southern areas are much more prosperous and populous.

China's major cities are found along the eastern coast. Along with the more favourable climate in these regions, proximity to the coast has allowed them to trade, and particularly to exploit the benefits provided by the fertile Yangtze River's delta. These areas are densely populated largely as a result of migration.

China's history has been full of major population movements, with events such as famines and political upheaval depopulating areas. Economic reforms that began in the 1970s encouraged rural-to-urban and west-to-east migration, with figures now estimating more than 140 million migrants have moved in this direction according to China's National Bureau of Statistics.

The people who move from west to east and from rural to urban areas are known as voluntary migrants – people looking for an improved quality of life and personal freedom, better jobs and health care. They are mostly young, poorly educated and male, and they make up approximately 40 per cent of the urban labour force.

Figure 6.5 The cities and provinces of China

Figure 6.6 Migrant worker in front of the iconic Bird's Nest stadium, preparing for the 2008 Olympic Games

ACTIVITY: Voluntary migration

ATL

- Communication skills: Use appropriate forms of writing for different purposes and audiences; Use a variety of organizers for academic writing tasks
- Critical-thinking skills: Consider ideas from multiple perspectives

Voluntary internal migration has a range of social, economic, political and environmental impacts on both the place of origin (where the migrants are from), and the destination (where the migrants settle).

1 Construct a table like Table 6.1 to **explore** both the positive (+) and negative (–) impacts of voluntary migration in China on the origin and destination. The following terms may provide a good place for you to start your research: hukou status, migrants Beijing 2008 Olympics, tough times for children left behind China's migrant workers, remittances internal migration China.
Use specific facts, figures and examples wherever possible when filling in your table.

Table 6.1 Impacts of voluntary internal migration in China

Geographic impacts of internal migration in China	Origin	Destination
+ Social impacts		
– Social impacts		
+ Economic impacts		
– Economic impacts		
+ Political impacts		
– Political impacts		
+ Environmental impacts		
– Environmental impacts		

2 Imagine you are a voluntary, internal migrant living and working in a Chinese city. Using your completed table, write an email or letter to your family back in the rural area where you grew up. Outline some of the positives and negatives that you experience as a migrant worker.

◆ Assessment opportunities

◆ In this activity you have practised skills that are assessed using Criterion A: Knowing and understanding and Criterion C: Communicating.

6 How does population change affect individuals and societies?

INTERNATIONAL MIGRATION

Voluntary migration can also occur internationally as well as internally or nationally. Many of the reasons for migration to another country are similar to those you have explored in relation to internal migration in China, with migrants seeking an enhanced way of life and economic opportunities. The advantages and disadvantages for both the countries of origin and destination are also similar but international migration may create additional challenges for both the migrants and the residents of the destination country, as has been seen in the case of migration from Mexico to the USA.

> **DISCUSS**
>
> What is the 'American Dream'? Is this something that is still relevant and/or desirable in today's society?

Mexico and the USA

The border between the USA and Mexico is 2,000 km long (see Figure 6.7), so it is perhaps not surprising that the USA receives in excess of 1 million Mexican migrants each year. It is difficult to calculate an exact figure as illegal migration is significant. US Border Patrol guard the border and in recent years strong restrictions on immigration have been introduced in an attempt to curb the flow. The assimilation of Mexican migrants into US communities has often proved problematic – the majority of migrants are poorly educated and do not speak fluent English, which makes integration difficult. To counteract this, and for stability and familiarity, many Mexicans live in closed communities of other Mexican immigrants. This reduces their need to assimilate with the USA but has led to tension between migrants and locals, which in extreme cases has led to segregation, violence and crime. Tensions have also risen between migrants and locals as the

■ **Figure 6.7** The USA/Mexico border

unemployment rate in the USA has risen. Since the majority of migrants have a low standard of education, they have traditionally taken low-paid, sometimes menial jobs. Although the wages are low in the US context, they are still higher than what they would earn in Mexico. As unemployment has risen, more Americans have needed these jobs and social tensions have increased as many Americans believe that the migrants have taken jobs that are rightfully theirs.

Despite this, there are undoubtedly upsides to the international migration between Mexico and the USA, in particular the introduction of Mexican culture and traditions. Mexican cuisine is now extremely popular in the USA and the foods and music that the Mexican migrants have introduced have helped to increase America's cultural diversity. Similarly, as the majority of Mexican migrants do not speak English fluently, Spanish is often taught in US schools and this widens the skill set of the younger population and broadens their future career opportunities.

However, international migration often takes its toll on the country of origin and Mexico is no exception. While it benefits economically from **remittances** sent home by the migrants, the lack of a young, working-age population means that Mexico increasingly has a **dependent population**, as the majority of people left are elderly and cannot work. The lack of young fertile couples is reducing the birth rate in Mexico, further increasing the **dependency ratio** as there is no workforce to pay taxes to support elderly people.

What are the causes and consequences of forced migration and internal displacement?

ACTIVITY: 'A world without border controls in a century'

ATL

- Media literacy skills: Locate, organize, analyse, evaluate, synthesize and ethically use information from a variety of sources and media (including digital social media and online networks)

Watch the TEDx Talk by Professor Danny Dorling 'A world without border controls in a century':

https://youtu.be/5TczgCTABII

In this video, Danny Dorling argues that there will be a world without borders and free migration within a century.

1. Take active notes in order to **summarize** the main views expressed in this talk.
   Consider how you will organize your notes. You could use mind maps, tables, line or flow diagrams. Clear organization of your notes will mean that they are easier to analyse – you could go through with a highlighter and pick out the key concepts and most relevant points – and help you in **evaluating** the views of Professor Danny Dorling.
2. To what extent do you agree with the views expressed in this talk? State and **justify** your viewpoint, using examples to support your arguments.

Assessment opportunities

- In this activity you have practised skills that are assessed using Criterion D: Thinking critically.

In Chapter 5 we briefly touched upon forced migration when examining the Sahel region (see page 128). **Push factors** for forced migration are likely to be environmental and political as opposed to the social and economic reasons that drive voluntary migrations, both internally and externally. These push factors have a huge impact on population change.

Migration terminology

Migrant: A person who moves from one place to another in order to find work or better living conditions.

Immigrant: A person who comes to live permanently in a foreign country.

Emigrant: A person who leaves their own country in order to settle permanently in another.

Internally displaced person (IDP): A person who is forced to flee their home but who remains within their country's borders.

Refugee: A person who has been forced to leave their country in order to escape war, persecution or natural disaster.

Asylum seeker: A person who has left their home country as a political refugee and is seeking asylum in another.

Internally displaced people (IDPs – see information box) often go on to become refugees, and later asylum seekers, if they are forced from their country's borders. There are currently twice as many IDPs as refugees in the world.

Take action

! Despite its global scale, the issue of internal displacement remains largely overshadowed by issues with refugees and migrants. Create a video and poster campaign to raise awareness of the issues of IDPs. Perhaps you could arrange to present in an assembly or to a group of your peers. This infographic may provide you with some useful information https://www.unhcr.org/global-trends

CASE STUDY OF FORCED MIGRATION FROM SYRIA

What are the push factors?

In March 2011, pro-democracy protests began in Syria after the arrest and torture of a group of teenagers who had painted revolutionary slogans on a school wall. These protests quickly spiralled as people demanded President Assad's resignation. The government's use of force to try to curb the protests made things worse and violence escalated. By 2012, the country had descended into civil war as rebel brigades were formed to battle government forces for control of cities, towns and the countryside. The rise of the **jihadist** group Islamic State (IS) added a further dimension to the civil conflict. The UN accused IS of waging a campaign of terror, as it inflicted severe punishments on those who transgressed or refused to accept its rules, including hundreds of public executions and amputations. Its fighters also carried out mass killings of rival armed groups, members of the security forces and religious minorities. In August 2013, a chemical weapons attack was launched on the city of Damascus which killed hundreds of people. The government denied the attack and blamed the rebel forces. Regardless of who is to blame for the use of chemical weapons and the continued state of political unrest, these conditions have led to a stream of forced migration as people fear for their lives. The continued attacks on schools, hospitals, water networks, electricity plants, places of worship and economic assets have made civilians extremely vulnerable.

Internally displaced people within Syria

As of 2016, according to a report produced by the **UN Office for the Coordination of Humanitarian Affairs**, 6.5 million people were internally displaced inside Syria, with

■ **Figure 6.8** Syria, showing international borders

1.2 million having been driven from their homes in 2015 alone. The report stated that the UN would need $3.2bn to help the 13.5 million people, including 6 million children, who would require some form of humanitarian assistance inside Syria in 2016. At the time, about 70 per cent of the population were without access to adequate drinking water, one in three people was unable to meet their basic food needs, more than 2 million children were out of school, and four out of five people were living in poverty. It is difficult for aid to reach those who most need it as humanitarian agencies have been refused access to civilians in need by rebel groups and the government. Up to 4.5 million people in Syria live in hard-to-reach areas, including nearly 400,000 people in 15 besieged locations who do not have access to life-saving aid.

Refugees

In addition to the IDPs, more than 5 million people have fled Syria since the start of the conflict, most of them women and children. Lebanon, Jordan and Turkey have struggled to cope with one of the largest refugee exoduses in recent history. About 10 per cent of Syrian refugees have sought safety in Europe, which has increased political tensions on a wider scale as countries argue over sharing the burden. The following link explores the number of refugees in neighbouring countries:
https://data2.unhcr.org/en/situations/syria

Humanitarian Needs Overview, 2016

- An estimated 13.5 million people in Syria, including 6 million children, require humanitarian assistance and protection.
- 8.7 million people have acute needs across multiple sectors.
- 4.5 million people in need in hard-to-reach areas and locations listed in UNSCR 2139, 2165, 2191, as updated by the UN.
- It is estimated that upwards of 250,000 people have been killed, including tens of thousands of children and youth.
- Almost 70 per cent lack access to adequate drinking water amid continuing water cuts.
- One in three people are unable to meet their basic food needs, with an estimated 8.7 million people in need of a range of food security-related assistance.
- 2.4 million people lack adequate shelter.
- Over 11 million people require health assistance, including 25,000 trauma cases per month.
- 1.7 million IDPs are living in camps and collective centres.
- An estimated 86,000 children aged 6–59 months suffer from acute malnutrition. A further 3.16 million children under the age of five and pregnant and lactating women (PLW) are considered at risk.
- Over 2 million children and adolescents are out of school. One in four schools are damaged, destroyed or occupied.
- Four out of five Syrians live in poverty. Competing over limited resources might create tensions in areas of displacement.
- Since the onset of the crisis the average life expectancy has fallen by 20 years.
- Nearly one in three Syrian households is now indebted, due mainly to food costs.
- Lack/loss of civil and personal documentation is a key concern.
- Up to 95 per cent of Palestine Refugees who remain in Syria are in continuous need of humanitarian aid.
- One in four children are at risk of developing mental health disorders.
- Three in five locations are affected by child labour, including in its worst forms.
- 1.5 million people have disabilities.
- An estimated 300,000 women are pregnant and need targeted support.

Source: UN Office for the Coordination of Humanitarian Affairs

DISCUSS

'The Western World has a moral obligation to take a more active role in addressing the refugee crises in Africa and Southwest Asia.'

Discuss this statement.

ACTIVITY: Forced migration in Syria case study

ATL

- Communication skills: Make inferences and draw conclusions; Organize and depict information logically
- Media literacy skills: Locate, organize, analyse, evaluate, synthesize and ethically use information from a variety of sources and media (including digital social media and online networks)

Using the information above as a starting point, compile a case study on the forced migration situation in Syria. Remember, case studies are useful tools for students of Individuals and Societies as they allow you to **demonstrate** your knowledge in the context of the real world.

Use the following as a guide for structuring your case study:
- Where is the event set?
- Who is affected?
- When did the event unfold?
- Why has it happened?
- How is it being managed?
- What impact is it having on the population of the country affected and of neighbouring countries? Is this event affecting the populations of other countries?

Illustrate your case study using photos, maps and diagrams where appropriate.

You could use the following search terms to help you find out more: **Syria news** and **UN Syria**.

◆ Assessment opportunities

- ◆ In this activity you have practised skills that are assessed using Criterion B: Investigating and Criterion C: Communicating.

How has population changed over time and how can it be measured?

THINK–PUZZLE–EXPLORE

Individuals and Societies for the IB MYP 3 explores the processes that contribute to population change and the ways in which population can be modelled, including birth and death rates, the demographic transition model and population pyramids. Using any prior knowledge you have from this book or elsewhere, answer the following questions:
- What do you think you know about this topic?
- What questions or puzzles do you have?
- How can you **explore** this topic?

MEET A SIGNIFICANT INDIVIDUAL: HANS ROSLING (1948–2017)

Communicator

■ **Figure 6.9** Hans Rosling

Hans Rosling was a statistician and professor of global health at Sweden's Karolinska Institute. He was often credited as 'the man who makes statistics sing' after developing the not-for-profit organization Gapminder as a way of 'unveiling the beauty of statistics for a fact based world'. *Time* magazine included him in its 2012 list of the world's 100 most influential people, saying his 'stunning renderings of the numbers … have moved millions of people worldwide to see themselves and our planet in new ways'. Rosling was an influential speaker and his series of Ted Talks are some of the most viewed.

See for yourself by exploring the links below:
- http://bit.ly/RosTEDtalk
- www.gapminder.org

You can also read more about Hans Rosling in *Mathematics for the IB MYP 4&5*, page 150.

Due to factors such as migration, populations are fluid and changing. In order to understand this change we need to measure key elements of population, and by looking at trends and patterns we should then be able to make predictions.

Population terminology

Birth rate: The number of live births per 1,000 people per year.

Total fertility rate (TFR): The average number of children a woman would have if she survives all her childbearing (or reproductive) years. Childbearing years are considered to be age 15 to 49.

Death rate: The number of deaths per 1,000 people per year.

Infant mortality rate: The number of deaths of children under the age of one year per 1,000 live births.

Life expectancy: The expected average life span of people in a particular population.

Natural increase: The rate of population growth calculated by subtracting the death rate from the birth rate.

Dependency ratio: A measure showing the number of dependents, aged zero to 14 and over the age of 65, to the total population, aged 15 to 64. It is also referred to as the 'total dependency ratio'. This indicator gives insight into the number of people of non-working age compared to the number of those of working age.

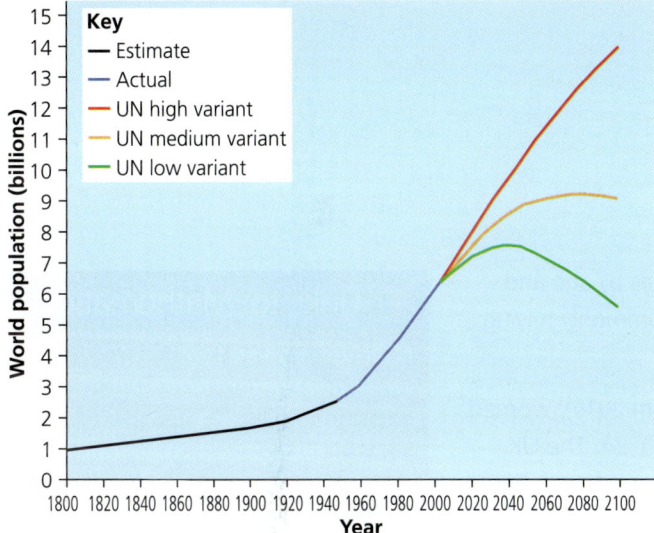

■ **Figure 6.10** World population growth

Global population levels, having grown slowly for the majority of human history, are now rising at a rapid rate. The total world population at the time of writing stands at approximately 8.05 billion. (The 8 billion mark was reached in 2022.)

Population change is dependent on births, deaths and migration. Births and deaths are natural causes of population change and the difference between the rates of both is called the natural increase (see information box). The rate of natural increase is given as a percentage, calculated by dividing the natural increase (given per 1,000 population) by 10. For example, if the birth rate is 12 per 1,000 population, and the death rate is 10 per 1,000 population, then the natural increase = 12 − 10 = 2. That is $\frac{2}{1000}$, which is equal to 0.2 per cent.

Although the world's population is growing, this growth (as with population density) is not equally distributed. Not all countries are experiencing growth: **MEDC**s generally have low population growth rates as a result of low death rates, high life expectancy and low birth rates.

Death rates are low because:
■ health care and education standards are high.

Birth rates are low because, compared to **LEDC**s:
■ there is better access to contraception and a lower infant mortality rate
■ women have higher levels of education and are therefore more likely to have children later in life.

Fertility rates

While a birth rate gives an overall figure of births in a country it is not the most accurate of measures as it deals with the whole population and does not account for males, children and elderly people, who are unable to have children. It is useful in that it provides a tool for comparing countries, but looking at age-specific fertility rates (ASFR) and the total fertility rate is much more useful.

A woman's childbearing years are considered to be between the ages of 15 and 49. To provide age-specific fertility rates, this age range is usually split into seven five-year age groups covering the reproductive years: 15–19, 20–24, 25–29, 30–34, 35–39, 40–44 and 45–49).

It is calculated using the following formula:

$$\frac{\text{Number of live births to women in specified age goup}}{\text{Number of women in same age group}} \times 1{,}000$$

ASFRs are important because the likelihood of having a child varies by age and they provide a tool to compare at what ages women are most commonly having children over different time periods and in different places.

As you can see from the Table 6.2 (based on UN fertility data from 2016), women are bearing children at young ages in Tanzania, peaking at age 20–24. The UK, by comparison, has a later age pattern of fertility with childbearing delayed and concentrated at the older ages of 30–34. The ASFRs are also considerably higher for Tanzania as compared to the UK.

■ **Table 6.2** Age-specific fertility rates in Tanzania and the UK, 2016

Country	Age-specific fertility rates						
	15–19	20–24	25–29	30–34	35–39	40–44	45–49
Tanzania	116	260	249	207	161	72	22
United Kingdom	25	74	108	110	59	12	1

> ### ▼ Links to: Mathematics
> Malthus showed that while population increased **exponentially** (as a **geometric series**), resources such as food could only be increased in a **linear** (**arithmetic series**) fashion. Use your mathematics knowledge and sketch graphs to show why this leads Malthusians and neo-Malthusians to believe there would be 'population crises' if the population is left unchecked. See *Mathematics for the IB MYP 4&5* Chapter 7.

Age-specific fertility rates also enable us to calculate the total fertility rate for a country. The total fertility rate (TFR) is the average number of children that would be born alive to a woman during her lifetime if she were to pass through her childbearing years having births according to the current schedule of age-specific fertility rates for a given year. It is a hypothetical measure but is very useful and is the standard way to compare fertility internationally.

A concept that is widely associated with TFR is replacement level fertility. A TFR of 2.1 is replacement fertility since an average of two births is needed to 'replace' a mother and father but only if the births survive to reproductive age. An extra 0.1 birth is added to offset the effects of premature death. If replacement level fertility is sustained over a sufficiently long period, each generation will exactly replace itself without any need for the country to balance the population through pro- or anti-natalist or changes to migration policies. Tanzania and the United Kingdom have TFRs of 5.44 and 1.95 respectively. This means that while both populations are growing, the UK's is below replacement level fertility and Tanzania's is way above.

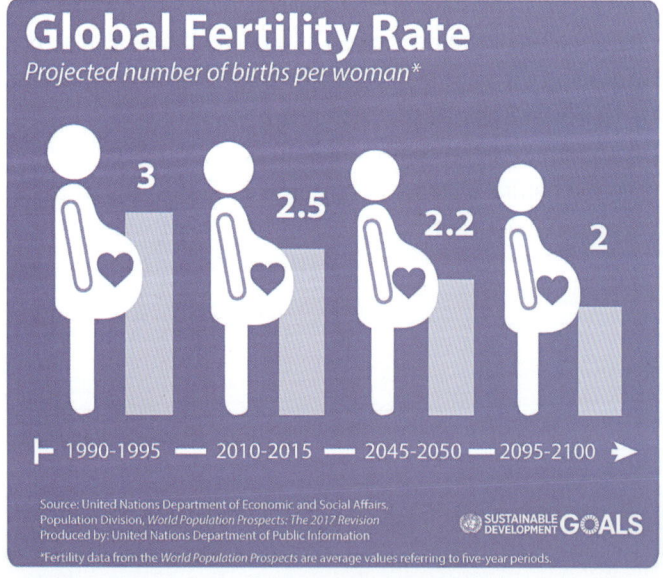

■ **Figure 6.11** Global fertility rate infographic produced by the UN

MEET A SIGNIFICANT INDIVIDUAL: THOMAS ROBERT MALTHUS (1766–1834)

Thinker

Thomas Malthus's *An Essay on the Principle of Population* (1798) set out his theory as to how and why the size of the population would change. Despite its age, Malthus' theory is still one of the most debated population theories.

Malthus thought that if the human population continued to grow, food production would not be able to keep up with demand and there would not be enough food to go around. The result, he warned, would be a terrible famine that would kill many people. He essentially believed that the human population was at risk of outgrowing its environment and that population growth was not sustainable.

Malthus believed that this catastrophic outcome could be avoided if the population stopped growing and outlined two types of check (relating to birth and death rates) that could stop population growth. A negative check, for example, an increased use of contraceptives, would cause a decline in the birth rate and a positive check, such as disease or war, would increase the death rate. These are sometimes referred to as Malthusian crises and many cite global epidemics such as AIDs and swine flu as well as diseases like cancer as types of positive check that serve to reduce the global population.

These checks, he argued, were more likely to take effect as the population got closer to exceeding its limits either because governments would take steps to stop the population getting any bigger or because of increased competition and hardship within the population.

The ideas of Thomas Malthus spawned a school of thought called Malthusianism and today there are many people who have developed his ideas and are proponents of this school of thought. Use the following search terms to find out more: **neo-Malthusian**, **Paul Ehrlich** and **Population Bomb**.

■ **Figure 6.12** Thomas Malthus

MEET A SIGNIFICANT INDIVIDUAL: ESTER BOSERUP (1910–1999)

Ester Boserup was a Danish economist who specialized in the economics and development of agriculture. She worked for the United Nations and this helped her develop her theories based on the relationship between population and food supply. She belongs to the anti-Malthusian school of thought as her ideas on population growth oppose those of Thomas Malthus.

In her work *The Conditions of Agricultural Growth: The economics of agrarian change under population pressure* (1965), Boserup challenged Malthus's ideas that the size of the human population is limited by the amount of food it can produce. She suggested that food production can, and will, increase to match the needs of the population. Boserup believed that 'necessity is the mother of invention' and that as the population neared a time of crisis, people would be inspired to innovate and create new forms of technology to help the population to continue to grow. Crops that fight diseases or survive with less water are examples of this.

Malthus and Boserup are often pitted against each other as the two opposing sides of the debate in population growth.

Who do you agree with more?

■ **Figure 6.13** Ester Boserup

While death rates are high in developing countries, the populations in these countries are expanding as birth rates are also high. Death rates are high because of a low life expectancy and a high infant mortality rate largely due to inadequate access to health care provision. Birth rates are high to offset the high levels of infant mortality, and there is often limited or no access to contraception. In addition to the limited access to contraception in some regions, in others, women are actively educated not to use contraception for cultural or ideological reasons. However, improving health care leads to death rates falling – while birth rates remain high.

> **DISCUSS**
>
> **Explain** the advantages of educating girls and women in LEDCs. Think about the impact a higher standard of education could have on all aspects of life, such as health care and employment. How are these factors interrelated?

■ **Table 6.3** Data in selected LEDC and MEDC countries (per 1,000 of the population per year)

Country	Birth rate	Death rate	Total fertility rate	Infant mortality rate	Natural increase	Rate of population growth (%)
UK	11	9	1.7	4	2	0.2
Germany	10	12	1.6	3	−2	−0.2
Brazil	14	6	1.7	10	8	0.8
China	11	7	1.6	10	4	0.4
South Africa	20	9	2.3	22	11	1.1
Tanzania	37	7	5.0	42	30	3.0

In Germany, the birth rate is $\frac{10}{1,000}$ and death rate is $\frac{12}{1,000}$. As birth rate is less than the death rate, Germany has a declining population.

In Tanzania, the birth rate is $\frac{37}{1,000}$ and death rate is $\frac{7}{1,000}$. Tanzania has an increasing population with a population growth rate of 3 per cent.

ACTIVITY: Interpreting population data

ATL

- Communication skills: Use and interpret a range of discipline-specific terms and symbols
- Critical-thinking skills: Interpret data; Identify trends and forecast possibilities

Using Table 6.3, complete the following data interpretation activities:
- **Identify** and **explain** the trends in birth rates, death rates and natural increase of high-income, low-income and middle-income countries.
- **Identify** any anomalies in the trends you have identified.
- **Suggest** reasons for the relatively high death rates of the more developed countries, Germany and the UK.
- **Explain** why despite a high infant mortality rate, the populations of South Africa and Tanzania show high levels of natural increase.
- **Compare and contrast** the potential difficulties that Germany and Tanzania may face with their differing levels of natural increase.
- Despite its below replacement level fertility rate, the UK has a growing population. Suggest reasons for this.

◆ Assessment opportunities

- In this activity you have practised skills that are assessed using Criterion A: Knowing and understanding.

THINK–PAIR–SHARE

What opportunities and challenges do ageing and youthful populations present?

Discuss with your partner and make a list. Be ready to share with the class.

You may already be familiar with the demographic transition model (Figure 6.14) from *Individuals and Societies for the IB MYP 3*. It is a model developed to illustrate population change over time and also differences been more and less developed countries, with a focus on how birth and death rates affect populations.

There are five stages to the model and countries usually pass through each stage on their way to becoming more economically developed, with countries in stage 4 being classed as MEDCs. As a country passes through each stage, the total population rises – most LEDCs are in stage 2 or 3 with growing populations and a high natural increase, whereas in stage 5 total population is high but beginning to decline as the population is ageing and birth rates are low. Germany is an example of a country currently thought to be in stage 5.

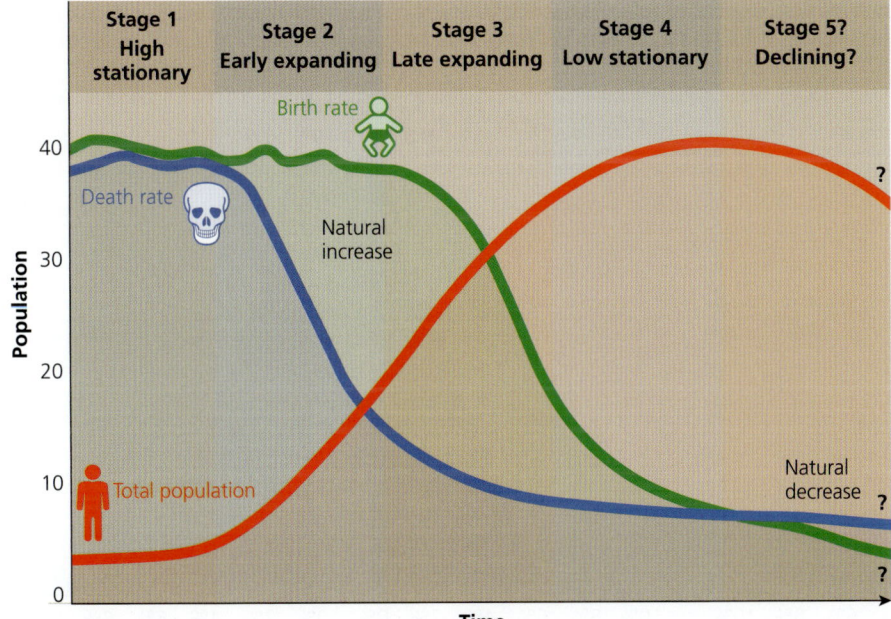

■ **Figure 6.14** Demographic transition model

6 How does population change affect individuals and societies?

ACTIVITY: Demographic transition model annotation

▪ ATL

- Critical-thinking skills: Use models and simulations to explore complex systems and issues

Using Figure 6.14, create a copy of the demographic transition model.

Annotate each stage of the model on your diagram, paying particular attention to the gap between birth and death rates and the total population. For example: 'In stage 1, total population is low but it is stable due to high birth rates and high death rates.'

Suggest reasons for the changes in birth and death rates as a country progresses through each stage.

◆ Assessment opportunities

♦ In this activity you have practised skills that are assessed using Criterion C: Communicating.

Population pyramids are another way in which population structure can be visually represented. They show the structure of a population by comparing numbers of males and females in different age groups. It is easy to identify LEDCs and MEDCs from the shapes of population pyramids and careful analysis can also inform us about: birth and death rates, life expectancy, dependents – young and old, and the proportion of economically active people in the population.

The following graphs show the population pyramids of an MEDC (the UK) and an LEDC (Tanzania) for 2017 and in 2055 using projected figures. The left side of each pyramid shows the number of men in each age group; the right side shows the number of women in each age group. A population pyramid that is very triangular (such as Tanzania in 2017) shows a population with a high number of young dependents and a low life expectancy. A population pyramid that has fairly straight sides (more like a barrel) shows a population with a falling birth rate and a rising life expectancy – this can be seen in the population pyramids for the UK. Over time, as a country develops, the shape changes from triangular to barrel-like. Places with an ageing population and a very low birth rate would have a structure that looks like an upside-down pyramid.

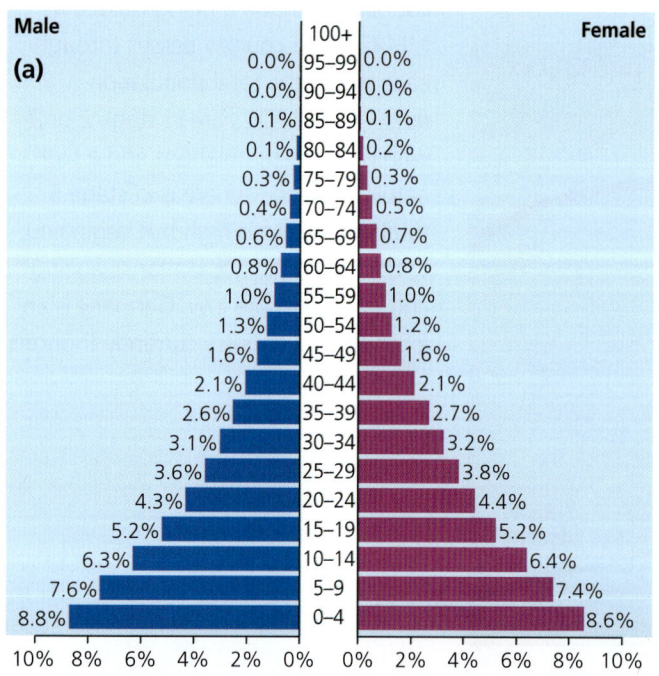

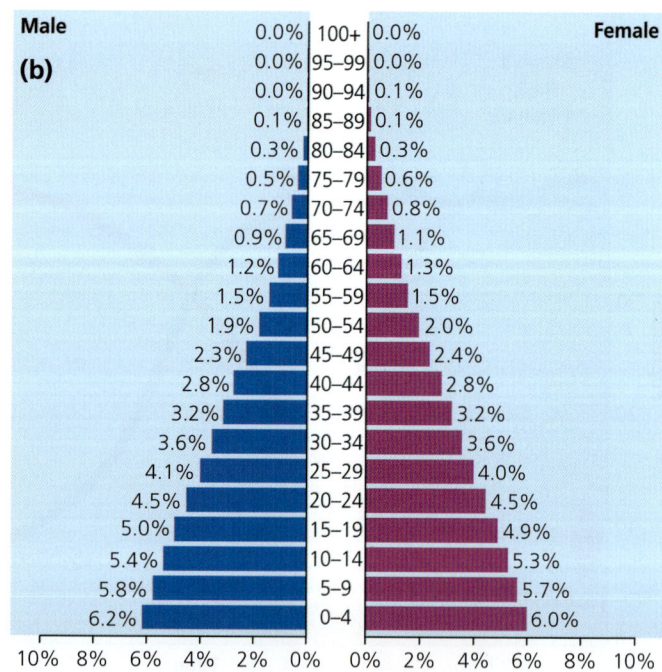

■ **Figure 6.15** Population pyramids for **(a)** Tanzania, 2017 and **(b)** 2055 and **(c)** the UK, 2017 and **(d)** 2055

EXTENSION

What is the **demographic dividend**? Find one example of a country benefiting from a demographic dividend. To what extent could population be considered a resource when contemplating possible futures?

ACTIVITY: Population pyramid analysis

■ **ATL**

■ Critical-thinking skills: Use models and simulations to explore complex systems and issues

Using Figures 6.15a–d, complete the activities below.

1 **Describe** the population pyramid for:
   a the UK in 2017
   b Tanzania in 2017
   c the UK in 2055
   d Tanzania in 2055.

> **Hint**
> Pay specific attention to birth rate, death rate, life expectancy and elderly, youthful and economically active populations in your descriptions. Give specific figures to support your description where possible.

2 For each of the population pyramids, state which stage of the demographic transition model you believe it to be in. **Justify** your answers.

3 Demographic structure can be used to **demonstrate** stages of development. **Explain** how the population pyramids show that the United Kingdom is more developed than Tanzania.

4 With reference to the population change shown between the UK in 2017 and 2055, suggest what considerations will need to be made by the government in the provision of services and employment between 2017 and 2055.

5 With reference to the population change shown between Tanzania in 2017 and 2055, suggest what considerations will need to be made by the government in the provision of services and employment between 2017 and 2055.

6 Using the website www.populationpyramid.net select another country of your choice and answer questions 1–4 for its population pyramids of 2017 and 2055.

◆ **Assessment opportunities**

◆ In this activity you have practised skills that are assessed using Criterion A: Knowing and understanding.

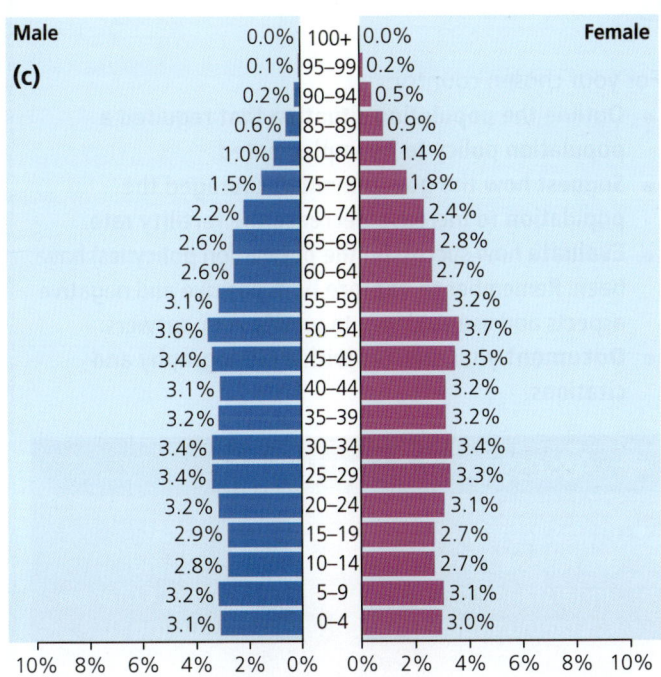

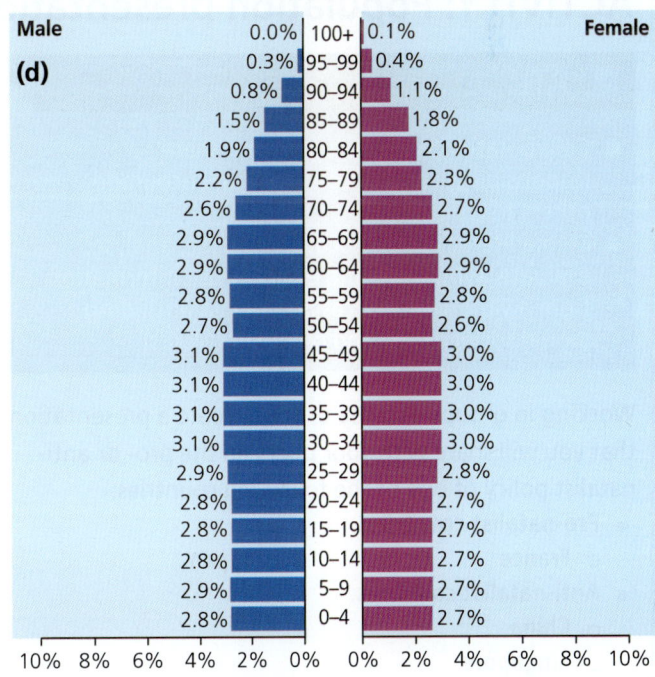

6 How does population change affect individuals and societies?

Can population change be managed?

■ **Figure 6.16** Population poster campaigns for Singapore and China

Demographers use models like the demographic transition model and population pyramids to make projections. These help governments in making plans and provisions for the future based on how the population is likely to change. Governments over time have implemented population policies to solve what they perceive to be future population issues, usually with a high or low birth rate. Of these pro- and anti-natalist policies, China's one child policy is one of the most famous and arguably successful, although its success has led to problems today.

EXTENSION

Explore countries that have gender equality policies and anti-trafficking policies in place. How do these impact population change? The UN Global Report on Trafficking in Persons 2016 will provide you with a good place to start your research: https://bit.ly/2h2jrVj

ACTIVITY: Population presentations

■ ATL

- Collaboration skills: Delegate and share responsibility for decision-making; Encourage others to contribute
- Media literacy skills: Locate, organize, analyse, evaluate, synthesize and ethically use information from a variety of sources and media (including digital social media and online networks)

Working in groups of three or four, create a presentation that you will share with your peers on the pro- or anti-natalist policy of one of the following countries:
- **Pro-natalist countries:**
  o France
  o Japan
- **Anti-natalist countries:**
  o China
  o Singapore

For your chosen country:
- **Outline** the population situation that required a population policy to be implemented.
- **Suggest** how the government encouraged the population to increase/decrease the fertility rate.
- **Evaluate** how successful the population policy(ies) have been. Remember to **explore** both positive and negative aspects and use evidence to **justify** your answers.
- **Document** your sources with a bibliography and citations.

◆ Assessment opportunities

◆ In this activity you have practised skills that are assessed using Criterion A: Knowing and understanding, Criterion B: Investigating, Criterion C: Communicating and Criterion D: Thinking critically.

What are the consequences of megacity growth for individuals and societies?

■ **Figure 6.17** Megacities **(a)** Tokyo; **(b)** Lagos

A megacity is a city of over 10 million people and as populations are continuing to increase globally, more and more megacities are developing. In the early 1970s, only Tokyo and New York fell into that category, joined by Mexico City in 1975. However, as of 2017, there are 37 megacities and the UN predicts that this will grow to 41 by 2030. Of the top ten megacities in Table 6.4, it is interesting to note that seven are in Asia. The concept of a megacity was introduced in *Individuals and Societies for the IB MYP 3* with a discussion of overcrowding in Lagos.

■ **Table 6.4** Top ten megacities

City	Population	Country	Continent
Tokyo	37,435,192	Japan	Asia
Delhi	29,399,141	India	Asia
Shanghai	26,317,104	China	Asia
São Paulo	21,846,507	Brazil	South America
Mexico City	21,671,908	Mexico	South America
Cairo	20,484,965	Egypt	Africa
Dhaka	20,283,552	Bangladesh	Asia
Mumbai	20,185,064	India	Asia
Beijing	20,035,455	China	Asia
Osaka	19,222,665	Japan	Asia

THINK–PAIR–SHARE

Read the extract below, from an article in the *Guardian* newspaper.

> 'Optimists see a new network of powerful, stable and prosperous city states, each bigger than many small countries, where the benefits of urban living, the relative ease of delivering basic services compared to rural zones and new civic identities combine to raise living standards for billions. Pessimists see the opposite: a dystopic future where huge numbers of people fight over scarce resources in sprawling, divided, anarchic "non-communities" ravaged by disease and violence.'

Source: 'How the Rise of the Megacity is Changing the Way We Live', The Guardian, January 2012

Think about which side you agree with. Are you an optimist or a pessimist?

Share your viewpoint with a partner and be ready to share with the class.

The relatively high birth rates in developing countries across Asia, combined with rising health care standards (which cause death rates to fall) are undeniably contributing factors in the growth of megacities, but it is the large stream of rural-to-urban migrants that have contributed most to the rapid swell in population in megacities. With the growth of megacities comes a range of impacts that affect both individuals and societies.

There are many perceived social benefits for individuals in megacities. In addition to the enhanced employment opportunities and earning potential, in terms of culture there is a wide and varied range of recreation activities to explore and modern technology in cities can make people's lives safer and more comfortable.

Even in the most developed and populous of megacities, people can find themselves alienated. In Tokyo, for example, rates of mental illness and suicide are rising. In 2015 more than 25,000 people took their own lives – this equates to a daily figure of more than 70, of whom the vast majority were men. Mental illness is still very much a cultural taboo in Japan and there is little understanding of depression. Those suffering its symptoms are often too scared to talk about it. Cultural practices may also play a role, in the form of **hikikomori**, a type of acute social withdrawal. The Japanese Ministry of Health, Labour and Welfare defines *hikikomori* as people who refuse to leave their house and isolate themselves from society in their homes for a period exceeding six months. The young person affected may completely shut himself – it is most often a male – off from the outside world, withdrawing into a room and not coming out for months or even years. In addition to this, Japan's booming technology industry may be making things worse, increasing young people's isolation as they interact more and more in a virtual environment. This has led to a boom in businesses such as 'rent a friend', where people employ someone from an agency to act as their friend to spend time with and to accompany them to social events.

ACTIVITY: How megacities are changing the map of the world

■ ATL

- Media literacy skills: Locate, organize, analyse, evaluate, synthesize and ethically use information from a variety of sources and media (including digital social media and online networks)

Search for **How megacities are changing the map of the world** at www.ted.com/talks/ Watch the talk.

Summarize the positive issues mentioned in the talk by creating a mind map that shows links and connections between issues.

◆ Assessment opportunities

- In this activity you have practised skills that are assessed using Criterion D: Thinking critically.

■ **Figure 6.18** Is technology isolating us further?

■ **Figure 6.19** The two sides of Mumbai

In the less developed megacities there are issues with inadequate housing and sanitation systems as densely populated slums form on the edges and within the cities. Due to a poor economy and weak infrastructure, cities such as Mumbai, India do not have the means to support the overwhelming urban population. Over half of Mumbai's residents live in slums surrounding the city, causing huge public health, environmental and land use problems. Slum dwellers survive with practically no sanitation, water, urban amenities, employment or security, and almost one-sixth of the world's population lives under these conditions. The lack of running water and sanitation, plus malnutrition and inadequate housing, leads to deadly conditions in the slums and shanty towns that surround many cities in Africa, Asia and Latin America. The spread of infectious diseases in these areas where so many people live in such close physical proximity is a critical public health issue. When combined with high unemployment rates and inadequate schools, these public health issues create a poor quality of life for many of the city's residents. In many cities, such as Lagos, Nigeria, residents of slums face eviction as the land on which they are built is valuable and needed for new developments by the government.

ACTIVITY: Life in a megacity: podcast it

ATL

- Collaboration skills: Delegate and share responsibility for decision-making; Make fair and equitable decisions

In pairs, and using the information on this page and your own research, create a 3–5-minute podcast that **explores** the positives and negatives of megacities and the impacts that they have on individuals and societies. You may wish to create your podcast in the style of an interview or discussion programme. Be as creative as you like! Listen to some examples, such as those in the BBC 'People Fixing the World' series, to give you an idea of style: http://bit.ly/FixWorld

You should include relevant examples and case studies where necessary and produce a script to accompany the recording of your podcast.

In general, the format of a podcast is:

1 **Welcome message**
Greet your listener and **identify** the name and purpose of your podcast.
2 **Theme music**
A short piece of music could help set the tone for your podcast.
3 **Preview**
Tell listeners what to expect from your podcast.
4 **Features**
The main content of the show.
5 **Conclusion**
The closing of your podcast. Outro music.

Think about:
- how long each segment of the podcast should last
- the order of presentation
- music excerpts to include between segments
- who will listen to the podcast (your audience).

◆ Assessment opportunities

◆ In this activity you have practised skills that are assessed using Criterion A: Knowing and understanding and Criterion C: Communicating.

Is population growth destructive or can it be viewed as a driver for development?

ACTIVITY: Population essay

■ ATL

- Communication skills: Structure information in summaries, essays and reports
- Organization skills: Use appropriate strategies for organizing complex information
- Critical-thinking skills: Consider ideas from multiple perspectives; Develop contrary or opposing arguments

Reflecting on what you have explored in this chapter, create a 1,000–1,500-word response to the following question:

'Is population growth destructive or can it be viewed as a driver for development?'

You should:
- **State your opinion in the introduction and refer back to it throughout your writing so that there is a clear thread to your response.**
- **Create a balanced response which considers both sides of the argument, coming to a clear and persuasive conclusion.**
- **Use evidence in the form of examples, figures and statistics to support your argument and justify your points.**
- **Consider the views of Malthus and Boserup and make reference to these in your response.**
- **Compile a bibliography of the sources you have used.**

◆ Assessment opportunities

- In this activity you have practised skills that are assessed using Criterion A: Knowing and understanding, Criterion C: Communicating and Criterion D: Thinking critically.

Reflection

In this chapter, we have **examined** the complexities of population change and **identified** how this impacts individuals and societies. We have **explored** how population change is measured with a focus on models and have **identified** some key significant individuals responsible for prominent demographic theories. We have **recognized** that population change is a key cause of social and environmental change and **considered to what extent** it can be viewed as a driver for development.

Use this table to reflect on your own learning in this chapter.					
Questions we asked	Answers we found	Any further questions now?			
Factual: How and why does population growth differ between different regions of the world? What are the causes and consequences of forced migration and internal displacement? What are the consequences of megacity growth for individuals and societies?					
Conceptual: How has population changed over time and how can it be measured? Can population change be managed?					
Debatable: Is population growth destructive or can it be viewed as a driver for development?					
Approaches to learning you used in this chapter	Description – what new skills did you learn?	How well did you master the skills?			
		Novice	Learner	Practitioner	Expert
Communication skills					
Collaboration skills					
Organization skills					
Media literacy skills					
Critical-thinking skills					
Learner profile attribute(s)	Reflect on the importance of being balanced for your learning in this chapter.				
Balanced					

6 How does population change affect individuals and societies?

Systems | *Sustainability, innovation and revolution* | *Scientific and technical innovation*

7 Can urban systems and environments be managed sustainably?

○ **Sustainable** living in future urban communities will require new ideas, **scientific and technical innovation** and **systems**, and a **revolution** in our way of life.

Figure 7.1 Sustainable Development Goal 11

CONSIDER THESE QUESTIONS:

Factual: What is sustainable development? What are the main problems urban areas face? Where can sustainable cities be found?

Conceptual: How can the city be viewed as a system? What is the relationship between innovation and sustainability?

Debatable: Can a truly sustainable city exist?

Now **share and compare** your thoughts and ideas with your partner, or with the whole class.

IN THIS CHAPTER WE WILL …

- **Find out** how cities can be viewed as systems and how some cities are taking steps to become more sustainable.
- **Explore** the concept of sustainability and how scientific and technological innovation are impacting on this.
- **Take action** by trying to raise awareness of the Sustainable Development Goals.

168 Individuals & Societies for the IB MYP 4&5: *by Concept*

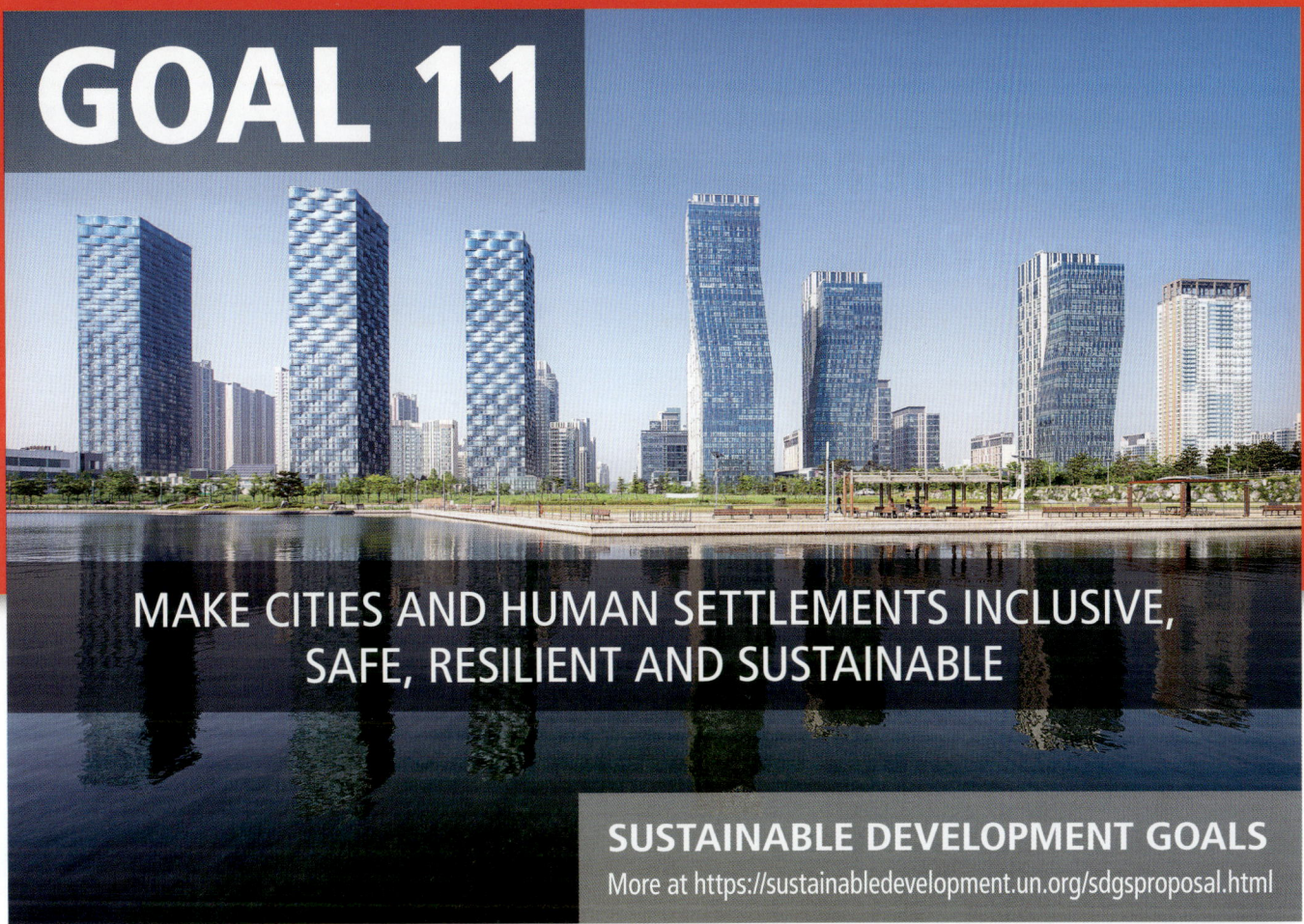

GOAL 11

MAKE CITIES AND HUMAN SETTLEMENTS INCLUSIVE, SAFE, RESILIENT AND SUSTAINABLE

SUSTAINABLE DEVELOPMENT GOALS
More at https://sustainabledevelopment.un.org/sdgsproposal.html

■ **These Approaches to Learning (ATL) skills will be useful ...**
- Communication skills
- Collaboration skills
- Organization skills
- Critical-thinking skills
- Creative-thinking skills

◆ **Assessment opportunities in this chapter:**
- Criterion A: Knowing and understanding
- Criterion B: Investigating
- Criterion C: Communicating
- Criterion D: Thinking critically

● **We will reflect on this learner profile attribute ...**
- Risk-takers – approaching uncertainty with forethought and determination; working independently and cooperatively to explore new ideas and innovative strategies; being resourceful and resilient in the face of challenges and change.

SEE–THINK–WONDER

Looking at the two images in Figure 7.1. What do you see? What do they make you think? What do they make you wonder?

We began to explore the issue of sustainability in cities in *Individuals and Societies for the IB MYP 1* and in the first chapter of this book. In this chapter, we will deepen our understanding of the concept and explore the notion that sustainable living in future urban communities will require new ideas, innovative systems and a revolution in our way of life.

KEY WORDS

carbon footprint
development
oxymoron
subjective
sustainable

7 Can urban systems and environments be managed sustainably?

What is sustainable development?

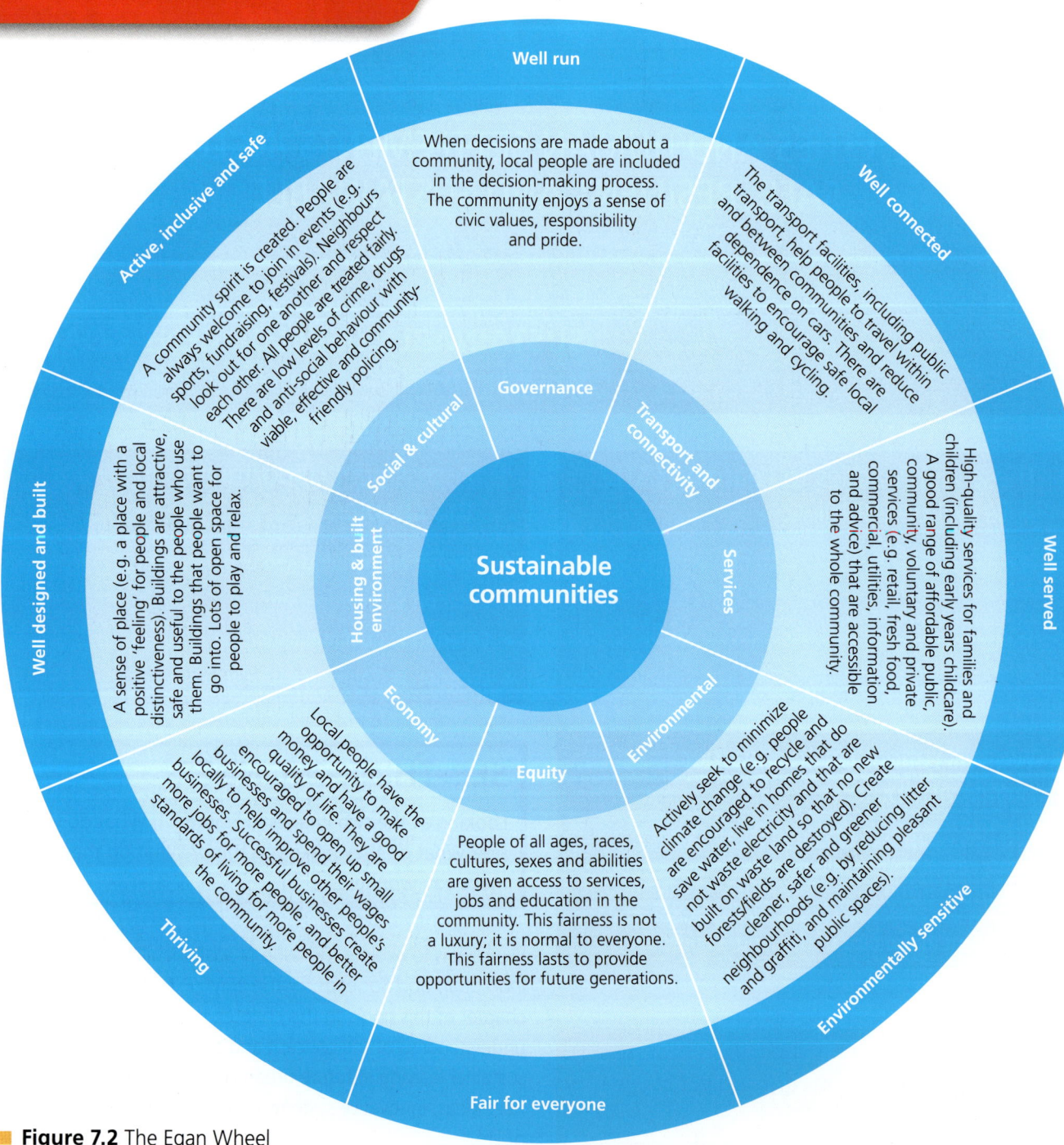

Figure 7.2 The Egan Wheel

THE EGAN WHEEL

In 2004, Sir John Egan was asked by the deputy prime minister of the UK to examine how communities could be more sustainable. Egan suggested that sustainable communities must meet 'the diverse needs of existing and future residents, their children and other users' by offering choice. As part of his work he introduced the Egan Wheel (Figure 7.2).

The Egan Wheel has eight components and can be used as a tool against which to **evaluate** cities and urban areas.

ACTIVITY: Applying the Egan Wheel to your local community

ATL

- Critical-thinking skills: Use models and simulations to explore complex systems and issues; Consider ideas from multiple perspectives

Taking the eight criteria of the Egan Wheel in Figure 7.2, develop a scoring system to grade your local community in terms of sustainability.

For example, your scoring system for the category of 'well served' may look like this, with 1 being low and 6 being high.

Criterion	6	5	4	3	2	1	
Quality nurseries and/or childcare	6	5	4	3	2	1	None
Quality primary school	6	5	4	3	2	1	None
Good range of local shops	6	5	4	3	2	1	No local shops
Easy to get local information	6	5	4	3	2	1	Difficult to get local information
Health services accessible	6	5	4	3	2	1	Health services not local
Good range of other services for all groups	6	5	4	3	2	1	Limited services for some groups, e.g. elderly, youth, family

Figure 7.3 Scoring system

After scoring your community for each category, reflect and suggest which of the eight aspects of the Egan Wheel you feel is in most need of improvement. **Justify** your reasons for this decision.

Remember, your opinions may be different from those of your classmates, even when you are considering the same community, and that is OK! There is no right or wrong answer as this is a subjective measurement – your views will be based on or influenced by personal feelings, tastes and opinions, and these obviously differ from person to person.

◆ Assessment opportunities

- In this activity you have practised skills that are assessed using Criterion C: Communicating and Criterion D: Thinking critically.

7 Can urban systems and environments be managed sustainably?

SUSTAINABLE DEVELOPMENT GOALS

In 2015, the United Nations replaced the earlier Millennium Development Goals with the 17 Sustainable Development Goals (SDGs). One of the targets for these goals is to create more sustainable cities and communities by helping urban areas to become more self-reliant and operate efficient systems for promoting the positive well-being of their citizens.

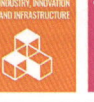

■ **Figure 7.4** Sustainable Development Goals

! Take action: SDG research and feedback

■ ATL

- Communication skills: Paraphrase accurately and concisely
- Collaboration skills: Take responsibility for one's own actions

! Watch this video 'Malala Introducing the World's Largest Lesson': https://vimeo.com/138852758

! With a partner, you will focus on some of the 17 goals. Find out three key things that make each of these global goals so important. Search **UN SDGs** to get you started.

! When you have completed your research, feed back to the class the importance of your goals and then, as a class, vote on which goal you think is the most important.

! It is important that everyone knows about the Sustainable Development Goals and the **British Council** are playing a big part in trying to raise awareness. They are encouraging young people to design a campaign poster to highlight a goal and why it is important to the public. You could choose one of the goals you researched or maybe the one that your class voted as the most important. Share your poster with a global audience by tweeting it @Schools-On-Line with the hashtag #sdgs.

◆ Assessment opportunities

◆ In this activity you have practised skills that are assessed using Criterion A: Knowing and understanding.

SDG goal 11

- Half of humanity – 3.5 billion people – live in cities today [2015]
- By 2030, almost 60 per cent of the world's population will live in urban areas
- 95 per cent of urban expansion in the next decades will take place in the developing world
- 828 million people live in slums today and the number keeps rising
- The world's cities occupy just 3 per cent of the Earth's land, but account for 60–80 per cent of energy consumption and 75 per cent of carbon emissions
- Rapid urbanization is exerting pressure on fresh water supplies, sewage, the living environment, and public health
- But the high density of cities can bring efficiency gains and technological innovation while reducing resource and energy consumption

Source: United Nations Development Programme

www.undp.org/content/undp/en/home/sustainable-development-goals/goal-11-sustainable-cities-and-communities/targets/

SOURCE A

'More than half of the world's population now live in urban areas. By 2050, that figure will have risen to 6.5 billion people – two-thirds of all humanity. Sustainable development cannot be achieved without significantly transforming the way we build and manage our urban spaces.

The rapid growth of cities in the developing world, coupled with increasing rural to urban migration, has led to a boom in mega-cities. In 1990, there were ten mega-cities with 10 million inhabitants or more. In 2014, there are 28 mega-cities, home to a total 453 million people.

Extreme poverty is often concentrated in urban spaces, and national and city governments struggle to accommodate the rising population in these areas. Making cities safe and sustainable means ensuring access to safe and affordable housing, and upgrading slum settlements. It also involves investment in public transport, creating green public spaces, and improving urban planning and management in a way that is both participatory and inclusive.'

Source: United Nations Development Programme

DISCUSS

Using Source A, what you have **explored** in Chapter 6 and your prior knowledge, think about and **discuss** whether the idea of a sustainable city is an **oxymoron**.

How can the city be viewed as a system?

> **▼ Links to: Sciences and Mathematics**
>
> Data analysis of this kind is an important source of information when looking at effects over large geographical regions and over time. Using graphs enables us to visually **identify** any trends, and also spot any anomalies (or 'outliers') in data – as seen in Chapter 6 with the work of statistician Hans Rosling (see page 154). In Chapter 2 of *Mathematics for the IB MYP 2* you may have explored the various ways in which statistics can be used to reveal the 'hidden' truth, but also to obscure the truth. In Chapter 2 of *Sciences for the IB MYP 3*, we explored the ways in which data have been used to **identify** human impacts on climate change. You can also find out more of the science behind these impacts in Chapters 10 and 11 of *Sciences for the IB MYP 4&5*.

It is evident that making urban areas more sustainable is a pressing concern for our society today but in order to begin to understand ways in which this may be realized we first need to understand how cities and urban areas can be viewed as a system.

In his 1997 work *Cities for a Small Planet*, Richard Rogers identified two major city types: the unsustainable linear city and the sustainable circular city.

As you can see from Figure 7.5, the linear system is seen as unsustainable whereas in the circular city system, the outputs are re-processed, therefore having less of an environmental impact and making the city more sustainable.

When thinking about the sustainability of cities, it is important to consider their **carbon footprints**. A carbon footprint is a measure of the impact our activities have on the environment. It measures all the greenhouse gases produced in all our activities and then compares them to an equivalent in units of carbon dioxide. While carbon dioxide (CO_2) is a very important contributor to **anthropogenic** global warming, it is not the only greenhouse gas – for example, methane (CH_4) causes 20–30 times the warming effect per unit mass, although there is much less methane in the atmosphere than carbon dioxide. The world average carbon footprint is about 6 metric tonnes of carbon dioxide per person per year.

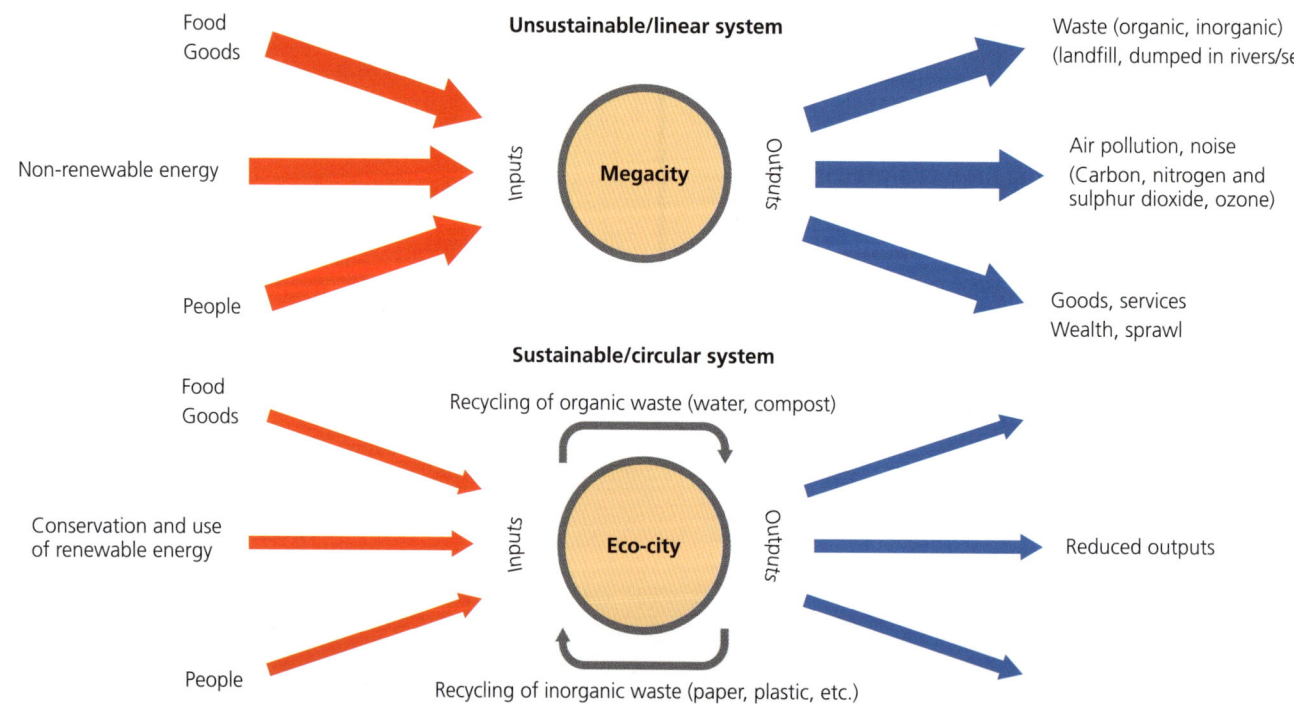

■ **Figure 7.5** A linear city and circular city

ACTIVITY: Carbon footprints

ATL

- Critical-thinking skills: Interpret data; Draw reasonable conclusions and generalizations

1. Use the following link to the WWF's carbon footprint calculator to work out an estimate for your own carbon footprint: http://footprint.wwf.org.uk/
   Share your results with the class and rank the results from highest to lowest.
   Reflect on the following and record your answers:
   - Are you surprised at your carbon footprint? Are you surprised where you ranked within your class?
   - List any areas you identified where you can make changes that would reduce your carbon footprint.
2. Look at Table 7.1, which shows the 20 countries with the highest metric tons of CO_2e per capita. CO_2e, or carbon dioxide equivalent, is a standard unit for measuring carbon footprints. The idea is to express the impact of each different greenhouse gas in terms of the amount of CO_2 that would create the same amount of warming. In this way, a carbon footprint consisting of lots of different greenhouse gases can be expressed as a single number.
   - **Identify** any general trends you think that the data shows.
   - **Identify** any anomalies in the data that do not fit the trends you have described.
   - **Discuss** what these countries may have in common that would cause them to have higher carbon footprints.
   - In your opinion, suggest the extent to which the carbon footprint is a reliable measure of the sustainability of a country.

◆ Assessment opportunities

◆ In this activity you have practised skills that are assessed using Criterion D: Thinking critically.

Table 7.1 Carbon footprint by country

Country	1990	1995	2000	2005	2010	2013
World	5.62	5.4	5.41	5.85	6.15	6.27
Kuwait	37.32	73.13	65.64	76.41	62.47	54.41
Brunei	48.33	46.38	46.49	44.83	46.88	46.84
Niue	16.4	16.8	19.05	24.3	28.65	45.6
Qatar	29.75	37.3	41.58	52.1	39.13	36.82
Belize	29.05	29.84	28.55	28.11	28.29	28.15
Oman	22.0	22.92	27.97	25.84	27.82	27.43
Bahrain	27.27	29.64	29.19	27.78	24.4	25.4
Australia	28.06	27.28	30.84	27.6	25.39	25.06
United Arab Emirates	40.13	38.81	34.89	32.13	23.73	24.59
Libya	21.16	19.43	18.66	20.91	22.63	21.47
Canada	20.22	20.69	22.12	21.94	20.47	20.94
Turkmenistan		13.39	14.51	18.13	19.44	20.93
Luxembourg			21.14	27.86	23.82	20.72
United States	23.23	23.26	23.86	22.92	20.97	19.9
Equatorial Guinea	0.52	2.7	13.89	25.83	21.33	19.15
Trinidad and Tobago	12.31	11.22	12.42	16.4	19.11	19.15
Grenada	16.29	16.63	17.28	17.82	18.39	18.89
Saudi Arabia	11.49	13.29	13.39	14.67	17.69	18.26
Kazakhstan		14.43	10.37	13.73	17.28	18.23
Estonia		14.4	13.53	15.77	17.3	17.66

Based on data for carbon dioxide, methane, nitrous oxide, perfluorocarbon, hydrofluorocarbon and sulfur hexafluoride emissions compiled by the World Resources Institute, divided by the population estimate by the United Nations (for July 1) of the same year

7 Can urban systems and environments be managed sustainably?

What are the main problems urban areas face?

Urban areas face a multitude of problems. The nature of these depends largely on whether the city is in a high- or low-income country, although some environmental issues such as air pollution and urban congestion, affect most cities. These issues, combined with overcrowding and noise, depletion of green space, waste overburden, poor quality housing, social deprivation, crime and inequality are often referred to as urban stress.

Urban congestion is broadly defined as demand for travel that exceeds the supply. This prevents free movement of traffic and many governments have been forced to revisit their policies in the face of growing demand for travel with a limited supply of services.

The rise in urban congestion can be attributed to rapid growth of cities in LEDCs, often without thorough forward planning in terms of infrastructure and more affluent populations which leads to an increase in vehicle ownership. In MEDCs, an increasing number of people live some distance from their place of work which means they are forced to commute and many choose to do this by car.

ACTIVITY: 3-2-1 Bridge

Before you watch the video on the right, think about the following question in relation to urban traffic congestion:

'Technology is driving change but will it change drivers?'

Copy the 3-2-1 Bridge template below and complete the first column. Write down three thoughts/ideas you have in relation to the statement above, then two questions and one analogy.

Now watch this video: 'What if everyone had a car' (**https://bbc.in/2IDQBTa**).

Complete your new responses to the statement after having watched the video.

Finally, create your bridge. **Explain** how your new responses connect to your initial ones.

YOUR INITIAL RESPONSES TO THE TOPIC	YOUR NEW RESPONSES TO THE TOPIC
3 Thoughts/Ideas	3 Thoughts/Ideas
3	3
2	2
1	1
2 Questions	2 Questions
2	2
1	1
1 Analogy	1 Analogy
1	1

■ **Figure 7.6** 3-2-1 Bridge template

Figure 7.7 Congestion in London and Mumbai

A 2016 study reported that the average US commuter wasted 42 hours a year stuck in traffic, and the case is similar, often worse, in LEDCS. As well as being an inconvenience to people and contributing to levels of **urban stress**, traffic congestion also contributes to air pollution.

Air pollution in urban areas is caused primarily by traffic idling in congestion. Exhaust emissions from vehicles result in the production of the main greenhouse gases: carbon dioxide, nitrogen oxides and particulate emission. This not only damages the urban environment by polluting the air but is possibly a cause of respiratory diseases. In developing countries, power plants, factories and in some cases forest fires also contribute to air pollution.

The World Health Organization (WHO) document 'Ambient air pollution: A global assessment of exposure and burden of disease' states that 'Air pollution represents the biggest environmental risk to health. In 2012, one out of every nine deaths was the result of air pollution-related conditions and of those deaths, around 3 million are attributable solely to ambient (outdoor) air pollution.'

Consequently, concerns about air pollution are reflected in the Sustainable Development Goals:
- Air pollution levels in cities is cited as an indicator for urban sustainable development in SDG 11.
- Access to clean energy – particularly clean household fuels and technologies – is highlighted as an indicator for sustainable energy in SDG 7.
- Mortality due to air pollution (ambient and household) is used as an indicator for health in SDG 3.

Air pollution is made worse by the depletion of green spaces in cities, which is driven by their growth and the need to improve infrastructure for their inhabitants.

Countries with the most and least polluted urban areas

Table 7.2 Most polluted urban areas (average PM 2.5 concentration)

1	Pakistan	115.7
2	Qatar	92.4
3	Afghanistan	86
4	Bangladesh	83.3
5	Egypt	73
6	UAE	64
7	Mongolia	61.8
8	India	60.6
9	Bahrain	56.1
10	Nepal	50
11	Ghana	49
12	Jordan	48
13	China	41.4
14	Senegal	40
15	Turkey	39.1
16	Bulgaria	38.6
17	Mauritius	38.1
18	Peru	38
19	Serbia	35.8
20	Iran	34.2

Table 7.3 Least polluted urban areas (average PM 2.5 concentration)

1	Australia	5.7
2	Brunei	6.6
3	New Zealand	6.8
4	Estonia	7.2
5	Finland	7.3
6	Canada	7.5
7	Iceland	8.2
8	Sweden	8.7
9	Ireland	8.8
10	Liberia	9.3
11	Japan	10
12	Bhutan	10
13	Norway	10.9
14	Malta	12
15	Portugal	12.3
16	Spain	12.4
17	United States	12.9
18	Monaco	13
19	Malaysia	13.2
20	Luxembourg	14

Figures above are micrograms per cubic metre of air ($\mu g/m^3$) PM 2.5 refers to fine particles (2.5 micrometres or smaller in diameter) produced by combustion, including motor vehicles, power plants, forest fires, and some industrial processes.

Source: www.telegraph.co.uk/travel/maps-and-graphics/most-polluted-countries/

▼ Links to: Sciences

You can find out more about the ways in which particulate air pollution is measured and its impact on health in Chapter 11 of *Sciences for the IB MYP 4&5*.

In addition to the environmental aspects of air pollution and urban congestion, urban areas also experience high levels of social and economic inequality. This inequality means extreme differences between poverty and wealth, as well as in people's well-being and access to jobs, housing and education. Inequalities occur in developed and developing countries. In MEDCs, inner-city areas usually experience the highest levels of inequality and deprivation because of the older housing and declining industry in these areas. Inner-city problems include: a high percentage of overcrowded households, higher death and infant mortality rates, social segregation and persistent unemployment. These social problems combine with a range of economic and environmental problems in the cycle of deprivation (see Figure 7.8).

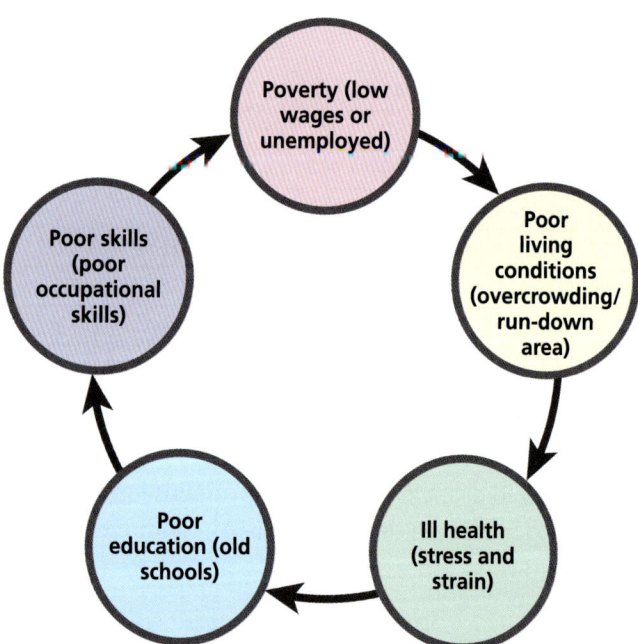

■ **Figure 7.8** The cycle of deprivation

LEDCs are troubled by overcrowding and the development of slums, shanty towns and squatter settlements, which are often the result of rural–urban migration, as discussed in Chapter 6. As well as the poor living conditions they afford residents, these settlements cause disputes about land use in growing cities where space is at a premium.

Where can sustainable cities be found?

'If you want to make life better for people make the cities better for people.' – Jaime Lerner (Mayor of Curitiba, see page 181)

Two main approaches are commonly used when exploring sustainable management in urban areas: to purpose build sustainable cities or towns, or to **retrofit** existing cities, including adapting systems and practices. We shall now consider the sustainable management of urban systems and environments through two case studies.

MASDAR CITY – AN EXAMPLE OF A PURPOSE-BUILT 'ECO-CITY'

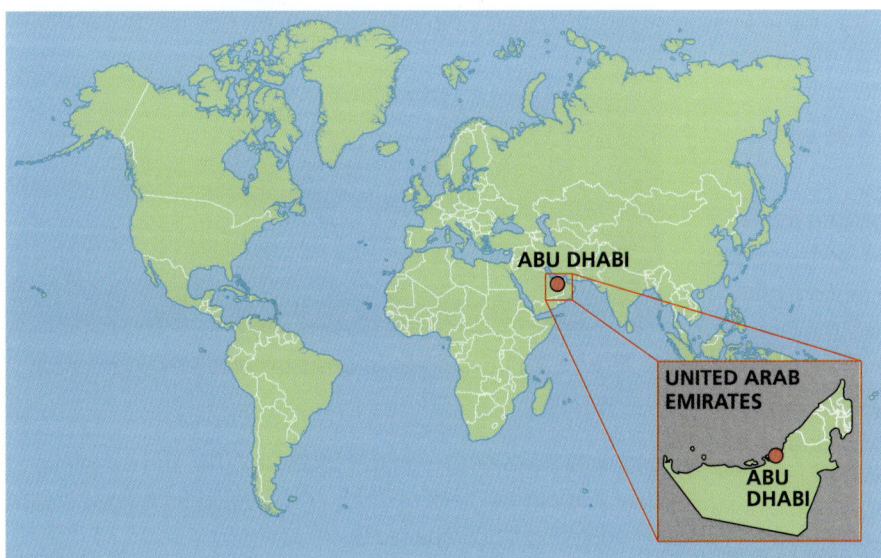

■ **Figure 7.10** Examples of sustainable technology in Masdar City

In 2008, Masdar City embarked on a mission to develop the world's most sustainable low-carbon city. Its overall aims were to:
- ensure a low carbon footprint during and after its construction
- be completely powered by renewable energy
- lead research and education into sustainable technology
- design the city streets and buildings to help create comfortable environments, reducing the need for air conditioning, heating and artificial light
- educate three-quarters of the 40,000 residents with five hours of sustainability education each year
- have pedestrianization within the city, without vehicles in the space. The transport network would be below ground.

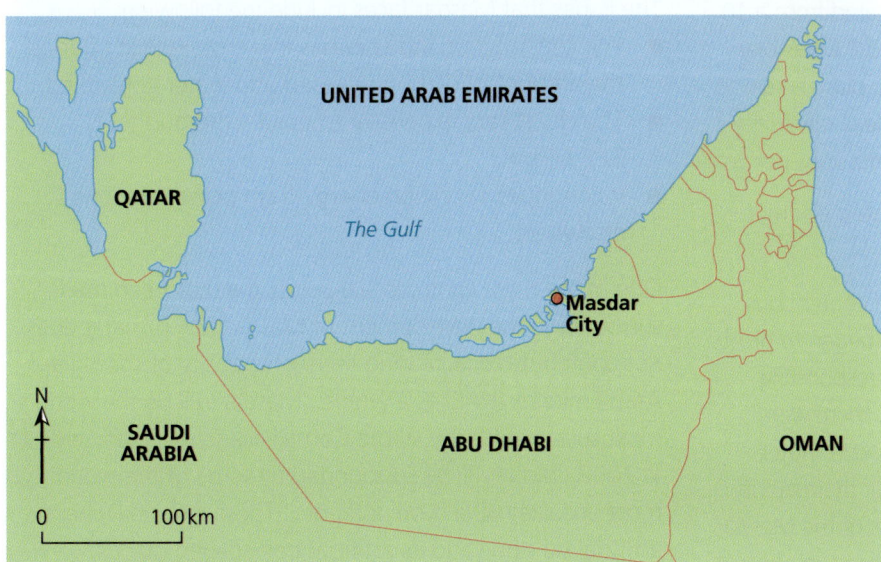

■ **Figure 7.9** Masdar City

Masdar City was designed to capture prevailing winds and offer naturally cool outdoor public spaces than those found elsewhere in Abu Dhabi. This was achieved with the help of traditional panelling and architecture to allow desert winds to circulate. It is reported by the company responsible for the design and building of Masdar City that the design of the walls of buildings has helped reduce demand for air conditioning by 55 per cent (https://masdar.ae/Site/ARCHIVE/Masdar-City/the-city).

Streets have been designed to be narrower than are usually found in similar environments, creating shaded, pedestrianized thoroughfares. The site of the development is raised slightly from the land, which architects say cools the air. The large public square at the centre of the development is cooled by a 45-metre-high wind tower, modelled on age-old Middle Eastern designs, which draws cool air from above and vents hotter air from below to push a cooling breeze through Masdar's streets. The buildings in Masdar on average consume 40 per cent less energy and water because Masdar City is in part powered by clean energy generated from a 10 MW (megawatt) solar power plant on site and 1 MW solar rooftop system. Harnessing the sun's rays, the plant is said to produce 17,500 MWh (megawatt hours) of clean electricity annually and divert 7,350 tonnes of carbon emissions per year.

Masdar is also almost car-free, using automated electric passenger cars and lorries.

So, has Masdar City been successful? This is a contentious issue as initial plans were changed as the city began to grow. The 2008 global crisis is thought to be partly responsible for the slow growth of Masdar City. By 2015, there were supposed to be 50,000 residents and 40,000 commuters but the population in 2017 was around 1,000, the majority of whom were students and faculty members of the Masdar Institute of Science and Technology, and Siemens employees. There were plans for windmills producing electricity on site,

Figure 7.11 Examples of unsustainable development in the UAE

and vegetables grown on its fringes. In 2010, the completion date was pushed back to 2025, and the project is now scheduled to be completed by 2030.

The issues that Masdar faces include the following:
- The construction industry has low sustainability due to the amount of carbon released and water consumed.
- The city is very expensive to build – the budget is $22 billion.
- It continues to rely on energy from power stations elsewhere.

One of the most controversial points that has been made surrounding the development of Masdar City is that it does not contribute to increasing the sustainability of the United Arab Emirates (UAE) as a whole. 'Masdar will be the world's most sustainable city,' wrote Cornell academic Brian Stilwell in 2008, 'but it will be surrounded by some of the world's most unsustainable developments.' These include Dubai's artificial ski slope and its artificial tree-shaped islands.

See www.masdar.ae/ for further information.

CURITIBA – AN EXAMPLE OF ADAPTING A CITY

Where?

Curitiba is the capital city of the Paraná state in southern Brazil.

> **Hint**
> Look at the way this case study on Curitiba is organized, using subheadings, and compare it with the case study on Masdar. Think about which you prefer and which you would find more useful when you are making notes.

What?

The city has a population of approximately 2 million. It has been transformed from an agricultural to a manufacturing city through sustainable planning and in 2010 was awarded the Global Sustainable City Award. The overall aims of its planners are to improve the environment, reduce pollution and waste, and improve the quality of life of residents.

When?

The city has had an urban master plan since 1968 and when Jaime Lerner became mayor. In 1971, he was instrumental in developing Curitiba's sustainability.

How?

The city has a budget of $600 million to spend every year and is moving towards sustainability in various different ways.

Reduced car use

There are five main arterial traffic roads into and out of the city. These routes have a central bus lane that is totally dedicated to two-directional public transport, rather than the car. This speeds up the journey for commuters on the bus and boosts the number of passengers per bus from 1,000 per day to 2,000. The arterial roads are also used as growth corridors for the urban and economic growth of the city.

Figure 7.12 Curitiba

The bus system is called the Bus Rapid Transit (BRT) and is cheaper to run than a tube system, making it more sustainable. The BRT, with its triple-section 'bendy buses' in the dedicated bus lanes, is used by 80 per cent of travellers. The same cheap fare is paid for all journeys, which helps poorer residents.

There are also over 200 km of bike paths in the city. The bus system and bike paths are so popular that car use is 25 per cent lower than the national average. The city has one of the lowest air pollution levels in Brazil.

Figure 7.13 A bus in Curitiba

7 Can urban systems and environments be managed sustainably?

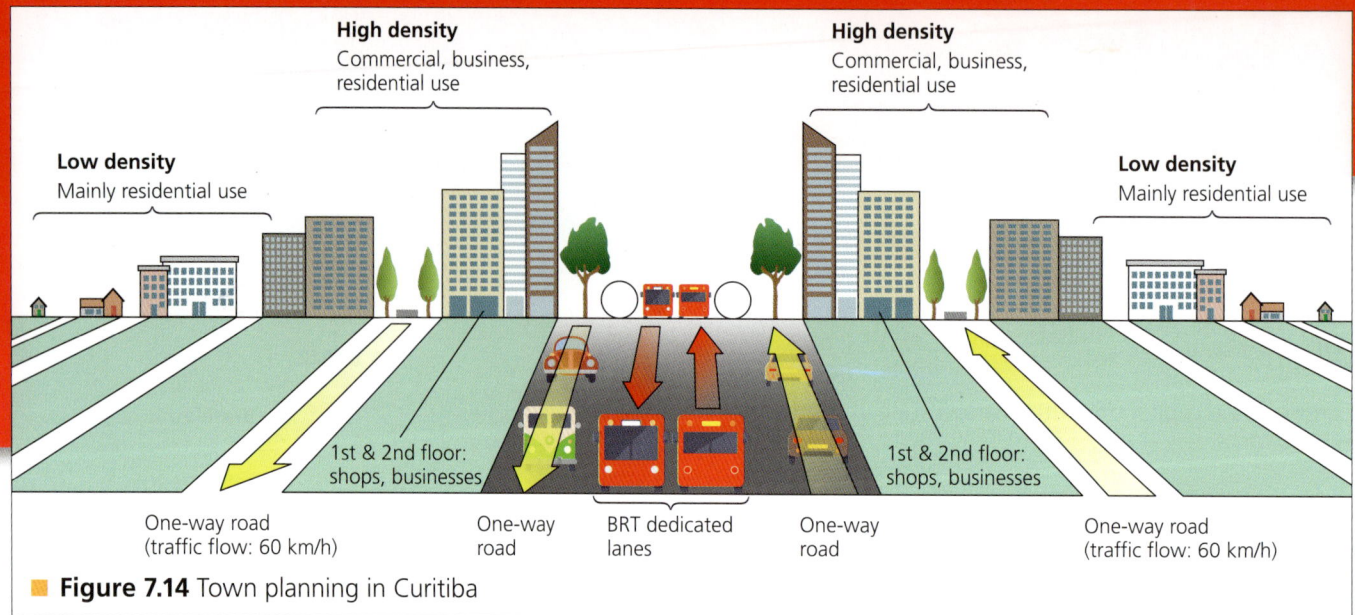

■ **Figure 7.14** Town planning in Curitiba

■ **Figure 7.15** Aerial view of an avenue in Curitiba

Open spaces and conserved natural environments

Green space has increased from 0.5 m² per person to 52 m² per person. The city has over 1,000 parks and natural areas, many of which are in areas prone to flooding so the land that cannot be used in other ways remains useful. Residents have planted 1.5 million trees and builders get tax breaks if their projects include green space.

Good recycling schemes

In Curitiba, 70 per cent of rubbish is recycled. Paper recycling saves 1,200 trees per day. Residents are given food and bus tickets for recycling in areas where rubbish collection is difficult.

In addition to the case studies we have explored, there are many examples of cities modifying elements of their systems to increase sustainability. Search **London's congestion charge**, **Hong Kong's vertical greening** and **Copenhagen city bikes**. Also see www.cyclescheme.co.uk for details of how the UK government is offering **incentives** for people to cycle to work.

MEET A SIGNIFICANT INDIVIDUAL: JAIME LERNER (1937–2021)

'Jaime Lerner is an architect and urban planner ... and three-time mayor of Curitiba, Brazil. He led the urban revolution that made the city renowned for urban planning, public transportation, environmental social programs and urban projects. He served as governor of Paraná State twice and conducted an economic and social transformation both in the urban and rural areas. His international awards include the highest United Nations Environmental Award (1990), Child and Peace Award from UNICEF (1996), the 2001 World Technology Award for Transportation, and the 2002 Sir Robert Mathew Prize for the Improvement of Quality of Human Settlements. In 2010 Lerner was nominated among the 25 most influential thinkers in the world by Time magazine.'

■ **Figure 7.16** Jaime Lerner

Source: http://jaimelerner.com.br

See what he has to say about sustainability here:
www.ted.com/talks/jaime_lerner_sings_of_the_city/transcript

DISCUSS

Which do you think is the most effective method of increasing sustainability in urban areas: building new eco-cities or retrofitting and improving old ones? Are the two methods even comparable?

What is the relationship between innovation and sustainability?

There is no question that innovation and technology play huge roles in many aspects of our lives today. Inventors and developers are always trying to harness new technologies to use in the quest to improve sustainability, particularly in urban areas.

In his talk, 'A future beyond traffic gridlock' (**https://youtu.be/MsLuQM5V3FA**), Bill Ford discusses his vision for a congestion-free future. His talk was published on 20 June 2011 and since then his vision has gone some way to being realized with the advent of **Waze**.

Figure 7.18 Bill Ford

Figure 7.17 The Waze app

The initial ideas behind Waze came about in 2007 although Waze was not created until 2009. On its webiste (**www.waze.com/about**), Waze claims to develop solutions that help people make better choices such as taking the fastest route or leaving at the right time, to sharing daily commutes using a global community of over 115 million people. Waze is 100 per cent powered by users who have the option to report information via hands-free voice control, which is activated by waving a hand in front of the smartphone screen (and initiating the phone's proximity sensor). Saying prompts such as 'report traffic' triggers the app to provide alerts on traffic flow. The app alerts users to reported obstacles on their route (e.g. road closures, accidents, police traps), and then redirects them to their destination. Waze was bought by Google in 2013 for US$1.3 billion, adding social data to its mapping business. It is thought that there are now as many as 50 million users.

Uber, founded in 2009, is another form of smart technology. It is essentially an app which connects drivers with passengers

Figure 7.19 The Uber app

directly, instead of through a centralized booking service or by hailing a car in the street. It was launched in San Francisco and now operates in excess of 644 cities in 77 countries. In 2019 it was valued at US$82.4 billion.

Uber claims that by reducing the need for car ownership, it contributes to a reduction in the overall number of cars on the road, thus reducing carbon emissions, minimizing traffic congestion on roads and eventually disincentivizing vehicle ownership in the first place. 'A city that welcomes Uber on to its roads will be a city where people spend less time stuck in traffic or looking for a parking space,' Uber CEO Travis Kalanick said at Uber's five-year anniversary celebration.

'It will be a cleaner city, where fewer cars on the road will mean less carbon pollution – especially since more and more Uber vehicles are low-emission hybrid vehicles.'

This claim has yet to be substantiated with strong evidence but environmental sustainability is an angle that Uber is keen to explore with their development of 'Uberpool', a ride sharing service which they claim helps the environment through further reducing the number of cars on the road and thus decreasing congestion and air pollution. They have also introduced a fleet of electric cars in Portland, Oregon and are carrying out controversial research into self-driving vehicles. Despite their sustainability claims, Uber have faced controversy in many places around the world over several issues including pricing, driver conditions and passenger safety. In 2017, and again in 2019, Uber was stripped of its licence to operate in London after Transport for London (TfL) found it was 'not fit and proper' to hold a private hire operator licence. In September 2020, it was granted an 18-month licence, and in March 2022, a 30-month licence was granted.

MEET A SIGNIFICANT INDIVIDUAL: VEENA SAHAJWALLA

■ **Figure 7.20** Veena Sahajwalla

Professor Veena Sahajwalla is the director of the Centre for Sustainable Materials Research and Technology (SMaRT) at the University of New South Wales and has been referred to as a 'waste warrior' and 'The woman who loves garbage'. She is the inventor of 'green steel', the environmentally friendly technology for recycling end-of-life rubber tyres to replace coal and coke in steelmaking. This has meant that more than 2 million tyres have been diverted from landfill and greenhouse gas emissions have been reduced. She continues her work in recycling and waste materials and strives to find ways to reuse waste, especially electronic waste. She is also passionate about raising the profile of females in the science and technology industry and has helped set up a programme to encourage and inspire Australian girls and young women to pursue degrees and careers in science and technology, so they can succeed in an innovation-driven future (see www.science.unsw.edu.au/50-50).

ACTIVITY: Design your own piece of smart technology

■ ATL

- Creative-thinking skills: Use brainstorming and visual diagrams to generate new ideas and inquiries; Consider multiple alternatives, including those that might be unlikely or impossible; design new machines, media and technologies

Working either on your own or with a partner, use the ideas on this page, elsewhere in this book and your prior knowledge to help you create a form of smart technology that aims to increase an element of sustainability in urban areas.

You could generate an idea for an app, a piece of machinery or a new technology, or find a way of improving a piece of existing technology.

You should:
- **Brainstorm** and/or mind map initial thoughts and ideas.
- Select one area to focus on.
- Develop a research question.
- Carry out some initial research into your chosen field, remembering to make a note of your sources.
- Outline how your invention will work and how it will increase sustainability in urban areas through the creation of an action plan.
- **Identify** any possible problems or limitations of your invention.
- **Evaluate** the process and results of the investigation.
- Be ready to share your ideas with the rest of the class in the form of a pitch to potential investors. How will you persuade people to get on board with your technology and invest money into your product? Don't forget to pre-empt potential questions any prospective investors may have and prepare answers for these.

Search **sustainable technology** and **smart cities** to **explore** websites which may provide you with some inspiration.

◆ Assessment opportunities

- In this activity you have practised skills that are assessed using Criterion B: Investigating and Criterion C: Communicating.

▼ Links to: Design

Criterion A: Investigate: explain the problem and discuss its relevance, critically investigate the problem, evaluating information from a broad range of appropriate, acknowledged sources.

Criterion B: Design: generate a range of feasible designs and justify the chosen design.

Criterion C: Plan: produce a plan that contains a number of detailed, logical steps that describe the use of resources and time.

You should also refer to the MYP Design cycle in developing your ideas.

Can a truly sustainable city exist?

ACTIVITY: Sustainability essay

■ ATL

- Communication skills: Structure information in summaries, essays and reports
- Organization skills: Use appropriate strategies for organizing complex information
- Critical-thinking skills: Consider ideas from multiple perspectives; Develop contrary or opposing arguments

Reflecting on what you have explored in this chapter and your prior knowledge, create a 1,000–1,500-word response to the following statement:

'With reference to named examples, discuss to what extent cites can be sustainable.'

- **Discuss:** Offer a considered and balanced review that includes a range of arguments, factors or hypotheses. Opinions or conclusions should be presented clearly and supported by appropriate evidence.
- *To what extent:* Consider the merits or otherwise of an argument or concept. Opinions and conclusions should be presented clearly and supported with empirical evidence and sound argument.

You should:
- **State your opinion in the introduction and refer back to it throughout your writing so that there is a clear thread to your response.**
- **Create a balanced response which considers both sides of the argument, coming to a clear and persuasive conclusion.**
- **Use evidence in the form of named case studies, examples, figures and statistics to support your argument and justify your points.**
- **Consider social, environmental and economic aspects of sustainable development.**
- **Compile a bibliography of all of your sources.**

◆ Assessment opportunities

- In this activity you have practised skills that are assessed using Criterion A: Knowing and understanding, Criterion C: Communicating and Criterion D: Thinking critically.

Reflection

In this chapter, we have **examined** the urban environment as a system and **explored** the ways in which innovation is playing a role in increasing sustainability. We have **discussed** the notion of sustainability – what it means and how it has been developed over time to encompass more than just environmental concerns. We must now continue to **evaluate** whether urban systems and environments can be managed sustainably in a way that allows the urban system to improve the lives of its residents while maintaining environmental integrity.

The significant individuals examined in this chapter have all approached uncertainty with forethought and determination, working independently and cooperatively to explore new ideas and innovative strategies, and being resourceful and resilient in the face of challenges and change.

Use this table to reflect on your own learning in this chapter.					
Questions we asked	Answers we found	Any further questions now?			
Factual: What is sustainable development? What are the main problems urban areas face? Where can sustainable cities be found?					
Conceptual: How can the city be viewed as a system? What is the relationship between innovation and sustainability?					
Debatable: Can a truly sustainable city exist?					
Approaches to learning you used in this chapter	Description – what new skills did you learn?	How well did you master the skills?			
		Novice	Learner	Practitioner	Expert
Communication skills					
Collaboration skills					
Organization skills					
Critical-thinking skills					
Creative-thinking skills					
Learner profile attribute(s)	Reflect on the importance of being a risk-taker for your learning in this chapter.				
Risk-takers					

Systems | *Resources; Choice; Perspective* | *Personal and cultural expression*

8 How do we decide what to produce?

○ **Different individual choices** by consumers and producers in a market **system** lead to the allocation of **resources**.

CONSIDER THESE QUESTIONS:

Factual: What economic systems exist to allocate resources? What is an economy?

Conceptual: How do markets work? Why and how do governments intervene in markets? What is a recession and why is it bad?

Debatable: To what extent do markets improve our lives? What is the role of the government in shaping the economy?

Now **share and compare** your thoughts and ideas with your partner, or with the whole class.

■ **Figure 8.1 (a)** A farm producing oranges in Valencia; **(b)** Motor vehicles as a significant source of pollution; **(c)** An open air primary school in Kenya

○ IN THIS CHAPTER WE WILL …

■ **Find out** how the market system works under capitalism to allocate limited resources.
■ **Explore** different markets for goods and services and how they might (or might not) allocate resources effectively.
■ **Take action** by using film in a creative way to campaign for the reduction of plastic pollution.

Individuals & Societies for the IB MYP 4&5: by Concept

SEE–THINK–WONDER

Look at the images on these pages. What do they make you think about how we produce and sell goods and services? What do they make you wonder about the effectiveness of our economic systems?

These Approaches to Learning (ATL) skills will be useful …

- Communication skills
- Information literacy skills
- Critical-thinking skills
- Media literacy skills

We will reflect on this learner profile attribute …

- Risk-takers – discovering that people take risks to start their own businesses and engage in the economy in a productive way.

KEY WORDS

economics	prices
government	resources
markets	society

Assessment opportunities in this chapter:

- **Criterion A:** Knowing and understanding
- **Criterion B:** Investigating
- **Criterion C:** Communicating
- **Criterion D:** Thinking critically

THINK–PAIR–SHARE

Think of examples of goods that have a positive impact on society.

- **Why do they have an impact?**
- **How are these goods different from other goods that might not have the same impact?**

Do the same for goods that have a negative impact.

We have access to limited resources on our planet – everything exists in a finite quantity. This is the fundamental economic problem and is referred to as scarcity. **Economics** is the study of how limited resources are allocated between competing demands by different groups in society. Throughout history, societies have evolved with different ways of making decisions about what to produce, how to produce and for whom to produce. These systems differ on the basis of how large a role the government has in making these decisions. There are two different types of economy:

- command economies
- market economies.

8 How do we decide what to produce?

What economic systems exist to allocate resources?

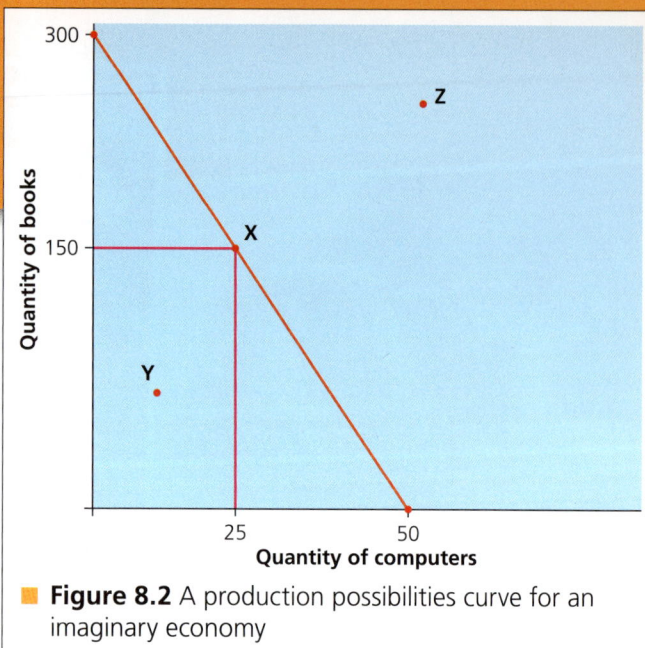

Figure 8.2 A production possibilities curve for an imaginary economy

Although there may be large quantities of some resources, nothing is limitless in volume. Scarcity is the fundamental economic problem – how do we satisfy the largest number of people in the best way possible with a limited quantity of resources? There are four main categories of resources, also known as the **factors of production**:

- Land – all the planet's natural resources
- Labour – the work we as individuals can do
- Capital – all resources produced by humans
- Entrepreneurship – the skills that some people possess, such as being creative and risk-taking, that enable them to start a business

Imagine that a country can only produce two goods, for example books and computers. We can plot what might be produced if the country uses all its resources. Figure 8.2 illustrates the country's production possibilities frontier or curve. It shows that, if all resources are used, then the country has various options; it can produce:

- 300 books and 0 computers
- 50 computers and 0 books
- 150 books and 25 computers (point X).

> ### THINK–PAIR–SHARE
>
> Look at Figure 8.2. What do you think points X and Y represent for the country and the way that it uses resources? How does the country make a decision regarding what to produce? What happens if the country changes its mind? What do you think point Z represents?

How resources are allocated and the methods that are used to distribute them are an important part of any society. These issues also cause some of the biggest tensions between different groups in society – they are related to the things we like to buy, the different incomes we earn, who gets what in life, and what we expect our government to do for us. The material we are about to explore also underlies major historical events such as the communist revolutions in Russia and China, and every national election that has ever taken place.

COMMAND ECONOMIES

A **command economy** is one in which decisions about what to produce, and how production is organized are made by individuals or groups of individuals who retain all the control over the production system. In the ancient world, and in civilizations such as Rome and Egypt, enslaved people were used to build large projects such as roads and the pyramids, and also to complete menial tasks in the home such as cleaning.

In medieval times, feudalism was the dominant system of production, in which the monarch and their lords retained ownership of all the land in the country, and the rest of the population existed as tenants of the land. The sole function of the tenants was to work the land, and grow food for the lords and their armies. Agriculture was the dominant economic activity.

The most recent system of production to develop that involved central planning was communism. In *The Communist Manifesto* (1848) and other texts, Karl Marx and Friedrich Engels responded to what they saw as the increasingly poor treatment of workers in major industrial cities such as London, Manchester and Paris. To them, capitalism did not seem to lead to the betterment of everyone's lives,

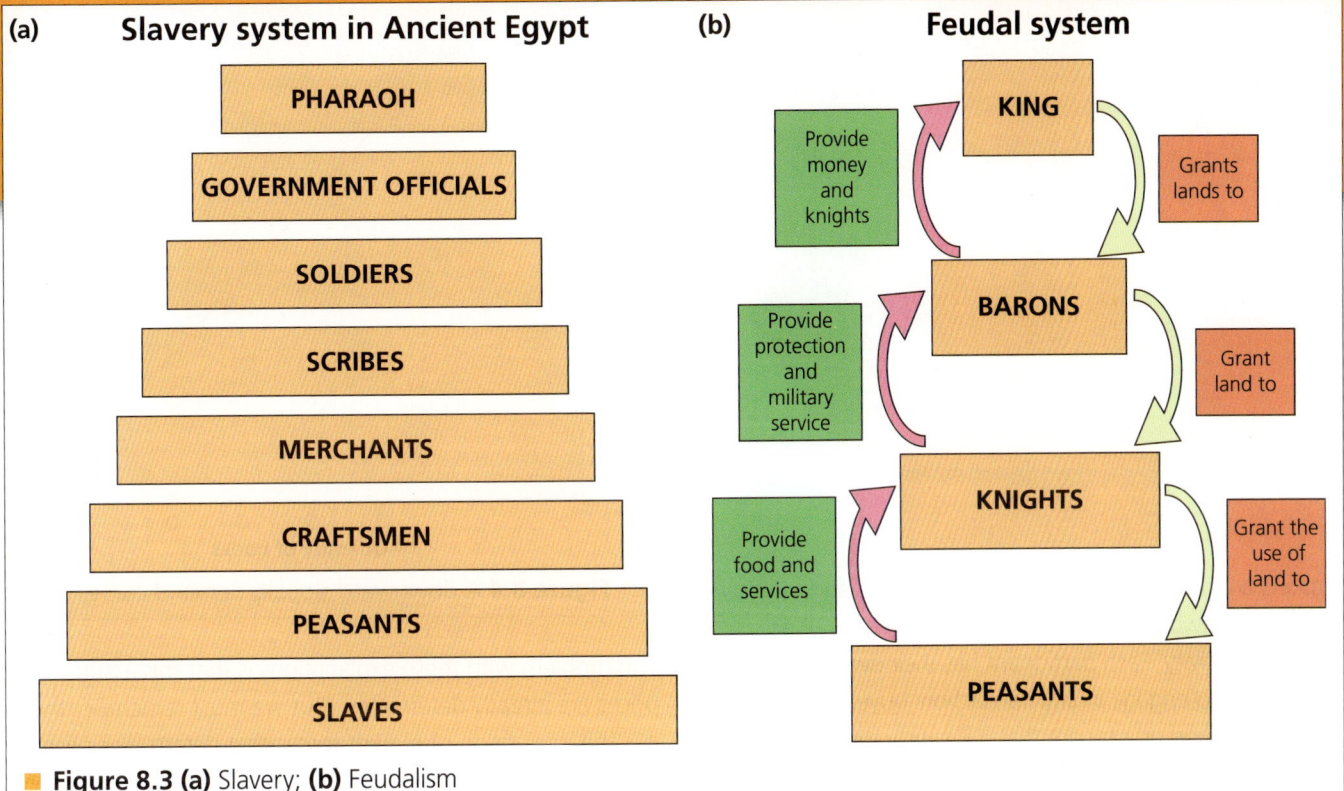

Figure 8.3 (a) Slavery; (b) Feudalism

rather to increasing inequality. They argued that capitalism would eventually lead to its own end: increased competition between businesses would lead to lower prices, and to businesses cutting workers' wages to save costs. This would eventually lead to a socialist revolution that would involve workers taking back control of production. You may remember from Chapter 6 in *Individuals and Societies for the IB MYP 3*, that in their original understanding, Marx and Engels predicted that after some time socialist government and the state would 'wither away', as all decisions would be made communally (collectively) by the people. However, no country that experienced socialist revolutions during the twentieth century reached this point and decisions about production continued to be planned centrally.

MARKET ECONOMIES

A market economy is the dominant system in the world today. Across much of Europe, from the Renaissance period onwards, a middle class of merchants, traders and skilled manufacturers began to grow. No longer tied to the land as peasants or serfs, they moved to the urban centres to work in manufacturing. This period – sometimes known as the early modern period – also saw civil war in Great Britain followed by a restoration of the monarchy, and a hundred years later, the American rejection of British monarchy and revolution in 1776. Shortly afterwards, the French Revolution removed King Louis XVI from the throne and beheaded him together with his wife, Queen Marie Antoinette. Important thinkers of the time included Adam Smith and Voltaire, for both of whom increased freedom from autocratic monarchies was crucial for the development of humankind. Growing groups of individuals who were neither peasants with no rights over private property, nor land-owning aristocracy, but working in or running secondary industries demanded the ability to determine their own economic futures and be able to make decisions about what to sell. We would now call this group within society the middle class.

THINK–PAIR–SHARE

True communist systems have never been achieved, and the world has mostly chosen market-based systems.

In pairs, choose one of the following questions. Think individually about your answers, and then share with your partner. **Summarize** your shared ideas and then share all the ideas as a class.

- For what reasons have groups of people wanted a socialist revolution?
- Why do some people still say they want a socialist revolution?
- Why do you think socialist revolutions might fail?
- Why might people prefer a capitalist to a communist economic system?

How do markets work?

MARKETS

Markets are defined as any place where buyers and sellers meet. These two groups of people form the basis of all economic activity. Each participant has their own reasons for wanting to engage in any transaction: buyers want to purchase a good or a service that will satisfy their wants or their needs, and sellers want to produce those goods in exchange for money that they keep as revenue and, after costs are covered, profit. People who are willing and able to be risk-takers and start their own businesses are called entrepreneurs.

When we make decisions about what we want to buy and sell, we must consider how much we value these items. It is extremely difficult to understand all the reasons why we are motivated to produce and buy the things we do, but how we value them is roughly captured by the price we are willing and able to pay for them or sell them for. In market systems, decisions over production are governed by the **price mechanism**.

DEMAND

We can represent the relationships between price and quantity graphically. For consumers, who **demand** goods and services, there is a negative or inverse relationship between the price of goods and the quantity that they want to buy. This is known as the **law of demand**: when the price increases, the quantity demanded falls, and vice versa. There are different ways of explaining why this is.

There are two reasons for the downward sloping demand curve, which require us to consider how prices determine the amount we buy. The first reason is that we will buy more of something because it is cheaper. The second reason is that lower prices make us relatively richer and goods that are similar, that could substitute the good in question, are relatively more expensive.

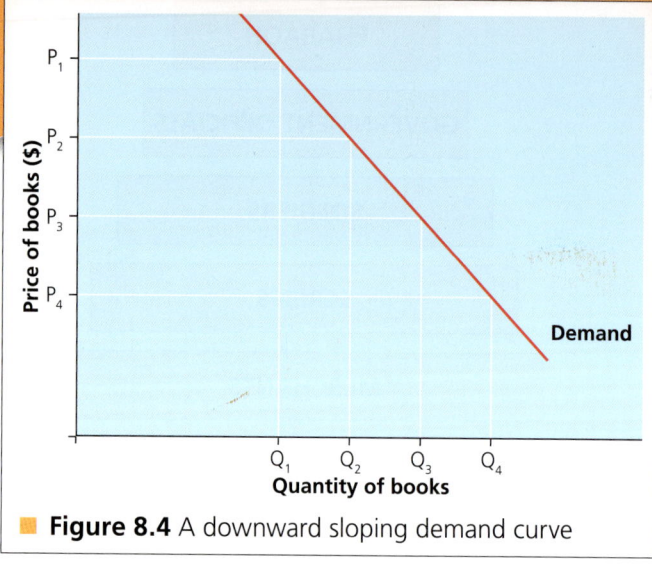

■ **Figure 8.4** A downward sloping demand curve

The problem with these explanations is that this assumes prices are already determined. But we must remember that it is the interaction of market forces that determines prices.

SUPPLY

Supply is a more straightforward part of the model, and there is only one explanation for the upward sloping curve (see Figure 8.5). There is a strong incentive to produce more goods when the potential to earn more revenue increases. Prices will have to rise to allow producers to cover their increased production costs.

THE SUPPLY AND DEMAND DIAGRAM

We are now ready to combine supply and demand and form our market. By plotting both curves on the graph, we can see how prices are determined. There is an intersection between supply and demand that results in an **equilibrium**, or balance. This point is where the market price and quantity sold are set.

Notice in Figure 8.6, which shows the market for rice, that it is only at the equilibrium price that the quantities demanded and supplied will be equal. At higher prices, at P_2, suppliers will want to increase production to Q_2 but this price is too expensive for consumers who will demand less at Q_3. This situation is called a *surplus*, an *excess in supply* or a *glut*. When this occurs, there will be downward pressure on the price of the good or service in order to correct the disequilibrium or distortion. The seller will not be able to sell all the goods, and so it makes sense to reduce the price and sell more.

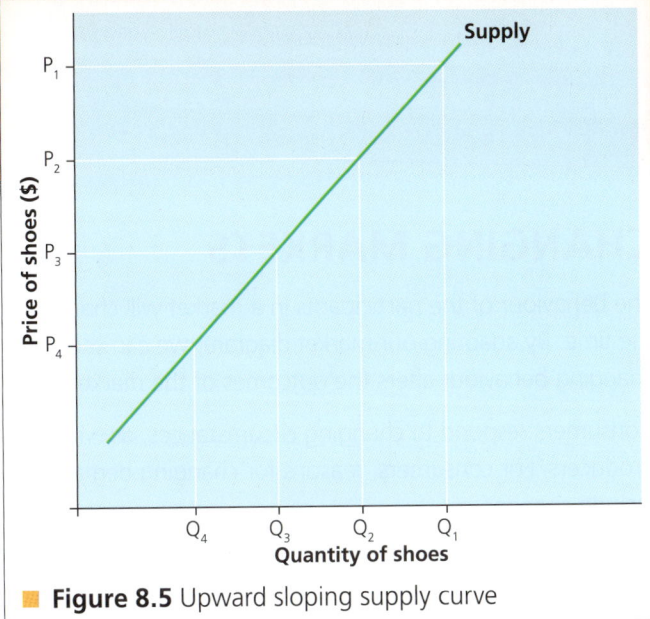

Figure 8.5 Upward sloping supply curve

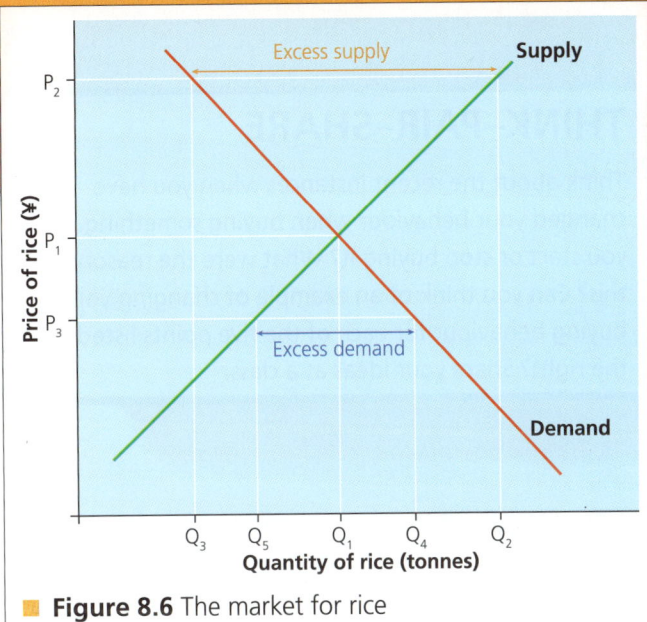

Figure 8.6 The market for rice

Conversely, when prices are set too low, in this case at P_3, quantity demanded will have risen because rice is now cheaper, but producers will struggle to produce the same volume as before. This situation is called a *shortage* or an *excess in demand*. Consumers will demand Q_4 volume of goods, but producers are only able to produce Q_5. When this happens, there will be upward pressure on prices. Think about it like an auction room – the goods will go to the highest bidder. If there is only a limited volume of goods with respect to the number of buyers, then the price will continue to rise until someone wins.

ACTIVITY: Find out about rice

ATL

- Information literacy skills: Access information to be informed and inform others

Rice is a **staple food** in 39 countries. Many people in these countries struggle on low incomes so the price of rice is very important.

Inquire further into the market for rice, and consider the following:
- **Identify** the current price for rice.
- **Explore** the recent changes to rice prices.
- **Explain** what happened to rice prices in 2008.
- **Analyse** the consequences of changing rice prices.

A useful source of information might be the Food and Agriculture Organization (FAO) and their Rice Market Monitor (RMM).

◆ Assessment opportunities

- In this activity you have practised skills that are assessed using Criterion A: Knowing and understanding and Criterion B: Investigating.

Figure 8.7 Rice paddy in Chiang Mai, Thailand

8 How do we decide what to produce?

THINK–PAIR–SHARE

Think about the recent instances when you have changed your behaviour when buying something. Did you start or stop buying it? What were the reasons for this? Can you think of an example of changing your buying behaviour for each of the five points listed on the right? Share your ideas as a class.

CHANGING MARKETS

The behaviour of the participants in a market will change all the time. By adapting our market diagram, we can see how changing behaviour alters the outcomes of the market.

Consumers respond to changing circumstances, as will producers. For consumers, reasons for changing demand include changes in:

- income
- taste
- prices of substitute and complementary goods
- the number of buyers
- consumers' expectations.

When any of these changes occur, there will be an increase or decrease in demand at each price. Figure 8.9 shows each determinant of demand and how it affects the position of the demand curve. For example, a new advertising campaign for clothing may change people's tastes towards that clothing (hopefully, for the business, the effect is positive). It is very important to remember that changing prices will only cause a movement *along* the demand curve (Figure 8.4), and so will not be included in our list of factors that cause the demand curve to shift.

The price that the market sets is known as the clearing price. At this price, there will be no shortages or surpluses, and all disequilibrium is corrected. However, prices will also change, often. When this happens, changing prices will be a sign that there is disequilibrium in the market, and you must try to establish the cause of the change. Rising prices will always be the result when the quantity demanded exceeds the quantity supplied, and falling prices will be the result of quantity supplied being larger. This price mechanism is what was originally referred to by Adam Smith as the 'invisible hand' in his *Theory of Moral Sentiments* in 1759, and in his seminal work, *The Wealth of Nations* published in 1776.

MEET A SIGNIFICANT INDIVIDUAL: ADAM SMITH (1723–90)

■ Figure 8.8 Adam Smith

Adam Smith was a Scottish economist who is known as the 'father of economics'. He was born in Kirkcaldy in Scotland in 1723. He went to one of the best schools in Scotland, and at the age of 14 went to study moral philosophy at the University of Glasgow. He went on to Balliol College, Oxford, as a postgraduate but found his studies there less stimulating than in Glasgow and so returned north. He was even punished at Oxford for reading materials that weren't approved of! His early works were the first to express economic ideas with the sole motive of understanding how nations acquire wealth. Prior to this point, most economic thinking was driven by wanting to understand morality, or issues of religious significance. For example, these 'moral economists' might have asked what kind of price setting or productive activity is accepted in the Bible? While the phrase 'the invisible hand' is only referred to three times across all of his work, he was the first to understand markets and the price mechanism as self-regulating and independent in the way that we are still familiar with today. He also understood the selfish behaviour that drives market participants to achieve their goals, and campaigned for the government to make appropriate interventions according to the principles he discovered. What learner profile attributes do you think Adam Smith most exemplified?

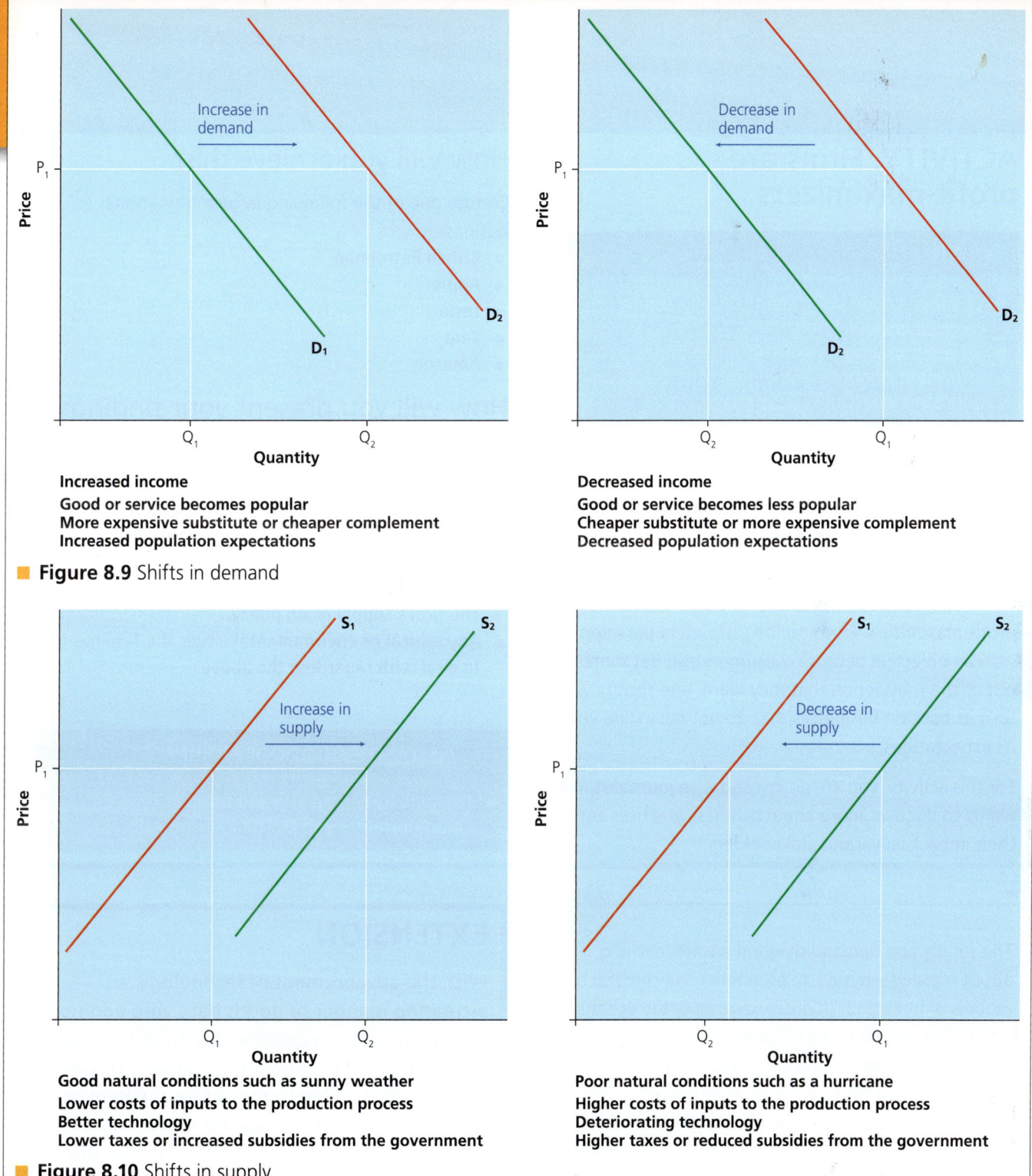

Figure 8.9 Shifts in demand

Figure 8.10 Shifts in supply

Producers also have their reasons for changing the amount they can supply at each price. The determinants of supply include:

- natural conditions, such as weather
- costs of inputs to the production process
- technology
- taxes and **subsidies** from the government.

All four of these determinants relate to production costs for the firm, and this is one of the major concerns for a business and its stakeholders. In economics, we often make assumptions about what drives behaviour, so that our models are a little more simple to work with. In the case of producers, we assume that all firms are profit-maximizers.

8 How do we decide what to produce?

ACTIVITY: Firms are profit-maximizers

■ ATL

- Communication skills: Read critically and for comprehension
- Information literacy skills: Evaluate and select information sources and digital tools based on their appropriateness to specific tasks

What is your goal?

What are the implications of firms being profit-maximizers? Are firms always capable of acting on the needs of their consumers and the wider community?

It is usually assumed in economics that all firms are profit-maximizers. Firms can be justified in pursuing such an objective because consumers also get something out of the transaction that they want, and society will turn its back on businesses that do not fall in line with its expectations.

For this activity, you are an investigative journalist, who wants to discover more about business practices and their impact on various stakeholders.

How will you achieve this?

Choose one of the following large multinational businesses:
- British Petroleum
- Apple
- Tesla
- Zara
- Amazon

How will you present your findings?

Write an editorial for a newspaper about your chosen business and its approach to corporate social responsibility. Your editorial should cover the following:
- Where the firm manufactures its products
- What kinds of workers the firm employs
- Where it sources component parts from
- The firm's supply chain policy
- Any ethical or environmental issues the firm has had to deal with regarding the above.

◆ Assessment opportunities

◆ This activity can be assessed using Criteria C: Communicating and D: Thinking critically.

The supply and demand diagram we are learning about is called a model. In economics, we construct models of behaviour in order to simplify the economic world that we live in. At all times, many forces will be acting on consumers, producers and markets. This is too complicated to study, so we must simplify it. This involves holding some variables constant to observe changes in others, and also involves making quite big assumptions about participants' behaviour. In science, it is much easier to control variables in experiments since we are able to conduct them in a controlled laboratory environment, but economists must develop models in the more complex environment of the real world.

EXTENSION

With the advancement of technology, an increasing number of goods have zero additional (marginal) cost to replicate, although they may have high costs of production initially. This means that it costs nothing to reproduce the item once it exists. These goods include TV shows on Netflix, downloadable tracks on iTunes, and scientific papers published on eJournal sites such as JSTOR and EBSCOhost. What are the implications of this? How might the idea of zero marginal cost goods fit with Marx's ideas about falling costs of production and problems for capitalism? For some answers and ideas watch the following video: https://youtu.be/3xOK2aJ-0Js or search **Rifkin Zero Marginal Cost Society**.

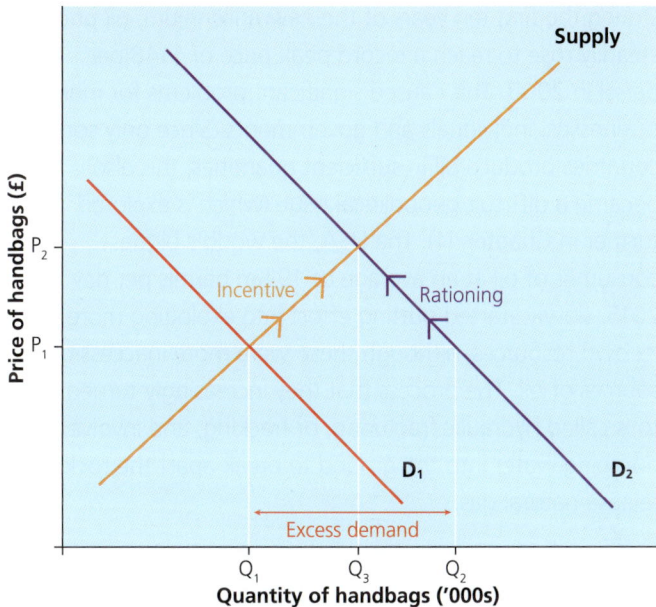

■ **Figure 8.11** The effect of an increase in demand on the market for handbags

Combining these factors affecting supply and demand, we are ready for the final stage in supply and demand analysis. Let's start with an increase in demand.

The handbag company Mulberry started in 1971, selling leather handbags to working women at fairly reasonable prices. The iconic 'Bayswater' handbag became popular during the 1990s with women who wanted luxury but didn't want to pay excessively high prices. As the company's sales grew, the decision was taken to remarket the brand to rival designers such as Dior, and prices for the handbag steadily climbed, for a time exceeding £1,000!

In Figure 8.11, you can see how increased demand for handbags affects the market. The increased popularity of the bag causes demand to increase from D_1 to D_2. At the old price level P_1, quantity demanded is now at Q_2, but the company is still supplying Q_1 number of handbags to the market. The disequilibrium, in this case excess demand, must be corrected by a price increase. There is an incentive for producers to increase production, causing an expansion along the supply curve from Q_1 to Q_3. In addition, the higher price will help to **ration** the limited number of bags between the increased number of people who want to buy them, and there will be a contraction in quantity demanded from Q_2 to Q_3.

Interestingly, the strategy to become an expensive luxury brand failed to win over its British consumers. Sales fell 29 per cent and profits reduced from £14m to £1.9m in 2015. Mulberry was eventually forced to rethink its pricing.

■ **Figure 8.12** A Mulberry store selling luxury handbags

During the first ten years of the new millennium, oil prices steadily rose to reach a record peak price of $148 per barrel in 2008. This caused significant problems for many businesses, individuals and governments. Since only some countries produce oil in sufficient quantities, this also became a difficult geopolitical issue (which is explored further in Chapter 11). The USA, the world's biggest consumer of oil at an average of 19.5m barrels per day in 2015, slowly started putting effort into exploiting more of its own resources, although these were more inaccessible sources of oil. The process that they increasingly turned to is called hydraulic fracturing, or fracking, and involves pumping water into the ground to break apart the rock and release natural gas.

In Figure 8.13, this practice corresponds to an outward shift in the supply curve from S_1 to S_2. A glut in the supply of crude oil to the world market, at the original high price of P_1, will exist until prices start to move downwards. There may be a time lag in this taking place, as contracts between businesses (and crude oil is sold business to business) are agreed long in advance and last for quite a long time. Eventually, however, prices will fall to P_2 and the market will clear at Q_3.

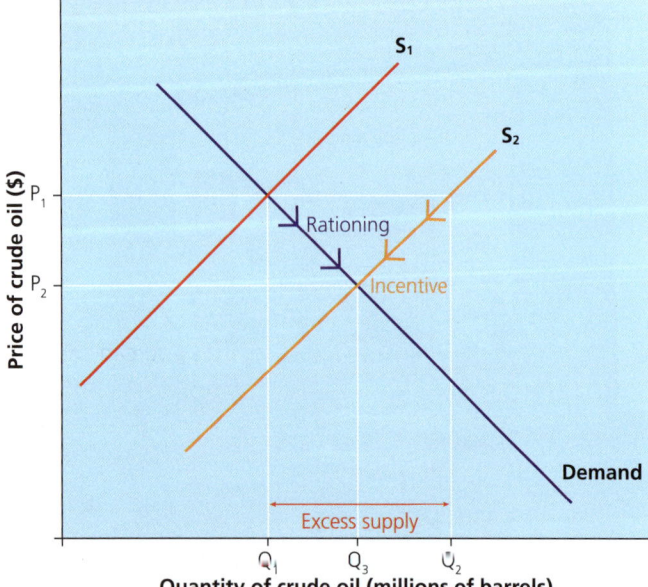

■ **Figure 8.13** The effect of a change in technology on the market for crude oil

■ **Figure 8.14** Pumpjacks extract oil from an oilfield in Kern County, California. About 15 billion barrels of oil could be extracted using hydraulic fracturing (fracking) in California

ACTIVITY: Practising the supply and demand diagram

ATL

- Information literacy skills: Use memory techniques to develop long-term memory

You will need:
- coloured pens
- a set of blank flash cards.
1 Make a **list** of some scenarios in which supply and demand is changing. You could include some real-life examples such as:
  - the market for olive oil in Italy in 2012
  - the global market for gold in 2011
  - crude oil prices in 2015
  - house prices in New Zealand since 2010.

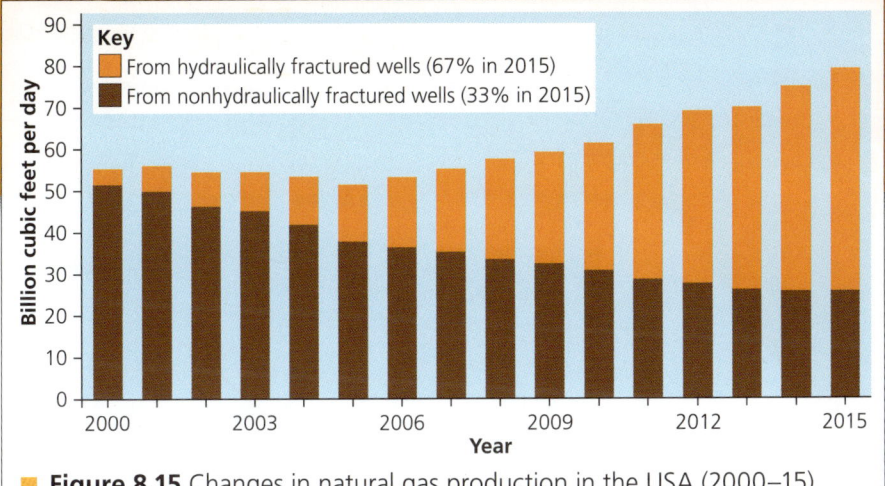

■ **Figure 8.15** Changes in natural gas production in the USA (2000–15)

Using flash cards to help you revise

Revision is a difficult, but important skill to master. It is important to be an active learner, not a passive one. Writing or reading notes once or twice will not ensure memory retention. Instead, you need to find ways to process the information and work with it. Flash cards are one good way of doing this. You can create flash cards for any subject and they can help you learn:
- quotations for literature
- verb conjugations and translations for language acquisition
- equations for maths and science
- definitions
- diagrams
- short explanations
- lists of facts.

2 On one side of the flash card write out what is happening in the scenario. For example, 'Italy experiences a particularly good season for growing olives in 2012'.
3 On the other side of the flash card, draw a diagram to **explain** the scenario.
4 Test yourself with your completed flash cards as often as possible, especially in the run-up to a timed assessment. You can also swap your flash cards with your friend and test each other.

Make sure you have enough flash cards completed to make a complete test of the material. You can also create flash cards for definitions, and the determinants of supply and demand.

◆ Assessment opportunities

♦ In this activity you have practised skills that are assessed using Criterion A: Knowing and understanding.

ACTIVITY: Supply and demand

■ ATL

■ Communication skills: Organize and depict information logically

Using Google News, find a news article about a change being experienced by a market. Prices could be changing, or there could be a shortage or surplus. Search terms might include **supply and demand**, **market** or any example of goods or services you can think of. Try to limit yourself to a simple example, like an agricultural crop, or a simple manufactured product. Once you have found your article:

1 Write a short **summary** of the article.
2 Using a supply and demand diagram, **explain** the scenario using the new price mechanism theory we have just acquired.

◆ Assessment opportunities

♦ In this activity you have practised skills that are assessed using Criterion A: Knowing and understanding.

8 How do we decide what to produce?

To what extent do markets improve our lives?

In an ideal situation, the outcomes of the market serve only those participating in the market – only the producers and consumers. However, there are instances in which people outside the transaction between consumers and producers are affected. When this occurs, the market is said to have failed. However, the situation can yield either positive or negative consequences.

An **externality** occurs when there is a positive or negative impact on someone outside of a transaction between buyers and sellers. This happens because other people might not value the production or consumption of goods in the same way as the buyer or seller.

Using a supply and demand diagram again (Figure 8.16), we can begin to see why market failure arises. An efficient market is one in which supply equals demand. At this point, the value or benefit that consumers derive from using each additional item or service, marginal private benefit, is the same as the additional cost of producing an additional unit, marginal private cost. Producers and consumers value the goods equally. If there are no positive or negative consequences of the goods, then society also values them in the same way. The private costs and benefits equal the social costs or benefits.

The diagram also shows how those participating in the market benefit from the market price and quantity. There are people who are lucky enough to afford more than the market price, and so the difference between that higher price (P_2 on this diagram, for instance) and the market price P_1 represents a surplus to those consumers. In addition, there will be producers who are productive enough to sell the goods at a lower price, such as P_3. These producers also enjoy a surplus. Every consumer along the demand curve down to the price, and every producer along the supply curve up to the price, experiences this. At the market price and quantity, the highest number of consumers and

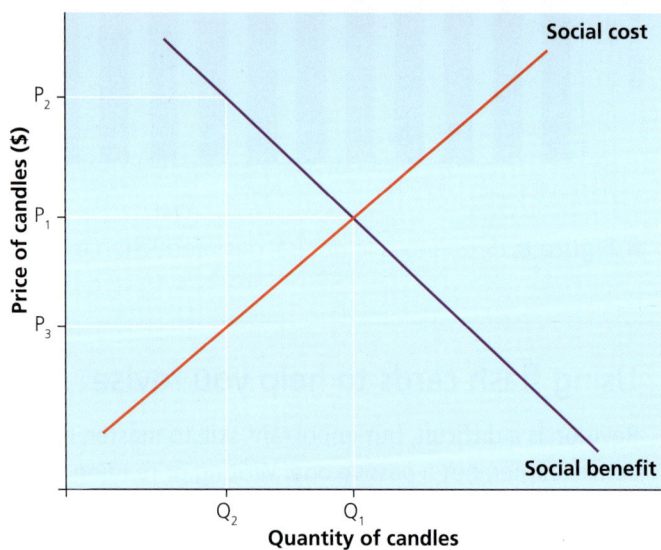
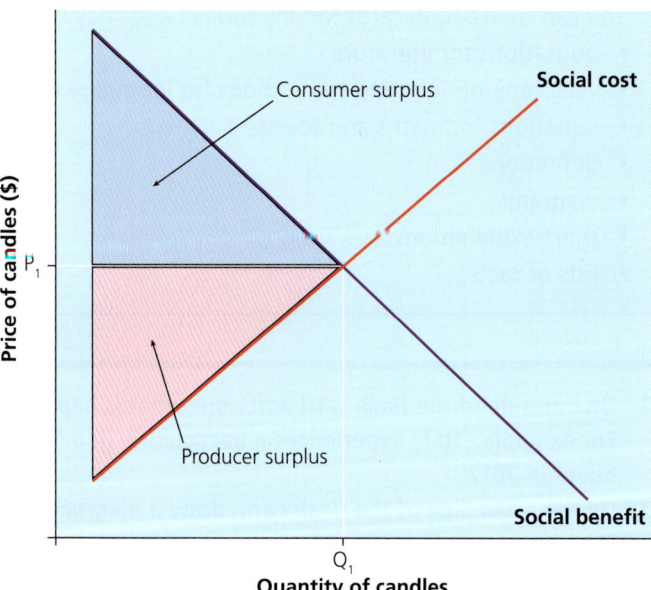

■ **Figure 8.16** An efficient market is one in which social costs equal social benefits, and supply equals demand

producers possible can enjoy the good, and **consumer surplus** and **producer surplus** is maximized. The sum of consumer and producer surplus is known as **community surplus**. This is considered **allocatively efficient** because resources have been used in the best possible way according to how market participants value this good or service.

But what happens when society does not value the market outcomes in the same way as private individuals and producers do?

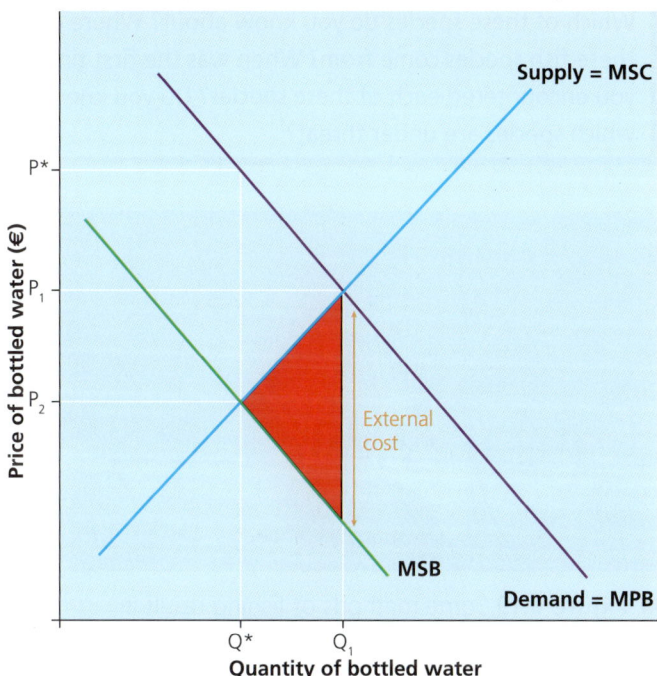

Figure 8.17 Negative externalities of consumption

NEGATIVE EXTERNALITIES

Negative externalities occur when society values the product or service less than producers or consumers of the goods. There are two types of negative externalities, those of:
- consumption
- production.

Negative externalities of consumption occur when the private benefit derived from the consumption of a product does not equal the social benefits of that private decision.

Every second, 20,000 bottles of water are produced for private consumption. While bottled water in many parts of the world is necessary, as so many parts of the world are still without safe water to drink, the developed world does have a suitable water system and bottled water is a luxury there. This is a tricky issue because regular consumption of clean water is necessary for maintaining your health.

The plastic that is discarded when we throw away plastic bottles has created a number of problems:
- Some chemicals used in plastic leak into the water system. Chemicals such as BPA (bisphneol A) are hormone disruptors and cause problems for our and the animal kingdom's reproductive systems.
- Plastic washes up on to beaches and ruins the natural environment.
- Plastic can break down into smaller particles (but does not biodegrade) and can be ingested by animals.

This is all represented in Figure 8.17. When we privately consume bottled water for whatever reason, the social benefits will not be the same as the private benefits – they will be less. This is because the price of bottled water does not cover the external costs of the plastic pollution. The external costs are represented by the vertical distance between the two parallel curves, and is indicated in orange. The overconsumption causes a failure to allocate resources efficiently, and community surplus is not maximized. This can be represented by the red triangle – this is the lost community surplus, which is also known as a **welfare loss**.

> ! **Take action**
>
> ! The Great Garbage Patch was mentioned in Chapter 5. It is an enormous pile of floating debris between the US coast and Hawaii, and contains mostly plastic.
>
> ■ **ATL**
>
> ■ Media literacy skills: Communicate information and ideas effectively to multiple audiences using a variety of media and formats
>
> 1 Visit the website https://www.youtube.com/watch?v=du7rE3sQ_tE and watch the video *Wasteland by Surfers Against Sewage*.
> 2 Consider the way in which Wasteland transmits its message. What is effective about the campaign. How can film and art be used to make a stronger impact?
> 3 Conduct an audit of your school's recycling methods, including the number of bins in each classroom, whether they are clearly marked and whether they are used by your classmates regularly.
> 4 Using the information you have gathered about your school's recycling habits, create a video to raise awareness about the issue of single-use plastics in your school community.
>
> ◆ **Assessment opportunities**
>
> ◆ In this activity you have practised skills that are assessed using Criterion A: Knowing and understanding, Criterion B: Investigating and Criterion C: Communicating.

THINK–PAIR–SHARE

Consider each of the following goods:
- cigarettes
- education
- a nightclub in a residential area.

If the free market produced these goods and sold them at a price without any government intervention, why might these goods be examples of market failure?

THINK–PAIR–SHARE

Consider each of the following commonly consumed species of fish:
- salmon
- cod
- tilapia
- prawns
- tuna
- mackerel
- pollock
- seabass.

Which of these species do you know about? Where do these fish species come from? When was the first time you encountered each of these species? Do you know which species are under threat?

Negative externalities of production refer to the external costs that arise from the production of a product.

With negative consumption externalities, private benefits exceed social benefits. In the case of negative production externalities, the marginal social costs (MSC) are bigger than the marginal private costs (MPC). This problem is shown using a supply curve (see Figure 8.18). The producers pay less to produce the product than society pays to deal with the consequences. A good example of negative production externalities is the market for fish.

Over 1 billion people are reliant on the seas and oceans as their primary source of income. Fish also forms an integral part of every country's cuisine and culture. In our globalized world, our knowledge of each other's cultures has changed profoundly, as has our interest in each other's food.

■ **Figure 8.19** Some methods of fishing result in overfishing

Our increasing interest in other cuisines means that our demand for fish species that come from far away has also increased. In addition, we have developed tastes for particular kinds of fish, and become less interested in types that are not familiar to us or are not readily available in plastic packaging in supermarkets.

In some parts of the world, there are no problems with using the resources that the seas provide, but, in addition to the overfishing described in Chapter 5, some industrial fishing methods have negative consequences:

- Using trawlers and nets results in more species being caught than are desired or allowed.
- Some species of seafood, such as scallops, are caught using dredgers. These are big claws that scratch along the bottom of the seabed to collect the produce.
- Dynamite or blast fishing uses explosives to kill large schools of fish. This ruins the surrounding environment.

POSITIVE EXTERNALITIES

It is not all negative, however. There are also positive externalities, and you are an example of one! Again, there are two types of positive externalities, those of:
- consumption
- production.

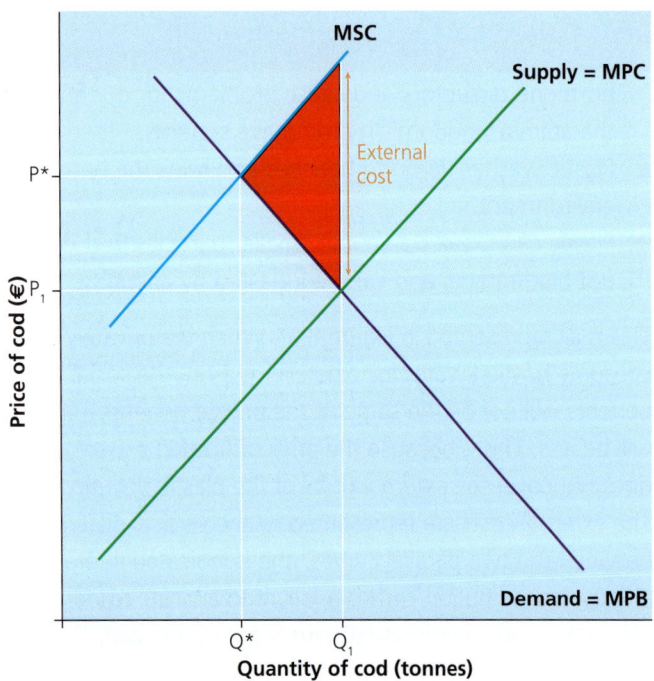

■ **Figure 8.18** Negative externalities of production

Positive externalities of consumption occur when the social benefits of someone consuming a product or service exceed the private benefits. Going to school means that, not only do you gain qualifications that will likely lead to a good job and income, but you will also contribute positively to society. More children becoming educated can lead to the following consequences:
- greater tax revenue for the government
- a more productive labour force
- lower rates of crime.

Returning to our market diagram, we only need to swap a few labels around. Positive consumption externalities are the result of greater social benefits than private benefits, and so the MSB (marginal social benefit) is placed above the MPB (marginal private benefit) or demand curve. The market produces where supply equals demand, and yields Q_1 number of school places. However, society would prefer a larger number of school places than the free market is able to provide. By setting a price for education, the market rations out education services and school places only to those who can afford the fees. Prices would need to fall along the demand curve to P* in order for Q_2 number of school places to be demanded.

Another very good example of positive externalities of consumption is a museum, and other such cultural venues or events. The free market would also under provide these to the market if a price was charged. Individuals gain knowledge of a country's history or gain positive feelings from looking at and appreciating art. There are many social benefits of individuals visiting these venues, including generating a happier and more aware society that might understand better what it means to be part of a social, national or cultural group.

Positive externalities of production occur when social costs are lower than private costs. This means that private firms pay for something that is enjoyed by others too. A great example is beekeeping. According to the Food and Agricultural Organization, we rely on pollinators, including 20,000 species of bees, for between US$235 billion and US$577 billion worth of annual global food production.

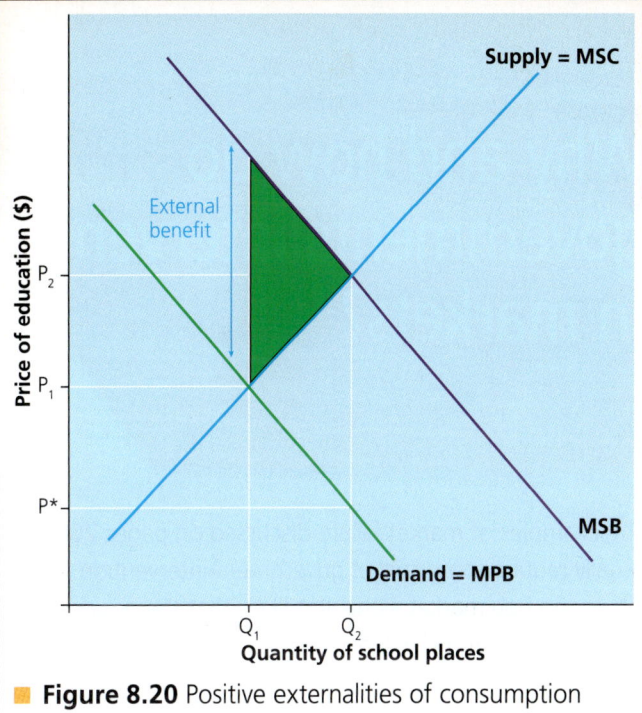

Figure 8.20 Positive externalities of consumption

When a farmer keeps bees for the production of honey, those bees will pollinate plants nearby. That includes such things as fruit trees. Apple growers, for instance, benefit greatly from having the bees nearby, while not having to pay the costs of keeping the bees themselves. Figure 8.21 shows that the beekeeper's costs in the market for honey will be MPC, but the apple grower, or grower of any other crop that requires the help of pollinators, will enjoy lower costs at MSC.

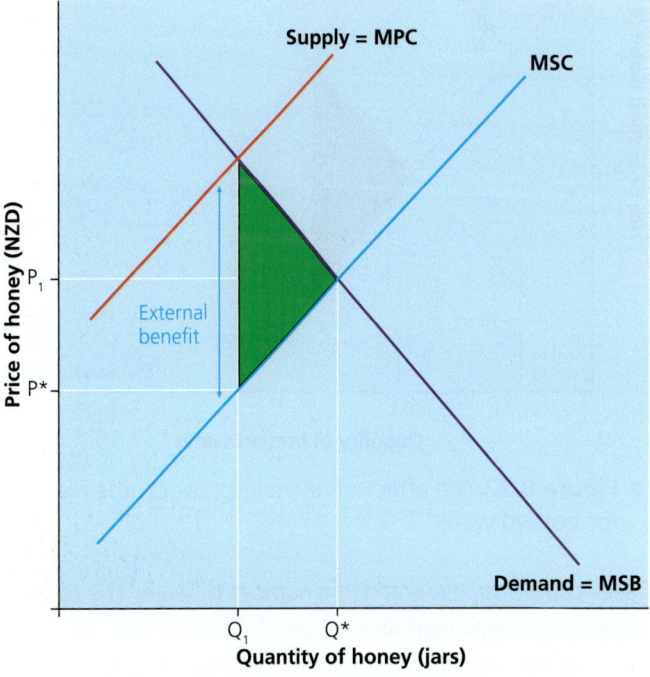

Figure 8.21 Positive externalities of production

Why and how do governments intervene in markets?

The examples of market failure discussed on pages 200–203 usually require some sort of government intervention. If left to the free market alone, it is likely that the goods will be under- or over-provided. In order to reduce production of the items we don't want, and encourage production of the items we do want, the government can influence the price mechanism to coax the market into behaving slightly differently.

as health care and the welfare system. There are usually different tax rates depending on the level of income.

The type of tax that is relevant to our discussion of markets here is called an **indirect tax**. An indirect tax works by taxing suppliers of goods or services, who then pass the tax on to consumers in the form of a price increase. The indirect tax is one of the non-price determinants of supply, and so shifts the supply curve inwards from Supply to S^{tax}.

This causes the equilibrium quantity of the product or service to fall to Q^*, in line with what society would consider allocatively efficient. In addition, prices will be forced upwards to P^*, but prices that producers receive fall to P_2 because $P^* - P_2$ has to be paid to the government.

TAXES

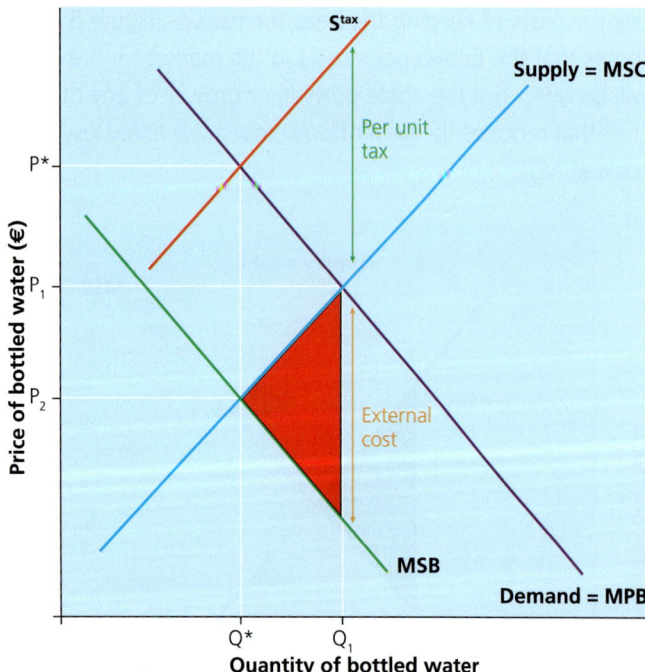

■ **Figure 8.22** The effect of an indirect tax on the market for bottled water

Taxes can be implemented in a number of ways. The most frequently complained about type of tax is income tax. Workers earning over a certain amount have to pay a share of their income to the government to pay for things such

SUBSIDIES

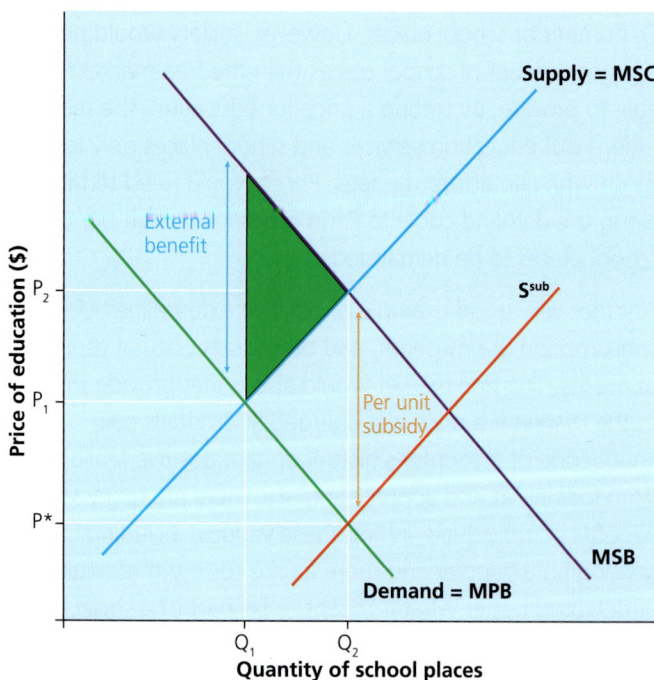

■ **Figure 8.23** The effects of a subsidy on the market for school places

Subsidies are used to increase the production of a product, when the effects of the product are positive for society. Subsidies are per unit payments that lower the production costs for producers, and so the market quantity is able to increase (from Q_1 to Q_2 in Figure 8.23). The price that producers receive also increases from P_1 to P_2, but the price that consumers pay falls to the socially optimum level P^*.

Governments have to use their tax revenues (from income taxes and sales taxes) to fund subsidies. They have to make careful decisions about how they spend taxpayers' money, and different groups in society will have different priorities.

PRICE CEILINGS

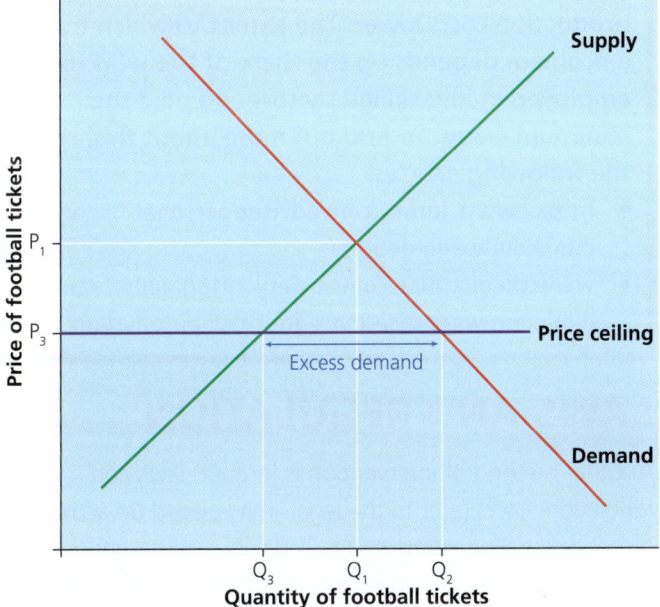

■ **Figure 8.24** The impact of a price ceiling, or maximum price, on a market

The government also has the ability to set the prices at which goods and services can be sold. **Price ceilings** are maximum allowed prices set below the equilibrium price.

A common example of the use of maximum prices is concert tickets. Going to see a favourite band or singer perform live is a popular activity, but because tickets are often in high demand, the prices could easily become unaffordable for most people.

For this reason, many venues and companies limit the prices they charge to customers. Football clubs and theatres also engage in this practice.

EXTENSION

Does quantity supplied really fall if we limit prices for concert tickets? What determines the number of tickets that can be sold to a football match? Can we draw the supply curve differently to represent this?

Figure 8.24 shows what happens when prices are set in this way. Because prices are set below the equilibrium price to keep them more affordable, the quantity demanded rises from Q_1 to Q_2. More people are willing and able to buy the football tickets at this lower price. However, the quantity supplied falls from Q_1 to Q_3 because the lower prices might not cover all the costs of providing the same number of seats. Because the quantity demanded will exceed the quantity of tickets supplied, there will need to be some way of trying to allocate those tickets.

ACTIVITY: What is the best way to allocate tickets to an event?

■ ATL

- Critical-thinking skills: Propose and evaluate a variety of solutions

Consider the following events:
- The Olympics
- The Wimbledon tennis tournament
- Chelsea Football Club playing at Stamford Bridge
- An Adele concert

You have been employed to **investigate** how effective the ticket sales process has been for one of the above events. Write a 500-word report **explaining** whether the current method is effective, and whether another method should be used. Your report should outline the advantages and disadvantages of the existing methods.

◆ Assessment opportunities

◆ In this activity you have practised skills that are assessed using Criterion A: Knowing and understanding and Criterion D: Thinking critically.

PRICE FLOORS

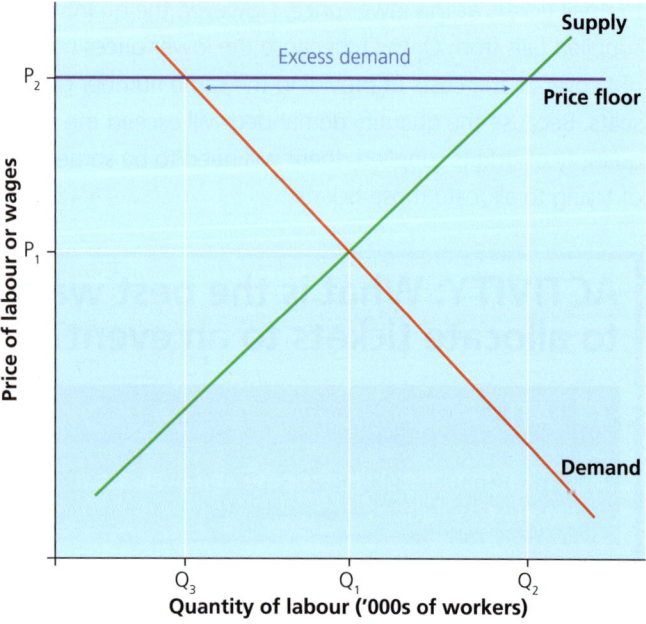

Figure 8.25 The effects of a price floor on the market for labour

The most frequently used price floor is a minimum wage. A price floor is a minimum price set by the government for a product or service, which is above the equilibrium price. This is labelled on Figure 8.25 at P_2. Of course, the number of workers willing and able to work at the new higher wage will increase from Q_1 to Q_2.

However, another theoretical consequence of minimum wages is that because they raise production costs, there will be a decrease in quantity of labour demanded from Q_1 to Q_3. This creates unemployment of workers (people who are willing and able to work but cannot find jobs) between Q_2 and Q_3.

EXTENSION

There is fierce debate as to whether minimum wages raise unemployment levels. The data does not always suggest that this is so, and this varies from country to country. However, some argue that above-inflation increases in the minimum wage may lead to some firms more rapidly resorting to automation as a way of keeping production costs lower. The extent to which this is a problem depends on the share of the workforce employed in low-skilled sectors and paid the minimum wage. To find out more about this, read the following articles:

- https://www.forbes.com/advisor/personal-finance/minimum-wage-debate/
- www.theguardian.com/society/2018/jan/04/fears-minimum-wage-rise-more-jobs-risk-automation

LAWS AND REGULATION

Another method of intervention is through laws and regulation. Laws refer to the legal limits placed on activity or behaviour. For example, it is illegal in most countries to sell alcohol to people under the age of 18, despite it being a socially acceptable activity, and for many countries an important part of food culture. It is important to consider the effectiveness of laws, and whether they actually achieve the objectives set out.

Regulation refers to the monitoring of industries and markets, usually by a government office. Any industry that has responsibility for people's health and well-being will be monitored in this way. These industries include health care, finance, education and food production. Regulation is costly, and often new measures introduced create additional costs in those industries and tend to be unpopular.

The free market system may so far be the best system that we have come up with to allocate resources. While capitalism has been able to achieve a lot in the last 200 years, there remain some problems that need to be solved by governments.

ACTIVITY: How effective are government solutions to market failure?

ATL

- Critical-thinking skills: Propose and evaluate a variety of solutions

What is your goal?

A new political party has been elected in your country. It campaigned on a platform of promising to reduce the negative effects of harmful consumption and production, and promote industries that have a positive impact. The newly elected Prime Minister wants you to **explore** the viability of solutions to market failure.

How will you achieve this?

You need to choose one of the examples of market failure from this chapter, or find another one if you can. You need to conduct research into this market in a particular country where it has caused market failure, and **investigate** what has been done so far.

How will you present your findings?

Construct a presentation to inform the rest of your class. In the presentation, you should:
- **Define** market failure and the type of externality relevant to your example.
- **Construct** the correct market failure diagram.
- **Explain** the market failure diagram.
- **List** possible solutions that have been attempted so far and **explain** each one.
- **Evaluate** the effectiveness of each solution.
- **Identify** the most effective solution, and **justify** your choice.

Assessment opportunities

- In this activity you have practised skills that are assessed using Criterion A: Knowing and understanding, Criterion C: Communicating and Criterion D: Thinking critically.

Presentation skills

There are common mistakes that students (and adults too) often make when they give presentations. You should avoid:
- writing in long and full sentences on the slides
- looking backwards and reading from the slides
- not rehearsing what you are going to say
- not citing sources on the slides themselves.

It is important to remember that the slides are only a visual support for you. Your audience can't read a lot of information and listen to you at the same time. The slides and what you say must complement each other, but not be the same.

EXTENSION

A lot of the news that we read is negative, and often gives us the feeling that not a lot is going well in the world and the economy. This has led to an increasing number of people wanting to focus on the positive effects of growth and capitalism. This group label themselves the 'New Optimists' and include people like Johan Norberg. Watch the following short interview with him: https://youtu.be/TvZqSqLDhxI.

What is an economy?

What has been discussed so far involves individual markets, but you will often have come across the word '**economy**' in the news or in conversations when it is used to refer to all of the productive activity taking place in a geographical location. It is possible to refer to the Shanghai economy, or the Colombian economy, or the global economy. This is referring to all markets in that area as a whole, or altogether.

All transactions between all buyers and sellers in an economy can be depicted in a simple diagram called the circular flow of income. There are two main exchanges that take place in this flow:

- Households acquire goods and services, and producers receive revenue from **consumer expenditure**.
- Producers buy factors of production, and households earn income from selling those resources.

People work in businesses and also act as consumers. When consumers stop consuming, producers stop earning and being able to pay their workers. This can become a vicious cycle.

So far, we have only considered two players – consumers and producers. But we must also consider three other very important participants, which are the government, banks and the foreign market. When we add them to the circular flow, income can flow out of and into the economy, allowing it to shrink or grow. When income flows out, we say that there are **leakages** from the circular flow, and when income flows in, we say that there are **injections**.

MEET AN ECONOMIST: KATE RAWORTH (1970–)

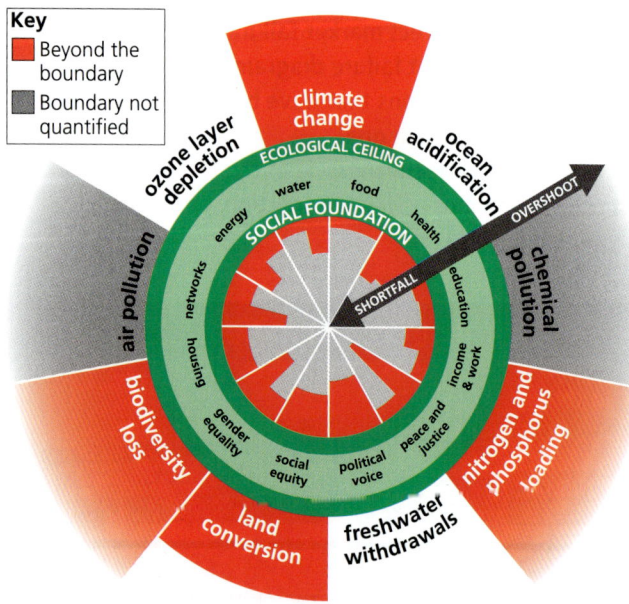

■ **Figure 8.26** We have to live within the doughnut!

Kate Raworth is an economist who works for the universities of both Oxford and Cambridge. She is the author of the popular book *Doughnut Economics*, published in 2017, which made an impact on the conversations regarding capitalism and its inability to prioritize the planet's environmental needs. She argues that the traditional goalpost of increased economic growth should be reassessed in light of the increasing difficulty to sustain our needs with the finite amount of resources available. Her work has been presented at and discussed by the UN General Assembly. She has also contributed to the UN Development Programme's Human Development Report, and worked as a researcher for Oxfam.

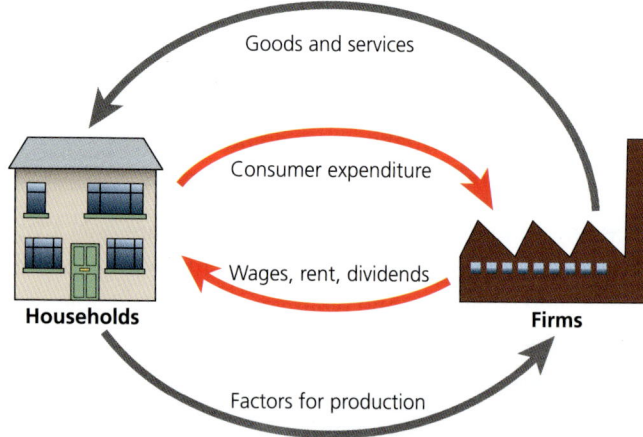

■ **Figure 8.27** The circular flow of income in a closed economy

DISCUSS

Watch the video 'Making Money Flow: The MONIAC' (https://youtu.be/rAZavOcEnLg). Do you think a machine can accurately depict the circular flow of income in an economy? What information can it capture? What information can it not capture?

THINK–PAIR–SHARE

What types of credit exist and what do you know about them? What types of credit might be considered more safe than others?

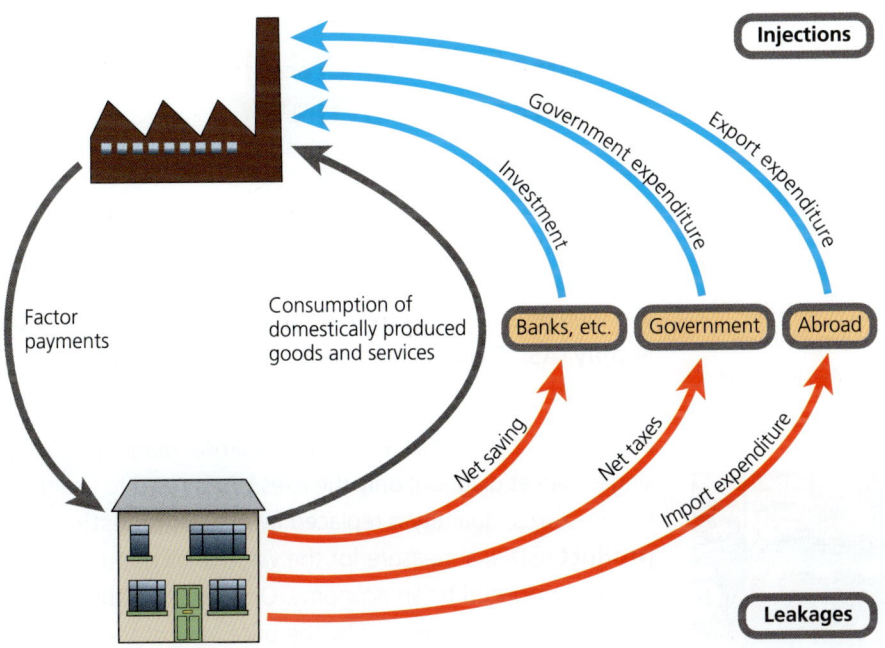

Figure 8.28 The circular flow of income in an open economy

GOVERNMENTS

Governments have an important role in the economy. Whether you live in a country that chooses its government democratically or not, the government has the potential to steer the economy in the right direction. There are two main ways the government can do this: it can raise revenue by taxing consumers and producers, either directly or indirectly, and it can spend this revenue on projects such as schools, the armed forces and roads. Using these tools, the government can influence how much income citizens have in their pockets to spend.

BANKS

One common reason for students to choose Economics in the Diploma Programme is that they develop an interest in banking. They may have watched a popular film or read about the financial crisis of 2008–9 in the news. Banking is an important development of the modern world. Starting in Italy, with Jewish moneylenders sitting on benches (the Italian for benches is *banco*) during the Renaissance, banking is now a crucial part of the modern economy, with everybody using some form of credit on a daily basis.

Banking works to channel surplus funds from those who don't currently need them, to those who could invest them in their entrepreneurial efforts. For this reason, banks are called financial intermediaries. To reward the lender, an **interest rate** is charged, which means that a percentage of the loan has to be repaid in addition to the amount borrowed. Income leaves the circular flow in the form of **savings**, but returns as investment in firms. Aside from the big firms that you are familiar with, most businesses are much smaller and have to approach banks for loans if they want to expand. This is an important source of finance for many firms.

FOREIGN MARKETS

Countries have traded with each other for a long time. Early groups probably exchanged goods in a rudimentary exchange, and as coinage developed so did more complex and formal markets for trading goods. By selling some of the goods they produce in foreign markets, firms gain access to new customers and can earn more revenue. This is called **export revenue**, as it is income injected into the economy. When income is spent on buying goods from abroad, this is called **import expenditure**, and is a leakage from the circular flow.

■ **Figure 8.29** A variety of goods on a supermarket shelf

SEE–THINK–WONDER

How much do we trade?

Look at Figure 8.29. What do you see? How many of these items do you think were imported from abroad? What does it make you wonder about your country's relationship with other countries? What questions does this image raise about sustainability?

AGGREGATE DEMAND AND AGGREGATE SUPPLY

The discussion of the circular flow of income can be extended to include demand and supply. When we talk about all firms and all households in an economy, we can also talk about all demand and all supply in the economy. We then refer to **aggregate demand** (AD) and **aggregate supply** (AS). The word aggregate simply means 'altogether' or 'added together'.

Both curves can be plotted on a very similar diagram as a single market diagram; only the axes labels need to change. On the *x*-axis, quantity is replaced by **gross domestic product** (GDP), a measure for the value of all goods and services produced by an economy. On the *y*-axis, the price of a single good is replaced by the price level of the entire economy. When the price level changes, the following terms are used to describe the change:

- inflation: the price level increases
- **deflation**: the price level decreases
- **disinflation**: the price level increases, but the rate at which it does so slows down.

EXTENSION

How do we measure the price level of an economy? How much data do we need to collect in order to know this? **Investigate** some of the measures of inflation and how they are constructed in your country.

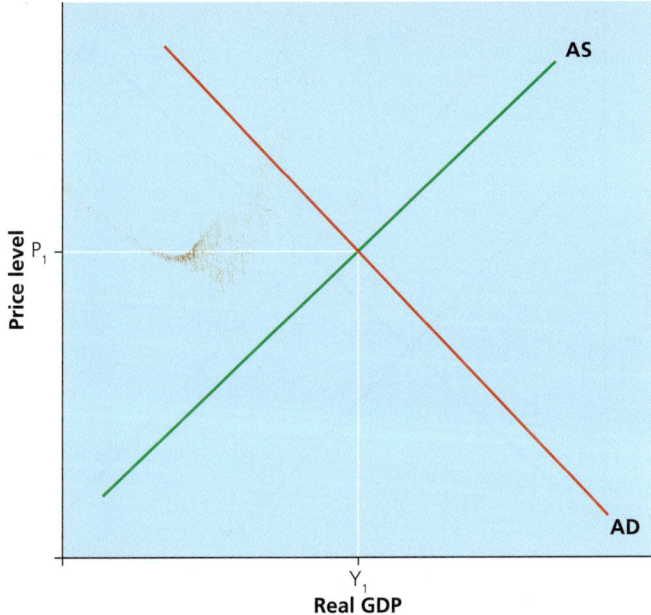

■ **Figure 8.30** The aggregate demand (AD)/aggregate supply (AS) model

Aggregate demand refers to demand from all the groups in society that demand goods and services. This includes households that consume, firms that invest, the government that spends money and foreign markets that buy our goods from us. This was already established in our circular flow model. We can therefore derive the following equation for aggregate demand:

$$AD = C + I + G + (X-M)$$

C – consumption by households

I – investment by firms

G – government spending

X – export revenue earned from foreign markets

M – import expenditure when goods and services are bought from abroad

THINK–PAIR–SHARE

Like the demand curve, the aggregate demand curve can also shift. **List** the things that you think will cause the demand curve to move outwards or inwards. Think in terms of the groups in society mentioned above. Compare this list with a partner and then share with the rest of the class.

The same downward slope is seen in the aggregate demand curve as is seen in the demand curve.

Aggregate supply refers to the ability of firms to produce output, given current prices in the country. Aggregate supply will shift when the costs of production change, allowing firms to produce more or less at any price level. Improvements in productivity are positive changes to aggregate supply that can reduce pressure on prices and result in more output. Costs can rise for any number of reasons, including increased resource costs, and tighter industrial regulations.

What is a recession and why is it bad?

The financial crisis of 2008–9, or the Great Recession, caused significant upheaval to the global economy, after many years of politicians and economists believing that such crises were a thing of the past.

There is still a lot of disagreement about what the most important factors were leading up to the crisis, but the following events were relevant:

- There were large increases in mortgage lending, especially to people with poor credit histories (known as subprime borrowers), and an extremely buoyant housing market in the 1990s and early 2000s led to house prices doubling over that period.
- Increases in interest rates in the early 2000s, and the fact that many subprime borrowers had unsustainable mortgages, led to many people defaulting on their mortgages and being evicted from their homes. This put downward pressure on property values.
- Much of this mortgage debt, together with car loans, credit cards and student loans, had been resold to investors all around the world as financial instruments known as derivatives.
- As people stopped paying their mortgages, and house prices started to fall, the banks and mortgage lenders started losing money.
- All the derivatives linked to mortgages and property values subsequently fell in value too.
- This led to the entire financial system severely restricting the lending of credit – a 'credit crunch'.

This credit crunch led to many countries' output, or GDP, starting to fall. When GDP falls for six months or more, the country's economy is said to be in **recession**. The financial crisis of 2008–9 was the worst the world had experienced since the Great Depression of the 1930s.

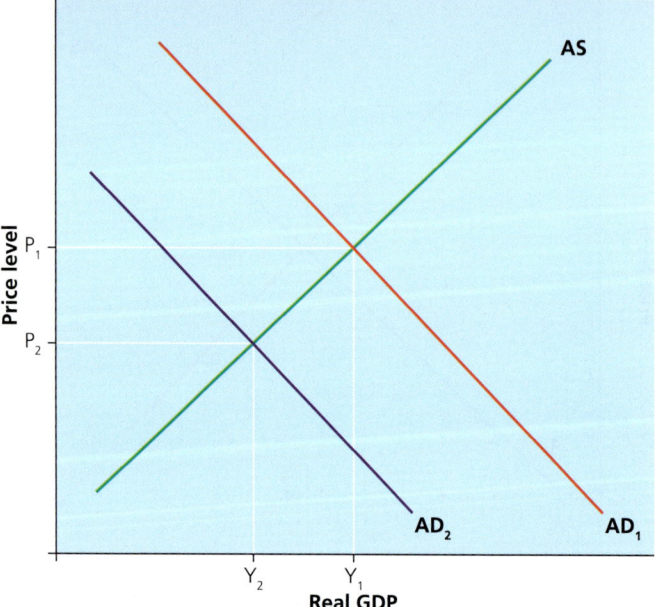

■ **Figure 8.31** Showing a recession using AD/AS

The banking crisis or credit crunch resulted in severe restrictions in lending to businesses and consumers. As shown in Figure 8.31, because consumption and business investments are components of aggregate demand (AD), AD will shift inwards from AD_1 to AD_2. This causes a decline in economic output from Y_1 to Y_2 and a recession.

To understand what happens to individuals during recessions, we must look at the labour market. The supply of labour is made up of individuals who are willing and able to work at each wage. The demand for labour is from firms that are willing and able to hire workers at each wage. During a recession, demand for workers will fall as firms struggle to make sufficient sales. In the short term, a gap between quantity demanded and quantity supplied of workers arises, and this is the resulting unemployment. Unemployment refers to the number of people who are willing and able to work but who cannot find work.

What is the role of the government in shaping the economy?

THE CLASSICAL SCHOOL OF THOUGHT AND FRIEDRICH VON HAYEK

■ **Figure 8.32 (a)** Friedrich von Hayek; **(b)** Ludwig von Mises

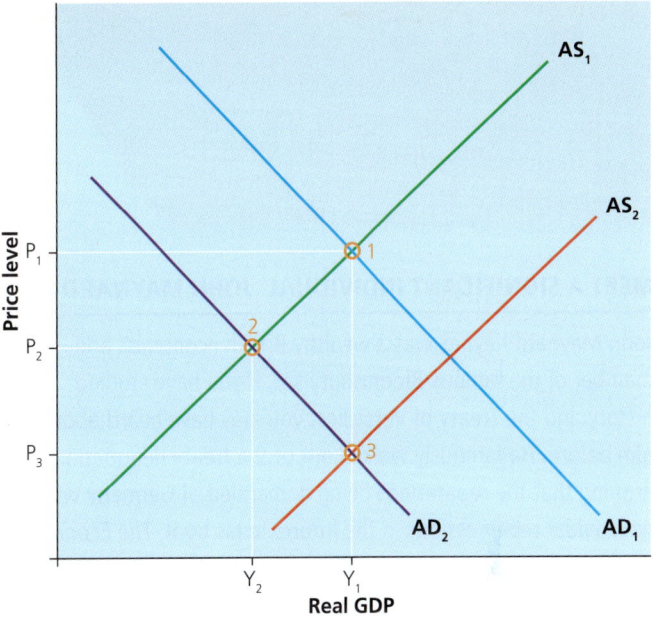

■ **Figure 8.33** How the economy corrects during a recession according to the classical view

After the First World War, some of the countries that had lost the war, including Austria and Germany, experienced an economic phenomenon known as inflation.

Prior to the Great Depression of the 1930s, economics was mainly occupied with individual markets. Any problems were seen as simply the result of disequilibrium in markets. Governments did not approach problems from a **macroeconomic** perspective (by looking at the economy as a whole). Instead, and as suggested by the classical economic theory, it was thought that disequilibrium would be corrected when prices changed. Governments believed that all they needed to do was to wait. This approach is called laissez-faire (leave it alone).

If we consider labour again, we can see why governments thought this. We already know that falling demand in the economy translates to a fall in demand for workers, and this is why unemployment arises. We also know that all markets, if left free to operate, will use a price change to correct disequilibrium, and the labour market is no different. When quantity supplied exceeds quantity demanded, then price for labour will fall.

Using the AD/AS model we can now see what happens to the economy when wages fall. At position 2 on Figure 8.33, there is high unemployment, and there will be downward pressure on wages. By allowing wages to fall from P_1 to P_2, however, the labour market corrects and aggregate supply can increase from AS_1 to AS_2. The result is that at position 3, the economy returns to the previous level of output at Y_1 and the labour market is in equilibrium, albeit with fewer workers than before the recession as there may be some workers who are discouraged from working at the new wage level. These 'discouraged' workers are not considered as unemployed, as it is only the people willing and able to work who are counted in that category.

The priority for classical economists is not the management of unemployment, as this is a problem that markets can fix on their own with a price correction, but instead the management of inflation. Given that von Hayek (1899–1992) and von Mises (1881–1973) experienced some of the worst inflation the world had ever seen (hyperinflation in Austria occurred between October 1921 and September 1922), it makes sense that their academic work focuses on understanding this problem.

MEET A SIGNIFICANT INDIVIDUAL: JOHN MAYNARD KEYNES (1883–1946)

John Maynard Keynes was a wealthy British economist and member of the famous Bloomsbury set. If you have studied history and the Treaty of Versailles, you may have heard about him before. He famously walked out of the treaty negotiations arguing that the reparations being demanded of Germany would have wider repercussions in the future. In his book *The Economic Consequences of the Peace* (1919), he wrote: 'If we aim at the impoverishment of Central Europe, vengeance, I daresay, will not limp'.

Later in his career he became better known for his macroeconomic policy recommendations. The interwar period for the United Kingdom was difficult in economic terms, and the Great Depression starting in 1929 led him to write the book *The General Theory of Employment, Interest and Money* (1936). This book was a gamechanger in the field of economics, and brought macroeconomics to the forefront of the government policy agenda. His ideas inspired mainstream economic thinking from the 1940s to the 1970s until Friedrich von Hayek and Milton Friedman's ideas became influential. Keynes' ideas informed many policy responses to the Great Recession of 2008/09.

■ **Figure 8.34** John Maynard Keynes

Keynes argued that the central problem was a lack of demand. Given that both producers and consumers had halted their demand for goods and services, and the Great Depression was affecting most of the world and therefore trade too, he argued that government is the only entity left with the ability (and in Keynes's eyes the responsibility) to do anything about the problem. He said that government, even if it had to borrow from financial markets, should spend money to create jobs, build new infrastructure and push the economy back into growth. This, he argued, would increase aggregate demand and return it and the demand for labour to their original levels. According to Keynes:

> 'We see … rising prices and falling prices each have their characteristic disadvantage …. Inflation … means Injustice to individuals … particularly to investors; and is therefore unfavourable to saving [and investment in capital] …. Deflation … is … disastrous to employment …. Inflation is unjust and Deflation is inexpedient. Of the two perhaps Deflation is, if we rule out exaggerated inflations such as that of Germany, the worse; because it is worse, in an impoverished world, to provoke unemployment than to disappoint the rentier [a person who lives on income from property or investments]. But it is not necessary that we should weigh one evil against the other. It is easier to agree that both are evils to be shunned.' – Keynes, John Maynard. 1923. A Tract on Monetary Reform

Of course, not everyone agrees with Keynes's ideas, and the rest of the twentieth century has been spent in fierce debate about whether governments should focus on making markets more free, or intervening in markets.

ACTIVITY: Stimulus packages during recession

■ ATL

■ Critical-thinking skills: Draw reasonable conclusions and generalizations

The following are examples of stimulus packages used as a response by various governments to recessions in their countries:
- The New Deal in the USA during the 1930s
- The American Recovery and Reinvestment Act, 2009
- 'Abenomics' in Japan from 2012 onwards

For one of the examples above:

1 **Explain** the causes of the economic problems.
2 **Describe** the main features of the economic policies used in response.
3 **Discuss** the effects of the policies on the country's recovery. Consider the length of time taken to return to growth and previous levels of GDP, the way in which people returned to employment (did the kinds of jobs they were doing change in any way) and the impact of government actions on the government's budget.
4 In your conclusion, decide whether you think the policy was effective and **justify** your decision.
5 Cite all your sources.

The following resources will be useful:
- The New Deal in the USA during the 1930s
  - www.bbc.co.uk/bitesize/guides/zcrdcwx/revision/1
  - www.loc.gov/rr/program/bib/newdeal/am.html
- The American Recovery and Reinvestment Act, 2009
  - www.thebalance.com/arra-details-3306299
  - https://brook.gs/2k646uI
- 'Abenomics' Japan from 2012 onwards
  - https://www.bbc.co.uk/news/business-62089543
  - https://bit.ly/2jYWiuw

To find charts providing information on gross domestic product and unemployment, and details of government spending, visit https://tradingeconomics.com.

◆ Assessment opportunities

◆ In this activity you have practised skills that are assessed using Criterion A: Knowing and understanding, Criterion C: Communicating and Criterion D: Thinking critically.

Several nations experimented with communism and state-run economic management during the twentieth century. Today, countries that still have communist governments typically allow the majority of economic activity to be organized by markets. This is because governments would struggle to process all the information necessary to determine the efficient quantity and price of all goods or services. In countries with democratically elected governments, the political debate takes place around the centre of the political spectrum. There is largely agreement that markets work well most of the time, but some require some intervention to bring them in line with society's expectations. The attitudes and perspectives that determine these expectations change all the time, however, and this is what explains how voters make their decisions to stick with a particular political party or change their minds.

Reflection

In this chapter, we have outlined how markets work to allocate scarce goods, and **discussed** examples where this system does and does not work well. We have also expanded our understanding of the market economy as a whole, what happens to economies in good and bad times, and **evaluated** possible government responses to different situations.

Use this table to reflect on your own learning in this chapter.					
Questions we asked	Answers we found	Any further questions now?			
Factual: What economic systems exist to allocate resources? What is an economy?					
Conceptual: How do markets work? Why and how do governments intervene in markets? What is a recession and why is it bad?					
Debatable: To what extent do markets improve our lives? What is the role of the government in shaping the economy?					
Approaches to learning you used in this chapter	Description – what new skills did you learn?	How well did you master the skills?			
		Novice	Learner	Practitioner	Expert
Communication skills					
Information literacy skills					
Critical-thinking skills					
Media literacy skills					
Learner profile attribute(s)	Reflect on the importance of being a risk-taker for your learning in this chapter.				
Risk-taker					

Global interactions | Causality; Identity; Processes | Fairness and development

9 Can we make a fairer world through trade?

○ **Global** trade **brings with it** global responsibilities to make a future that is **fair** for all.

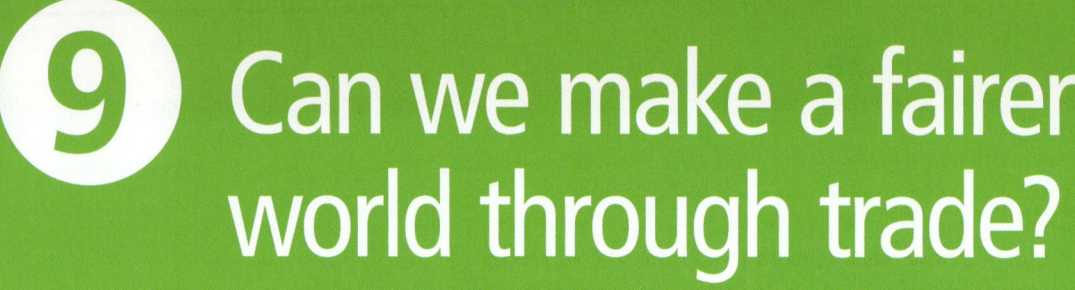

■ Figure 9.1 How do we transport goods, services and people?

CONSIDER THESE QUESTIONS:

Factual: What do we mean by globalization? What are trade agreements? How do countries restrict trade? How is a currency's value determined? What kind of trade agreements do countries form with each other?

Conceptual: Why do we trade? How important can trade be to the success of a society? Why do countries sometimes want to restrict trade?

Debatable: Is globalization good or bad? What are the pros and cons of aid and trade?

Now **share and compare** your thoughts and ideas with your partner, or with the whole class.

○─ IN THIS CHAPTER WE WILL …

- **Find out** about how countries trade goods, services and currencies with each other, and what agreements they form to do so.
- **Explore** different countries' trade balances, and trade agreements that are formed between countries.
- **Take action** by conducting an audit of your family's shopping habits.

■ These Approaches to Learning (ATL) skills will be useful …

- Information literacy skills
- Media literacy skills
- Critical-thinking skills

● We will reflect on this learner profile attribute …

- Inquirers – nurturing our curiosity, developing skills for inquiry and research; knowing how to learn independently and with others; learning with enthusiasm and sustaining our love of learning throughout life.

◆ Assessment opportunities in this chapter:

- ◆ **Criterion A:** Knowing and understanding
- ◆ **Criterion B:** Investigating
- ◆ **Criterion C:** Communicating
- ◆ **Criterion D:** Thinking critically

KEY WORDS

exchange rate
trade
trade agreement

THINK–PAIR–SHARE

Look at the three photographs.

Can you **identify** similarities and differences between the types of societies depicted here?

Discuss the differences you have identified with your learning partner. What has changed? What might have stayed the same?

Share your ideas as a class and **summarize** your ideas.

9 Can we make a fairer world through trade?

■ **Figure 9.2** Armana letters from the fourteenth century BCE. They show the correspondence between Ancient Egypt and diplomats in Canaan and Amurru, in an internationally recognized language, Akkadian. One of the things they mention is trade restrictions between the territories

People have been trading together for a very long time. In traditional societies that had not yet developed a monetary system, it was long thought that people engaged in a barter system, and traded goods in exchange for other goods or services that they needed. The system works in theory because people find some way to reach an agreement – people have things that other people need. This exchange could take place within or between small villages.

David Graeber, a social anthropologist, challenges the assumption that people engaged in simple bartering in his book *Debt: The First 5,000 Years* (2011). He argues that this system is far too simplistic, and would have failed to enable each small group to access all the goods they would have needed to survive. Instead, he argues that basic societies would have worked together more collectively, and stored goods needed for the entire group to survive. As long as everyone contributed what they could, then everyone would enjoy the benefits of living in a social group. Marx referred to this as 'primitive communism'.

As societies grew, so did their need for more sophisticated systems for trade, both within their own communities and between themselves and others. People realized that it was possible to make payment by exchanging promises that represented how much something was worth (its value), rather than by exchanging actual objects. For example, by inscribing a clay tablet with the number of goods held in

■ **Figure 9.3** This looks more familiar! This is a coin bearing the head of Alexander the Great

stock, as the ancient Sumerians did, the clay tablet could be traded, instead of the items themselves. As long as the clay tablet is accepted by anyone for anything to the value of those goods, the system works as an intermediary between people engaging in trade. This was the first money! Today, we use coins, notes, cheques and plastic debit and credit cards. We don't demand money because of any properties that money itself possesses, but because of the promise that it can be exchanged for something of use or value.

The increasingly close relationship between countries has enabled many positive things, such as exposure to other cultures, lower production costs for our goods and services, and access to new technology. However, there are also other consequences of living in today's globalized world that we need to understand.

In many cases, increased trade promotes peace and security between nations. Economic integration in Europe since the Second World War has been seen as a permanent remedy to the conflict that arose between European nations during the first half of the twentieth century. During the inter-war period, however, trade relations soured in Europe and are cited as one of the contributing factors to the outbreak of another war in the 1930s. Protectionist measures were deemed necessary in many countries around the world to prevent catastrophic decreases in prices and wages. A cycle of retaliation, deteriorating trust and further economic difficulties resulted in worsened economic and political relations between countries that had not long before experienced the worst war the world had ever witnessed. Outside Europe, countries that were beginning to cast off the shackles of colonialism saw protectionist measures as a way to avoid dependence on outside powers for resources or goods. Latin American countries favoured policies that would allow import substitution, or the use of protectionism to stop the import of manufactured goods that these countries wanted to develop industries for themselves. Import substitution is one method that can help nations industrialize.

What do we mean by globalization?

Globalization is not a term that has a precise definition, and there are many arguments over what it is, what causes it and what the most important consequences of it are. The modern concept of globalization has its roots in the writings of Karl Marx and others during the late nineteenth century, but the processes that cause it have been at work for much longer.

For most of us, globalization means that 'the things we use in our daily lives are derived more and more from an increasingly complex geography of production, distribution and consumption, whose scale has become, if not totally global, at least vastly more extensive, and whose choreography has become increasingly intricate' (Peter Dicken, *Global Shift*, 2007). Figure 9.4 shows all the types of firms or businesses that can exist in an economy.

Increasingly, a business's success has been defined by how large it has become. While some organizations are held in public or government ownerships (as is often the case with important industries such as communication, transport, energy and sometimes raw materials), most businesses today are privately owned. On the right of Figure 9.4 you can see types of private organizations, and the ways in which they interact with each other and with publicly owned enterprises.

Because of the concerns over loss of jobs, the merging of cultures and the unequal spread of income and gains from economic growth across the world, there is a growing tendency to view the effects of globalization negatively.

> **THINK–PAIR–SHARE**
>
> Look at Figure 9.4. In pairs, think of an example of a publicly or state-owned enterprise, a small and a large national firm, and a global corporation. Share your examples with the rest of the class.

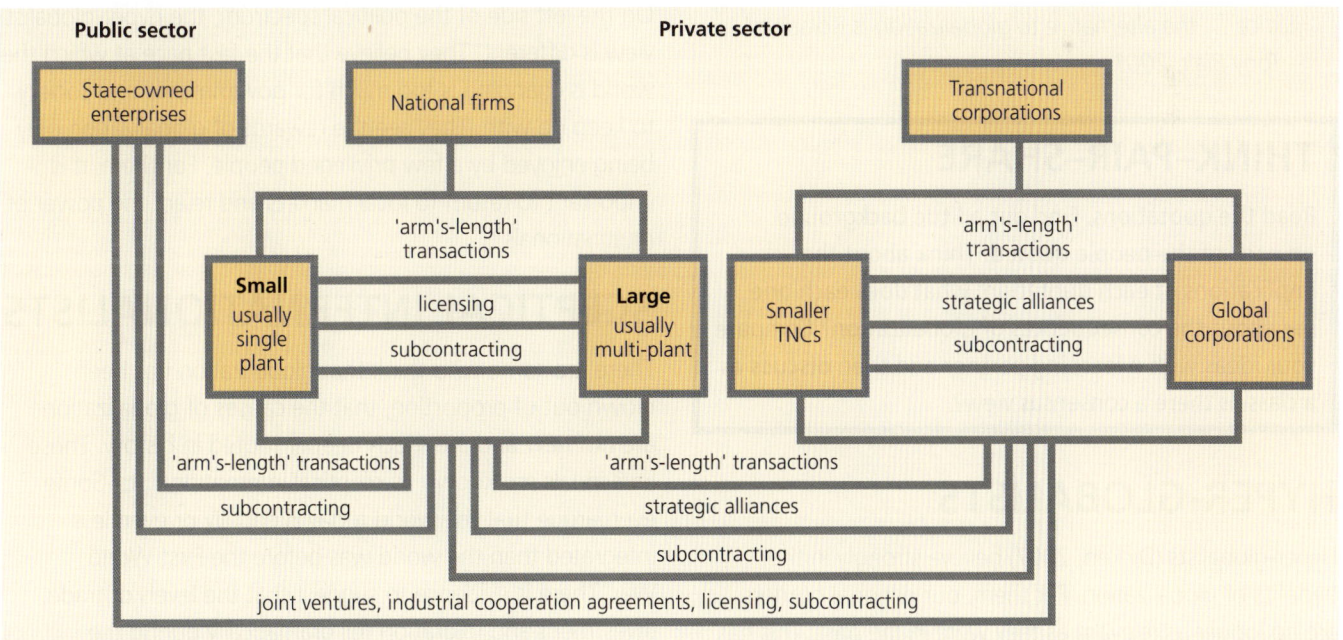

■ **Figure 9.4** Types of firms in an economy

9   Can we make a fairer world through trade?

Is globalization good or bad?

'Wild globalization has benefited some, but it's been a catastrophe for most.' – Marine Le Pen

'Globalization has made us more vulnerable. It creates a world without borders, and makes us painfully aware of the limitations of our present instruments, and of politics, to meet its challenges.' – Anna Lindh

'Globalization is a fact … Not just in finance, but in communication, in technology, increasingly in culture, in recreation. In the world of the Internet, information technology and TV, there will be globalization. And in trade, the problem is not there's too much of it; on the contrary there's too little of it … The issue is not how to stop globalization. The issue is how we use the power of community to combine it with justice … the alternative to globalization is isolation.' – Tony Blair, 2001

> **THINK–PAIR–SHARE**
>
> Read the quotations. Find out a little background on each of the people quoted. Think about the implications of each quotation: what does each one say about the consequences of globalization? Compare your ideas with a learning partner and then **discuss** as a class. Is there a consensus view?

HYPER-GLOBALISTS

Hyper-globalists (Dicken, 2007) believe strongly in the benefits of globalization. For them, our national borders are no longer as relevant as they were in the past. This has positive and negative implications, and so there are two camps of hyper-globalists.

> **EXTENSION: EXPLORE FURTHER**
>
> In Chapter 1 we were introduced to Émile Durkheim. Use the Internet Encyclopedia of Philosophy to find out more about Émile Durkheim, often described as one of the 'fathers of sociology' (the other two being Karl Marx and Max Weber). Read the section 'The Division of Labor and the Emergence of Modernity in Europe', in which his ideas about the development of complex societies are explained. What do his ideas tell us about living in a globalized society today? How is life in a societal group today different from life in prehistoric, ancient or medieval times? To what extent do you agree with his views?

On the right side of the political spectrum, or for those in favour of free market capitalism on the whole, globalization represents the power of markets to create growth, raise incomes, improve product quality and choice, and lower prices for consumers. They believe that we stand to gain from global communication networks, shared research and development, and closer economic integration.

On the left side of the political spectrum, the hyper-globalist view is different. They believe that the fast pace at which the world is changing is too much for governments and society to keep up with. They see the rewards of globalization only being enjoyed by a few privileged people. For them, it is important to return to local markets and reject the power of multinationals.

SCEPTICAL INTERNATIONALISTS

There are some who think that globalization has been blown out of proportion, that the causes of globalization are not new and are much deeper rooted in history. These individuals are known as sceptical internationalists. Some even argue that the world today is equally or even less integrated than the world was before the First World War. There is evidence to suggest that the levels of trade, investment and migration fell dramatically during the interwar period, and didn't recover to levels seen before the First World War until the end of the twentieth century.

Why do we trade?

THE THEORY OF COMPARATIVE ADVANTAGE

Prior to the Industrial Revolution (c.1760–1840), European countries adopted what are known as mercantilist policies. This means that any trade that took place was taxed in order to increase the stock of gold and silver the government had in its possession. This is what made countries wealthy. Eventually it was understood, thanks to the writings of Adam Smith and David Ricardo, that countries had more to gain from trade than just an opportunity to raise tax revenue.

David Ricardo tried to understand what would happen if two countries tried to trade with each other, when one country produced greater volumes of goods and services than the other. To illustrate this, we can use a production possibilities curve (see Figure 8.2 on page 190).

Figure 9.6 shows the production possibilities for Panama and Mexico. Mexico is the more economically developed country, and has much greater capacity to produce goods and services, in this case blenders and avocados. Looking at this, it seems as though Mexico should just produce both goods because it produces 300 avocados where Panama only produces 100, and produces 100 blenders where Panama only produces 50. However, Ricardo developed the theory of comparative advantage in order to explain why this is misleading.

■ **Figure 9.5 (a)** Adam Smith (1723–1790); **(b)** David Ricardo (1772–1823)

To understand Ricardo's theory we must learn a new term: **opportunity cost**. When we are faced with various options and decisions to be made in order to choose between those options, something will always need to be sacrificed. The options not chosen are the opportunity cost of making the decision. To work out the opportunity of one good in terms of the other, we must perform the following calculation:

$$\text{Opportunity cost of good X in terms of good Y} = \frac{\text{Production volume of good Y}}{\text{Production volume of good X}}$$

The two countries' opportunities costs have been calculated and are presented in Table 9.1 below:

■ **Table 9.1** Opportunity costs for avocados and blenders in Mexico and Panama

	Avocados	Blenders
Mexico	$\frac{100}{300} = 0.3$ Mexico must give up 0.3 blenders to produce 1 avocado	$\frac{300}{100} = 3$ Mexico must give up 3 avocados to produce 1 blender
Panama	$\frac{50}{100} = 0.5$ Panama must give up 0.5 blenders to produce 1 avocado	$\frac{100}{50} = 2$ Panama must give up 2 avocados to produce 1 blender

Looking at it this way, we can now see which country sacrifices the least when they produce each of the goods, or which country has the lowest opportunity in the production of each of the goods. For the production of avocados, Mexico sacrifices fewer blenders than Panama does to produce each avocado. Panama sacrifices fewer avocados when it produces blenders than Mexico does.

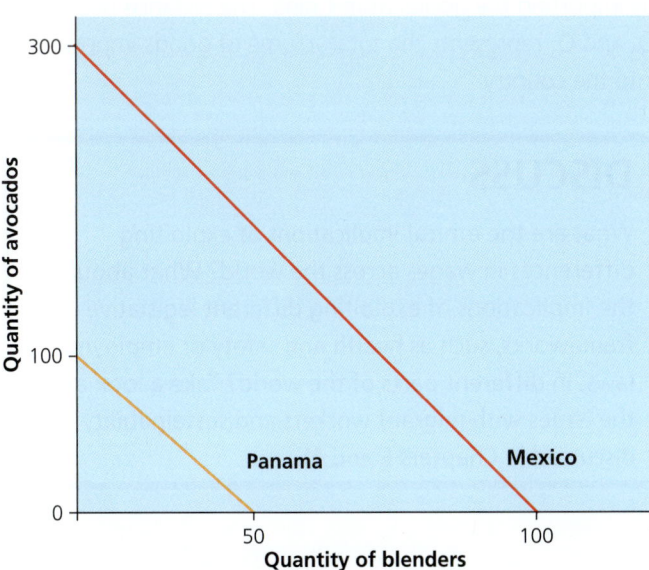

■ **Figure 9.6** Production possibilities for Panama and Mexico, for avocados and blenders

9 Can we make a fairer world through trade?

USING SUPPLY AND DEMAND

Returning to our supply-and-demand model from Chapter 8 (see page 200), we can see how a nation might benefit even more from engaging in trade with another country. With its rapid progress towards industrialization during the second half of the twentieth century, China has become the world's leading producer of low-tech manufactured goods. China's government has created Special Economic Zones (SEZs) such as the one in Shenzhen, and many government policies are in place to support the manufacturing industry. Low-tech manufactured goods include air conditioning units, toys and component parts for more complex manufactured goods.

Australia, on the other hand, has a lot of agricultural land, and considerable natural resources like tin and copper. The country has chosen to focus primarily on exporting these, and imports low-tech manufacturing from countries like China. Figure 9.7 shows Australia's market for low-tech manufactured goods.

When a country as big as China becomes the world's largest producer of low-tech manufacturing, it is able to produce those goods at much lower costs than a country like Australia. China also benefits from a large labour force that for a long time was paid a relatively low wage. If Australia were to produce these goods, it would produce Q_1 volume of goods at a price of P_1.

China is a better producer of these goods, and can produce them in greater quantities, such that Australia cannot compete. Whatever Australia does, it cannot compete with the low prices P_2 that China can produce at. China's supply curve must be drawn horizontally to indicate that Australia has no ability to impact the prices of low-tech manufactured goods coming from China.

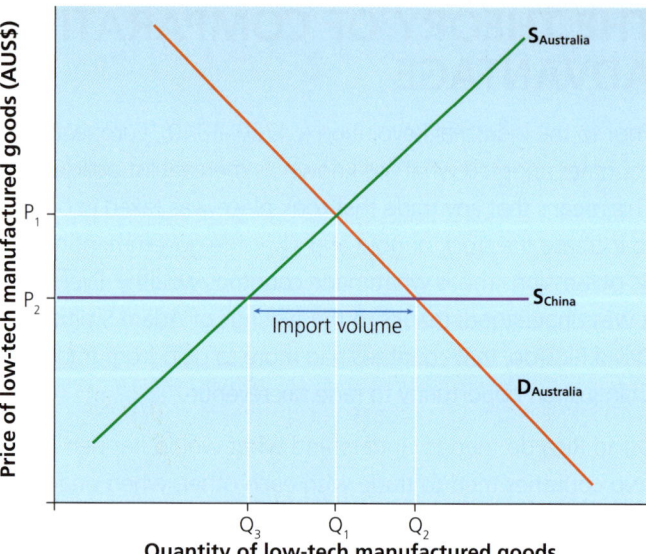

Figure 9.7 Using supply and demand to illustrate international trade

At these lower prices, the quantity demanded of low-tech goods increases from Q_1 to Q_2. However, domestic producers in Australia will struggle to compete with Chinese prices, and so the quantity supplied by Australian producers falls from Q_1 to Q_3. You will remember from Chapter 8 that this mismatch between quantity supplied and demanded is called a shortage, but in this case the shortage can be fixed by importing the goods from China. The distance between Q_2 and Q_3 represents the total volume of goods imported into the country.

DISCUSS

What are the ethical implications of exploiting differences in wages across the world? What about the implications of exploiting different legislative frameworks, such as health and safety or employment laws, in different parts of the world? Take a look at the issues with migrant workers and sustainability discussed in Chapters 6 and 11.

ACTIVITY: How does your country trade?

■ ATL

■ Information literacy skills: Collect and analyse data to identify solutions and make informed decisions

Use the Harvard Atlas of Economic Complexity http://atlas.cid.harvard.edu/ to find out about a country's trade patterns.

1 **Describe** the country's geographical location, making references to neighbouring countries, access to seas and other geographical features that might be relevant to trade.
2 **Identify** your chosen country's main exports and imports.
3 **Identify** your chosen country's main trading partners.
4 **State** whether your chosen country exports a diverse set of goods and services.
5 **Explain** the likely reasons for the kinds of goods and services that it exports.
6 To what extent would your chosen country benefit from a different trade strategy?

◆ Assessment opportunities

◆ In this activity you have practised skills that are assessed using Criterion A: Knowing and understanding and Criterion D: Thinking critically.

THINK–PAIR–SHARE

In pairs, **list** all the food that you and your families regularly buy that is not grown or produced in the country where you live. Think about the factors that determine where food is produced or grown. Share these factors with the class. Were there any factors you didn't think of?

Trade lowers prices and provides consumers with increased choice from other countries. We like to be able to shop around and find the best deal, and trading with other nations gives us this opportunity.

We learned about community surplus in Chapter 8 (see page 200). Figure 9.8 shows that before engaging in trade, Australian consumers pay a price P_1, and anyone more willing and able to pay that price will enjoy a consumer surplus represented by the dark blue shaded triangle. When prices lower to P_2, and the increased quantity demanded of Q_2 is satisfied by imports, consumer surplus can increase by the light blue shaded area.

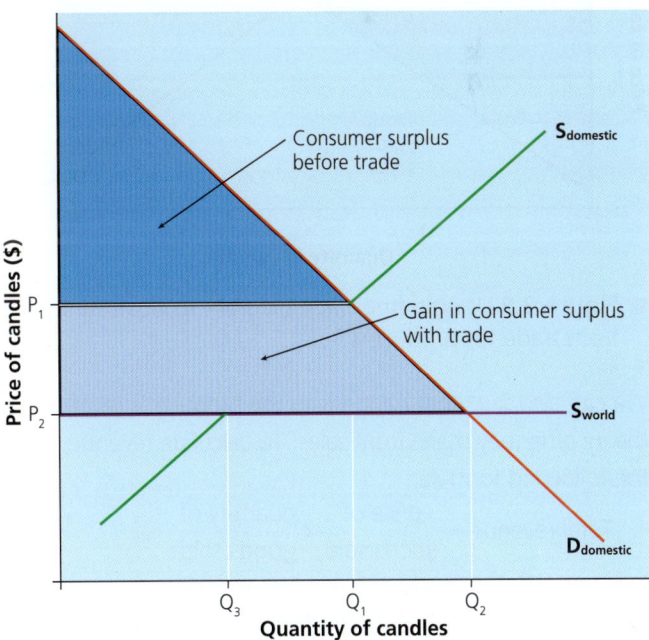

■ **Figure 9.8** Using a free trade diagram to illustrate gains from trade for consumers

IMPACT OF TRADE ON CONSUMERS

Trade is great for consumers. Trading with other nations means that consumers benefit from the variety of goods that other countries are better able to produce.

Links to: Mathematics

Some of the skills you have acquired in Mathematics can be useful when studying these diagrams. To work out the changing areas of consumer and producer surpluses, you need to work out the areas of triangle and trapezoids using the following formulae:

$$\text{Area of a triangle} = \frac{1}{2} \text{ base} \times \text{height}$$

$$\text{Area of a trapezoid} = \frac{(a + b)}{2} \times \text{height}$$

IMPACT OF TRADE ON PRODUCERS

Domestic producers are unlikely to benefit from this competition from abroad, unless they can find ways to innovate and compete. Figure 9.9 shows that the producer surplus before trade was introduced to the market was the sum of the coloured shapes; both the pink triangle and purple trapezoid. With the price decrease, and loss of sales to foreign producers, producer surplus falls to only the pink triangle.

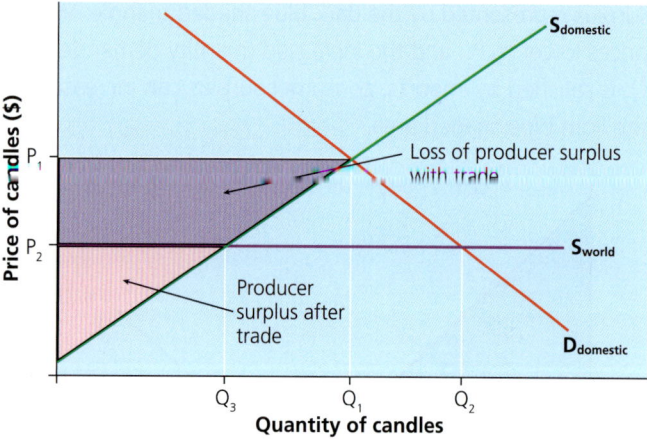

■ **Figure 9.9** Using a free trade diagram to illustrate losses from trade for producers

We can also see what happens to the producer's revenue, or the income they make from sales. To calculate revenue, use the following formula:

$$\text{Total revenue} = \text{price of goods sold} \times \text{quantity of goods sold}$$

In Figure 9.9, the producer's revenue would be represented by P_1 multiplied by Q_1. After trade starts to take place, the producer's revenue falls to P_2 multiplied by Q_3.

ACTIVITY: Calculating the impact of free trade on the domestic market

■ **ATL**

■ Critical-thinking skills: Use models and simulations to explore complex systems and issues

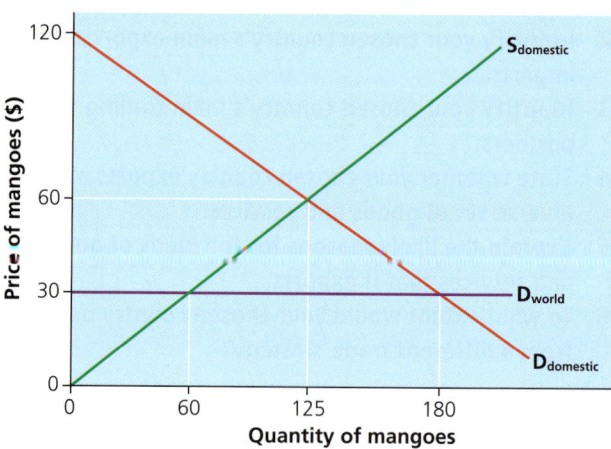

■ **Figure 9.10** Using a diagram to help calculate the effects of free trade

Using Figure 9.10, calculate the following before and after free trade is introduced:
- Consumer expenditure
- Consumer surplus
- Producer revenue
- Producer surplus.

◆ Assessment opportunities

◆ In this activity you have practised skills that are assessed using Criterion A: Knowing and understanding.

How important can trade be to the success of a society?

■ **Figure 9.11** The city of Petra was built into difficult-to-navigate rock formations

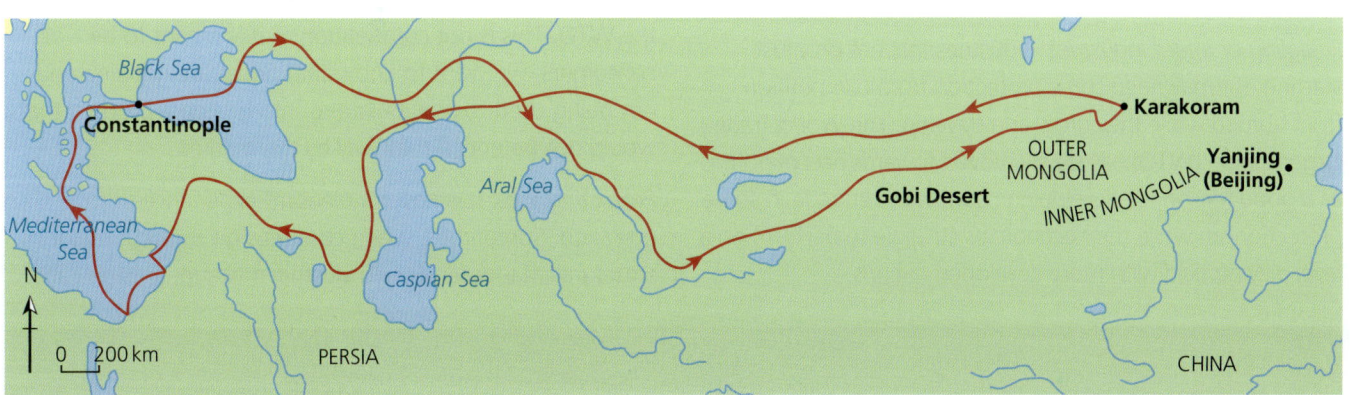

■ **Figure 9.12** The Silk Road

Petra was the home of the Nabataeans, an ancient society that lived in present-day Jordan. Its location was along a route that provided incense from Asia to places like Gaza, Jerusalem and Damascus. This was an important commodity for religious and cultural purposes.

Looking at the images in Figure 9.11, we can see that this terrain was difficult to navigate. The Nabateans knew the area better than anyone, and this gave them a distinct advantage when it came to the trade of incense. The monopoly that they eventually gained allowed them to accrue enormous wealth, and build cities and monuments (see Figure 9.11). The wealth also enabled modernization in areas such as the carving into rock and harvesting of rainwater for the improvement of agriculture. This latter development was of particular importance in the dry desert climate of the region, and resulted in significant population growth and the building of relatively large cities.

EXTENSION: EXPLORE FURTHER

Use the search terms **Petra** and **Jordan** in Google Maps, and use the Street View function to navigate the ancient city. See if you can locate all of the following ancient sites:
- the Nymphaeum
- the Street of Facades
- the Tomb of Aaron
- the Tomb of the Roman Soldier
- Petra Theater

Explain how these sites indicate Petra's importance as a centre of trade.

Why do countries sometimes want to restrict trade?

While there are major gains from trade for consumers, not everyone in society is happy to allow foreign products to compete with domestically produced goods. Policies that are used to restrict trade are called **protectionist policies**. There are many different reasons that may justify a government using policies to protect domestic industries.

Fledgling or infant industries: Industries that are only just starting out may need some protection from competition from abroad while they grow and develop. The World Trade Organization (WTO) has slowly moved towards accepting this as a good reason for developing countries to engage in some protectionism while their economies struggle to perform on a level playing field with more developed nations.

Sunset industries: The reasoning here is similar to that above, but these are dying industries that are at risk of disappearing because of new innovations or competition from abroad. Examples include the car and steel industries in Europe and the USA that became sunset industries in response to Japan becoming a major car producer, and China becoming a producer of steel. The UK experienced significant upheaval during the 1980s when the steel and coal mines were closed, and miners and steelworkers went on lengthy strikes.

Anti-dumping: Foreign producers sometimes sell at unfair prices. If the prices are lower than production costs, then this is called **dumping**. This is against the rules set out by the WTO. This is not competition as it is meant to be – as consumers, we want to know that prices are genuine and not being used to manipulate us into buying a product that would not be priced that way by the market.

Protecting jobs: It is never a pleasant experience to lose one's job. Sometimes, when countries go through major structural changes in their industrial makeup, tension can

■ **Figure 9.13** Abandoned steel factory in Steubenville, Ohio

arise between policymakers and the workers in industry. Policymakers want to ensure their economy is competitive, and that inefficient industries are not being subsidized unnecessarily. Workers want to make sure their jobs and income are not at risk, and that they can still support their families. Competition from abroad can make this difficult.

Health, safety and environmental regulations: A roundabout reason for restricting trade can be to enforce certain health and safety requirements in the country. This is not necessarily done to protect domestic industries, nor does it have to mean restricting imports from a particular place, but it still works as protectionism. Countries can limit goods if they fail to meet requirements for manufacturing processes, or chemicals used. These requirements may have been imposed for health or environmental reasons.

Security: For security and reasons of defence, it might be sensible to retain some industries domestically. This includes food, as it is unwise to be reliant on food imports if prices rise or trade relations deteriorate. A more controversial industry that is important for strategic reasons is defence and military equipment.

Independence: During the first half of the twentieth century, some countries in Latin America restricted trade in an attempt to gain full independence from their colonial past. Countries such as Brazil wanted to stop being reliant on other countries for simple goods such as textiles and clothes. Countries often want to make sure that they are not reliant on imports for food.

Preventing loss of culture: Some goods, particularly food items, are such important parts of a country's culture that they receive special protections from the government. Some foods are so special that there are even international protections for them. For example, you cannot produce Parmigiano-Reggiano outside particular regions in Italy. If it is produced elsewhere, it must be called something else. The same is true of Champagne from the Champagne region. In England, a similar product is called English sparkling wine. In fact, Champagne is so important to the French people there was even a clause about it in the Treaty of Versailles.

■ **Figure 9.14** Champagne and Parmesan are both legally protected goods. Sparkling wine cannot be called Champagne unless it is made in the Champagne region of France

DISCUSS

Under what circumstances do you think it is acceptable to protect industries?

How do countries restrict trade?

Using the free trade diagram (see Figures 9.7 and 9.8), we can see how **tariffs** work to restrict trade. A tariff is one of the most commonly used protectionist measures, and imposes a tax on each unit of imported good. This raises the price of the good by the amount of the tax to P_2 in Figure 9.15c. By raising prices, two things happen. First, domestic producers are able to increase the quantity that they can supply to the market from Q_2 to Q_4. Thus, the tariff achieves its objective of protecting domestic producers. Second, consumers will be less able to afford the product, so the total quantity demanded will fall from Q_1 to Q_3.

The result is that imports are drastically reduced from Q_1–Q_2 to Q_3–Q_4. In addition, the government gains revenues from the tariff that are worth the per unit tariff multiplied by the new quantity of imports. In Figure 9.15c, this is represented by the yellow square. This value is calculated using the following equation:

$$\text{Total revenue} = \frac{\text{tariff}}{\text{per unit}} \times \frac{\text{new volume}}{\text{of imports}}$$

ACTIVITY: Calculating the effects of a tariff

ATL

- Critical-thinking skills: Interpret data

Using Figure 9.16, calculate the following figures for before and after the tariff is introduced:
- Consumer expenditure
- Consumer surplus
- Producer revenue
- Producer surplus
- Tax revenue for the government

With reference to the figures you have calculated, **discuss** the impacts of the tariff on various stakeholders.

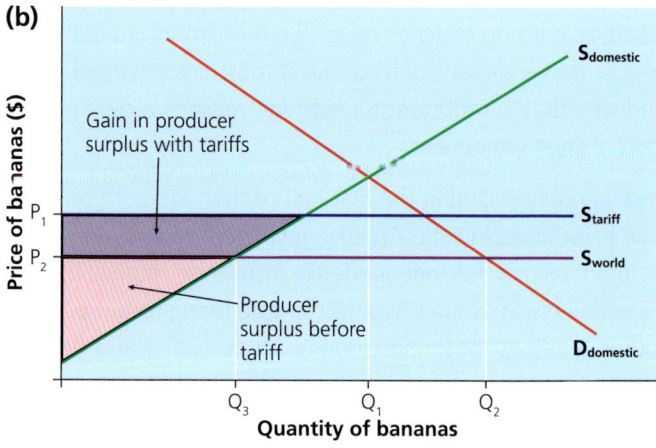

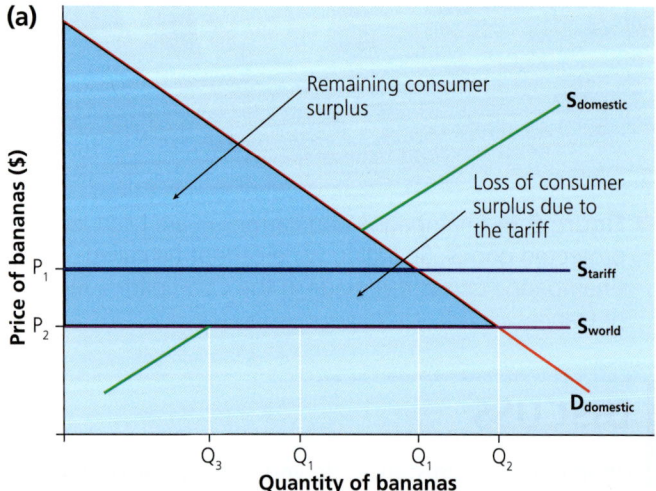

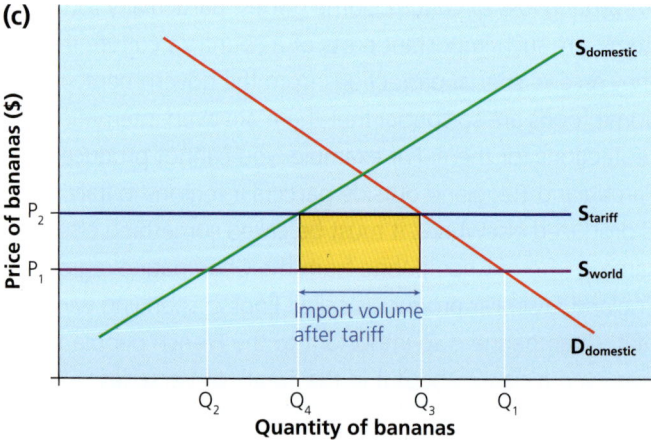

■ **Figure 9.15** Showing how tariffs work to restrict trade from abroad

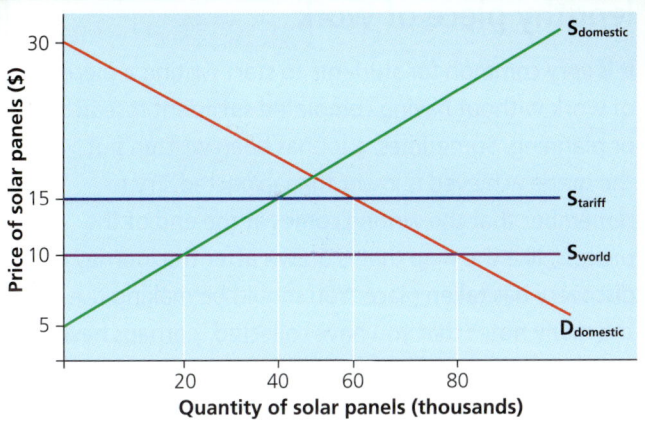

Figure 9.16 Using a diagram to help calculate the effects of tariffs

◆ Assessment opportunities

♦ In this activity you have practised skills that are assessed using Criterion D: Thinking critically.

SHOULD PROTECTIONISM BE USED?

There are some instances when tariffs can be justified, and, indeed, the World Trade Organization has in recent decades relaxed its views regarding the use of protectionist measures by some countries. Less economically developed countries can benefit from using tariffs. This is because these countries often struggle to compete with better developed global industries that already exist. Implementing tariffs can give these countries some time to build up their infant (small and growing) industries, and provide revenues to the government for investment purposes. More economically developed countries also belong to many trade agreements that give advantage to trade between member nations, often leaving out less economically developed countries.

However, protectionism can also be unfair and create tensions between countries. A very recent example is the rising tensions between the USA and China. The two countries have a difficult trading relationship, and tariffs implemented in 2018 made global stock markets very nervous because of the chances of the 'trade war' escalating. Protectionism can create such strong tensions between countries that it contributes to a complete breakdown in trust. Many countries employed strong protectionist barriers during the Great Depression in the 1930s, and historians often cite this as a contributing factor to the breakdown of relationships before the Second World War.

ACTIVITY: To tax or not to tax?

■ ATL

■ Media literacy skills: Locate, organize, analyse, evaluate, synthesize and ethically use information from a variety of sources and media

Government ministers need to think very carefully about whether tariffs they propose will be successful. There are a number of reasons why countries try to limit the trade of some goods with other countries. Not all of these reasons are always justified, and your opinion will depend on whose perspective you are considering. Write a report for your country's Minister of Trade that discusses the advantages and disadvantages of a particular tariff.

1 Conduct some research into tariffs that countries set, and find an example. You may find the following website helpful: http://bit.ly/WTOtariff (see the instructions at the bottom of the page). You can also find the tariff profile for each country if you scroll down to the bottom of the page and click the link to 'list of members'. It may be worth selecting a substantial tariff so that its impact is more significant and easier to explore.
2 **Explore** the reasons why the country has set the tariff.
3 Research other countries' responses to this tariff, using news media sites.
For example, you could do an online search using the words US+steel+tariff+china.
4 Once you are happy that you have sufficient information, write your ministerial report, including the following:
   • Background to the country's economy and the industry that is being protected
   • The reasons why the tariff was implemented
   • Who the main affected stakeholders are
   • The responses from other nations
   • A judgement of the effectiveness of the tariff and whether you think the tariff is justified.
5 Cite all your sources according to a recognized convention.

◆ Assessment opportunities

♦ In this activity you have practised skills that are assessed using Criterion A: Knowing and understanding, Criterion B: Investigating, Criterion C: Communicating and Criterion D: Thinking critically.

9 Can we make a fairer world through trade?

What kind of trade agreements do countries form with each other?

When to start writing a lengthy piece of work

It is very common for students to start writing a piece of work without having completed sufficient research or planning. Sometimes, a lot has been written but the grade achieved is lower than expected. Try to remember that the writing comes at the end of the process, like the map that is drawn after the journey of discovery has taken place. You should be making use of the many notes that you have collected, perhaps having structured the information into a plan or a mind map. Only when you are happy that you have structured the parts of the argument that you will use to answer the question, and have enough evidence to back up each part of that argument, do you start writing. Not before.

Countries have always made agreements with each other, to support one another in war, or – more often in the past – to make arrangements between royal families to marry off their children. In the case of trade, regions go through phases of wanting to trade with other countries and also of wanting to prevent trade with them. Trade agreements can have positive consequences for those involved, but also sometimes create tension between the **trade bloc** and others, or within the trade bloc itself.

FREE TRADE AREA

Countries can agree to reduce trade barriers for certain goods. This is called a **preferential trade agreement**. A **free trade area** (FTA) goes one step further, with countries promising to remove all barriers to trade in goods and services between participating countries.

The following are some examples of FTAs:
- North American Free Trade Agreement (NAFTA)
- South Asian Free Trade Area (SAFTA)
- ASEAN–Australia–New Zealand Free Trade Area (AANZFTA) (ASEAN: Association of Southeast Asian Nations)
- Central Europe Free Trade Agreement (CEFTA)
- Common Market for Eastern and Southern Africa (COMESA)

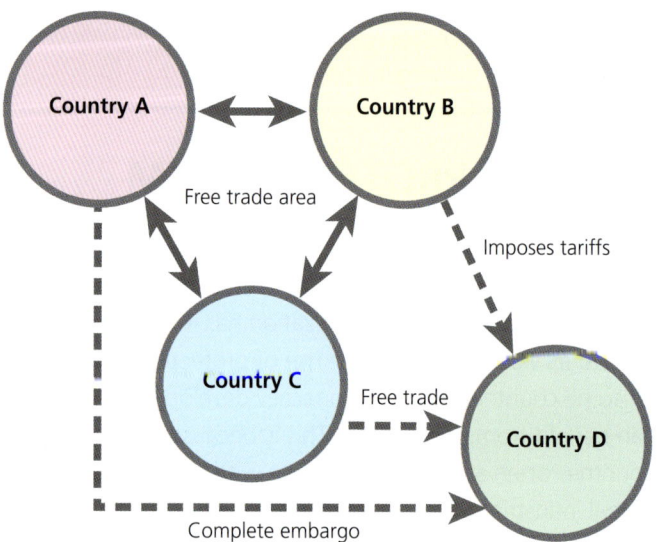

■ **Figure 9.17** Visualizing a free trade area

Being a member of a free trade area is not restrictive and members can still engage in trade or a trade agreement with any non-member country. Countries can also choose not to trade with non-members or erect barriers that are different from those in the FTA.

CUSTOMS UNION

A **customs union** is an agreement between members of a free trade area that requires members to set exactly the same trade policy with non-member countries. This means that if the bloc finds a reason to set a trade barrier against a non-member, then all the countries must agree to set the same barrier.

While the customs union does promote free trade between its members, such an agreement can be seen as not promoting free trade with the outside world. However, it does make it easier for outside countries to negotiate trade agreements with the entire bloc, as opposed to having to make these arrangements with each country separately.

COMMON MARKET

A **common market** includes the characteristics of an FTA and a customs union, but there is also free movement of all goods, people and services across borders within the common market. This means that you don't need to show your passport when you cross a border, and trucks and other goods vehicles are also free to drive across these borders. Workers and students do not need visas to live, work or study in countries within the common market. This significantly reduces costs for businesses. Examples include:
- MERCOSUR (Argentina, Brazil, Paraguay, Uruguay and Venezuela)
- The Gulf Cooperation Council (GCC)
- The European Union (EU).

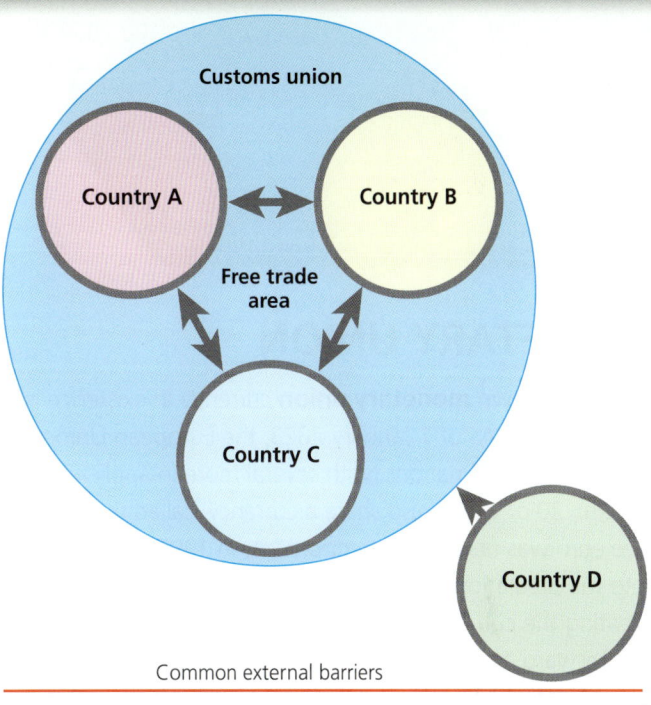

■ **Figure 9.18** Customs union

■ **Figure 9.19** Some trade blocs around the world

9 Can we make a fairer world through trade?

MONETARY UNION

The best known **monetary union** currently in existence is the Eurozone. As of 1 January 2023, the European Union is made up of 27 nations (with several more in application to join), 20 of which also share a currency, called the euro. The euro was first issued electronically in 1999 and went into full circulation on 1 January 2002. The process of creating the currency took a long time. The idea was first put forward as early as a formal agreement signed in 1992 (the Maastricht Treaty), and the name was determined in 1995. The currency and all monetary policy is set by the European Central Bank (ECB), which has its headquarters in Frankfurt, Germany.

For some years, the currency union gave a large number of benefits to the participating nations. These benefits included:
- lower trade costs because currencies did not need to be exchanged
- better pricing information for consumers, because consumers now had access to a wider choice of goods and services all being sold in the same currency
- price stability in all countries
- better relations between all participating nations because of the requirements to work together to manage institutions like the European Central Bank.

However, there have been some issues experienced with sharing a currency in Europe, particularly in 2012 when there was a risk that Greece would need to leave the union. In 2010, it was announced that the Greek government had borrowed much more than was allowed by the original agreements of the euro (and double what the government had previously stated). The borrowing had been exacerbated by the 2008–9 financial crisis, but on top of this, Greece had only been able to collect half the tax revenue due from its citizens and businesses. Financial markets responded to the news very negatively, and interest rates on Greek government debt rose to unsustainable levels.

■ **Figure 9.20 (a)** Euros; **(b)** the ECB in Frankfurt, Germany

■ **Figure 9.21** Two faces of European monetary union: **(a)** the idyllic island of Santorini and **(b)** protests taking place in Athens in 2012

In order to qualify for assistance from both the International Monetary Fund (a multilateral organization whose purpose is to provide assistance to countries in financial difficulties) and the European Stability Mechanism, Greece had to agree to measures to reduce the amount that it spends on the public sector (including on government offices and functions, public sector wages, and pensions, among many other things), raise taxes and improve the methods used to collect taxes. These measures have been difficult for the entire Greek population to endure, and there has been much debate about whether this was the right response.

> ### EXTENSION: EXPLORE FURTHER
>
> Watch the following video of an interview with the Greek Finance Minister George Papaconstantinou who was in office when the crisis first started: https://youtu.be/o2v5o-wHGgk.

Another monetary union is being planned in Africa, between nations belonging to the West African Monetary Zone (WAMZ). The currency will be called the eco. The currency was due to be introduced in 2003, but it has been postponed several times because the member nations have struggled to meet all the convergence criteria set out for certain aspects of the economy. In order for the monetary union to go ahead, the countries must all agree to having:

- an inflation rate that is no higher than 10 per cent
- annual government borrowing that does not exceed 4 per cent
- financing of government debt by the central bank that does not exceed 10 per cent of the government's tax revenues
- export revenues that can cover import expenditure for three months.

Further criteria include **exchange rate** stability and other aspects that ensure each country can participate in the monetary union with low risk. So far, Ghana is the only country to have managed to meet the criteria.

> ### DISCUSS
>
> How easy will it be for the countries participating in the WAMZ to achieve the convergence criteria? What problems might there be in knowing that all countries have met the criteria?

COMPLETE ECONOMIC INTEGRATION

There is only one example of complete economic integration. The history of the United States of America's progress in becoming a single nation state was long and gradual, and involved the coming together of parts of the country that were initially the territory of Native Americans, then controlled by Great Britain, the Netherlands, France and Spain. Once the 13 original colonies ceded from the British empire in 1776, the United States of America took another century to become what we know it as today. What is special about the USA is that it slowly merged together different political and economic systems to form a single nation, including its currency. It took from 1776, when the first 13 former colonies of Britain signed the Declaration of Independence, until 1959 when Alaska and Hawaii became the 49th and 50th states of the USA (before that, they both were territories).

■ **Figure 9.22** A map showing how the United States formed since 1776

■ **Figure 9.23** The US dollar

The US currency, the US dollar, is today's most circulated and most widely held currency.

Today, there is a Federal Government of the entire country, and each of the 50 states that makes up the USA has a separate state government. This system of organizing the USA is left over from the way that Great Britain ran its vast empire, installing a governor in each territory that it controlled.

> ## DISCUSS
> According to some, the Eurozone Debt Crisis highlighted the need for closer economic and political integration. It might be that there will someday be a 'United States of Europe'. Do you think this is a good idea? What are the advantages and disadvantages of forming a closer union between the countries that make up the EU? Read the following articles and watch the video to get some more background about the EU and this debate:
> - http://bit.ly/EuropeTimeline
> - https://youtu.be/JIqxY04D-Uc

Did you know that the root of the word 'dollar' comes from the sixteenth century, when a Bohemian count created a coin named after the area where the metal was mined called the Joachimsthalers, where the word *thaler* meant valley (similar to the English word 'dale'). The word has migrated into several languages:
- Danish and Swedish as *daler*
- Norwegian as *dalar* and *daler*
- Dutch as *daler* or *daalder*
- Ethiopian as *talari*
- Hungarian as *tallér*
- Italian as *tallero*
- English as dollar

The Dutch used a coin called a *leeuwendaler* (*leeuw* is the Dutch for lion, which featured on the coin) in the Dutch colony of New Netherland (known as New York today). English settlers in the region referred to it as the lion dollar. The US dollar was first minted by the United States Mint in 1792. Spanish, Dutch and Mexican currencies remained in circulation until the Coinage Act in 1857.

How is a currency's value determined?

The foreign exchange market deals with trillions of dollars' worth of transactions every day. London is where most of these transactions take place, with most of them being for investment purposes (so not simply the kind of currency exchange we might need for going on a summer holiday, although this can have an impact too). Exchange rates, or the value of one currency expressed in terms of another currency, are determined by the interaction of market forces.

The way we think about supply and demand in this particular market has to change slightly, however. With currencies, nothing is really produced. The central bank keeps tight control over the number of physical notes in the system and most currency is traded simply from those who have it to those who want it.

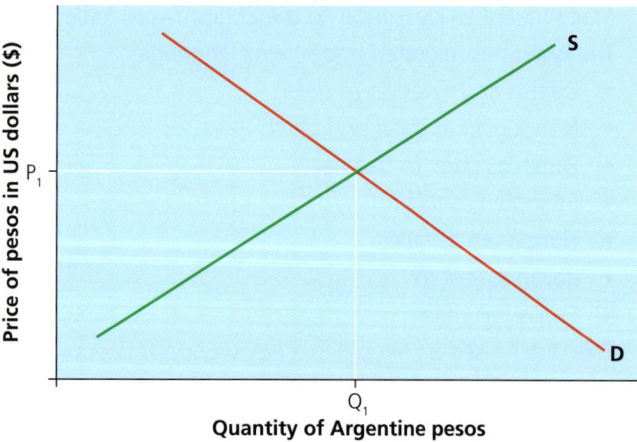

Figure 9.24 Showing how currencies are determined using supply and demand

CHANGING CURRENCY VALUES

Currency values change every day. This is largely because financial markets can place 'bets' on the movements of currencies, and make agreements to buy currencies at certain rates in the future. In addition, the news that we receive about different countries can heavily influence these financial markets, as well as consumer demand to buy goods from or visit that country.

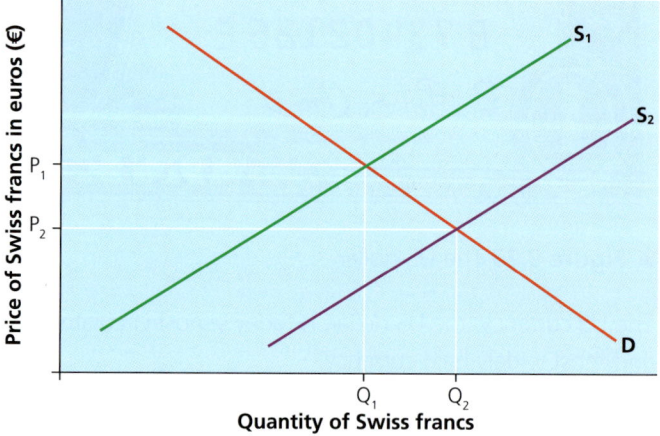

Figure 9.25 A currency depreciating

When people stop wanting to hold a currency, often when there is some negative economic news like poor growth forecasts or rising unemployment, they will want to sell what they hold of that currency. When this happens, there will be an increase in supply of currency to the market from S_1 to S_2 (see Figure 9.25). Because there will be many people unwilling to buy the currency, there will have to be a price decrease from P_1 to P_2, in order for the market to correct.

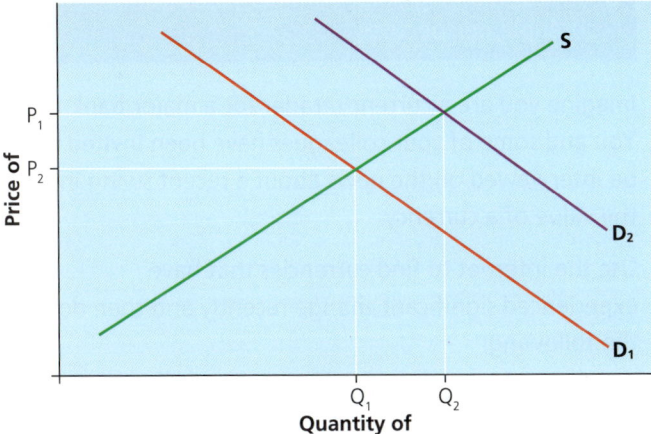

■ **Figure 9.26** A currency appreciating

When a currency experiences an increase in demand from D_1 to D_2 (see Figure 9.26), it will appreciate. This is because the currency must now be allocated between an increased number of people who want to hold the currency for whatever reason.

EVALUATING CURRENCY CHANGES

Currency movements can be analysed in different ways, and it is important to think very carefully about whether the effects of the change are good or bad. It is often assumed that a currency depreciation is a bad thing, when in fact there can be positive impacts too. This depends on the structure of the economy, what is produced and what is traded.

Trade balance: With a depreciating currency, exports can become relatively cheaper. This is because buyers need to exchange fewer units of their currency to buy the same good or service. This means that it is possible that the quantity demanded can rise. The opposite is true for anything we import, as we will need more foreign currency to buy the same goods, and this may lead to a fall in imported volumes. It is extremely difficult to know exactly what will happen to the trade balance, however, because consumers do not necessarily respond to a price change immediately.

■ **Figure 9.27** Day-to-day movements in exchange rates are caused by currency speculation by financial firms and these days are completed electronically. Trillions of dollars are traded on markets per day

Take petrol, for example. Just because it becomes more expensive to import does not mean we will reduce the amount we buy, because it is such an important part of our economy. In fact, the amount we spend on imported fossil fuels will probably rise with a currency depreciation. We must therefore always look at what the country imports and exports before being able to understand what will happen to the trade balance, and consider how sensitive buyers will be to the changes in relative prices.

Employment: Linked to the above point, a currency change can affect employment in the economy. When the quantity demanded of our exports rises with a currency depreciation, there may be an increase in the demand for workers. As with the point above, not all price changes immediately correspond to a response by consumers.

Inflation: Currency changes will affect the cost of imported raw materials. While a currency depreciation can have a positive impact on exports, imported goods become relatively more expensive. If the country relies heavily on imported raw materials, like copper or crude oil, both of which are important inputs into production, the costs of production will rise. Producers using these more expensive resources will either have to absorb the price increases and lose some profit, or raise the selling price of the goods they produce. A significant price increase of raw materials can cause inflation in the whole country to rise – a real burden if incomes are not rising.

Economic growth: Depending on all the above points, and how responsive consumers are to price changes, currency changes can affect economic growth, both positively and negatively. As long as demand for exports rises with a cheaper currency and demand for non-essential imports falls, domestic production can rise and result in increased gross domestic product.

What are the pros and cons of trade and aid?

Since the end of the Second World War, when most former colonies gained their independence, a lot of effort and research has gone into development theory to determine the best policies to help standards of living improve globally. In particular, there is a big debate about how effective it is to send aid to developing countries.

ARGUMENTS FOR AND AGAINST TRADE

As we have discussed previously, free markets are pretty good at allocating resources. Where there is supply of a product, there will probably be demand for it or it would not have been produced. To quote classical economist, Jean-Baptiste Say (1767–1832):

> 'As each of us can only purchase the productions of others with his own productions – as the value we can buy is equal to the value we can produce, the more men can produce, the more they will purchase.'

In other words, we must use the income generated from our production to buy the production of others. Say's ideas are most commonly paraphrased as 'Supply creates its own demand'. By engaging in trade, and opening up to foreign markets, opportunities for production in the developing country will increase. With this, opportunities for entrepreneurs to start businesses will improve, and further support industries will develop, thereby raising incomes for those employed in these new fledgling industries.

However, most developing countries export primary goods, or those derived solely from resource extraction. This includes farming and mining. It is very difficult to generate large amounts of surplus through selling these goods, and so it is likely that developing countries trade only an undiversified set of products. Too many resources end up being allocated to too few industries, and the country is at greater risk if anything happens to those industries, such as a price shock or problem with its currency. These types of industries are not sustainable in the long term, as they can lead to soil erosion, and damage to a beautiful natural environment. By specializing in the production of only primary goods, less economically developed countries will eventually run out of the ability to rely on trading those goods because the land has been exploited of all its resources. Over the longer term, countries need to invest in manufacturing and services to be able to cope.

In addition, the EU and USA protect some of their industries, such as dairy and crops like wheat and corn. This makes it very difficult for developing countries to compete with them. While agricultural industries in MEDCs are **capital intensive**, the majority of workers in developing countries might be employed in agriculture and earning much lower wages.

ACTIVITY: What's happening to currencies today?

■ ATL

- Critical-thinking skills: Consider ideas from multiple perspectives

Imagine you are a currency trader for a major bank. You and some of your colleagues have been invited to be interviewed on the news about a recent swing in the value of a currency.

Use the internet to find currencies that have experienced significant change recently and then do the following:

1 **Plan and film a video in the style of a news interview.**
2 Using a relevant diagram, **explain** what has happened to the currency.
3 **Explain** the main factors that have led to the currency change.
4 **Evaluate** the impact of the currency change on different stakeholders in the economy.

◆ Assessment opportunities

- In this activity you have practised skills that are assessed using Criterion A: Knowing and understanding, Criterion C: Communicating and Criterion D: Thinking critically.

ARGUMENTS FOR AND AGAINST AID

Aid refers to the transfer of money, goods and services, without the need for something in exchange, with the purpose of helping a country to develop or supporting people in meeting their basic needs. Governments send what is called Official Development Assistance (ODA).

Non-Governmental Organizations (NGOs) carry out what is called humanitarian aid, which provides support in cases of extreme emergency such as famines, wars and natural disasters.

Arguments for aid include:
- Aid is able to provide necessary items directly to those in need.
- Aid can target particular geographical areas, distinguishing between areas where it is needed more or less.
- Aid is effective when basic infrastructure or institutional frameworks are not in operation, such as during a natural disaster or war.
- https://bit.ly/2m0kY6G
- https://youtu.be/8eJRRCBiTOs

ARGUMENTS FOR THE USE OF OTHER METHODS SUCH AS MICROFINANCE

Microfinance is the industry that tries to provide financial services like banking and insurance to people or businesses who usually would not qualify for finance. Most businesses and entrepreneurs in developed countries will approach a bank to take out a loan to finance the start of their business or a major project. This is not always an option in developing countries, however, where credit institutions are limited in number and size. Microfinance therefore gives greater access to credit which can then fuel new business start-ups and thus economic growth.

The most famous example of a microfinance institution is the Grameen Bank. Microfinance is credited with being able to help people start their own businesses and escape the poverty cycle (see Chapter 10) and has become very popular.

MEET AN ECONOMIST: ESTHER DUFLO (1972–PRESENT)

Figure 9.28 Esther Duflo

You may have encountered in your studies in MYP Sciences how researchers prove the effect of a drug on the human body in the field of medicine, by conducting blind trials of the drug. One group of people is given the drug and the other group a placebo; neither group knows which they received. The groups are then compared. This is called a Randomized Control Trial (RCT). Esther Duflo, a French economist who teaches at the Massachusetts Institute of Technology (MIT), is well known for using RCTs in her academic work. She is interested in trying to quantify the effects of policies and initiatives, especially in cases where the existing evidence is anecdotal. One area where this is particularly relevant is microfinance. In a paper called 'The miracle of microfinance? Evidence from a randomized evaluation' (2014), Duflo and her co-authors conclude that:

'Small business investment and profits of pre-existing businesses increased, but consumption did not significantly increase. Durable goods expenditure increased, while "temptation goods" expenditure declined. We found no significant changes in health, education, or women's empowerment. Two years later, after control areas had gained access to microcredit but households in treatment area had borrowed for longer and in larger amounts, very few significant differences persist.' – Esther Duflo et al, 'The miracle of microfinance? Evidence from a randomized evaluation' (2014)

ACTIVITY: Trade or aid?

ATL

- Information literacy skills: Gather and organize relevant information to formulate an argument

Many argue that the best road to development is not through aid, but through a free market approach of pursuing increased trade. They suggest that only this approach creates the incentives for people to participate in work, and start businesses that generate revenue and grow.

Read the following two articles:
- **'The Case for Aid' by Jeffrey Sachs:** http://foreignpolicy.com/2014/01/21/the-case-for-aid/
- **'Seven Moral Arguments for Free Trade' by Daniel Griswold:** www.cato.org/commentary/seven-moral-arguments-free-trade

Prepare a speech arguing for or against aid as a means to development. You must **justify** your argument with credible evidence both from and in addition to that given in the two articles.

◆ Assessment opportunities

◆ In this activity you have practised skills that are assessed using Criterion B: Investigating and Criterion D: Thinking critically.

ACTIVITY: Investigating supply chains

ATL

- Information literacy skills: Process data and report results

As we saw in the beginning of the chapter, globalization has led to a large number of multinational or transnational corporations taking advantage of differences in resources availability, labour costs and institutional frameworks (laws, tax systems, government) between countries. Supply chains have become increasingly complex as a result, and it can be difficult for consumers to know for certain where their things come from and how they were made.

Choose one of the following options:
- Nestlé
- Nutella
- Apple
- Asos
- Nike
- Volkswagen

Conduct an investigation into and write a report about your company's supply chain for some of its products. In your investigation and report, consider the following question:

'To what extent are businesses able to act ethically without the need for government intervention?'

Your report should be no more than 1,500 words in length. Include information about the following:
- Incidents of unethical behaviour
- Any government action against the company
- Incidents of the company taking responsibility for its actions
- Processes that led to the discovery of a problematic incident
- Changes companies made themselves to improve their supply chain management

Conclude your work by suggesting the most effective ways governments might better regulate production that takes place across borders.

◆ Assessment opportunities

◆ In this activity you have practised skills that are assessed using Criterion A: Knowing and understanding, Criterion B: Investigating, Criterion C: Communicating and Criterion D: Thinking critically.

Reflection

In this chapter, we have **explored** how the exchange of goods and services between countries can improve cooperation and international relations, perhaps preventing the outbreak of war and conflict. We have **analysed** how trade improves the competitiveness of firms. We have **evaluated** the extent to which trade can be positive for all participating countries, and **explored** the various reasons why protectionist measures might sometimes be justified.

We have **investigated** the various trade agreements that can exist, and the difficulties that can sometimes arise when countries align themselves so closely with each other. We can now **explain** the kinds of mechanisms, like currencies and exchange rates, that facilitate trade.

Use this table to reflect on your own learning in this chapter.					
Questions we asked	Answers we found	Any further questions now?			
Factual: What do we mean by globalization? What are trade agreements? How do countries restrict trade? How is a currency's value determined? What kind of trade agreements do countries form with each other?					
Conceptual: Why do we trade? How important can trade be to the success of a society? Why do countries sometimes want to restrict trade?					
Debatable: Is globalization good or bad? What are the pros and cons of aid and trade?					
Approaches to learning you used in this chapter	Description – what new skills did you learn?	How well did you master the skills?			
		Novice	Learner	Practitioner	Expert
Information literacy skills					
Media literacy skills					
Critical-thinking skills					
Learner profile attribute(s)	Reflect on the importance of being an inquirer for your learning in this chapter.				
Inquirers					

9 Can we make a fairer world through trade?

Change | Equity; Resources | Fairness and development

10 How can developing countries successfully increase standards of living?

○ **Improved standards of living** can be achieved through **equitable** distribution of **resources**.

CONSIDER THESE QUESTIONS:

Factual: What do we mean by growth and development? What are the characteristics of a developing country? How much progress has been made towards international development goals?

Conceptual: What challenges do developing countries face? How do we measure development?

Debatable: To what extent does development require intervention in markets? To what extent does economic growth result in development?

Now **share and compare** your thoughts and ideas with your partner, or with the whole class.

■ **Figure 10.1** People live in very different homes in different countries, regions and cities

○ IN THIS CHAPTER WE WILL …
- **Find out** about the characteristics of developing countries.
- **Explore** the challenges faced by different developing countries and what solutions might work.
- **Take action** by investigating how difficult it can be to live below the poverty line.

WHAT MAKES YOU SAY THAT?

What do the images suggest to you about the places where they might be found? What makes you say that?

- These Approaches to Learning (ATL) skills will be useful …
  - Communication skills
  - Information literacy skills
  - Media literacy skills
  - Critical-thinking skills

- We will reflect on this learner profile attribute …
  - Caring – showing empathy, compassion and respect; having a commitment to service, and acting to make a positive difference in the lives of others and in the world around us.

- Assessment opportunities in this chapter:
  - Criterion A: Knowing and understanding
  - Criterion B: Investigating
  - Criterion C: Communicating
  - Criterion D: Thinking critically

KEY WORDS

development   fairness   statistics

Why is the quality of life different in different countries and how can we raise standards of living in countries where basic needs are not being met? This is a question that economists, geographers, historians and sociologists have been trying to answer for decades. When colonial powers relinquished controls over their colonies, starting in the 1940s, the only goal of economic policy was to achieve high rates of economic growth. It was thought that if incomes were raised, all the other features of a developed country would follow. Now that we are in the twenty-first century, and we know that there are still countries where people's basic needs are not being met despite many years of positive economic growth, we understand that it is not only economic growth that brings happiness. This chapter will explore the shared characteristics of developing countries, and the different circumstances that they face.

THINK–PAIR–SHARE

Remind yourself of Maslow's hierarchy of needs (see Chapter 1, page 4). Which elements of the hierarchy do you think are achieved when incomes increase? Share your thoughts with a partner, and then with the rest of the class.

10 How can developing countries successfully increase standards of living?

What do we mean by growth and development? How can we measure development?

Economic growth is defined as an increase in economic output (measured by increases in gross domestic product). In Chapter 8 we learned that our income is derived from the production of goods and services – owners of capital might earn interest, labourers earn a wage, owners of land earn rent and entrepreneurs earn profits. By putting our resources to productive uses, and by becoming better able to produce more goods and services, our incomes rise. It is through increased investment, government spending and export revenues that the circular flow of income grows in size.

Development is a multi-faceted concept that refers to the improvement in people's standards of living, which means they are not prevented from reaching their own personal potential. Development means that people have the freedom to access basic goods and services, that they have the freedom to 'be' and 'do' the things they want in life.

> **EXTENSION: EXPLORE FURTHER**
>
> Take a look at the following website:
>
> http://hdr.undp.org/en/content/what-human-development
>
> and watch the video. Take notes of the meaning of the term 'development', considering the focus on people rather than solely economic factors.

> **DISCUSS**
>
> How strong might the relationship be between growth and development? Are there circumstances in which high growth rates might not lead to development?

ECONOMIC GROWTH AND THE POVERTY CYCLE

The poverty cycle isn't a model in the strictest sense, but it is a diagram that helps to visualize the reasons why it is so difficult to break out of a situation of low income. The diagram (see Figure 10.3) particularly helps us to understand the relationship between economic growth and development.

The cycle on the left of the diagram is the growth cycle, and links low incomes to low economic growth. If people are only earning enough to consume basic goods such as food and shelter, they have no money to save. One of the injections to the circular flow of income is investment, which is generated by savings in the financial market. Investment is needed in an economy to start new businesses and to fund businesses during their expansion. The incentive to lend to new businesses is the interest that is paid on the loans, but without developed financial markets and institutions there will be little channelling of funds from savers to investors. The result is low rates of economic growth and so limited chances for incomes to grow.

On the right-hand side of the diagram, low incomes can be linked to a lack of development. When families don't earn a lot of money, they will struggle to send their children to school. It may be that the family cannot afford the school fees, or an expensive uniform, or the children may be needed to help earn money or farm the land to produce food. In addition, low incomes also limit the government's ability to use tax revenues to fund education and health services. This means that the labour force is of lower quality, without the means to be innovative or entrepreneurial, and there will be low levels of what economists call human capital. Human capital is essential for improved productivity levels, workers are needed to enable businesses to become more efficient in using their resources – helping them make more with less. Without these gains in productivity, the chances of increased incomes are low.

To what extent does economic growth result in development?

It must be remembered that economic growth has resulted in major positive change for the world since 1800. In his book *Utopia for Realists* (2017), Rutger Bregman reminds us that the following major changes have taken place:

- In 1820, 84 per cent of the world population lived in absolute poverty; in 2017 that figure was less than 10 per cent.
- Life expectancy has more than doubled since 1900.
- In 1965, 51 per cent of people were living on fewer than 2,000 calories per day; in 2015 it was 3 per cent.

It is no coincidence that this has all taken place since the Industrial Revolution. Prior to that, income remained roughly the same for most people, whether they were born in the year 1300 or 1600. The Industrial Revolution created a major surge in productivity and output. Above we discussed how economic growth might raise living standards for individuals. Governments use economic growth as a target for government policy because of the increased economic potential and improvements to living standards that it brings. However, relentless pursuit of economic growth also creates problems. Both more and less economically developed countries experience these, but in less economically developed countries the difficulties experienced by individuals will be more acute.

INCOME INEQUALITY

It is a necessary reality of capitalism that there is some income inequality in the economic system. It is only pure communism that aims to give everyone an equal share of the country's resources and income. One central feature of capitalism is the right to private property (the opposite of communism). With private property rights, people are free to make decisions about how to deploy the resource they own. Consumers seek to maximize their utility (or satisfaction) and producers want to maximize profits. While some people are or will become business owners, the majority of the population earns an income by working and earning a wage. For most people, earning a wage will probably earn them a lower income than earning profits, as the risk taken by workers is lower.

With the promotion of free markets in developing countries, there is a risk of increasing income inequality, however. There are a number of reasons for this, including control of the country being left in the hands of certain ethnic groups and not others, poor and unequal access to education and credit systems, poorly developed infrastructure, and unsupportive institutional frameworks (such as government corruption and heavy bureaucracy).

■ **Figure 10.2** 'Breaker boys' (who separated impurities from coal, by hand) during a break at a South Pittston Pennsylvania coal mine

ACTIVITY: Wealth inequality: How bad is it and what can we do about it?

■ ATL

- Communication skills: Make effective summary notes for studying

The French economist, Thomas Piketty, has done a lot of work on the relationship between economic growth and income inequality. His central idea is that wealthy people (those who become rich from assets other than income from a paid job, such as property, stock market investment, business profits) find it much easier to accumulate more wealth than someone who just ▶

earns an income. The reason for this is that the rate of return on capital (the money made from investing) has historically been much greater than rates of economic growth (which are responsible for rising incomes).

Watch his TED Talk called **New thoughts on capital in the twenty-first century**.

Look back at Chapter 1 to structure your page using the Cornell note-taking method. Here are your questions for the left-hand column:

- What is the interesting lesson that Piketty has learned from historical data?
- What database will he refer to?
- What has happened to income inequality in the USA compared to Europe in the last century (the first fact)?
- Why has income inequality changed in the USA?
- What is the second fact that Piketty discusses?
- What is the third fact?
- What is the dynamic dynastic model that explains why wealth inequality is so much worse than income inequality?
- When $r > g$ is $5 > 1$, what does he say will happen to wealth inequality?
- What has the rate of g been historically?
- What is the important conclusion that can be made about the impact of the Industrial Revolution and increased growth rates on wealth inequality?
- What happened to r and g during the first and second halves of the twentieth century, or pre and post the Second World War?

EXTENSION

What are some of the factors that influence $r > g$?

What can be done about wealth inequality?

Check your understanding of the video by taking the quiz, which you will find below the video in the section 'More resources' (you may need to create a TEDEd account for this).

If you struggled with the video, you can read the article '$r > g$: explained'.

EXTENSION

Do you agree with Piketty's main idea that income inequality will worsen if economic growth is always less than the rate of return on capital? What do you think about his ideas for redistributing income?

◆ Assessment opportunities

- In this activity you have practised skills that are assessed using Criterion A: Knowing and understanding.

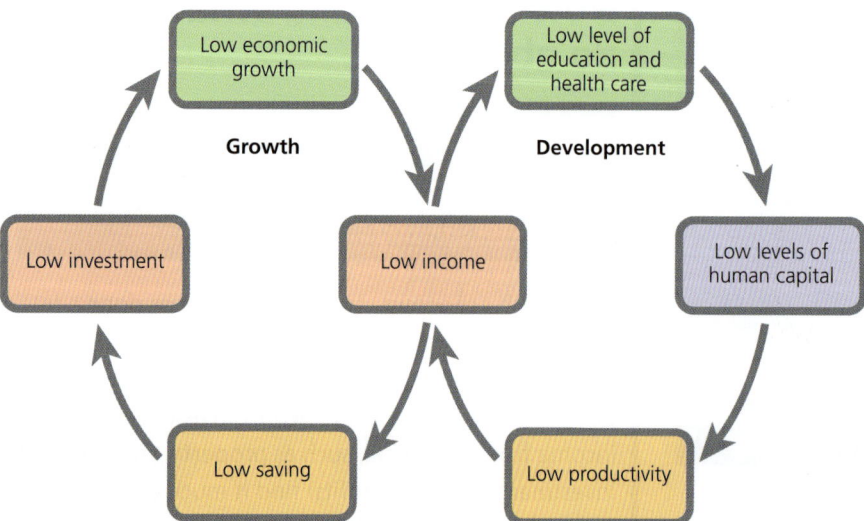

■ Figure 10.3 The poverty cycle

NEGATIVE EXTERNALITIES

We came across this concept in Chapter 8. Negative externalities occur when the price of a good or service does not cover the real costs associated with the production or consumption of a good that is not desirable for societies. Without taxes, the price of cigarettes would only compensate the tobacco companies, and not help towards the costs of cancer treatment and other negative consequences. The same is true for pollution, alcohol, recreational drugs and anything else that causes damage to society.

Developing countries often lack the institutional frameworks to manage fast-paced growth and development. For example, is local government able to cope with and recycle the waste generated by local businesses? How well entrenched are regulations regarding pollution? How easy is it to weigh the needs of a growing mining industry that supplies most of a country's exports against the need to be sustainable and have a longer-term outlook?

UNSUSTAINABLE USE OF RESOURCES

In Chapter 5, we discussed the sustainable use of natural environments for their resources (see pages 136–41). Many developing countries have large quantities of natural resources that can be sold on international markets. Resource gathering is a simple form of economic activity, which often makes use of labour rather than machinery. Because labour is relatively inexpensive in developing countries, this can be a profitable industry. Historically, this has been at the heart of the relationship between countries and their colonies – colonies were exploited for their resources by colonial powers to sustain economic growth and increased incomes. This is explored further in Chapter 2.

However, resource gathering such as mining can be very detrimental to the natural environment. For example, rainforests in Indonesia are being cut down at alarming rates to make way for palm oil plantations. The images in Figure 10.4 show the impact on land resources as a result of intensive use.

ACTIVITY: The tobacco industry's fight for survival

■ ATL

- Communication skills: Read critically and for comprehension

Search online to read the newspaper article **'Threats, bullying, lawsuits: tobacco industry's dirty war for the African market'** published in the *Guardian* on 12 July 2017 and then do the following:
- **Explain** what the tobacco industry is trying to accomplish in African countries.
- **Suggest** reasons for the increased tobacco use in African countries.
- **Suggest** to what extent the tobacco industry should continue to be allowed to do business selling tobacco products.

◆ Assessment opportunities

◆ In this activity you have practised skills that are assessed using Criterion A: Knowing and understanding and Criterion D: Thinking critically.

OVERDEPENDENCE ON NARROW RANGE OF INDUSTRIAL OUTPUT

Industrial output from developing countries is simple and not very varied, and creates little surplus value or profit. To be able to sell something useful, activity has to take place over a large scale to make sufficient revenues, and enable those revenues to increase and contribute to economic growth. For example, large amounts of land have to be used if a country's main export is coffee.

When demand for primary resources is growing, this can be an important contributor to growth for any developing nation which is reliant on those resources for income. For example, when oil prices rise, this can be very good for countries like Nigeria and Saudi Arabia. However, prices for these types of goods are highly volatile (see Chapter 11, page 285 to understand why), and subject to dramatic declines. It is during these periods of falling prices that the economies of developing countries are hit hard, and this leaves them more vulnerable to other shocks such as droughts or political instability.

SEE–THINK–WONDER

Look at the images in Figure 10.4. What environmental damage do you see is being done to the land? What do you think will be the consequences of such economic activity? What does that make you wonder about the ease with which we sacrifice our environment for economic gains?

■ **Figure 10.4 (a)** Large-scale animal farming; **(b)** mining; **(c)** palm oil plantations

What are the characteristics of a developing country?

The characteristics of a developing country can be shown through various indicators that demonstrate what life is like for those people who live in the country. These indicators are calculated by gathering statistics on the residents. The characteristics are shared by most developing countries and all link to lack of development (as defined on page 246).

You have been introduced to some of these statistics in Chapter 6, which dealt with the impact of population change on indicators like the birth and death rate. Here we are going to spend a little more time with these indicators, but look at them in the context of development, trying to understand how a lack of development in a country results in these outcomes, and how they in turn prevent development from occurring.

SINGLE INDICATORS

High birth rates: Developing countries tend to have high birth rates. The birth rate measures the number of live births per 1,000 of the population. There are a number of factors that affect whether women in a country tend to have many or few children. These include how wealthy they are, their education levels, their religiosity (for example, whether their religion forbids the use of some types of birth control), and the availability of maternal support and family planning advice.

High infant and maternal mortality rates: Pregnancy in any part of the world carries risks. In 1800, 43 per cent of children on average failed to reach their fifth birthday. In 2017, that rate was 4.25 per cent, but this varies greatly from country to country. In developed countries, even difficult births can be easily managed with the supervision of the mother in a hospital by doctors. If necessary, children are born by caesarian section instead of being delivered naturally. In developing countries, the number of doctors and midwives is much lower, and the risk of infection after delivery extremely high. A caesarian section in an LEDC is a more dangerous procedure, and natural births also carry a higher risk.

Low life expectancy: On average, people will live shorter lives in developing countries. Reasons for this include poor nutrition, low access to medical care, poor sanitation and high prevalence of communicable diseases.

Low access to medical care: This links very closely to the previous two indicators of development, and is typically measured by the number of doctors per 1,000 people. Without enough doctors, people do not have access to information about health, treatment when they are ill, or the supervision of medical expertise during childbirth.

Low literacy rates and education levels: The literacy rate is the share of the population that can read. Significant progress has been made with this indicator, so we tend to use measures for the amount of schooling received by children. Statistics for this include the expected years of schooling, and the mean years of schooling achieved by children.

Low incomes: It is highly likely that a significant proportion of people living in a developing country earn just enough or not enough to cover basic needs such as food and shelter. An internationally defined level of income is used to indicate absolute poverty. Since October 2015, you are considered to be in absolute poverty if you earn below $1.90 per day.

High rural–urban migration: Less economically developed countries tend to have large proportions of their populations still living in rural areas, working in informal economic sectors such as subsistence farming. As economic growth and development takes off in a country, it is usually cities that are located near ports or other regions through which goods and services are transported that experience significant change. This results in cities growing rapidly in size as workers move from the countryside to the cities in search of better opportunities.

> ! **Take action: Living on one dollar a day**
>
> ! In 2013, four university students from the USA went to live in Guatemala for three months to experience the realities of living on one dollar a day. See their YouTube channel 'Living on One'. What do you think about what these young men decided to do? Do you think you could conduct such an experiment? How valuable do you think what they learned is?
>
> ! Find out what the level of income is in your country below which a person is considered to be in poverty.
>
> ! Put together a presentation that includes the following information:
> - Average rent for housing in the area where you live
> - Average energy costs for electricity and gas
> - Average food costs
> - Any other costs that you think are necessary where you live
>
> ! Then do the following:
> 1. **Describe** the statistic used by your country's government to measure poverty.
> 2. **Explain** the challenges faced by people on low incomes in your country.
> 3. **Suggest** three government policies that might be effective in reducing levels of poverty in your country.

ACTIVITY: Developing country profile

■ **ATL**

- Communication skills: Find information for disciplinary and interdisciplinary inquiries, using a variety of media

There has been a tendency in the past to group all developing countries together as though they have shared experiences and problems. When looking at economic and social data, developing countries may look very similar, but the reasons why they find themselves in that predicament and why it is difficult to escape low standards of living will be different.

Choose two countries that are considered to be less economically developed.

1. Using relevant statistics that you find from a credible source online, **describe** the current state of development in the countries up to now.
2. **Suggest** the main reasons for the two countries' lack of development.
3. **Compare and contrast** the two countries in terms of their developmental background and current states.

◆ Assessment opportunities

- In this activity you have practised skills that are assessed using Criterion A: Knowing and understanding.

Low access to technology: Technology can dramatically improve productivity for businesses, especially if they make use of machinery and computing to lower production costs. Of course, it is important that any technology is appropriate in that country. For example, does it make sense to introduce an email system when businesses' suppliers, distributors and customers don't use emails? The internet is useful for both consumers and producers, as it can provide accurate information about the availability and price of goods and services. Mobile phone masts are much cheaper to install than landlines, so it was only when mobile communications took off in the early 2000s that developing countries were able to start introducing the infrastructure necessary for making use of the internet. Search for the *Guardian's* series of photographs called 'Bringing phone reception to a remote mountain town in the Democratic Republic of the Congo' to see what is involved in erecting a mobile phone mast.

COMPOSITE INDICATORS

A composite indicator is one that is made up of, or composed of, several different indicators. The best known composite indicator for development is the **Human Development Index** (HDI). The HDI was developed by economists at the United Nations Development Programme (UNDP) as part of the annual Human Development Reports. It combines statistics for health, income and education levels. The current **methodology** uses:

- average life expectancy
- gross national income per capita
- mean and expected years of schooling.

THINK–PAIR–SHARE

Take a moment to think about what things make you truly happy. How many of these things are related to money, and which cannot be bought? If you feel open to sharing these, then do so with a partner. Have a **discussion** with the rest of the class about what it means to 'be happy' and how this affects the goals you set for yourselves.

▼ Links to: Sciences

In your Sciences subjects, you no doubt do experimental work in which you measure many variables and consider the direction of causality between them. In your lab reports you reflect on this process, and consider the reliability and validity of your method and measurements. In Economics and Geography we must do the same.

MEET TWO SIGNIFICANT INDIVIDUALS: AMARTYA SEN AND MAHBUB UL HAQ

■ **Figure 10.5** Amartya Sen and Mahbub ul Haq

Amartya Sen and Mahbub ul Haq are credited with developing the Human Development Index in 1990 when they worked together for the UNDP. Haq was from Pakistan, educated at the University of Punjab and the University of Cambridge, and worked as the Minister of Finance for Pakistan. Nobel Laureate Sen is from India and was educated at the Presidency College of the University of Calcutta, and at Trinity College, Cambridge. Haq led a team, that included Sen, at the UNDP to write the very first UN Development Report, and over time they both developed new understandings of what development meant and how to measure it. It is they who defined development as having the freedom to make choices about being and doing (see page 2). Sen developed his ideas from his work about famines, having experienced the Bengal famine of 1943 himself. He cared deeply about what happened to his family and to his country during that time, and this led him to want to study these things in more detail. He noticed in his research that food supplies during famines didn't necessarily fall, but that instead there were inherent inequalities in access to and distribution of food.

The HDI is one of the best composite indicators that we have. Because development is a multi-faceted concept, we need a statistic that captures more than one dimension. For example, looking at GDP on its own as a measure of economic progress can be misleading as in some countries, the high incomes earned by small groups suggest that the whole population earns a sufficiently high wage. By including other measures, HDI is able to iron out such problems. The three components that are used in HDI are likely to be low in most developing countries.

There are criticisms of HDI, however. In developed countries, each person's ecological footprint is dramatically bigger than those in developing countries. Despite all the improvements in quality of life that development gives, developed countries do more harm to the environment than LEDCs. Does becoming a developed country mean that more plastic must get used to contain all our food, that we need to regularly go out and shop for new clothes to replace the ones we don't like anymore, or that we must all stop walking to places and each own a flashy car?

ACTIVITY: Is development sustainable?

■ **ATL**

■ Communication skills: Make inferences and draw conclusions

Figure 10.6 shows the correlation between HDI and the ecological footprints of every country. Study the graph and answer the questions below.

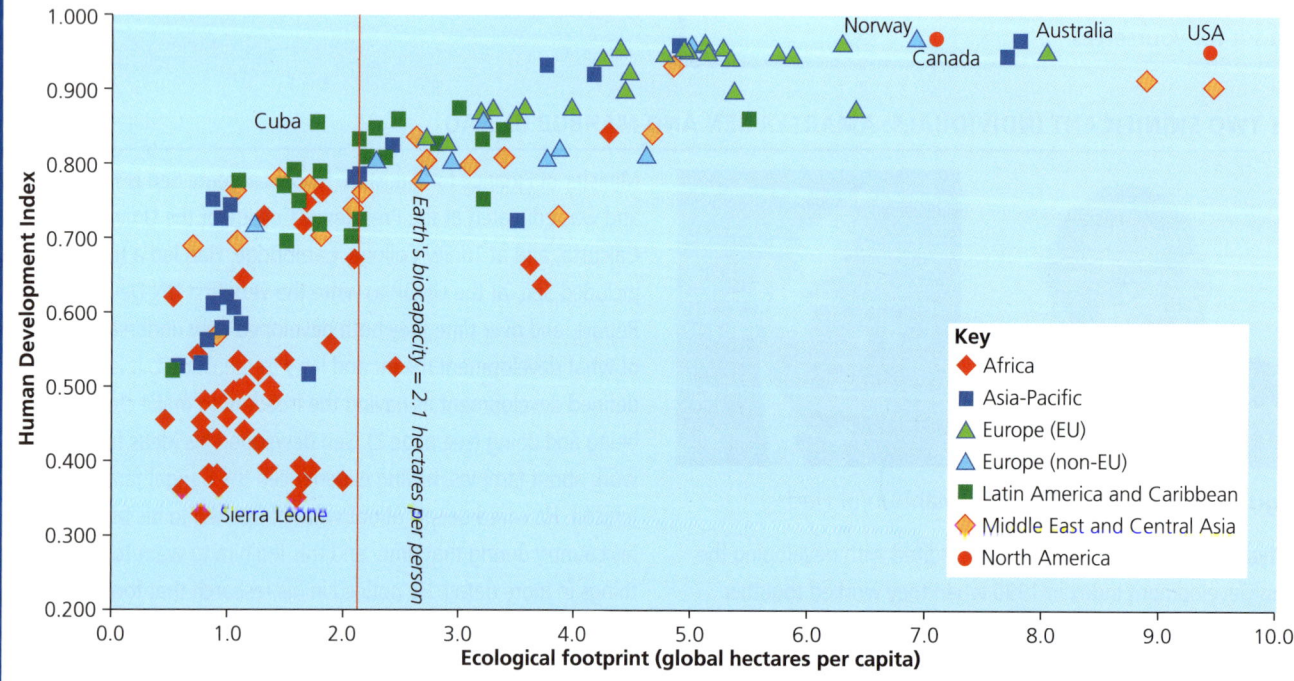

Figure 10.6 The correlation between HDI and the ecological footprints of every country

1 **Describe** the patterns you see for each region of the world.
2 **State** the trend between a country's Human Development Index and its ecological footprint.
3 **Suggest** possible reasons for this trend.

◆ **Assessment opportunities**

◆ In this activity you have practised skills that are assessed using Criterion A: Knowing and understanding.

All attempts to measure something are limited by the effectiveness of the methods that are used. In developing countries, roads and communication systems are rudimentary, and systems for gathering information about the general population involve lots of paperwork (rather than technological systems).

How much progress has been made towards international development goals?

In recent years, the UNDP has set out various development goals to be achieved by set deadlines. We have already come across these in Chapter 7, but it is a good idea to return to them again. The first set of these was the Millennium Development Goals (MDGs), which were agreed to by 191 countries in the year 2000, with a deadline set for 2015. They included:

1. To eradicate extreme poverty and hunger
2. To achieve universal primary education
3. To promote gender equality and empower women
4. To reduce child mortality
5. To improve maternal health
6. To combat HIV/AIDS, malaria, and other diseases
7. To ensure environmental sustainability
8. To develop a global partnership for development

Goals and Target	Africa		Asia				Oceania	Latin America and the Caribbean	Caucasus and Central Asia
	Northern	Sub-Saharan	Eastern	South-Eastern	Southern	Western			
GOAL 1 | Eradicate extreme poverty and hunger									
Reduce extreme poverty by half	low poverty	very high	low poverty	moderate poverty	high poverty	low poverty	—	low poverty	low poverty
Productive and decent employment	large deficit	very large deficit	moderate deficit	large deficit	large deficit	large deficit	very large deficit	moderate deficit	small deficit
Reduce hunger by half	low hunger	high hunger	moderate hunger	moderate hunger	high hunger	moderate hunger	moderate hunger	moderate hunger	moderate hunger
GOAL 2 | Achieve universal primary education									
Universal primary schooling	high enrolment	moderate enrolment	high enrolment	high enrolment	high enrolment	high enrolment	high enrolment	high enrolment	high enrolment
GOAL 3 | Promote gender equality and empower women									
Equal girls' enrolment in primary school	close to parity	close to parity	parity	parity	parity	close to parity	close to parity	parity	parity
Women's share of paid employment	low share	medium share	high share	medium share	low share	low share	medium share	high share	high share
Women's equal representation in national parliaments	moderate representation	moderate representation	moderate representation	low representation	low representation	low representation	very low representation	moderate representation	low representation
GOAL 4 | Reduce child mortality									
Reduce mortality of under-five-year-olds by two thirds	low mortality	high mortality	low mortality	low mortality	moderate mortality	low mortality	moderate mortality	low mortality	low mortality
GOAL 5 | Improve maternal health									
Reduce maternal mortality by three quarters	low mortality	high mortality	low mortality	moderate mortality	moderate mortality	low mortality	moderate mortality	low mortality	low mortality
Access to reproductive health	moderate access	low access	high access	moderate access	moderate access	moderate access	low access	high access	moderate access
GOAL 6 | Combat HIV/AIDS, malaria and other diseases									
Halt and begin to reverse the spread of HIV/AIDS	low incidence	high incidence	low incidence	low incidence	low incidence	low incidence	low incidence	low incidence	low incidence
Halt and reverse the spread of tuberculosis	low mortality	high mortality	low mortality	moderate mortality	moderate mortality	low mortality	moderate mortality	low mortality	moderate mortality
GOAL 7 | Ensure environmental sustainability									
Halve proportion of population without improved drinking water	high coverage	low coverage	high coverage	high coverage	high coverage	high coverage	low coverage	high coverage	moderate coverage
Halve proportion of population without sanitation	moderate coverage	very low coverage	moderate coverage	low coverage	very low coverage	high coverage	very low coverage	moderate coverage	high coverage
Improve the lives of slum-dwellers	low proportion of slum-dwellers	very high proportion of slum-dwellers	moderate proportion of slum-dwellers	moderate proportion of slum-dwellers	moderate proportion of slum-dwellers	moderate proportion of slum-dwellers	moderate proportion of slum-dwellers	moderate proportion of slum-dwellers	—
GOAL 8 | Develop a global partnership for development									
Internet users	moderate usage	low usage	high usage	moderate usage	low usage	high usage	low usage	high usage	high usage

The progress chart operates on two levels. The text in each box indicates the present level of development. The colours show progress made towards the target according to the legend below:
- Target met or excellent progress
- Good progress
- Fair progress
- Poor progress or deterioration
- Missing or insufficient data

■ **Figure 10.7** Progress towards the Millennium Development Goals in 2015 (Source: the UN)

10 How can developing countries successfully increase standards of living?

When the MDGs expired, countries met again and set out the Sustainable Development Goals. These were put in writing in paragraph 54 of United Nations Resolution A/RES/70/1 of 25 September 2015. There are 17 goals and 169 indicators for the measurement of their success, with the deadline being 2030.

ACTIVITY: How successful were the MDGs?

ATL

- Communication skills: Read a variety of sources for information and for pleasure

Using the information in Figure 10.7 and your own research, do the following:

1. Suggest which region in the world made the most progress and which region the least progress towards the MDGs. Give reasons for your answer.
2. Suggest which of the goals we are closest to achieving and which we are furthest away from. Give reasons for your answer.
3. Download the Millennium Development Goals Report 2015. Choosing one goal, **explain** what progress has been made.
4. For the same goal, **explain** the reasons why the goal was not fully met.

Assessment opportunities

- In this activity you have practised skills that are assessed using Criterion A: Knowing and understanding.

ACTIVITY: The Sustainable Development Goals

ATL

- Media literacy skills: Compare, contrast and draw connections among (multi)media resources

While some progress was made towards the MDGs, there is still much to be done.

Using the website **http://bit.ly/UNsustaingoals**, write an essay on the following:

Compare and contrast the Millennium Development Goals and the Sustainable Development Goals (see page 137).

Assessment opportunities

- In this activity you have practised skills that are assessed using Criterion A: Knowing and understanding and Criterion D: Thinking critically.

What challenges do developing countries face?

While developing countries share characteristics, such as a high birth rate, countries are much less likely to share the circumstances that led them to being underdeveloped and that hinder their current development.

ECONOMIC BARRIERS

There are a number of factors that prevent countries from being able to generate increasing incomes while they are still developing. These include:
- undeveloped banking and finance sectors
- an inability to compete in international markets
- currency instability.

These factors make it difficult for businesses to start and operate. They also mean that foreign companies are unlikely to do business there. Without the assurance of economic stability, entrepreneurs will not have the confidence that stable revenues and hence profits will be earned – it is too big a risk to take. In addition, banks provide a pivotal role in lending startup and investment capital to businesses. Without sizable banks, and a proper legislative framework to support them in case of economic difficulties, the rate of growth of industry will be low, and it is likely that productivity will be low also.

CORRUPTION AND POLITICAL INSTABILITY

Many developing countries have only gained independence from colonial countries within the last century or even few decades. Occupying countries took advantage of the resources and people in their colonies to the detriment of quality of life and sustainability. This has left a legacy of problems that remain difficult to deal with. Today, many less economically developed countries struggle with establishing stable democracies and transparent frameworks for government. (Remember that some of these took centuries to establish in Western democracies.)

Corruption is dishonest or fraudulent conduct by people in positions of responsibility for personal gain. Instances of corruption might include:
- taking a bribe
- using friendships or connections in an inappropriate way in a business or political environment, to gain an unfair advantage
- faking or doctoring documents.

Corruption acts as a leakage from the circular flow of income, without necessarily returning those wasted resources to society in a positive way. Government officials, or people employed in the public sectors such as the military or the police, can use their positions of power to accept money, or make decisions that are not in the best interests of society. This means that taxpayers' money is not used in the best way possible.

Most governments in the world function as democracies, meaning that adults in the country decide who will represent them in government. There are different ways of organizing this, but on the whole democracies are considered a stable way to run a country. This is because governments become directly responsible to the people – they will be re-elected if they are deemed successful by voters and will be voted out if not considered successful.

Not all countries are governed in this way, however, and there are currently some countries, such as China and Cuba, that are growing relatively strongly, and meeting many of the development goals, with single-party states. This challenges the view that the best road to development is through democracy.

HIV AND AIDS

There are more than 35 million people living with HIV/AIDS worldwide. Since 2001, the annual rate of new infection has fallen 38 per cent but this still means the number of people living with HIV/AIDS is continuing to rise. It is possible today to lead a full life with an HIV/AIDS diagnosis, with the proper medication and monitoring, and the cost of this is coming down. However, there are many factors that affect the rate at which HIV/AIDS is spread and how well it is treated in different countries, including the:
- understanding of the disease and how it is spread
- stigma attached to receiving an HIV/AIDS diagnosis
- religiosity of people, and their use of family planning and birth control as a result
- availability of medical care
- cost and availability of antiretroviral drugs.

MEET A SIGNIFICANT INDIVIDUAL: DAMBISA MOYO (1969– PRESENT)

Dambisa Moyo was born in Lusaka, Zambia, in 1969. She started her degree in Chemistry at the University of Zambia, and completed it when she moved to the American University in Washington DC. She continued with her studies and gained an MBA in Finance from the same institution, completed a Masters in Public Administration from Harvard and a DPhil from St Antony's College, Oxford. From 1993 to 1995 she worked for the World Bank, and after earning her doctorate she worked for Goldman Sachs, advising developing countries on issuing government bonds (a type of investment instrument that allows governments to borrow) to international markets. She has written bestselling books including *Dead Aid: Why Aid Is Not Working and How There Is Another Way for Africa*. Her background has led her to be supportive of a pro-capitalist approach to development, harnessing the power of free markets to bring growth, increased incomes and improved living standards to LEDCs. She argues that Official Development Assistance (aid coming directly from governments, not humanitarian aid) causes dependence and corruption, and is not the right route to development. She uses the economic successes of Brazil, China and India to illustrate her arguments. This is quite a controversial position to take, given that most governments in developing countries view their economic model (one of free market capitalism) as the model for the developing world to emulate.

Search for her presentation **Is China the new idol for emerging economies?** at www.ted.com/talks/ and watch to see her explain her ideas.

■ Figure 10.8 Dambisa Moyo

ACTIVITY: Zambia and the HIV/AIDS epidemic

ATL

- Information literacy skills: Access information to be informed and inform others

One of the countries worst affected by the HIV/AIDS epidemic is Zambia. Since its independence in 1964, at the start of its journey towards development, it has experienced significant challenges despite its enormous mineral wealth.

Conduct research about the following in Zambia:
- Average life expectancy and how it has changed over the last 20 years
- The percentage of adults infected with HIV/AIDS
- The share of the population who are younger than 20
- The share of government spending that goes to health care

What prospects does Zambia have for economic development? How will the country's population pyramid change over the coming years? What kinds of policies might be needed to avert some of the problems that HIV/AIDS creates for the economy?

◆ Assessment opportunities

- In this activity you have practised skills that are assessed using Criterion A: Knowing and understanding and Criterion C: Communicating.

GEOGRAPHICAL BARRIERS

Tim Marshall, author of *Prisoners of Geography*, explains that Africa's geography has not helped its circumstances and identifies two features in particular that make things difficult: the lack of natural harbours and navigable rivers.

Natural harbours that are sufficiently deep for large vessels to sail through help to enable seagoing trade. This is one reason why Vikings from Scandinavia during the late first millennium CE, and countries such as the Netherlands during the sixteenth century and England during the seventeenth century, were able to become wealthy. They were able to engage in boat building and start to exchange goods with groups of people from much further away than if they had travelled by land. Deep harbours are safe places to keep boats during bad weather, and large towns and cities were therefore built as the area benefited from the trade that arrived.

In addition, Africa has very few large rivers (with the exception of the Nile) that are navigable along their entire length. This has meant that settlements and countries along the rivers find it more difficult to trade with one another and have no choice but to use land routes which take longer and are not as well suited to transporting large quantities of products.

There are other problems for developing countries as a result of their location. A climate with little rainfall that never cools down is one in which disease and bacterial infections are greater risks. In addition, a cooler climate is better for growing crops and easier to work in. (See Chapter 5 for more detail about the relationship between climate and development.)

THINK–PAIR–SHARE
Can you think of any other towns or cities that have large harbours? How does the existence of the harbour link to the history of those cities?

■ **Figure 10.9 (a)** Copenhagen; **(b)** Amsterdam

To what extent does development require intervention in markets?

There is disagreement over how strong the role of government should be in pushing a country towards its development objectives (see also Chapter 8, page 213). While free markets have the ability to organize and distribute goods and services to where they are demanded and needed, some people believe that with all the knowledge we have accumulated about economics, governments should be in a position to drive their economies in the direction that the country needs. In particular, there are examples where the free market fails to provide socially optimum levels of goods or services, such as health care and education.

MARKET-BASED POLICIES

In Chapter 8, we saw that markets can be one of the best ways for resources to be allocated efficiently (see page 200). When it comes to developing an industry or industries, markets will form where there is a need for goods and services, and additional industries will develop nearby. In particular, there will be growing demand for better roads, telecommunications and other such essential services. Offices need places nearby where people can eat. Factories need suppliers nearby to deliver parts, as well as transport companies to take finished goods away.

Markets and the price mechanism respond to all the information that exists to indicate what is needed, where it is needed, in what quantities and what methods to use. While developed countries can improve the efficiency of markets by removing strong legislation and reducing minimum wages or trade union power, developed countries have to focus on making the business environment a safe and secure one in which businesses want to operate.

ACTIVITY: Linking the AD/AS model with development

■ ATL

- Critical-thinking skills: Use models and simulations to explore complex systems and issues

The aggregate demand (AD)/aggregate supply (AS) model can be used here to explain how the government can help stop the poverty cycle.

1 Review the section on the AD/AS model in Chapter 8 (see page 210).
2 Construct an AD/AS model to show the impact of an increase in government spending on the size of the economy.
3 **Explain** how an increase in government spending might impact the size of the economy.
4 Using a poverty cycle diagram (see page 248), **explain** how an increase in government spending might help bring an end to the poverty cycle.
5 With reference to examples, **discuss** possible limitations to using increased government spending in a developing country.

◆ Assessment opportunities

- In this activity you have practised skills that are assessed using Criterion A: Knowing and understanding and Criterion D: Thinking critically.

ACTIVITY: Ease of Doing Business

ATL

- Communication skills: Read a variety of sources for information and for pleasure

Imagine you are an employee of a major corporation. You have been instructed by your boss to find a new location for the business to expand to, and have been asked to **investigate** the extent to which the business environment in that country is a safe place to do business.

Conduct some research about the Ease of Doing Business index, published by the World Bank.

1. **Explain** how it is constructed and the factors used to decide on a country's ranking.
2. **List** some of the factors that it does not include.
3. For two of the factors used to compile the index, **explain** what can be done in a country to improve the country's score.
4. For one developed and one developing country, compare and contrast the Ease of Doing Business. You can find this information by clicking on the country name when on the rankings page of: www.doingbusiness.org/rankings

Assessment opportunities

- In this activity you have practised skills that are assessed using Criterion A: Knowing and understanding and Criterion D: Thinking critically.

INTERVENTIONIST POLICIES

While markets have their definite strengths, it is generally acknowledged that there are some things that markets do not do so well. In addition to some of the weaknesses discussed in Chapter 8 (see pages 201–202), markets are not always good at providing the following elements of development:

- *Education:* The UN Declaration of Human Rights states that 'Education shall be free, at least in the elementary and fundamental stages'. Providing education for free is not something that markets will do, because markets work by setting a price and allocating the good or service to those who are willing and able to pay that price. Education is a market that requires government intervention because the price set by a market will mean that some children will not get the chance to go to school.
- *Health care:* For the same reason as education, private health care is not going to be able to provide services sufficiently to a whole population. Health care is not the same as a simple private product like a mobile phone, and there are clear benefits to everyone when people are healthy. We want people to not spread illnesses and want them to be able to work and pay their taxes.

Review to remember!

Success in the IB MYP and later in the DP depends to a large extent on the amount of revision undertaken throughout the course. You cannot expect your busy brain to remember everything from your lessons and so you must revisit the material in your own time. The sections on market-based and interventionist policies refer to material from Chapter 8, so it would be a good idea to return to that chapter to revise the material.

DISCUSS

What might you suggest are some of the reasons why developing countries struggle to build and maintain infrastructure?

Public goods: These are goods that the free market will never provide, because it does not make sense to charge a price for them. They are not called public because of the government, but it is true that the government ends up having to provide them. Examples include the army and street lights. The reason why they will not be provided by the free market is that you cannot exclude people from their consumption, and there is no rivalry in consumption of them. The concept of rivalry can be explained as follows. An apple is rivalrous because once it is consumed by one person, it cannot be consumed by another. A street light is non-rivalrous however, as one person using it does not diminish the next person's ability to use it. Public goods have to fulfil both conditions of non-rivalry and non-excludability, and will not be provided by a free market because a price cannot be charged for their use.

Infrastructure: Infrastructure is any large-scale capital project that is essential for economic activity to take place, and is usually provided by the government. Infrastructure includes:

- roads
- railways
- airports
- ports
- clean water and sewage systems
- electricity networks
- telecommunications, including landlines, mobile and internet.

These are projects that could be privately built and owned, as long as the private company could charge for their use. However, there needs to be demand for the service – there is no point erecting mobile phone masts when no one owns a mobile phone. It is common for the government to intervene here, and use tax revenues to build the projects, but this is a significant hurdle for governments of developing countries.

ACTIVITY: The best of both worlds?

ATL

- Critical-thinking skills: Consider ideas from multiple perspectives

You are going to write a newspaper article for your school magazine about development policies that will **explain** the strengths and weaknesses of market-based and interventionist policies in various countries.

Read the following articles, and **summarize** the main points from each one.

www.bbc.co.uk/news/business-23041513

https://bit.ly/2k1pwZM

www.devpolicy.org/is-tourism-the-answer-for-kiribati-20190805/

https://bit.ly/2k0fYOD

Now write your article. It should **discuss** and **evaluate** some of the development policies employed in some example countries in recent years. Your article should include sufficient data and statistics as evidence, as well as a range of quotations covering a variety of perspectives.

Remember to cite and reference all your research using the referencing standards your school recommends.

Assessment opportunities

- In this activity you have practised skills that are assessed using Criterion A: Knowing and understanding, Criterion B: Investigating, Criterion C: Communicating and Criterion D: Thinking critically.

Welfare: A welfare system, or the benefits system, refers to the systems in place to protect citizens from adverse circumstances. In most countries, these would include payments from the government to people on low incomes, or who find themselves without work or unable to work (such as in the case of illness or disability). In many countries, families also receive child support payments, and help with housing costs if necessary. The amount of money that families receive is often the subject of intense debate.

Reflection

In this chapter, we have **defined** development and **explained** the barriers that some countries face in achieving better standards of living. We have **discussed** policies available to governments for promoting development.

Use this table to reflect on your own learning in this chapter.						
Questions we asked	Answers we found	Any further questions now?				
Factual: What do we mean by growth and development? What are the characteristics of a developing country? How much progress has been made towards international development goals?						
Conceptual: What challenges do developing countries face? How do we measure development?						
Debatable: To what extent does development require intervention in markets? To what extent does economic growth result in development?						
Approaches to learning you used in this chapter	Description – what new skills did you learn?	How well did you master the skills?				
		Novice	Learner	Practitioner	Expert	
Communication skills						
Information literacy skills						
Media literacy skills						
Critical-thinking skills						
Learner profile attribute(s)	Reflect on the importance of being caring for your learning in this chapter.					
Caring						

10 How can developing countries successfully increase standards of living?

Time, place and space — *Resources* — *Globalization and sustainability*

11 Is our exploitation of the Earth sustainable?

Since **resources** are **unevenly distributed** around the world, reliance on resource extraction as a source of growth and development can threaten a country's **sustainability and security**.

CONSIDER THESE QUESTIONS:

Factual: Who produces oil? How are resources extracted? What are the alternatives to oil?

Conceptual: How has the world become so reliant on crude oil? Why are oil prices so volatile?

Debatable: How far can resource extraction be relied upon as a source of development? To what extent do the benefits of resource extraction outweigh the costs? How sustainable are resource extraction industries?

Now **share and compare** your thoughts and ideas with your partner, or with the whole class.

■ Figure 11.1 The Earth's resources are exploited in many different ways

IN THIS CHAPTER WE WILL …

- **Find out** how we have become so reliant on crude oil.
- **Explore** the costs and benefits of the oil industry.
- **Take action** by advocating for migrant workers' rights in the construction industries in the Middle East.

Individuals & Societies for the IB MYP 4&5: by Concept

These Approaches to Learning (ATL) skills will be useful …

- Communication skills
- Collaboration skills
- Organization skills
- Information literacy skills
- Critical-thinking skills

We will reflect on this learner profile attribute …

- Balanced – understanding the importance of balancing different aspects of our lives – intellectual, physical and emotional – to achieve well-being for ourselves and others; recognizing our interdependence with other people and with the world in which we live.

Assessment opportunities in this chapter:

- ◆ **Criterion A:** Knowing and understanding
- ◆ **Criterion B:** Investigating
- ◆ **Criterion C:** Communicating
- ◆ **Criterion D:** Thinking critically

KEY WORDS
conflict
crude oil
reliant
sustainable

As our population continues to grow, the resources we use and the way in which we use them need to be examined. The issue of over reliance on fossil fuels is a much debated one and the focus throughout this chapter will be on oil.

Oil is formed deep underground from the decomposition of organisms such as plankton and algae. Over millions of years, heat and geological pressure transform this organic matter into oil and gas, hence oil is known as a fossil fuel. Oil has been produced commercially and refined since the 1850s and is now one of our most important fuels. Oil refining produces transport fuels such as petrol (gasoline), diesel and jet fuel, as well as heating oils such as kerosene. By-products from oil refining are also valuable as they are used in the production of plastics and chemicals, as well as many lubricants, waxes, tars, pesticides and fertilizers. As we strive to meet the Sustainable Development Goals, the issues of resource security and sustainability are key. This chapter will consider to what extent reliance on resource extraction, in this instance oil, as a source of economic growth and development threatens a country's sustainability and security.

11 Is our exploitation of the Earth sustainable?

Who produces oil?

There are approximately 90 million barrels of oil produced each day globally, with the top ten producers being responsible for 60 per cent of this crude-oil production.

The importance of the Middle East as a supplier of oil is critical. Involvement in the Gulf War (1991) is a case in point. The Organization of the Petroleum Exporting Countries (OPEC) is made up of 14 countries that have controlling shares in the global supply of oil, six of which are Middle Eastern countries. It regularly influences the price of crude oil at which member nations sell, and this has increased its economic and political power. It has also increased dependency on the Middle East by all other regions, which provides an incentive for rich countries to increase energy conservation or develop alternative forms of energy. Countries therefore need to:
- maintain good political links with the Middle East and strive for political stability in the region
- involve the Middle East in economic cooperation
- reassess coal and nuclear power as energy options.

Oil is a global commodity, vulnerable to any event that impacts on its supply and demand. All countries that depend on oil imports are defenceless against external events affecting its supply.

It is unlikely that the pattern of oil production will change significantly in the near future; the major producers at the start of the twenty-first century are still major suppliers in 2020.

■ **Table 11.1** Top 25 producers of oil globally (2016)

Country	Oil – production (barrels/day)
Russia	10,550,000
Saudi Arabia	10,460,000
United States	8,853,000
Iraq	4,452,000
Iran	4,068,000
China	3,981,000
Canada	3,679,000
United Arab Emirates	3,106,000
Kuwait	2,924,000
Brazil	2,515,000
Venezuela	2,277,000
Mexico	2,187,000
Nigeria	1,871,000
Angola	1,770,000
Norway	1,648,000
Kazakhstan	1,595,000
Qatar	1,523,000
Algeria	1,348,000
Oman	1,007,000
United Kingdom	933,000
Colombia	886,000
Azerbaijan	833,500
Indonesia	831,100
India	734,500
Malaysia	666,900

Source: CIA World factbook

ACTIVITY: Create a choropleth map

ATL

- Communication skills: Organize and depict information logically

A choropleth map is a map that shows regions or areas that have the same characteristics. It shows patterns that a list of data cannot clearly indicate.

To make a choropleth map, data is grouped or categorized and colour-coded by either colouring or shading. The darker colour is more intense and shows a greater value; the lighter shading is less intense and shows a lower value.

Create your own choropleth map for the data in Table 11.1, the top 25 oil-producing nations.

◆ Assessment opportunities

- ◆ In this activity you have practised skills that are assessed using Criterion C: Communicating.

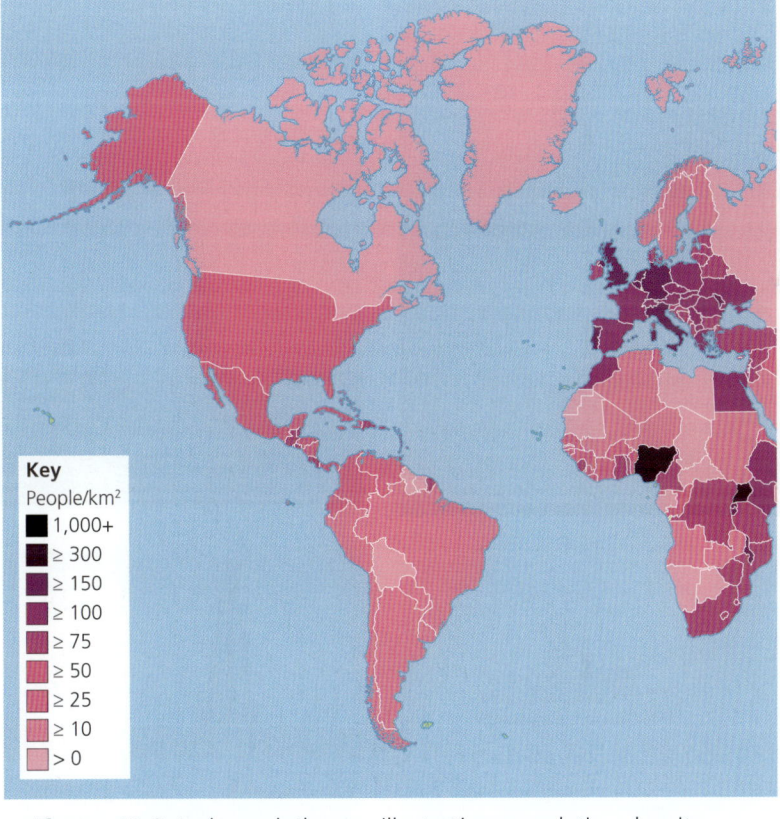

■ **Figure 11.2** A choropleth map illustrating population density

11 Is our exploitation of the Earth sustainable?

How are resources extracted?

The process of extracting oil is complex and depends largely on the type of raw materials found in an area and how close they are to the surface.

Drilling via oil sands, extracting petroleum from oil or tar sands and hydraulic fracturing or 'fracking' are some of the most commonly used extraction techniques.

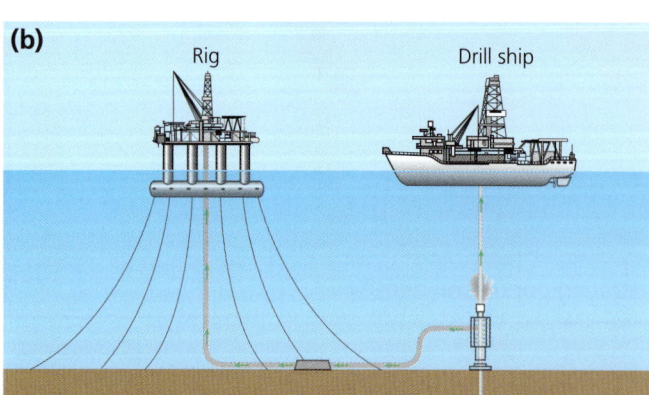

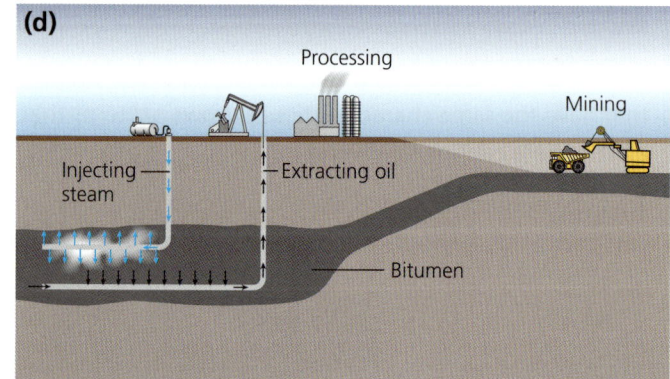

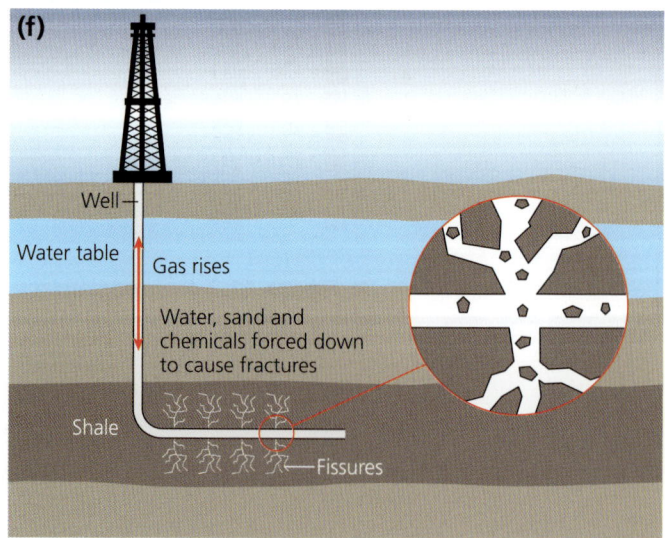

■ **Figure 11.3 (a)** Offshore oil drilling rig; **(b)** Offshore oil drilling; **(c)** Open pit bench mining; **(d)** Natural gas extraction; **(e)** Hydro-fracking derricks; **(f)** Shale gas extraction using fracking

268   Individuals & Societies for the IB MYP 4&5: *by Concept*

How has the world become so reliant on crude oil?

SOURCE A

'At the beginning of the 1990s – almost eighty years after Churchill made the commitment to petroleum, after two World Wars and a long Cold War, and in what was supposed to be the beginning of a new, more peaceful era – oil once again became the focus of global conflict. On August 2, 1990, yet another of the century's dictators, Saddam Hussein of Iraq, invaded the neighboring country of Kuwait. His goal was not only conquest of a sovereign state, but also the capture of its riches. The prize was enormous…

But the stakes were so obviously large that the invasion of Kuwait was not accepted by the rest of the world as a fait accompli, as Saddam Hussein had expected. It was not received with the passivity that had met Hitler's invasion of the Rhineland, or Mussolini's assault on Ethiopia. Instead, the United Nations instituted an embargo against Iraq, and many nations of the Western and Arab worlds dramatically mustered military force to defend neighboring Saudi Arabia against Iraq and to resist Sadam Hussein's ambitions. There was no precedent for either the cooperation of the United States and the Soviet Union or for the rapid and massive deployment of forces into the region. Over the previous several years, it had become fashionable to say that oil was no longer 'important'. Indeed, in the spring of 1990, just a few months before the Iraqi invasion, the senior officers of America's Central Command, which would be the linchpin of the U.S. mobilization, found themselves lectured to the effect that oil had lost its strategic significance. But the invasion of Kuwait stripped away the illusion. In early 1991, when peaceful means failed to secure an Iraqi withdrawal from Kuwait, a coalition of thirty-three nations, led by the United States, destroyed Iraq's offensive capability in a five-week air war and one hundred hours of ground battle, which forced Iraq out of Kuwait. At the end of the twentieth century, oil was still central to security, prosperity, and the very nature of civilization.'

From *The Prize*, by Daniel Yergin

THINK–PAIR–SHARE

Read the excerpt from the Pulitzer Prize winning book *The Prize* by Daniel Yergin. Do you think oil has become less important? Can you think of all the industries that rely on oil as an input to production? Make a **list** of those industries and see if a partner can add to your list.

ACTIVITY: How is oil extracted?

ATL

- Organization skills: Use appropriate strategies for organizing complex information

Using the pictures in Figure 11.3 as a starting point, copy and complete Table 11.2 below.

◆ Assessment opportunities

- ◆ In this activity you have practised skills that are assessed using Criterion A: Knowing and understanding and Criterion C: Communicating.

■ Table 11.2 Extraction techniques

Extraction technique	How it works	Positives of method	Negatives of method	Example of a place where this happens
Oil drilling				
Extraction from oil/tar sands				
Hydraulic fracturing or 'fracking'				

11 Is our exploitation of the Earth sustainable?

■ Figure 11.4 (a) *Panther*; (b) HMS *Dreadnought*

THE IMPORTANCE OF OIL IN THE NAVAL ARMS RACE OF THE EARLY TWENTIETH CENTURY

Winston Churchill, who was in 1911 First Lord of the Admiralty of the United Kingdom, expressed deep concern about German militarism, in particular Kaiser Wilhelm's determination to build a powerful navy. Previously, Germany had never seen naval power as a major military consideration but the Kaiser's plans seemed to represent something more sinister than battleship envy. Churchill's concerns were amplified in July 1911 when a new German gunboat, *Panther*, sailed into the Moroccan port of Agadir.

▼ Links to: Sciences

Crude oil, when it is found naturally in the ground, contains hydrocarbons of many different lengths. Heating crude oil at different temperatures evaporates the different lengths of hydrocarbons, allowing them to be collected. Short chains evaporate quickly, and can be used as fuel for cars. Longer chains evaporate at higher temperatures, and are much more viscous (a thick and sticky consistency). Longer chains are used for surfacing roads. This process is called fractional distillation.

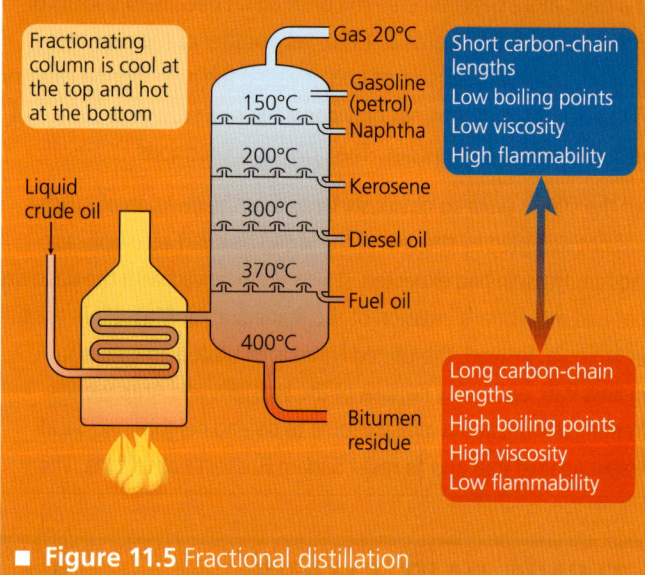

■ Figure 11.5 Fractional distillation

Churchill, in his bid to modernize the British Navy in order to retain supremacy, became obsessed with a need for greater speed on the part of their battleships, cruisers and especially the new HMS *Dreadnought*. Ships had become considerably heavier due to the weight of the armour that they were forced to carry in an effort to protect themselves against a new weapon, the torpedo. They were now encased in 35 centimetres of steel armour plating and both guns and their shells were getting bigger (38-cm guns, each firing an 870-kg shell). The Navy was powered by coal, and despite efforts to make ships lighter by having fewer turrets and more boilers, the 25 knots that Churchill saw as the magic speed necessary for superiority in battle was not achievable.

Churchill sought advice from John Fisher, a retired Admiral, and they concluded that new engines running on new fuel were needed. Oil is more combustible and burns hotter than coal, meaning steam would be produced more quickly, allowing a ship to accelerate and move more rapidly while at the same time needing fewer turrets and boilers (as the volume of oil needed to generate the desired power would be less). In trials, oil-powered destroyers could go for twice as long at top speed (8 hours rather than 4 hours), carry more guns and still be 15 per cent lighter and cheaper to run than their coal-powered counterparts. They also required less manpower, as there was no need to shovel coal into the furnaces. An added benefit was that the smoke output from burning oil was far less visible to the enemy than coal smoke. New battleships (called the Queen Elizabeth class) were to be oil-fired.

A major hurdle in the conversion was a reliable supply of oil – Britain produced coal not oil. Churchill took the gamble, however, declaring that if it paid off 'we should be able to raise the whole power and efficiency of the Navy: better ships, better crews, high economies, more intense forms of war power – mastery itself was the prize of the venture'. In 1914, one month before the start of the First World War, Churchill paid £2.2 million on behalf of the British Crown for a 51 per cent controlling interest in the Anglo-Persian Oil Company. This gamble was a master stroke, securing British naval supremacy for the duration of the war.

ACTIVITY: The significance of Manchuria

ATL

- Information literacy: Make connections between various sources of information

Use the information on pages 271 and 272, as well as Figures 11.9 and 11.10 and your own research, to write a paragraph that **describes** and **explains**:
- Why Manchuria was so desirable to Japan
- Why the USA was so heavily involved in the peace negotiations
- If Japan's ambitions extended beyond Manchuria, where might they continue their expansion and why.

Assessment opportunities

- In this activity you have practised skills that are assessed using Criterion B: investigating, Criterion C: Communicating and Criterion D: Thinking critically.

DISCUSS

Why are large battleships no longer being built and aircraft carriers being favoured along with smaller ships?

JAPANESE EXPANSIONISM

Japan, until 1853, had deliberately isolated itself from the outside world in an attempt to preserve its cultural and religious heritage. The relative ease with which better armed and organized British forces had overcome China in the Opium Wars of 1839–42 and 1856–60 had woken the Japanese government up to the realization that, at least technologically, it had to open itself up to the West in order to ensure its long-term future. The Treaty of Kanagawa, signed in 1854 between the USA and Japan, opened up two of Japan's ports to American vessels. (Previously no foreign vessels were allowed into any ports.) At much the same time, Japan underwent political change too, with the feudal system being replaced by a limited democracy, though the Meiji ('Enlightened Emperor') still held decision-making powers. By 1872, Japan had introduced conscription, and modernized and restructured its armed forces, following British principles for its navy and Prussian methods for its land army. The Sino-Japanese war of 1894–5 showed these methods to be effective against a Chinese army that had not taken the same steps to modernize. While this success put Japan on the map as a military force to be reckoned with, it exposed the lack of strategic resources available in Japan itself. In order to sustain its changed military position, it adopted a more expansionist and imperialist foreign policy. From 1900, a government restructuring meant that ministers for the army and navy had to be either retired generals or admirals. The outcome of this change was a more aggressive foreign policy.

Japan was particularly interested in the resources that China and Korea possessed: iron, coal and land in Manchuria and a wide range of metal ores and coal in Korea, but was also aware that Tsarist Russia had expansionist ideas for the same areas. An Anglo-Japanese alliance was signed in January 1902 in the hope of deterring Russian ambitions. This did not work, however, and by 1904 the Russo-Japanese War had begun.

Russo-Japanese War, 1904–5

Figure 11.6 The Russo-Japanese War, 1904–5 (countries shown as they were at the time)

This war was fought on both land and sea.

The most important naval battle was on 27 May 1905 in Tsushima Strait where the Russian fleet, which had sailed 29,000 km from St Petersburg round the Cape of Good Hope, was destroyed within 20 hours, with 12,000 Russian sailors dying. Japan lost just 116 men.

The two most important land battles were at Liaoyang in August 1904 and Mukden in March 1905, both of which resulted in Japanese victories. Reports were that the Japanese army's courage, training and quality of artillery (more technologically advanced) were the decisive factors.

Figure 11.7 Painting of the Battle of Tsushima, showing the Japanese Navy sinking the Russian Fleet, 27 May 1905

The Treaty of Portsmouth, which ended the Russo-Japanese War, was signed on 5 September 1905 with an agreement that:
- troops from both sides had to leave Manchuria
- Japan would keep the Liaodong Peninsula and Port Arthur (under 'lease' from China)
- Japan would retain Korea
- Japan could also 'lease' the Russian-built Southern Manchuria railway from China
- Japan retained the southern half of Sakhalin island.

While this undoubtedly improved the Japanese position, they felt they should have received more in the peace settlement.

Figure 11.8 The Treaty of Portsmouth, signed 5 September 1905

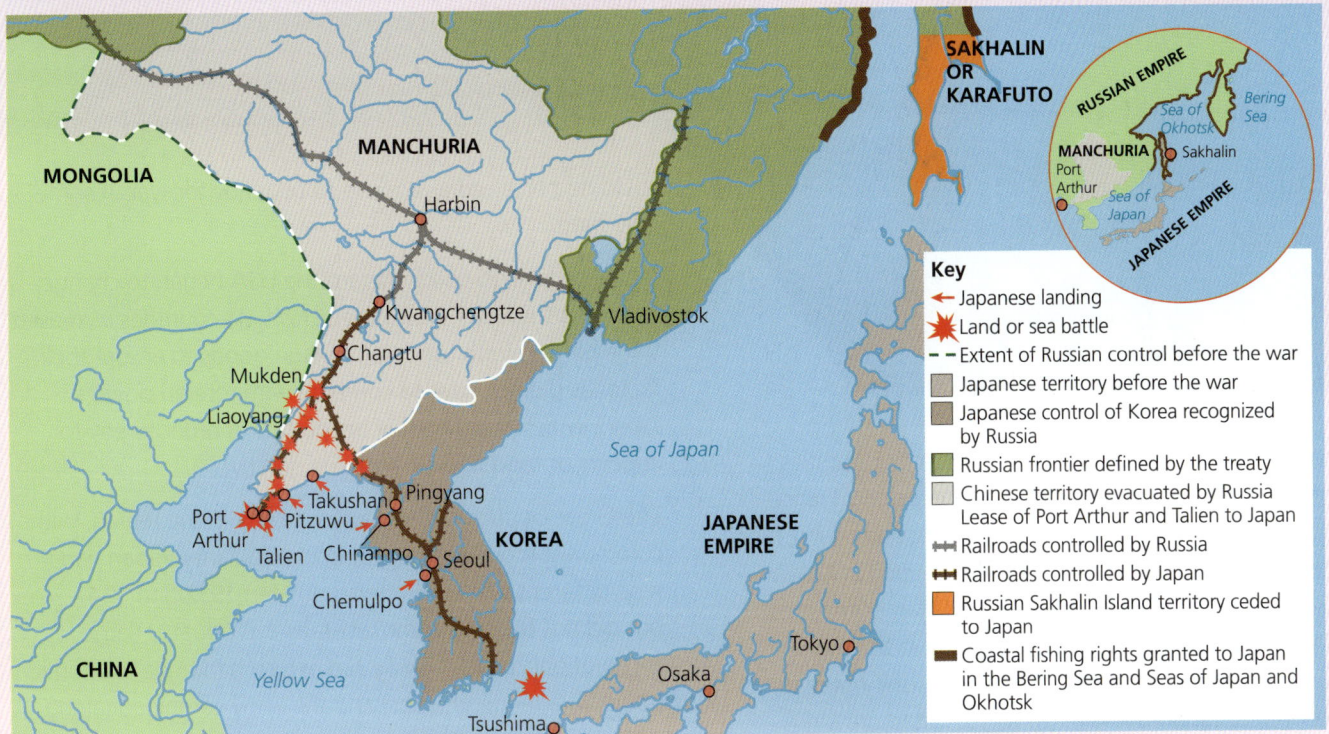

■ **Figure 11.9** The Russo-Japanese War and the outcomes of the peace treaty (Treaty of Portsmouth, signed September 1905)

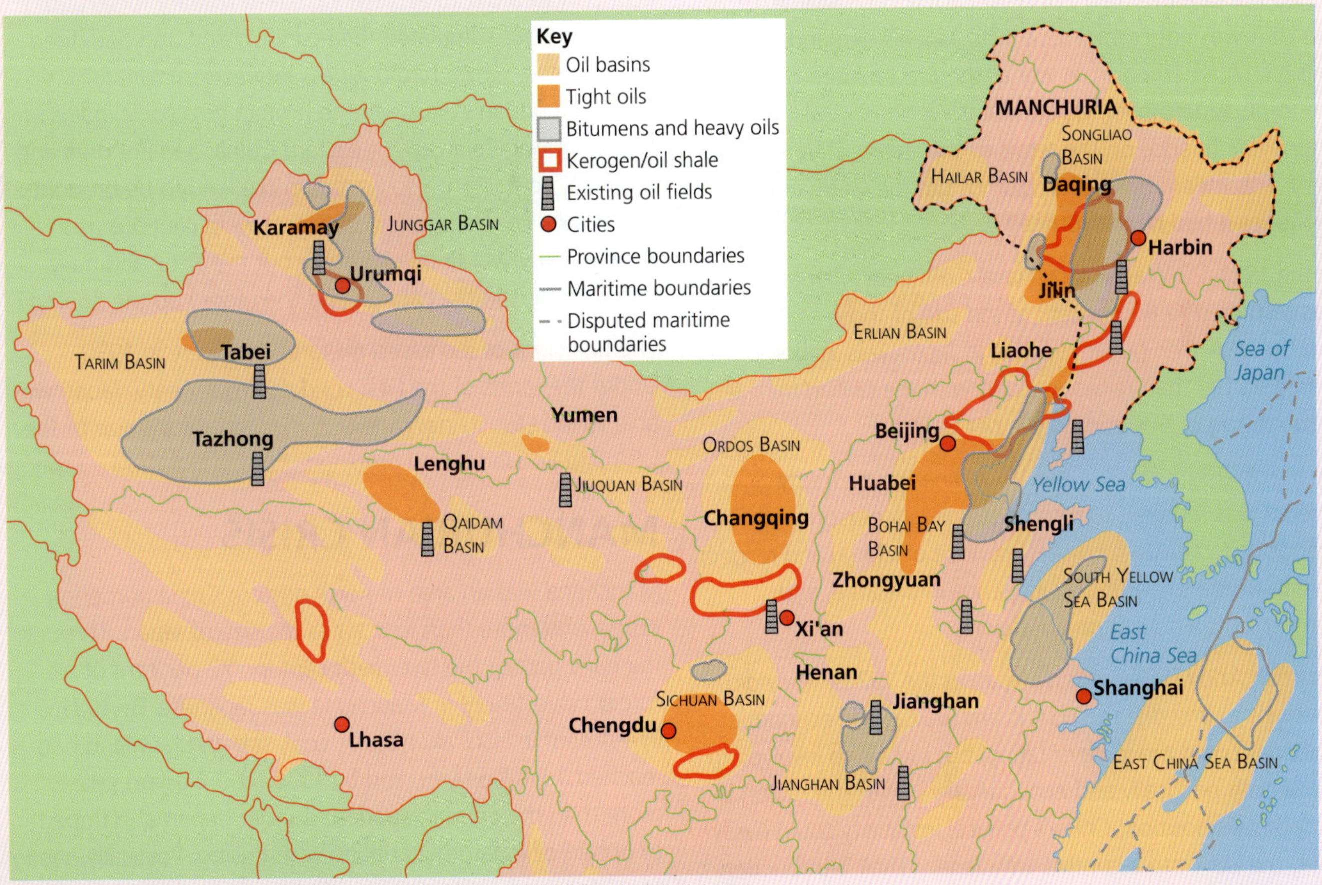

■ **Figure 11.10** Map showing oil resources in the Pacific and China

11 Is our exploitation of the Earth sustainable?

The First World War gave Japan further opportunities to expand – they joined the Triple Entente (Britain, France, Russia), demanding German colonial possessions in China if their side secured victory. They also issued China with 'Twenty-One Demands', establishing Japan as the most influential economic and political nation in the region. The USA, which had signed the Lansing-Ishii Agreement, recognizing Japanese gains up to 1917, had growing interests in the area as they entered the war on the side of Britain, France and Japan (Russia had surrendered and signed the punitive treaty of Brest Litovsk on 3 March 1918). The USA was not comfortable with Japan's demands and as the USA emerged from war as the pre-eminent global economic superpower, US President Woodrow Wilson had extensive influence on the terms of the Treaty of Versailles in 1919. This meant that Japan did not get the German Pacific Territories it had been promised.

At the 1921–22 Washington Naval Conference, Japan's navy was restricted to 60 per cent of the size of those of Britain and the USA. The public reaction in Japan was 'national shame' rather than rejoicing along with the civilian ministers at the saving of 500 million yen per year.

Japan suffered further at the 1922 Nine Power Treaty when it was required to remove all military personnel from Shandong (an eastern coastal province of China) and respect China's borders, diluting its influence in the area, and making it more reliant on US exports.

Historian Andy Dailey says of Japan in the 1920s, 'they did not want to provoke the USA in any way as any economic sanctions could prove devastating, but were also involved in China both politically and economically'. It left the region in a precarious position; China's political instability could easily bring the USA into a conflict with Japan. Their introduction of universal conscription for all 20-year-old males from 1927 could be perceived as a move to be ready for war at some later date.

Japanese foreign policy toward the USA began to change following the 1929 Wall Street Crash. As countries increased trade barriers with tariffs on foreign goods to ensure their factories did not have to compete with foreign powers, Japan, which relied heavily on exports in order to pay for imports of food and oil, suffered greatly.

The Great Depression created instability in the region, with communist movements surging in popularity. Japan had nine different prime ministers between 1932 and 1941 but did not become communist, as the Zaibatsu (large corporations, usually family run, which had huge economic power in a range of areas) and the army combined (along with support from the Emperor) to suppress this.

There was however a massive reorganization of the economy in order to achieve increased military focus and spending. This stimulated the economy and also benefited the Zaibatsu, which had business interests in military hardware. Japan's aims were to protect its colonial gains of the Shandong Peninsula of eastern China, and in Korea and Taiwan. The military also wanted more land to be brought under their control. Civilian ministers were cautious as a large military would be expensive but the army and navy had members in the cabinet and therefore had the final say.

The first signs of increased militarization were in 1930. Under the terms of the First London Naval Treaty, Japan was able to increase its navy to 69.75 per cent of the size of the USA and British navies combined.

MANCHURIAN CRISIS

Manchuria was an area of north eastern China bordering Korea, and more than four times the size of Japan. Through the early part of the twentieth century, 72 per cent of all foreign investment in Manchuria was Japanese. By 1931, investment in iron, aluminium, coal, salt and farmland had reached 1.5 billion yen, and by 1936 hit 3.7 billion yen – more than the annual Japanese budget. Japan also hoped to obtain oil in large quantities from drilling. Politically, Japan saw Manchuria as an area for the peasant population to expand into and also as a buffer zone to communism.

On 18 September 1931, a bomb exploded on the Russian-built, Japanese-run South Manchurian Railway outside Mukden, the biggest city in Manchuria. While the explosion did not even stop trains from using the railway, a Japanese garrison stationed nearby, which historians such as Sandra Wilson believe possibly even created the explosion, claimed an act of sabotage by Chinese rebel soldiers and used it as an excuse to occupy the whole of Manchuria in order 'to protect Japanese interests'. In an attempt to make this look less like an invasion, Japan renamed Manchuria, Manchukuo (land of the Manchu), although over 90 per cent of population in the area were Chinese not Manchu. Japan appointed the last Emperor of China as a **puppet head of state** and sponsored Manchuria in applying for separate Olympic and League of Nations membership.

Despite Chinese appeals, the League of Nations response was limited. The Lytton Commission was formed in December 1931 and sent to investigate but the report was only finally submitted in October 1932, a full year after the invasion. The USA published the Stimson Doctrine protesting at Japan's actions but was still following its policy of **isolationism** and was therefore never going to commit troops to mainland China; thus it had no effect on the crisis. The USSR also did not act as it was in the middle of its own industrialization programme as set out in the first of its Five Year Plans. In February 1933, Japan left the League of Nations in protest against the League's demand that they should leave Manchuria.

■ **Figure 11.11** The Doormat

■ **Figure 11.12** Trial by Geneva

THINK–PAIR–SHARE

What do Figures 11.11 and 11.12 suggest about Japan's reaction to the League's demand for them to leave Manchuria, relative to their desire for oil resources?

Discuss this with your partner and formulate ideas for steps the League could have taken to handle the Manchurian Crisis more effectively.

Share these ideas with the class.

TRIPARTITE PACT, 27 SEPTEMBER 1940

The Tripartite Pact, signed in Berlin in 1940, created an alliance between Germany, Italy and Japan. These countries were wary of the USA possibly joining the Allies (Britain, France and Poland to begin with, but eventually Commonwealth countries, the Netherlands, Belgium and European nations), and it was hoped this pact would cause the USA to hesitate. Until this point, the USA had remained neutral and would not officially join the war effort until after the attacks on Pearl Harbor in December 1941. According to the agreement, Germany and Italy would take charge in all European matters, and Japan would oversee East Asia.

From 2 August 1941, US President Franklin D. Roosevelt introduced an embargo of oil exports to Japan. Finally, as historian George Morgenstern wrote in his essay 'The Actual Road to Pearl Harbor', on 26 July 1941, Roosevelt 'froze Japanese assets in the United States, thus bringing commercial relations between the nations to an effective end. One week later Roosevelt embargoed the export of such grades of oil as still were in commercial flow to Japan.' When the British and Dutch governments enacted similar bans on exporting goods from their southeast Asian colonies to Japan, it forced Japan's hand, as it realized its economy would collapse without these resources. Japan would have to take oil- and rubber-rich territories by force. The Japanese government was concerned that the USA might provide support for China who had been fighting them since their invasion in 1937 following the Marco Polo Bridge incident. To provide realistic quantities of support involved long lines of communication across the Pacific, so destruction of the American Pacific fleet would give Japan a relatively free hand in China and elsewhere in Indochina.

Despite its territorial gains, Japan found that the production of oil (and coal) was far lower than had been hoped. The absence within its territories of critical raw materials, particularly oil and rubber, acted as a major barrier to Japanese military expansion. Rubber was imported from British Malaya while oil was imported from the USA. Japanese oil reserves amounted to its requirements for about six months.

In January 1935, Japan withdrew from the Second London Naval Treaty talks. These talks were aimed at limiting the growth of international naval armaments.

The Japanese army and navy initially disagreed on where to expand. The army favoured a continued push north through Manchukuo, taking on the Soviet Union, while the navy wanted a southern invasion of the Dutch East Indies to secure oil supplies and British Malaya for the rubber. Although the army pursued its campaign from 1937 to 1940, a combination of Chinese, Soviet and French Indochinese resistance stretched, dragged and drained Japanese resources further in China to the point where the army agreed to abandon its plans and focus on the navy's southern campaign.

Figure 11.13 A map to show the invasion of Manchuria which began in 1932 and was soon renamed Manchukuo by Japan

ACTIVITY: Who is to blame?

ATL

- Communication skills: Make inferences and draw conclusions

Choose one of the following questions:
- To what extent was Japanese pursuit of oil to blame for the start of the war in the Pacific in 1941?
- To what extent was Roosevelt's embargo on oil to blame for starting the war in the Pacific?

It may be helpful to consider the following points:

Japan to blame for starting the war in the Pacific:
- Historians such as David Bergamini have argued that Japan had planned a war from the early 1930s and was therefore clearly the aggressor (for example, their invasion force into Russia numbered 70,000 men).
- Other historians believe that Japan was pursuing a traditional 'European style' imperialist policy in Asia, and took too many risks in their diplomacy (in the same way, one could argue, that Hitler did in Europe), thereby stumbling into a war with both the USA and Britain.
- James William Morley documented how Japanese military spending rose from 3 to 9 million yen between 1936 and 1939.

Japan not to blame:
- Japan's declaration of war stated that the USA was to blame for the war.
- Historians argue that Japan was aiming to 'liberate' Asia from Western domination.
- Japan's 'sphere of influence' was not dissimilar to what the USA was also doing.
- Japan had been continually provoked and mistreated by the west (for example, in the form of US trade embargoes). They entered a defensive war in order to preserve their existence.
- Lack of a clear leader makes it more difficult to decide whether Japan had any intention to cause the war in the Pacific.

◆ Assessment opportunities

- In this activity you have practised skills that are assessed using Criterion B: Investigating and Criterion C: Communicating.

ACTIVITY: Why was the war in the Pacific so difficult?

■ ATL

■ Collaboration skills: Listen actively to other perspectives and ideas

Task 1

Using the maps in Figure 11.14 to help you, create a summary of Japanese expansion in southeast Asia from December 1941 to August 1942.

Task 2

Using the maps in Figure 11.14 and any other sources, make a **list** of reasons why it was so difficult and took so long for the USA and its allies to win the war in the Pacific.

Task 3

The bombing of Hiroshima and Nagasaki has remained controversial for over 70 years. What were the justifications for it and what were the alternatives? (When researching this, make a point of looking at the work of Leo Szilard who, among other things, drafted the letter to President Roosevelt, which Albert Einstein signed, that led to the development of the atomic bomb.)

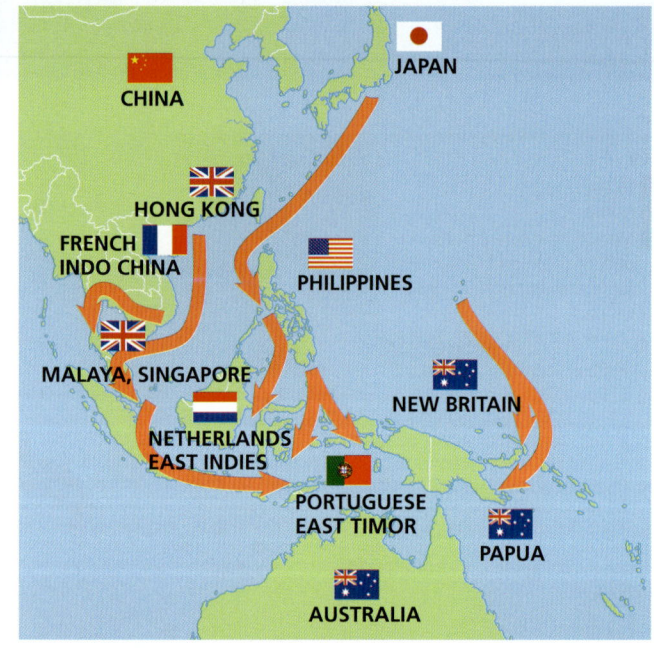

◆ Assessment opportunities

◆ In this activity you have practised skills that are assessed using Criterion B: Investigating, Criterion C: Communicating and Criterion D: Thinking critically.

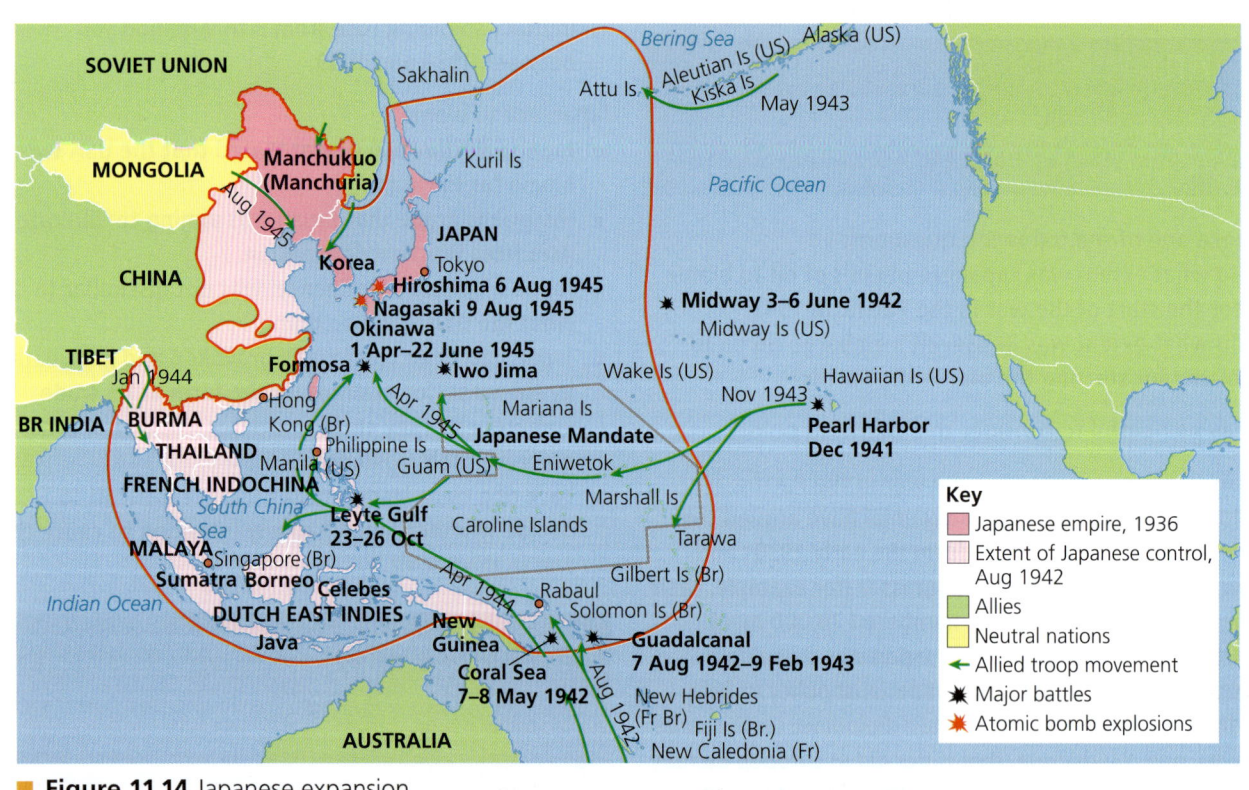

■ Figure 11.14 Japanese expansion

Figure 11.15 Someone is taking someone for a walk – Hitler and Stalin with guns behind their back

Figure 11.16 The signing of the Molotov-Ribbentrop Pact

GERMAN EXPANSIONISM – OPERATION BARBAROSSA

The Nazi–Soviet Non-aggression Pact was signed by Molotov, the Soviet Minister of Foreign Affairs, and the German Foreign Minister Joachim Ribbentrop on 23 August 1939. The pact stated that the two countries would not attack one another and that Poland would be divided between them, thus paving the way for the 1.5 million soldier-strong German invasion of Poland on 1 September 1939. This then resulted in the British ultimatum delivered by Prime Minister Chamberlain telling Berlin (via the British Ambassador to Germany) that unless the Nazis announced a withdrawal by 11am on 3 September, Britain and France would uphold their promise of support to Poland. Von Ribbentrop referred the message to Adolf Hitler. Chamberlain's subsequent speech to the British public when Germany ignored the ultimatum ended with the words 'and consequently this country is at war with Germany'. https://youtu.be/t2qlZHW-fDI

The Nazi–Soviet Pact was an uneasy agreement between ideologically polar opposite countries: fascist Germany and the communist Soviet Union. It lasted until 22 June 1941 and Germany's invasion of the Soviet Union, under Operation Barbarossa.

So, why did Germany not begin the war with Operation Barbarossa rather than an invasion of Poland, the Netherlands, Belgium and France? In the 1930s, Germany could only supply itself with 25 per cent of the oil that it needed. Trade deals and the resulting imports from the Soviet Union were able to fill much of this void. Hitler knew that the oil, grain, wood and other metals that Germany received from the Soviet Union would cease immediately if they went to war with them, and Germany only had reserves for two months of fighting. The quantities of raw materials and food imported into Germany before the start of Operation Barbarossa were enormous and reduced the effect on Germany of the British naval blockade which had been in place since the start of the war. Soviet imports did, however, become increasingly expensive and at the time of the invasion, Germany was quite heavily in debt to the Soviet Union. Armaments minister Albert Speer, when captured in 1945 and asked how much economics came into military decision-making, particularly with Barbarossa, said 'the need for oil was certainly a prime motive'. Hitler stressed the absolute necessity of the quick capture of key oilfields, particularly those in the Caucasus region (especially Baku in modern-day Azerbaijan, which was one of the most productive in the world) which accounted for almost 90 per cent of all oil produced in the Soviet Union.

Germany deployed 4.5 million soldiers in 148 combat divisions, penetrating hundreds of kilometres into Soviet territory. Some 600,000 Red Army troops were captured, killed or wounded but Germany failed to shatter Russia 'to its roots with one blow' as Hitler had promised. By December of 1941, German troops were within sight of Moscow, but the advance along the whole front slowed to a halt when winter set in. Casualties on both sides were staggering and the fighting around Stalingrad, which lasted until early 1943, was brutal beyond belief. A key factor was that Germany was unable to get the Caucasus under its control. Soviet goods were not being imported any longer and the German war machine ground to a halt. The length of supply lines into the Soviet Union was too great and the perishingly cold winters wrecked both mobility and morale. By the time Field Marshal Paulus' Southern Group surrendered on 31 January 1943 and General Schreck's surrender of the Northern Group two days later, the loss of human life had run into millions. It has been estimated that the war as a whole cost the lives of 25 million Soviet soldiers and civilians.

■ **Figure 11.17** The Eastern Front (22 June – 5 December 1941)

Figure 11.17 shows the scale of the German invasion, both in terms of the length of the front (over 3,000 km) and also depth the German military managed to go into Soviet territory (and therefore the length of supply line needed). This supply line was hampered in no small part by Russian railroads that could at first not be used (until a sufficient number of trains had been seized) due to a difference in their gauge compared to German trains. Also, most Soviet roads were unpaved, making them virtually impassable during winter.

Hitler said at the beginning of the second summer of Operation Barbarossa, 'If I do not get the oil of Maikop [near the Black Sea] and Grozny [near the Caspian Sea] then I must end this war.' The output of these two oilfields was estimated at 2.5 million tons per year and Hitler, perhaps rightly, considered a reliable oil supply such as this a non-negotiable requirement in order to wage a prolonged **war of attrition** on many fronts. Hitler was aware that a shortage of oil during 1916–18 was of decisive importance and was determined not to be hampered in his ambitions by a repeat of the problem.

It is interesting to note that on 23 June 1941, J. Edgar Hoover, head of the FBI, wrote that the 'FBI discovered various payments to oil companies [indicating] that the Standard Oil Company of New Jersey has been receiving money from German oil sales by order of the Reichsbank'. Effectively, US companies were selling oil to Germany during the war.

How did the Allies respond to the German need for oil?

The reliance of Germany on oil and oil products for its war machine was identified before the beginning of the Second World War and strategic bombing started from 1940 with the British Royal Air Force (RAF) targeting German (and European Axis power) factories, refineries and storage depots. The United States Army Air Force (USAAF), as their involvement in Europe increased from 1943, launched systematic bombing raids of their own, even conducting daytime raids in order to be more precise. They also expanded the range of attacks to include oil fields in Austria and Romania.

Examples of attacks included Operation Tidal Wave on 1 August 1943, during which the USAAF were able to use airfields in Southern Italy and Libya to bomb nine oil refineries around the city of Ploieşti in Romania (see Figure 11.18).

Figure 11.18 Operation Tidal Wave, 1 August 1943

As the war progressed, intelligence reports resulted in the targeting of Nazi oil production, storage and transport becoming a higher priority. Both before and after D-Day, targets across the whole continent were relentlessly attacked through to January 1945 when their priority was lowered. For example, four months after the D-Day landings, on 16 October 1944, USAAF bombers destroyed the oil plant at Linz in Austria, causing serious disruption to the German war effort.

Table 11.3 Attacks by the RAF and USAAF against oil targets, 1944–45

Month	USAAF Eighth Air Force	USAAF Fifteenth Air Force	RAF Bomber Command
May 1944	11	10	0
June 1944	20	32	10
July 1944	9	26	20
August 1944	33	23	20
September 1944	23	8	14
October 1944	18	10	10
November 1944	32	19	22
December 1944	7	33	15
January 1945	17	5	23
February 1945	20	20	24
March 1945	36	24	33
April 1945	7	1	9
Total	233	221	200

Source: Hall, R. Cargill, Case Studies in Strategic Bombardment, 1998

Table 11.4 Short tons dropped on oil targets (short tons are a measure of explosive power)

Month	USAAF Eighth Air Force	USAAF Fifteenth Air Force	RAF Bomber Command
May 1944	3,883	1,540	0
June 1944	3,689	5,653	4,562
July 1944	5,379	9,313	3,829
August 1944	7,116	3,997	1,856
September 1944	7,495	1,829	4,488
October 1944	4,462	2,515	4,088
November 1944	15,884	4,168	16,029
December 1944	2,937	6,226	5,772
January 1945	3,537	2,023	10,114
February 1945	1,616	4,362	15,749
March 1945	9,550	6,628	21,211
April 1945	1,949	124	5,993
Total	66,497	48,378	93,691

Source: Hall, R. Cargill, Case Studies in Strategic Bombardment, 1998

ACTIVITY: How were bombs used towards the end of the Second World War?

■ ATL

■ Critical-thinking skills: Interpret data

Describe the pattern of bombing of USAAF and RAF forces during the Second World War.

Explain why the number of bombing raids on oil targets dropped off in April 1945.

In a paragraph, **explain** why successful bombing raids on oil facilities would have been of such importance to Allied commanders and of such concern to Axis commanders.

◆ Assessment opportunities

♦ In this activity you have practised skills that are assessed using Criterion D: Thinking critically.

THE SUEZ CANAL AND THE SUEZ CRISIS, 1956

In 1854, Mohamed Said, the then Viceroy of Egypt, agreed, following persuasion from the former French diplomat Ferdinand de Lesseps, to the construction of a 160 km stretch of canal through the desert between Africa and Asia. The Universal Company of the Suez Maritime Canal (UCSMC) was created in 1858. Work began on 25 April 1859 and after ten years of construction, much of which was initially done by hand, the Suez Canal was officially opened in November 1869.

The Suez Canal provided a route to India and the Far East that was far shorter than the original route that required ships to round the Cape of Good Hope in South Africa. A trip from Mumbai to London was now less than 60 per cent of the original distance, meaning trade links were strengthened and trade generally increased.

■ Figure 11.19 The Suez Canal

In the first year after its opening, around 75 per cent of all shipping through the Suez Canal was British; this was despite their declining to take shares in the UCSMC and encouraging companies not to finance the company, which resulted in Egypt owning 44 per cent of the shares. At this time, massive debts were being run up by Ismail the Magnificent (the viceroy of Egypt and Sudan, 1863–79) in attempts to modernize the country. In order to raise money, Egypt's shareholding was sold to the British government under Disraeli for £4 million, which secured for them an enormous influence over the management of the canal.

■ Figure 11.20 George Reynolds struck oil in a remote part of modern-day Iran

In 1882, Britain invaded Egypt, beginning a long occupation of the country. The canal was crucial to trade with the Far East but there was relatively little trade with countries of the Middle East until 1908 when George Reynolds, financed by the Burmah Oil Company and the Englishman William D'Arcy, who in 1901 had obtained a licence to explore for oil in Persia, struck oil in a remote part of modern-day Iran (see Figure 11.20). D'Arcy and the Burmah Oil Company reorganized their holdings more formally in 1909 as the Anglo-Persian Oil Company.

This was a game changer as the Suez Canal now provided not only a shorter sea route to India, Australia and Britain's other colonies in the Far East, but also easy access to the oilfields of the Persian Gulf, cementing the British requirement to protect the canal. It is important to remember that motor cars were growing in popularity at the time, following Karl Benz's invention in 1885–86, and ships were moving towards the use of oil as their main fuel source (see Churchill's decision, page 270). Following General Allenby's defeat of Turkey in 1918, the old Ottoman empire was divided between France and Britain, leaving the latter in possession of the oilfields in what became Iraq.

Even following the Anglo-Egyptian treaty of 1936, which made Egypt all but independent, Britain still reserved its right to protect the canal, withdrawing troops from everywhere except around the canal. For strategic reasons, this continued during the Second World War. Britain had 36,000 soldiers guarding the canal and the Arabian oil fields.

At the end of the war, Egypt pressed for evacuation of British troops from the Suez Canal Zone, which Britain resisted. Tensions grew and in July 1956, Gamal Abdel Nasser, the Egyptian President at the time, nationalized the canal, in the hope of charging tolls to commercial shipping in order to finance an enormous dam construction project on the Nile River.

Historian Daniel Yergin wrote about the canal's changing role but retained significance stating:

'In 1948, the canal abruptly lost its traditional rationale. … [British] control over the canal could no longer be preserved on grounds that it was critical to the defence either of India or of an empire that was being liquidated. And yet, at exactly the same moment, the canal was gaining a new role – as the highway not of empire, but of oil. By 1955, petroleum accounted for half of the canal's traffic, and, in turn, two thirds of Europe's oil passed through it.' – Daniel Yergin, *The Prize*.

Israel, which had become an official country on 14 May 1948, wanted to secure its interests in the canal and so in collusion with Britain and France attacked Egypt on 29 October 1957. French and British forces launched an assault on 5 November in order to occupy the canal zone and keep it open to their shipping. While it was a military success, the assault was a political disaster, viewed by many, including the USA, as old-fashioned imperialism at its worst. The United Nations stepped in and Egypt agreed to reopen the canal to commercial shipping provided Israeli, British and French troops withdrew, which they did by March 1957.

The importance of the canal remained high on European agendas, and events such as the Six-Day War (Israel's occupation of the Sinai Peninsula) created anxiety for European premiers who relied on the route to sustain their oil demands, as well as other goods, from the Middle East and beyond. It retains such status to this day.

■ Figure 11.21 The Suez Canal

11 Is our exploitation of the Earth sustainable?

ACTIVITY: Why did the USA and Britain invade Iraq in 2003?

■ **ATL**

- Critical-thinking skills: Evaluate evidence and arguments

SOURCE A

■ **Figure 11.22** The Four Horsemen of the Drillocalypse

SOURCE B

'Iraq is currently the world's second largest source of oil, but the majority of subterranean oil reserves have never been tapped. After the war, when US oil corporations have fully developed the oil industry's potential, Iraq is expected to become the largest single supply of oil on Earth. The new oilfields, when developed, could produce up to eight million barrels a day within a few years – thus rivalling Saudi Arabia, the present kingpin of oil.'

Evening Standard, *Is this war all about oil?*, 11 March 2003

SOURCE C

'If Iraq was invaded for oil… then the US was remarkably negligent in securing the prize. Iraq awarded its first major post-invasion oil concessions in 2009, and the big winners? Norway, France, China and Russia. Of the 11 contracts signed only one went to a US company (Exxon Mobil).'

Muhammad Idrees Ahmad, *The Road to Iraq: The Making of a Neoconservative War*

SOURCE D

'President Bush's Cabinet agreed in April 2001 that "Iraq remains a destabilising influence to the flow of oil to international markets from the Middle East" and because this is an unacceptable risk to the US "military intervention" is necessary.'

Sunday Herald, *Official: US oil at the heart of Iraq crisis*, 6 October 2002

1. What is the message of Source A?
2. Compare and contrast the views expressed in Source B and Source C.
3. With reference to its origin, purpose and content, evaluate the values and limitations of Source D to a historian studying the origins of the 2003 Iraq War.
4. Using the sources and your own research, write an essay of 1,000 words on what motivated the USA and Britain to invade Iraq.

◆ **Assessment opportunities**

- ◆ In this activity you have practised skills that are assessed using Criterion A: Knowing and understanding, Criterion C: Communicating and Criterion D: Thinking critically.

THE IRAQ WAR

In early 2003 around 36 million people worldwide took part in 3,000 anti-war protests, most of which were centred around the proposed invasion of Iraq by the USA and its allies (including Britain). While there is continued debate about the reasons for the invasion, there is evidence to suggest that economic interests in the area, particularly oil, played a part in the decision to go to war.

Why are oil prices so volatile?

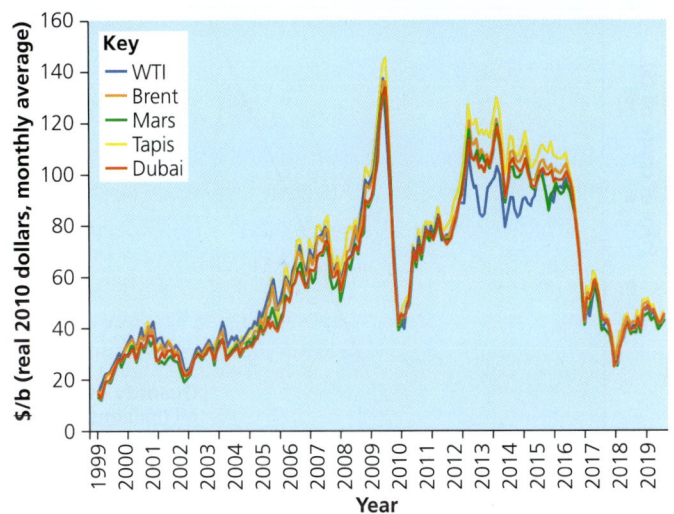

Figure 11.23 World oil prices from 1999 to 2017, quoted in 2010 dollars (Source: EIA)

The price of oil can change dramatically from year to year, wreaking havoc on oil-producing companies and countries. Between 1999 and 2008, oil prices rose from below $30 per barrel to more than $140 per barrel. Oil prices crashed in 2008 at the onset of the financial crisis, and recovered between 2010 and 2015. The most recent price change has been the dramatic fall during 2015, and who knows what other price fluctuations may be around the corner. But why does the price of oil change so much and so fast compared to the prices of most goods we consume on a daily basis? The concept that explains why this happens is called elasticity.

PRICE ELASTICITY OF DEMAND

Price elasticity of demand (PED) is a concept that explores the sensitivity of consumers' demand to changes in price. It is calculated using the following formula:

$$\text{PED} = \frac{\text{(per cent change in quantity demanded)}}{\text{(per cent change in price)}} = \frac{(\%\Delta Qd)}{(\%\Delta P)}$$

When we calculate PED, we are able to work out by how much the quantity demanded for a product or service will change when the price changes by 1 per cent.

If a 1 per cent price change results in a more than 1 per cent change in quantity demanded, the demand for the good is said to be price elastic. In this case, consumers have responded significantly to the price change. Goods for which demand is price elastic include anything that is not very important to us, or that represent a large portion of our income so we are motivated to shop around.

If a 1 per cent price change results in a less than 1 per cent change in quantity demanded, the demand for the good is said to be price inelastic. In this case, consumers have not responded significantly to the price change. Goods for which demand is price inelastic include anything that we depend greatly on, or that does not take up a significant portion of our income.

Determinants of PED include:
- number of substitutes available or how narrowly defined the good is
- proportion of income spent
- whether the good is a luxury or a necessity
- whether the good is addictive or habit forming
- the time period available to make the buying decision.

Figure 11.24 shows what the demand for crude oil will look like if we draw it to correctly show its price elasticity of demand. Because crude oil is such an important input into the production process, we will be relatively insensitive to price changes. For every 1 per cent change in price, we will change our quantity demanded by less than 1 per cent – we will continue to buy oil in the similar quantities as before. Notice how the changes in quantity look relatively smaller than the changes in price.

> **THINK–PAIR–SHARE**
>
> In pairs, make a **list** of three goods that you think have a low PED (PED<1) and three goods that have a high PED (PED>1). Share these with the rest of the class.

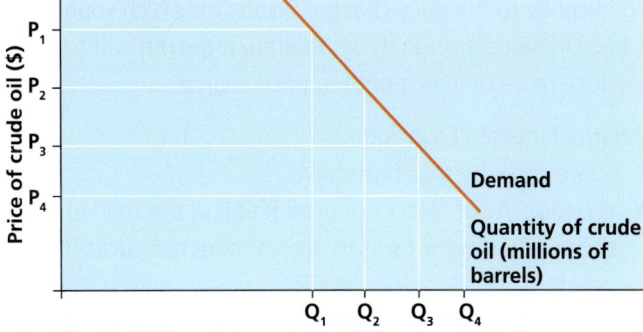

Figure 11.24 Demand for crude oil

EXTENSION: EXPLORE FURTHER

In 2015, crude oil prices started dropping dramatically from above $100 per barrel to less than $40 by January 2016. Some countries are extremely dependent on oil production for their government revenue and the health of their economy. For different oil exporting countries, try to find out how high oil prices need to be for those countries to break even.

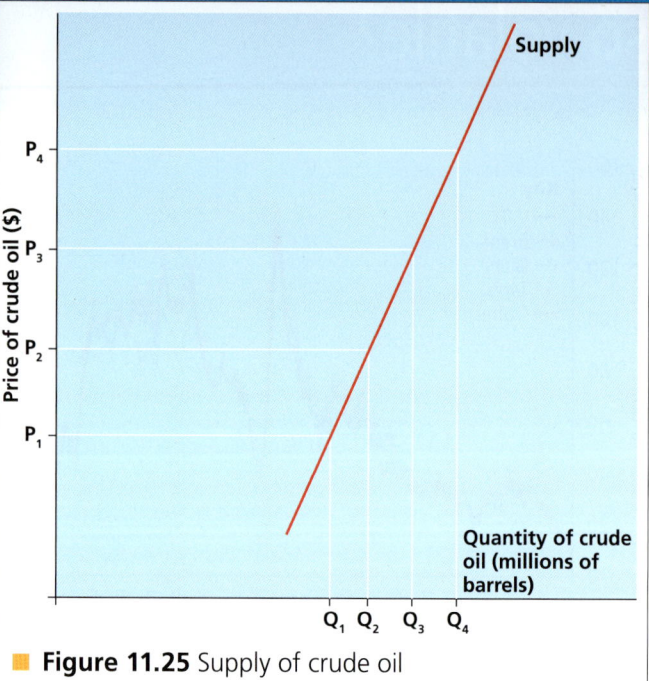

Figure 11.25 Supply of crude oil

PRICE ELASTICITY OF SUPPLY

Price elasticity of supply (PES) is a concept that explores the sensitivity of producers' supply to changes in price. It is calculated using the following formula:

$$PES = \frac{\text{(per cent change in quantity supplied)}}{\text{(per cent change in price)}} = \frac{(\%\Delta Qs)}{(\%\Delta P)}$$

When we calculate PES, we are able to work out by how much the quantity supplied of a good or service will change when the price changes by 1 per cent.

If a 1 per cent price change results in a more than 1 per cent change in quantity supplied, the supply for the good is said to be price elastic. In this case, firms have responded significantly to the price change. Goods for which supply is price elastic include anything that can be manufactured relatively easily in increased volumes.

If a 1 per cent price change results in a less than 1 per cent change in quantity supplied, the supply for the good is said to be price inelastic. In this case, firms cannot respond significantly to the price change. Goods for which supply is price inelastic include things that are more difficult to produce more of in response to price changes.

Determinants of PES include:
- spare capacity that firms have
- the mobility of factors of production in the market (how easy it is for firms to access more resources if they need to)
- the ability to store the good once it has been produced
- the time period available to produce.

ACTIVITY: How can global events influence oil prices?

ATL

- Information literacy skills: Access information to be informed and inform others

In groups, you will be assigned one of the cases in the table below to research. **Investigate** how your global event impacted oil prices. Then share your information with the rest of the class.

Copy Table 11.5 and complete it with the information provided by each group.

Table 11.5 Impact of global events

Name of case	Geopolitical impact/effect
The 1973 oil crisis	
The Exxon Valdez oil spill, 1989	
Hurricane Katrina, 2005	
Syria instability, 2011	

Assessment opportunities

- In this activity you have practised skills that are assessed using Criterion B: Investigating.

How far can resource extraction be relied upon as a source of development?

The discovery and extraction of oil has been a huge driving force for development in many countries, including Dubai in the United Arab Emirates (UAE). Oil was first discovered offshore there in 1966 and the first exports of oil left the country in 1969. Further exploration took place from 1972 onwards, and since then Dubai has become a major producer.

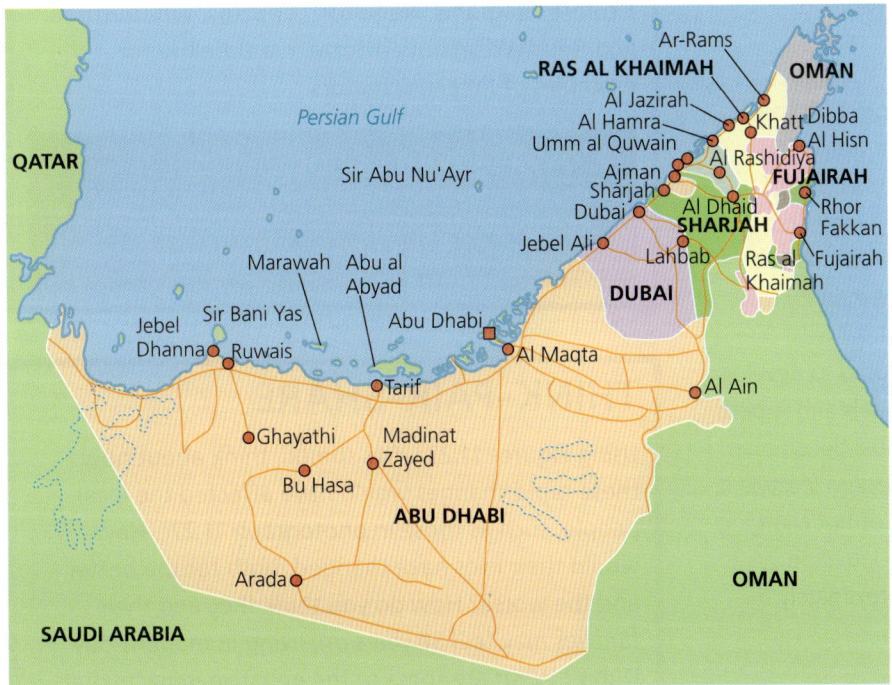

■ **Figure 11.26** UAE

■ **Figure 11.27** How the emirate went from desert backwater to the Manhattan of the Middle East in just 50 years

11 Is our exploitation of the Earth sustainable?

Figures 11.27a–f show the huge changes that Dubai underwent in a relatively short period of time, with the black and white photographs being taken in the 1960s. In the eighteenth century, Dubai's function was that of a fishing and pearl-cultivating village. In the nineteenth and twentieth centuries it became a trading partner with Iran and India and in 1960 its population reached 20,000. In 1966 everything changed for Dubai when oil was discovered. A huge increase in wealth was used to develop Dubai with up-to-date roads, schools, hospitals and superb communications and transport facilities. Dubai became an attractive place to expatriates due to the modern lifestyle it afforded them and it had the added bonus of not charging workers tax on their earnings. In 2006 its population reached 1.1 million people and in 2017 approximately 2.78 million – a phenomenal rate of growth.

RELIANCE ON PRIMARY GOODS

For many countries that are fortunate to have oil reserves, specializing their industrial output around the oil industry has yielded significant benefits for their economies. When oil prices are high, the revenues that can be gained from the sale of crude oil to the rest of the world will also be high. Profits can be reinvested into growing industries, increasing employment in the country and generating economic growth. The government can raise more tax revenue which it can spend on essential public services such as health and education, raising the living standards in the country over the longer term. Countries like Qatar have used their revenues from natural gas to build a modern city in Doha, with hotels, shopping malls, new schools and collaborative university projects with other countries. Countries have also taken advantage of the expertise of existing petroleum corporations, inviting them to extract the resources for a share of the revenue streams.

ACTIVITY: Dubai timeline

■ ATL

- Information literacy skills: Present information in a variety of formats and platforms

Using the dates and statistics above, as well as extra research, create an online timeline that details Dubai's growth from the eighteenth century until the present day.

Explore programs like **Sutori**, **Capzles**, **whenintime** and **ReadWriteThink interactive timeline** for examples of timeline creators.

◆ Assessment opportunities

- In this activity you have practised skills that are assessed using Criterion B: Investigating.

THINK–PAIR–SHARE

Using Figures 11.27a–f as stimuli, think about how these rapid changes would have affected the local people, such as those in photograph 11.27c. How would their lives have changed, both for the better and the worse? How do you think they and their families may feel 50 years on, living in modern-day Dubai? What are some of the negative impacts that this phenomenal growth and development may have brought with it? Once you have thought about these questions, **discuss** with a partner and be ready to share with the class.

When prices fall, however, these streams of revenue for firms and the government start to decrease. Such volatility can disrupt or reverse the progress that primary-resource-dependent countries make towards poverty reduction. In addition, primary resources do not create as much surplus value, or profit, as secondary (manufacturing) or tertiary (services) industries. Therefore, as a long-term growth and development strategy, reliance on oil is very risky. A final and important point to raise is the industry's environmental impact. The equipment needed for resource extraction is unattractive, refining crude oil involves the use of harmful chemicals, and the use of fossil fuels in the transport and energy industries is a major contributor to climate change.

How sustainable are resource-extraction industries? To what extent do the benefits outweigh the costs?

Global industrialization has benefited oil-producing nations in many ways but there are undoubtedly major concerns regarding the long-term sustainability of the industry which they supply. In Chapter 5, we discussed the impacts of the Trans-Alaska Pipeline including disruption to ecosystems, the potential melting of the permafrost, chemical contamination and issues regarding transporting the oil (see pages 130–31). Nigeria is also an oil-rich nation which has experienced some very specific environmental and social impacts of oil exploration.

Oil was first discovered in Nigeria in the late 1950s and, as with Dubai, has ever since been the major source of foreign exchange for the country, making Nigeria the wealthiest country in Africa (by GDP).

Royal Dutch Shell (Shell) is one of the world's largest oil TNCs (transnational corporations) and is the largest of the companies extracting oil in the Niger delta region of Rivers State, operating six oil fields in this area. Despite the wealth oil has brought to Nigeria, these oil fields have caused much controversy, largely relating to the effects experienced by local Ogoni people.

In 2011, the United Nations Environment Programme (UNEP – www.unep.org) carried out a study in the Ogoni region and found that the Ogoni farmers are competing with Shell for the fertile land in the delta. Food production has declined drastically since Shell became established in the region and the Ogoni are now net importers of food where once they were exporters. Government support for the Ogonis has been limited as Shell's presence can offer many benefits to the country in terms of investment in infrastructure. Pollution has had a drastic impact on the region. Oil spills have damaged land and wildlife, gas flaring has released toxic gases and oil has bubbled into local water supplies.

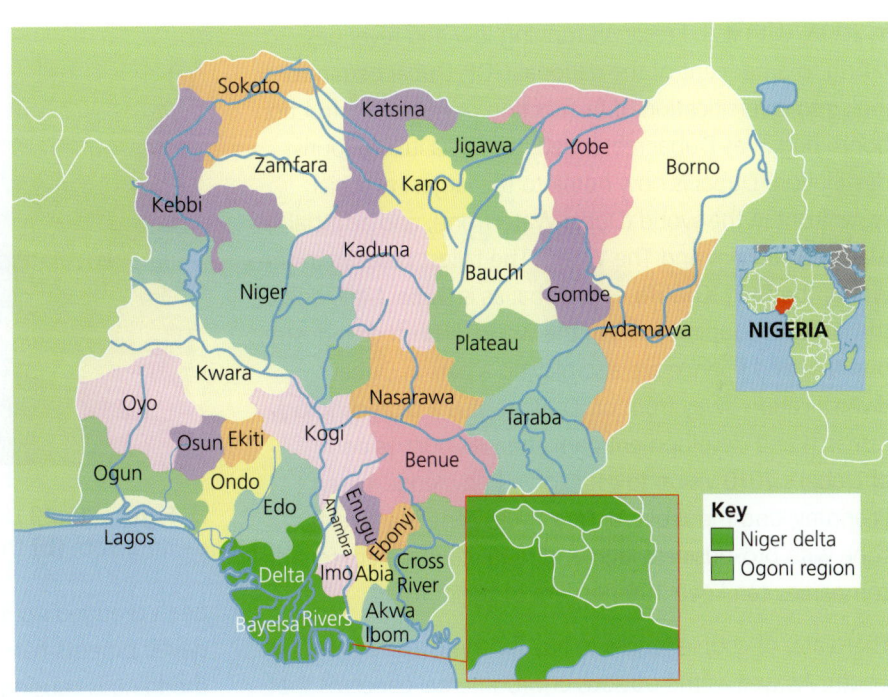

■ **Figure 11.28** Nigeria

11 Is our exploitation of the Earth sustainable?

In 2016, Nigerian Vice-President Yemi Osinbajo set in motion a $1 billion clean-up and restoration programme of the Ogoniland region, announcing that financial and legislative frameworks had been put in place to begin implementing recommendations made by the 2011 report. Work continues on this today.

As well as environmental concerns over the sustainability of oil extraction, there are also economic issues and Dubai has realized that economic reliance on oil is unsustainable. In 2006, with its oil reserves running low and revenues falling to 3 per cent of the national GDP, Dubai began to look into diversification of its function. A huge construction boom began as Dubai rebranded itself as a luxury tourist destination. Dubai is now home to the largest artificial waterfront in the world (Dubai Waterfront), and artificial islands, The Palm and The World. The tallest building in the world, the **Burj Khalifa**, is in Dubai as is Dubai Mall, one of the largest shopping malls in the world. High-tech industry, business and finance are also playing a part in Dubai's diversification away from oil. DuBiotech is a biotechnology research and development park and was built as part of Dubai's 2010 vision to establish a knowledge-based economy, and the Jebel Ali Free Trade Zone is a zero-tax zone with pro-business laws and regulations where foreign companies can keep 100 per cent of their profits.

There are, of course, prices to pay for this construction boom. As well as the obvious environmental concerns that increased construction brings, such as increased noise and air pollution which contributes to the greenhouse effect and in turn global climate issues (see Chapter 5 and *Sciences for the IB MYP 4&5*, Chapter 11), the buildings created also contribute to the heavy reliance on air conditioning and desalinated water. In the reclaiming of land to make the artificial islands, The Palm and The World, 3 million cubic metres of sand and shell from the seabed have

■ **Figure 11.29** Development in Dubai: **(a)** The Palm Jumeirah; **(b)** the Burj Khalifa; **(c)** Jebel Ali port

been dredged up. Plumes of sediment disturbed by the developments have smothered sparse coral outcrops and dredging is causing permanent changes to current systems in the Gulf that carry developing fish and coral through the marine ecosystem. The low-lying reclaimed land that has been created, and Dubai's coastal location, mean that the area is at increased risk from flooding as sea levels rise. Building work is expensive and, in the wake of the 2008 global financial crisis, many proposed projects have been halted or not started (see Masdar City in Chapter 7, page 179).

There are also social issues that must be addressed, in particular Dubai's questionable treatment of migrant workers. In Chapter 6 we discussed some of the issues faced by voluntary migrants seeking a better way of life for themselves and their families (see page 149), and those coming to Dubai as construction workers often face similar issues to those in China and Mexico. Most of the construction workers in Dubai are poorly paid migrants, mainly from India, Pakistan, Bangladesh and Nepal, who can end up working in dangerous conditions, such as 12-hour shifts in 50°C heat with full sun exposure, as well as living in squalid accommodation. Labourers were not allowed to strike or form unions to protect themselves from poor treatment in the construction industry until 2007 when the UAE drafted a law that allows labourers to form unions and pursue collective bargaining.

ACTIVITY: Annotation and comprehension

ATL

- Communication skills: Paraphrase accurately and concisely; Organize and depict information logically

1 **Explain** how local people, such as the Ogonis in the Niger Delta, may benefit from the exploitation of natural resources on their land.
2 **Explore** the possible conflicts of interest over the need to exploit natural resources for national development and the needs of the local communities where resources are located. **List them in detail.**

Assessment opportunities

- In this activity you have practised skills that are assessed using Criterion A: Knowing and understanding.

ACTIVITY: Creative writing

ATL

- Communication skills: Write for different purposes
- Information literacy skills: Access information to be informed and inform others

Research the labour and human rights issues in Dubai. Search **Dubai migrant workers** to get you started. Produce a piece of creative writing, for example a poem, exploring the lives of the Asian construction workers – pay close attention to the style of your writing, making sure it is appropriate for the task and your audience.

Assessment opportunities

- In this activity you have practised skills that are assessed using Criterion A: Knowing and understanding and Criterion C: Communicating.

Take action

! As we have seen in both this chapter and Chapter 6 there are global issues around the treatment of migrants. With a partner, **explore** what can be done to begin to tackle these.
! Can any of the UN's Sustainable Development Goals be related to the treatment of migrant workers?
! Are there any charities that deal with this issue? If so, are there ways in which you could become involved?
! Are there issues with migrant workers in your local area or country? Can you raise awareness of their plight?

What are the alternatives to oil?

As we have seen throughout this chapter, reliance on oil, and other fossil fuels, is not sustainable so alternatives are being developed and used. In Chapters 5 and 7, we looked at renewable energy when we examined the Three Gorges Dam and hydroelectric power (see page 133) and the use of solar panels in Masdar City (see page 179). However, there are other alternative energy sources that are important to explore, including nuclear power which, despite not being a renewable source of energy, is often grouped with renewables since the amount of raw material (plutonium) needed to produce a large amount of energy is very small.

■ **Figure 11.30** Alternative sources of energy

ACTIVITY: Group presentations on alternative energy

■ **ATL**

- Collaboration skills: Negotiate effectively; Exercise leadership and take on a variety of roles within groups; Encourage others to contribute

In groups, you will be assigned an alternative source of energy: solar, wind, tidal or nuclear power, (not hydroelectric as this is covered in the case study on the Three Gorges Dam in Chapter 5), and will create a presentation that you will share with your peers.

For the source of energy you have been assigned:
- **Outline** what it is and how it works.
- **Explain** its advantages.
- **Discuss** its disadvantages.
- **Identify** countries in which it is used as a source of energy.

Consult the ATL skills cog in Chapter 8 that outlines presentation skills (see page 207).

◆ **Assessment opportunities**

◆ In this activity you have practised skills that are assessed using Criterion A: Knowing and understanding, Criteria C: Communicating and Criterion D: Thinking critically.

Reflection

In this chapter, we have **described** the distribution of oil reserves in the world, and **explained** how oil is extracted. We have **explained** the significance of oil as a resource for production, and its role in affecting global events during the nineteenth, twentieth and twenty-first centuries. We have **explained** why oil prices change so easily, and what impact those changes can have on countries. We have constructed supply and demand diagrams to learn about the concept of price elasticity. We have **evaluated** how reliance on oil exports can bring positive and negative effects for some less economically developed countries. We have **discussed** the sustainability of the oil industry and the effects of oil extraction on local communities.

Use this table to reflect on your own learning in this chapter.					
Questions we asked	Answers we found	Any further questions now?			
Factual: Who produces oil? How are resources extracted? What are the alternatives to oil? .					
Conceptual: How has the world become so reliant on crude oil? Why are oil prices so volatile?					
Debatable: How far can resource extraction be relied upon as a source of development? To what extent do the benefits of resource extraction outweigh the costs? How sustainable are resource extraction industries?					
Approaches to learning you used in this chapter	Description – what new skills did you learn?	How well did you master the skills?			
		Novice	Learner	Practitioner	Expert
Communication skills					
Collaboration skills					
Organization skills					
Information literacy skills					
Critical-thinking skills					
Learner profile attribute(s)	Reflect on the importance of being balanced for your learning in this chapter.				
Balanced					

Time, place and space   Causality; Perspective   Orientation in space and time

How has our perspective changed now?

○ Our **perspective** changes **over time**; reflection allows us to see the causes and impacts of events in **different times and places**.

CONSIDER THESE QUESTIONS:

Factual: What have you learned so far? What else do you need to know? How is the knowledge you have learned connected to the aims of MYP Individuals and Societies? How will it prepare you for your Diploma courses?

Conceptual: What approaches to learning skills will I need next? How do we gather our own data? How do I develop research questions based on current issues? How do our perspectives change as we learn through different subjects? How do we know the information we read is true? How do we answer exam-style questions? How has your understanding of Individuals and Societies been transformed?

Debatable: Can we ever be sure that we have mastered the topics we learned?

Now **share and compare** your thoughts and ideas with your partner, or with the whole class.

■ **Figure 12.1 (a)** Exploring the world can change our perspective; **(b)** Pieces of the Berlin Wall remind us of recent events in history; **(c)** Rubbish from more economically developed countries becomes a source of income in less economically developed countries; **(d)** Shanty towns sit beside wealthy areas in some cities

○ IN THIS CHAPTER WE WILL …

- **Find out** how much you've learned and where you need to revise or refresh.
- **Explore** the most appropriate course in Individuals and Societies for you.
- **Take action** by considering ethical, moral and social implications of Individuals and Societies.

■ These Approaches to Learning (ATL) skills will be useful …

- Communication skills
- Organization skills
- Collaboration skills
- Critical-thinking skills
- Research skills
- Information literacy skills
- Media literacy skills

● We will reflect on this learner profile attribute …

- Reflective – our learning is enriched and deepened if we reflect on it, connecting new discoveries to existing understanding.

◆ Assessment opportunities in this chapter:

- Criterion A: Knowing and understanding
- Criterion B: Investigating
- Criterion C: Communicating
- Criterion D: Thinking critically

KEY WORDS

dataset
hypothesis
primary source
research question
secondary source

I USED TO THINK … NOW I THINK …

Take a look at Figure 12.1 above. What are our aims when we study Individuals and Societies? Use your ideas to help you reflect through this visible thinking routine:

- I used to think that …
- Now I think that …
- What I would like to know next is …

12 How has our perspective changed now?

What approaches to learning skills will I need next?

HOW DO WE GATHER OUR OWN DATA?

ACTIVITY: Urban heat island effect

ATL

■ Research skills: Process data and report results

In Chapter 7 we explored the concept of urban stress as part of our focus on sustainability in urban systems. A concept relating to urban stress is the phenomenon of the urban heat island (UHI). This is an urban area that is significantly warmer than its surrounding rural areas due to human activities. Figure 12.2 shows that as distance from the centre of the city decreases, so does temperature.

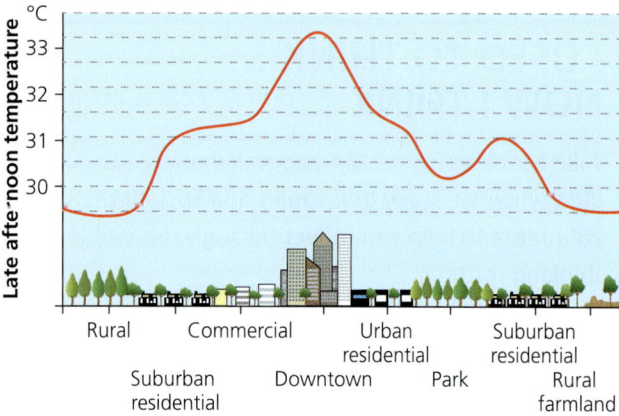

■ **Figure 12.2** An urban heat island profile

DISCUSS

Why do you think urban areas are hotter than their surrounding rural areas? What things do they have or lack that may make them warmer?

Fieldwork investigation

Your task is to carry out a fieldwork investigation in your own, or nearest, urban area.

Your teacher will manage this so that you are sharing data with your peers as this is the most effective way of data collection.

You will then produce a report that can be assessed on all four of the MYP Individuals and Societies criteria.

You will need to take the following steps:
- Carry out some initial research into the urban heat island effect, for example what the causes are said to be and any examples of places said to experience one.
- Develop a research question, relating to UHIs that you would like to **explore**.
- **Justify** the relevance of your research question and why it is important to study it.
- Make a brief preliminary judgement (prediction/hypothesis) answering the research question for your fieldwork, linked to the urban heat island profile in Figure 12.2 (geographical theory).

Methodology

- Plan with your teacher how you will carry out the fieldwork as a class. This may involve a whole-class trip or you may be assigned some data collection to complete as homework.
- An example of how you could carry out the fieldwork would be to divide your city, or an area of your city, into zones along a transect running north to south or east to west (or both). Different groups of students could then be assigned to each area along the transect to collect their data and then the data could be shared so you have a picture for the whole city, from the centre to the fringe.
- Think about and plan what data you will collect and what equipment you will require – variables you could measure include temperature, humidity, noise pollution, traffic count, pedestrian count, percentage of concrete visible, percentage of vegetation visible and function of the area. You can use a mix of **primary** and **secondary data** and **qualitative** and **quantitative data**. Your school science department may have equipment you can borrow or you could

explore ways in which you could use smartphones (if you have access to them) to help you gather data.
- When you have decided on your plan, you should **explain** in your report where the fieldwork investigation was carried out.
- A map of the data collection locations used is essential.
- You may wish to use photos to show the area you studied, any equipment you used or anything else you feel is relevant to the study.
- In your report, you should **describe** the methods used to collect your data and **justify/evaluate** the methods used and the quality of the data collected.

Advice on the use of maps

- You must add value to maps you include – just sticking in a photocopied map or a printed map from the internet is of little value unless you have used it as a base map to show other information.
- You must acknowledge the source of the map.
- You must give the map a title, scale (or state not to scale), key/legend and border.

> **EXTENSION**
>
> You may wish to research and **discuss** sampling techniques as part of your discussion on data collection.

> **EXTENSION**
>
> You may wish to research statistical tests you could use to help display your results and findings – your maths teacher may be able to help you with this.

Data presentation and analysis

- The presentation of your data (graphs, etc.) and the written analysis must be integrated – there should be no random graphs on a single page.
- You should treat and display the data collected using the most appropriate techniques.
- You must **demonstrate** your knowledge and understanding of the fieldwork investigation by **interpreting** or **explaining** the information you have collected.
- You should **describe** and **explain** your results and look for any anomalies that may be present – **explain** these too.

Conclusion

- In your conclusion, you should **summarize** your findings and make a clear, concise statement answering the fieldwork question.
- Ensure your conclusion to the fieldwork question is consistent with the outcomes of your analysis.
- Ensure any recommendations for improvements are realistic.
- Make suggestions for modifying the fieldwork question.
- Compile a bibliography of any sources you have used throughout this investigation. These may be research into the UHI effect, different methods, sampling techniques, etc.

◆ Assessment opportunities

- ◆ In this activity you have practised skills that are assessed using Criterion A: Knowing and understanding, Criterion B: Investigating, Criterion C: Communicating and Criterion D: Thinking critically.

HOW DO WE FRAME AN INVESTIGATION?

As you are aware, in Individuals and Societies, Criterion B is dedicated to investigation. But what does this really mean? As we read in the first chapter, there is a set of skills in Individuals and Societies that are important to all disciplines within the subject, especially investigating (see pages 22–3). Sometimes the different subjects can take slightly different approaches when conducting investigations, particularly in terms of the types of sources used, but there are some core principles that they all share. In this activity, you will be practising those core principles of investigating.

You will draw on concepts and content discussed in Chapter 5 in planning your own investigation into sustainability in ecosystems. You will be guided through all the strands of Criterion B: formulating a research question; creating an action plan; effective and relevant research and reflecting on the process.

ACTIVITY: Sustainability investigation

ATL

- Organization skills: Plan short- and long-term assignments; Meet deadlines; Create plans to prepare for summative assessments (examinations and performances)

You are to conduct an investigation into sustainability in an ecosystem of your choice. You should choose an ecosystem that you are interested in and that allows you to find helpful evidence through research.

You will produce a report or presentation that answers your research question. Your teacher may choose to assess this using Criteria A, C and/or D in addition to the planning element of Criterion B.

Choose a topic

You can choose one of the following ecosystems or find another that is not on this list:
- **Savanna grassland**
- **Rainforest**
- **Polar**
- **Freshwater**
- **Marine**

Formulate your research question

Do some quick research to get ideas about the issues faced by your chosen ecosystem. These could be due to human impact or natural phenomena.

Research question 'must haves':
- **Clear: does it make sense?**
- **Focused: does it identify the what, where, when and who?**
- **Un-Googleable: does it require information from multiple sources in order to be answered? (It should not be easy to answer.)**
- **Relevant: is it connected to the task itself (the concept, the statement of inquiry, the task instructions)?**

Combine your chosen ecosystem with your chosen issue to create a clear and focused research question.

Explain your choice

Answer the questions below:
- **Why did you choose this focus?**
- **Does it fit the research question 'must haves'?**
- **Does it allow you to meet the task requirements?**

Research methods

Copy and complete Table 12.1 to record your ideas and help order your notes.

- **Guiding questions:** Identify questions to guide your research. What information must you have in order to respond to your research question?
- **Notes:** Information you find that answers the key questions. These notes can be copied from your sources.
- **My notes:** Your own words – usually in bullet points.
- **Sources** – The sources you have used.

Table 12.1 Questions, notes and sources

Guiding questions	Notes	My notes	Sources

Report or presentation structure

Your report or presentation will be made up of four main sections, and has a 1,000-word limit/8-minute time limit.

Introduction (100 words or 1 minute)

- **Identify** the purpose of your investigation.
- **Identify** and **explain** your *research question*.

Overview (250 words or 2 minutes)

- Include the *core facts and information* about the ecosystem and your specific area of focus (evaluating sustainability).
- Aim to answer the *5Ws* (see Creating a geographical case study, page 124) + H (how) regarding sustainability (both positive and negative actions) on your chosen ecosystem.
- Use *visuals* to show/**demonstrate** information (maps, graphs, photos, quotations).

Analysis (400 words or 4 minutes)

- This is where you answer or respond to your research question. It requires you to think and draw conclusions.
- Aim to *identify three main points*. You have to *process* the information you have found in your research to identify these points.
- Use *evidence* from your research to support each point. Use clear sections or paragraphs.
- Aim to include *multiple perspectives* in your explanations of each point.
- Use some *visuals*.

Conclusion (150 words or 1 minute)

- **Summarize** your main points using your research question as your basis.
- Aim to give a concise response to your research question.

Structure requirements

- Your report/presentation should have a cover/title page/slide, four main sections with sub-headings, and a bibliography.
- Include a variety of relevant pictures/photos, graphs, tables, diagrams, statistics and maps and explicitly reference each one. These should also be included in your bibliography if they are taken from another source.
- All presentations should have minimal words on the screen, useful images and a bibliography on the last slide. Practise your presentation and write out notecards before you make your presentation to ensure your communication is clear.

Reflection

Evaluate the process and results of your investigation.

- What interested you about the topic you chose? Are you glad you chose it? Why?
- Which resources did you find especially helpful and why?
- What was difficult about the process?
- Did you find it difficult or easy to follow your action plan? Why?
- What did you enjoy about the investigation? What didn't you like?
- What new skills did you develop during this investigation?
- What did you find challenging about this investigation?
- What problems did you encounter during the investigation and how did you fix them?
- In your next investigation, what will you do differently?
- What did you think of the product you made?
- Is it your best work? Why/why not?

Remember, this should be a *critical evaluation* of your process and result. Use specific examples throughout.

◆ Assessment opportunities

♦ In this activity you have practised skills that are assessed using Criterion A: Knowing and understanding, Criterion B: Investigating, Criterion C: Communicating and Criterion D: Thinking critically.

How do I develop research questions based on current issues?

We know that to find the right answers we need to start out with the right questions. You will have worked on developing research questions in all your MYP subjects as this is a key approaches to learning skill. In Individuals and Societies our questions are very often prompted by what is happening in the world right now.

ACTIVITY: Austerity – does it do more harm than good?

ATL

- Information literacy skills: Collect and analyse data to identify solutions and/or make informed decisions

Austerity refers to a set of government policies that involve cuts in government spending or increases in tax rates (or both) in order to reduce the total level of borrowing by the government. These policies have a direct effect on the level of aggregate demand in the economy, but in some circumstances are necessary to prevent bigger economic problems. Countries that have implemented these policies recently include:

- Brazil
- Greece
- Portugal
- Spain
- the United Kingdom
- Latvia.

The aim of the task is to write a 1,200–1,500-word essay arguing for or against the use of austerity in one of the countries listed. You will need to select a narrow focus for the research (you will not be able to deal with the entire country's economy in 1,500 words) and develop a research question.

Preliminary research

You will need to carry out preliminary research before you start your project. Make notes on the following:

- How do governments borrow money? (Find out what a government bond is.)
- What do the terms 'bond yield' and 'bond price' mean?
- Why do bond prices rise and fall?
- Why do bond yields rise and fall?
- How do governments raise more revenue?
- How do governments cut their spending?

Research question

Once you have chosen your country, you need to develop your research question. The best research questions are open ended, debatable and do not already indicate the direction of your answer.

Your research question will need a narrow focus, and you will need to start gathering your evidence at this stage, before you start the writing process, so that you know whether you will be able to answer your quotations. You need to know that you have enough data, quotations from credible sources, and other evidence first.

To find a more narrow focus, think about an aspect of the country you want to **investigate**. Consider an industry or an aspect of life in the country.

Once you have developed your research question, submit it to your teacher for approval. Take on any feedback from your teacher about the question, and revise it if necessary.

Research and planning

This part will take the most time, and it is a mistake to think otherwise. When it comes to writing the actual essay, you will have already gathered all the material you need, and will have a clear plan for how your argument will be broken down into parts. The research process will include:

- gathering data from reliable sources, such as government statistics organizations
- reading newspaper articles from the relevant period of time (try using the advanced search function of Google News)
- finding quotations from important economists or politicians to support any argument that you want to make.

You will need to plan the main arguments that you will make to answer the question. Each argument and section of your essay will be based on the evidence you have gathered. Submit your essay outline to your teacher. It should include the following:

- **Introduction**
  - Give some background to the country's economy during the period in question. Information that might be relevant includes: the country's GDP and rank in terms of relative size, its main industries and a short timeline prior to austerity being implemented.
  - **Justify** the relevance of your research question and why it is significant.
  - Make a brief preliminary judgement (prediction/hypothesis) that answers the question, and **explain** the approach you will take to answer it.
- **Three main sections to your argument**
  - The main sections of the essay should be structured in such a way that enables the reader to follow what you are saying, and that presents the reader with credible and sufficient evidence for the argument being made. Use the PEEL paragraph structure as follows:
    - *Point*: The first sentence should make a clear point, and express a particular controlling idea. The rest of the paragraph should not stray from this idea.
    - *Explain*: You will need to develop this point further, by **explaining** any economic theory fully or by making any link between cause and effect clear. If you are suggesting that one particular group is affected, in what way are they affected and why?
    - *Evidence*: You will need to present the evidence that you have gathered to support this point that you are making. This makes the work more believable and so you must choose your evidence carefully. Make sure the facts or quotations are from credible sources. This evidence needs to **demonstrate** your scholarship, not your ability to type a few words into a search engine and hope for the best!
    - *Link*: The link between this point and the question you are answering needs to be made explicit. You should also set out the end of each paragraph to lead nicely on to the next.
- **Conclusion**
  - Your conclusion should present your answer to the question, outlining the reasons why austerity is or is not effective as a government policy in your chosen country. It is important to be clear about why your answer can be argued for over and above any possible counter-arguments.

◆ Assessment opportunities

- In this activity you have practised skills that are assessed using Criterion A: Knowing and understanding, Criterion B: Investigating, Criterion C: Communicating and Criterion D: Thinking critically.

ACTIVITY: Educating citizens of a country or the world?

ATL

■ Organization skills: Create plans to prepare for summative assessments (examinations and performances)

Education policy is a hotly debated topic in every country. The following questions are often asked:
- What is the purpose of education?
- What skills should students leave school with?
- Should we prioritize some kinds of learning/some subjects over others?
- What proportion of the government's budget should be spent on education?
- Should there be private schools?
- Should there be standardized testing? At what ages?

Imagine you are a university lecturer interested in studying education policy. You would like to publish research for the Organisation for Economic Co-operation and Development (OECD) about the effectiveness of education systems. Select one of the OECD countries (see **OECD.org**), and carry out an investigation into the successes and weaknesses of its education system.

As part of your preliminary research you need to:
- keep an active notebook containing all your research and making note of any sources as you go along
- submit an action plan to your teacher, using a copy of Table 12.2 below.

Your report should include:
- an *outline* of the education system that currently exists in the country
- a section that **analyses** the effectiveness of current practices, including statistics for attainment, literacy and shares of the population who leave education with qualifications
- a section that **explains** the current government's plans for improvement
- a section that **discusses** government plans and suggests other approaches that might be used.

◆ Assessment opportunities

◆ In this activity you have practised skills that are assessed using Criterion A: Knowing and understanding, Criterion B: Investigating, Criterion C: Communicating and Criterion D: Thinking critically.

■ **Table 12.2** Action plan

Task	Resources, e.g. books, specific webpages, databases	Due date	Complete
Date to submit completed work:			

How do our perspectives change as we learn through different subjects?

Individuals and Societies is the study of social relationships; but by now you will probably have recognized the different approaches taken by the different subjects within this subject area. Each of the subjects has its own methodology, and each looks at different conceptual relationships, even within the same social events. As a consequence, each subject produces a different set of understandings or answers to the questions we have about societies.

An example might be the Wall Street Crash of 1929.

Causes:
- Historians' perspective of the roaring '20s
  - [ ] Renewed optimism since the First World War
  - [ ] The new industrial age of steel and electricity
  - [ ] Rapid growth in incomes
  - [ ] Increasing use of the radio in the home
  - [ ] The cultural exuberance of the period, with changing tastes in music, fashion and leisure activities
  - [ ] Protectionism during the interwar period that contributed to an increase in manufacturing
  - [ ] Republican government policies supported business growth and investment
- Economists' perspective:
  - [ ] Market optimism and overconfidence
  - [ ] The rise of American Consumerism leading to the overproduction of consumer goods that were attained as a result of easy credit schemes
  - [ ] The stock market boom and the 'long bull market' which led to the system of buying stocks 'on margin' with loans from stock brokers
  - [ ] The fall in demand for consumer products and the unequal distribution of wealth across America
  - [ ] Weaknesses in the American banking system
  - [ ] Panic-selling of massive amounts of stocks and shares

Effects:
- Geographers' perspective:
  - [ ] High levels of unemployment
  - [ ] Bankruptcies
  - [ ] Suicides
  - [ ] Starvation
  - [ ] Migration
  - [ ] Evictions and wage cuts that led to the Great Depression
  - [ ] Reduction in trade between countries (higher trade barriers)
- Historians' perspective:
  - [ ] Breakdown in communication between countries, generating suspicion
  - [ ] Countries become insular (forcing people to buy national goods in order to create jobs and rebuild the economy)
  - [ ] Global nature of the crisis results in a loss of confidence in democracy and a rise in extremist groups promising to solve a nation's problems, e.g. Nazism in Germany (Hitler), Fascism in Italy (Mussolini) and Spain (Franco)
  - [ ] A cause of the Second World War

12 How has our perspective changed now?

ACTIVITY: Taking a viewpoint

> **ATL**
>
> - Media literacy skills: Seek a range of perspectives from multiple and varied sources

Choose any twentieth-century event and **analyse** the event in two clear sections: causes and effects.

Your project will be made up of five sections, all of which will be assessed:

1 Research question and justification – 100 words
2 Action plan – 200 words
3 Investigation essay – 1,000 words
4 Reflection – 200 words
5 References

The perspectives of *two* of the Individuals and Societies subjects we have explored in this book (historian, geographer and economist) must be given in your *investigation* section.

1 Research question and justification
   - **Formulate** your own research question.
   - Include a short paragraph to **justify** the relevance of the topic and question as being important to **investigate**.
2 Action plan
   - **Formulate** an action plan for how you will complete the investigation from start to finish. Include a time frame for how long you think each section might take you.
   - **Describe** the methods you will use to find the information you require.
3 Investigation essay
   a **Describe** the event and give it context.
   b **Analyse** the causes from the different perspectives.
      - **Identify** the opinions of academics who have a view on the causes.
   c **Analyse** the consequences from different perspectives.
      - **Identify** the opinions of academics who have a view on the consequences.
   d Conclusion
      - **Summarize** the key points of your investigation.
      - **Evaluate** what the most influential cause and most impactful consequence was, based on the weight of evidence.

In this section you should:
- use a wide range of terminology in context
- **demonstrate** knowledge and understanding of subject-specific content and concepts through developed descriptions, explanations and examples
- communicate information and ideas effectively using an appropriate style for the audience and purpose
- structure information and ideas in a way that is appropriate to the specified format
- **discuss** concepts, issues, models, visual representation and theories.

Evaluation of sources

You should choose two sources that you used most prominently and, with reference to their origin, purpose and content, **discuss** the values and limitations of each source.

You may wish to structure your evaluation like this:

Source A

Values paragraph:
- The origin is of value because …
- The purpose can be considered a value to an individual studying the Wall Street Crash because …
- The content of the source is valuable due to …

Source A

Limitations paragraph:
- The origin can be seen as a slight limitation due to …
- The purpose is limited because …
- The content has limitations because of … which requires the individual to seek out further sources.

Source B

Values paragraph: follow the same structure as the Source A values paragraph

Source B

Limitations paragraph: follow the same structure as the Source A limitations paragraph

In this section you should:
- **synthesize** information to make valid, well-supported arguments
- **analyse** and **evaluate** a wide range of sources/data in terms of origin and purpose, examining values and limitations
- **interpret** different perspectives and their implications.

4 **Reflection**
   - **Explain** why the chosen research question and topic were relevant and appropriate.
   - **Explain** the research methods you used to collect and record appropriate, varied and relevant information.
   - **Evaluate** the process and results of your investigation.

5 **References**

Your investigation should include in-text citations (Harvard) or footnotes (MLA) as well as a bibliography to show that you have **documented** sources of information using a recognized convention.

It is very important to reference your work in order to:
- **demonstrate** to your readers that you have conducted a thorough and appropriate literature search, and reading
- **acknowledge** that you have used the ideas and written material belonging to other people/authors in your own work.

If you do not do this, you can be accused of plagiarism, which has serious consequences. The IB MYP provides further guidance on this at:

www.ibo.org/globalassets/publications/become-an-ib-school/myp-general-regulations-2015-en.pdf

You may find it useful to use a framework to 'scaffold' or direct your writing towards the MYP Individuals and Societies assessment criteria. Table 12.3 provides a framework that you could use for this project.

◆ **Assessment opportunities**

- In this activity you have practised skills that are assessed using Criterion A: Knowing and understanding, Criterion B: Investigating and Criterion D: Thinking critically.

■ **Table 12.3** Framework with assessment criteria

Criteria being assessed	Section name and guidance	Score / 8
B i	**Research question and justification:** Identify your research question / the title of your investigation. Explain why you believe your question to be appropriate to investigate.	
B ii & iii	**Action plan:** Formulate an action plan for how you will complete the investigation from start to finish. Include a time frame for how long you think each section might take you. Describe the methods you will use to find the information you require.	
C i & ii	**Investigation essay:** Communicate your information in a clear and concise manner ensuring you follow a structure of regularly paragraphing and linking back to the question at the end of each paragraph. You may wish to use the PEEL paragraph structure: • Point: make it clear. • Evidence: ensure you support your point with evidence from academic sources. • Explanation: explain how the evidence supports the point you made. • Link: this should point back to the main question and show how the paragraph has helped to partly answer it (or give a perspective on it).	
A i & ii	Where appropriate, use technical vocabulary and write in detail, but remember you are writing an analytical piece not a narrative one.	
D i	Identify the author's opinions and concepts as part of your analysis.	
D ii	Bring together your knowledge gained from this book and the course as a whole, as well as the opinions of academics, to help you support the points and opinions you are trying to make.	
D iv	Explore the different perspectives: economic, geographical and historical, as well as those of academics, and identify what they are implying in relation to your question.	
B i	**Evaluation of sources:** Identify and name the two sources that were most prominent in your investigation. Evaluate and justify why they were so prominent in your investigation.	
D iii	Analyse and evaluate the two sources (separately) in terms of their values and limitations, linking these to their origin and purpose.	
B iv	**Reflection:** Evaluate what went well in your investigation and how you could have made it even better.	
C iii	**Bibliography:** Document all the sources that you used in your investigation. Ensure this is done using either the Harvard or MLA system – use the same one throughout.	

ACTIVITY: Competing claims

■ ATL

- Collaboration skills: Build consensus

Imagine you are a leading a committee of two members (one from the USA and one from Canada) that has been set up to **evaluate** the proposed building of a new ski resort on the US–Canadian border, linking the Cascade Range in the USA and the Coast Mountains in Canada at coordinates 49°N, 120°W (as denoted by the blue square in Figure 12.3).

The proposed site for the resort is on Native American land (belonging to the Sanpoil, Salish and Shuswap tribes) and the plans are to build the resort to a state-of-the-art specification that would allow the town to bid for the Winter Olympics in 2030.

Conduct a debate in class in which the main issues of building such a resort are discussed. Your teacher will allocate you to a side of the debate. During the debate, everyone should take notes on what is being said and what evidence is used.

After the debate, you will individually write a summary of the issues, and the different arguments set out by each side during the debate. You will finish your summary with a conclusion in which you **justify** your own view.

Prior to beginning the debate, you should conduct some research into:

- the physical geography of the area – rainfall, snowfall, days of sunshine per year, topography
- the population of the area
- the economics of the area in terms of percentage unemployment, money currently received in tourism, any other major industries
- the history of the area, particularly relating to the activities of the Sanpoil, Salish and Shuswap tribes and how they view the land
- the multiplier effect
- diversification in tourism.

◆ Assessment opportunities

◆ In this activity you have practised skills that are assessed using Criterion A: Knowing and understanding, Criterion B: Investigating and Criterion D: Thinking critically.

■ Figure 12.3 Native American tribal territories across North America

How do we know the information we read is true?

ACTIVITY: The role of the news media today

ATL

- Critical-thinking skills: Identify obstacles and challenges

Read the following extract from an interview with a British television news producer in 2018.

In a world with 'information' at your fingertips, how can you tell what is legitimate and what is not?

Historically if, for example, a Washington Post [American broadsheet newspaper] article had quoted 30 separate sources, it was easy to see it was more credible than an article from, say, the Mirror [British tabloid paper] quoting one unnamed source.

When writing an essay, your teachers ask you to show text citations or footnotes to demonstrate the credibility of what you are saying – the same cannot be said when social media is used. It makes evaluating the credibility/validity of evidence even more important.

The 'Fake News' era is constantly evolving and shifting. President Trump wants people to believe it is misreporting and therefore wrong – is this a tactic or a genuine thought, i.e. the journalist has a political motive? This creates scepticism of real information.

President Trump's aim is to create an atmosphere of suspicion around any story about him ... to create an unavoidable cacophony of misdirection where people do not know what to believe – this undermines what the free press brings to a democracy.

Republicans and Trump supporters may consider this to be wrong however, and that Trump is being unfairly targeted. Either way, it has resulted in a lack of trust in the press. A testament to the public's confusion is that, in 2018, CNN had both its highest approval and disapproval rating of all time.

Collins Dictionary lexicographers said that use of the term 'fake news' had increased by 365 per cent since 2016.

In April 2018, it was stated in the *Telegraph* that '"Fake news" was not a term many people used 18 months ago, but it is now seen as one of the greatest threats to democracy, free debate and the Western order.'

Create a 6–8 minute presentation describing and analysing the role that the news media play in shaping public opinion and keeping governments to account and how you, as students, can use your research skills to validate the legitimacy of what you read, see and hear. Be sure to address the following points in your presentation:

- Using a formal definition of 'fake news', **justify** why it is important to address this issue.
- **Describe** and **explain** how this issue has come to our attention in recent years.
- **Evaluate** the role that the news has played in recent times and in some example countries.
- **Explore** how we can ensure we **identify** the differences between credible and untrustworthy sources, and find out the real facts, for use in our written work.
- **Identify** the methods we can use to find out where a source comes from.
- **Use** a conclusion to **summarize** your key recommendations on how to validate the legitimacy of information in the era of fake news.
- **Document** the sources you have used in a bibliography at the end of your presentation.

The topic of 'fake news' overlaps with recent political events that have caused some contention between people in their countries. We must always remember that people's political views are their own, and that there are ways to engage in debate with people without upsetting them (see the *Guardian*, 2019, 'The science of influencing people: six ways to win an argument'). It is important to remain objective and balanced when discussing such issues.

◆ Assessment opportunities

- ◆ In this activity you have practised skills that are assessed using Criterion A: Knowing and understanding, Criterion B: Investigating, Criterion C: Communicating and Criterion D: Thinking critically.

How do we answer exam-style questions?

As you progress towards the Diploma Programme (DP) it is increasingly important that you become familiar with answering exam-style questions. The DP exams follow this format in many subjects – the subjects you are familiar with from Individuals and Societies especially. The activity below relates to the population topics covered in Chapter 6.

ACTIVITY: Answering exam questions

ATL

- Communication skills: Use appropriate forms of writing for different purposes and audiences

1 a **Define** the term 'population density'. [1 mark]
   b **Define** the term 'population distribution'. [1 mark]
   c **Explain** the meaning of the term 'densely populated'. [2 marks]
   d Using examples of places you have studied, **describe** the physical factors that may cause areas to be sparsely populated. [6 marks]

2 a **Define** the term 'birth rate'. [1 mark]
   b **Define** the term 'death rate'. [1 mark]
   c **Explain** why LEDCs often have a high birth rate. [3 marks]
   d On a copy of the diagram below (the demographic transition model) **draw** three lines to represent the birth rate, death rate and total population. (Make sure you label them or use different colours.) [3 marks]

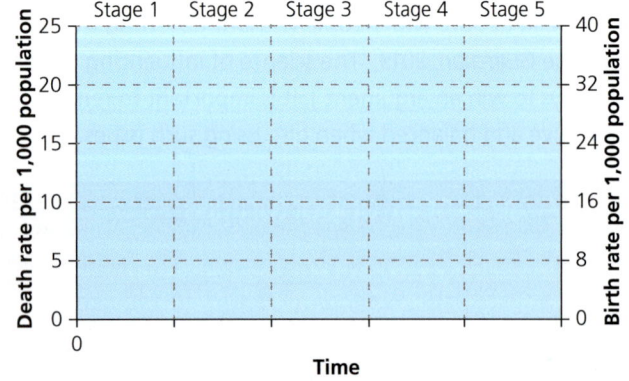

3 a Look the population pyramid below. **State** whether it shows Sweden or India. [1 mark]

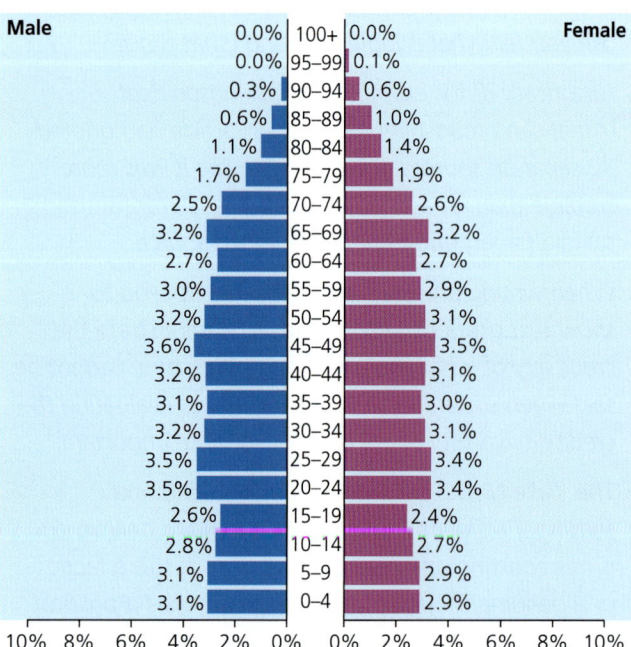

   b **Examine** the pyramid and **explain** what you can **identify** about the country from its structure. [5 marks]

◆ Assessment opportunities

◆ In this activity you have practised skills that are assessed using Criterion A: Knowing and understanding.

Answering exam questions

Read the question carefully! Pay close attention to the command term at the start of the question as this is your biggest clue as to what the examiners are wanting you to do.

If you are asked to **explain**, give reasons and say why something is the case.

If you are asked to **describe**, you should use the information in front of you (often in a graph, table or photograph) and simply say what you see.

Look at how many marks each question is worth to guide you as to how much detail is needed. Generally in Individuals and Societies subjects, for each point you make you are awarded 1 mark and if you develop that point, it could gain you a further mark.

Your teacher will be able to advise you on how much time you should spend on specific questions and sections of assessments as this differs between the Individuals and Societies subjects, but it is important to get into the habit of paying attention to time so that you allow yourself enough time to complete all the tasks.

Reflection

In this chapter we have practised all the skills required to be successful in an MYP Individuals and Societies course. We have **explained** complex concepts and problems, we have gathered research to support our writing with evidence, we have **evaluated** claims and constructed counter-arguments. We have considered ideas from multiple perspectives and **analysed** the implications of those views. We know how to cite our sources in-text and how to construct our reference list at the end of our work.

Use this table to reflect on your own learning in this chapter.						
Questions we asked		Answers we found	Any further questions now?			
Factual: What have you learned so far? What else do you need to know? How is the knowledge you have learned connected to the aims of MYP Individuals and Societies? How will it prepare you for your Diploma courses?						
Conceptual: What approaches to learning skills will I need next? How do we gather our own data? How do I develop research questions based on current issues? How do our perspectives change as we learn through different subjects? How do we know the information we read is true? How do we answer exam-style questions? How has your understanding of Individuals and Societies been transformed?						
Debatable: Can we ever be sure that we have mastered the topics we learned?						
Approaches to learning you used in this chapter		Description – what new skills did you learn?	How well did you master the skills?			
			Novice	Learner	Practitioner	Expert
Communication skills						
Organization skills						
Collaboration skills						
Critical-thinking skills						
Research skills						
Information literacy skills						
Media literacy skills						
Learner profile attribute(s)		Reflect on the importance of being reflective for your learning in this chapter.				
Reflective						

Glossary

absolute poverty A person is considered to be in absolute poverty when they earn an income that falls below internationally defined levels. The World Bank set the level to $1.90 per day in 2015

aggregate demand The total amount of goods and services demanded by consumers, firms, government and the foreign market in an economy at any given price level

aggregate supply The total amount of goods and services that firms are willing and able to supply to the economy at any given price level

agro-industrialization The industrialization of farming to include large-scale intensive farming techniques and heavy machinery

allied states Countries that agree to work together for a common goal

allocatively effective When community surplus is maximized

annexation When a state declares that an area that was previously outside their geographic borders now belongs to them, and seizes control of this area

annotate To mark up or add labels to a diagram or map

anomaly An outlying piece of data that does not fit a pattern

anthropogenic Something which is caused by humans

appanage A grant of land given by a ruling emperor, king or other monarch, which allowed that land to be ruled by another individual but to remain under the ultimate authority of that monarch

archive A collection of records, usually dealing with a particular place, institution or group of people

arid Extremely dry

arithmetic series This is a sequence of numbers or quantities, each term of which differs from the succeeding term by a constant amount, such as 3, 6, 9, 12

Aromanian An eastern Romance language descended from Latin that is spoken in some areas of southeastern Europe

Augustus, The A title given to Roman emperors that means 'exalted' or 'venerable', first used by the founder of the Roman empire, Gaius Octavius

austerity In economics, austerity refers to a set of policies a government can employ to reduce the size of their budget deficit and eventually total public debt. This usually involves cuts in government spending, sales of government assets and/or increases in tax rates

average rate of tax The share of a person's total income paid in tax

biome A large, naturally occurring community of flora and fauna occupying a major habitat, e.g. forest or tundra

bubonic plague One of three types of plague caused by the bacterium *Yersinia pestis*, and spread primarily by small, infected fleas from small animals or contact with the bodily fluids of a dead infected animal

bureaucracy A system of government where important decisions are decided by, or with the advice of, state officials

Caesar (The) A Roman title for the emperor derived from the family name of the first emperor, Gaius Octavius Caesar

caliph The title of the leader, religious and civil, of the world Muslim community until 1924, at which point the title was abolished

caliphate A system of governance in the Islamic world led by a caliph, the religious and government leader of a predominately Muslim state

capital intensive Industries that make heavy use of capital (machinery) as opposed to relying mostly on labour

capitalism A system of organizing production in which owners of capital employ wage workers to convert resources into goods and services that can be sold for a profit

caravan A large train of pack animals such as camels, donkeys or horses that carry goods and people, usually for great distances

carbon footprint The calculation of all the carbon emissions created by your daily life. Where you buy your food from, how and how often you travel and how you buy your clothes can all affect your carbon footprint

chariotry The unit of a military force that uses chariots for combat

city-state A sovereign state that is centred around a city and its surrounding area, e.g. Venice during the Renaissance, and modern-day Monaco and the Vatican City

climatic Relating to climates, such as temperature or precipitation

command economy An economy where decisions about what to produce are made centrally by a government

common market A customs union agreement between countries that includes free movement of labour and capital across borders

communism A system of running the economy in which there is no private property, and all decisions about production are made on a local level in communes

community surplus The sum of consumer and producer surplus

composite bow A traditional bow made of horn, wood and sinew that was known for its great range and strength. This type of bow has existed since the second millennium BCE, and was used by the militaries of several empires, including the New Kingdom Egypt and the Mongol empire

constitution A body of fundamental principles, laws or rules that govern a state or empire, and that acts as a foundation for the laws of that state or empire

consumer expenditure The amount spent on goods and services by individuals in society

consumer surplus Anyone more willing and able to pay the market price, or who can afford more, enjoys a consumer surplus. This is represented by the distance between the demand curve and the market price, up to the market quantity

cultural diffusion The spread of cultural ideas from their place of origin to other regions, groups or nations

customs union An agreement between countries to remove trade barriers between them and to set a common set of barriers to non-member countries

deflation When the price level decreases

demand The willingness and ability of consumers to buy goods and services at any given price

demography The study of statistics such as births, deaths, income or the incidence of disease, which illustrate the changing structure of human populations

dendrochronology The science of analysing tree growth rings in order to determine age, amount of growth and other environmental data over time

dependency ratio A measure of the number of dependents aged 0–14 and over the age of 65, compared with the total population aged 15–64

dependent population The part of the population that does not work and relies on others for the goods and services they consume – generally those below the age of 15 and above the age of 65

diasporas The spread of people beyond where they originally come from

disinflation When the price level increases, but the rate at which it does so slows down

dumping When foreign goods are sold in a country at a price that is below the average costs of production

echo chambers Figurative or metaphorical 'chambers' created by being exposed to media that largely expresses just one view, perspective or set of beliefs, e.g. what you 'like' or look at on the internet determines what you are shown, creating an echo chamber which limits other views to which you might be exposed

economic growth An increase in economic output (measured by increases in gross domestic product)

economics The study of how limited resources are allocated between competing demands by different groups in society

economy An area where productive activity takes place. This can be a country, but also a town or smaller area

ecosystems A biological community of interacting organisms and their physical environment

ecotourism Tourism to places that have unspoiled natural resources, with minimal impact on the environment being a primary concern

equality When referring to income, equality means that everyone earns the same

equilibrium In supply and demand diagrams, the equilibrium occurs where the supply and demand curves intersect. This point determines the market price and quantity of goods or services

equity When referring to income, equity means that everyone earns fair amounts of income

exchange rate The value of a currency expressed in terms of another country's currency

exponentially Growing or increasing very rapidly

export revenue The amount earned when firms sell goods or services abroad

externality A cost or benefit that affects people outside of the transaction between buyer and seller

factors of production The resources necessary for production to take place: land, labour, capital and entrepreneurship

federation An alliance of several sovereign states or city-states that allows them to maintain semi-independence while remaining connected politically

feudalism A system of production and government, largely based on agriculture, in which control is retained by a monarch and nobles, with the rest of the population forced to work the land

flowstones Thin layers of rock created by minerals found in flowing water

fort A fortified, or heavily defensible, building or strategic position

free trade area (FTA) An agreement between countries to remove barriers to trade between them completely

fresco A painting on plaster

geometric series This is a geometric progression written as a sum, as in $1 + 2 + 4 + 8$

globalization The increasing interaction of people, companies and governments across the world, facilitated by trade and the media

glocalization The practice of expanding business models globally, while simultaneously maintaining local considerations, e.g. the differences in McDonald's menus between different countries

gross domestic product (GDP) A measure for the value of all goods and services produced by an economy

hikikomori A type of acute social withdrawal

hominids or **hominins** Any member of the taxonomic family *Hominidae*, which includes humans, gorillas, orangutans and chimpanzees, and also our extinct ancestors *Homo habilis* and *Homo erectus*

homogenize To become the same or similar

Human Development Index (HDI) A compositive index that uses Gross National Income (GNI) per capita, mean and expected years of schooling, and life expectancy to measure the development of a country

imperialism The formation of an empire, or the policy of extending a state's power or influence through military, political or economic conquest

import expenditure The amount spent when an economy buys goods or services from abroad

incentive A reason for doing something

indirect tax Price increase caused by suppliers of goods or services being taxed and passing the cost on to consumers

inflation When the price level increases

infrastructure Any large-scale capital project that is essential for economic activity to take place

inherited Passed on (of a characteristic or object), e.g. you inherit your eye colour from your parents

injections Spending that comes into the circular flow of income, such as investment, exports and government spending

interest rate A percentage that has to be repaid in addition to the value of the loan, or the cost of borrowing

investment When firms spend on capital (machinery) for the purposes of expansion

isolationism A policy of disengaging or keeping out of the political activities and interests of other countries (or groups)

jihadist An Islamic fundamentalist movement that favours the pursuit of jihads in defence of the Islamic faith. A jihad is a holy war

juries Committees, or small groups of individuals, that preside over a legal case and make a decision about the guilt or innocence of the person on trial

khanates States such as the Mongol empire that are led by a khan (a title meaning ruler)

kinship The shared characteristics or origin between people

law of demand When the price increases, the quantity demanded falls, and vice versa

leakages Flows of income from the circular flow. They include savings, taxation and import expenditure

LEDC Less economically developed country

Levant An approximate historical term to describe the eastern Mediterranean

linear A linear process or development is one in which something progresses straight from one stage to another, and has a starting point and an ending point

mace A blunt weapon, similar to a club, that was made primarily using metal or wood. Maces typically had heavy heads of stone, bone, iron or steel, and were used to deliver heavy blows to an opponent

macroeconomic An approach or branch of economics that considers the national economy as a whole, rather than individual participants or markets. Macroeconomics concerns issues such as economic growth, and unemployment

magistrate A civil or legal officer for a state or empire

marginal rate of tax The percentage of each additional unit of income earned that must be paid in tax

market economy An economy in which the decisions about what to produce, how to produce and for whom to produce are answered by the interaction of market forces

market failure When a market fails to reach a point of allocative efficiency. Resources allocated by private individuals and firms do not take into account any external costs or benefits or effects to the wider society. Community surplus is not maximized

mechanical solidarity A term coined by Émile Durkheim, describing the close interaction between people who belong to small social groups. Clothing, customs and belief are similar in the entire group

MEDC More economically developed country

methodology A set of steps needing to be taken to carry out data collection and research

migration The movement of people between countries, sometimes temporarily but usually permanently

Mithraism A religion that was based on the worship of the god Mithras. Mithraism was particularly popular in the Roman military during the first three centuries CE, but it also had a following in other places including Syria, Britain and the areas that are now Germany and Austria

monetary union A common market that also shares a currency, e.g. the Eurozone

moral density A term coined by Émile Durkheim that refers to the amount of interaction between people in social groups. Increased moral density allows societies to progress from mechanical solidarity to organic solidarity

mortuary temple A temple in ancient Egypt built for the ka or soul of a dead pharaoh where the soul could live and the pharaoh could be worshipped by his followers

natural increase The difference between the numbers of births and deaths in a population; the rate of natural increase is the difference between the birth rate and the death rate

negative externalities of consumption The external costs that arise from the production of a product

Neolithic Period An era starting approximately 12,000 years ago when the use of stone tools and pottery expanded and developed. This era ended at different times in different parts of the world, such as 4500 BCE for parts of the Middle East and Asia when they developed metal working, and in the 1500s CE in parts of North and South America. Some people continue to live in the Neolithic cultures in remote areas of the Amazon and in other areas of the world

opportunity cost The cost of the next-best alternative forgone. If you choose to eat an apple instead of an orange, your opportunity cost is the orange

organic solidarity A term coined by Émile Durkheim, describing the distant interaction between people belonging to large social groups. Clothing, customs and beliefs are more diverse and people's roles in the society are more specialized

oxymoron Something that combines two opposite qualities or ideas and therefore seems impossible

Pax Mongolica The period of peace that followed the Mongol empire's conquests, and the stabilizing effect the empire had on the economic, social, cultural and political lives of those living within its borders

pharaoh The most common title for the emperors of Ancient Egypt; the term implied absolute political, military and religious power within the empire

policy statement A brief statement that indicates the position, beliefs or objectives of a country

population density Population refers to how many people live in a specific geographic area on average, e.g. the Netherlands had a population density of 418 people per km^2 in 2018

positive externalities of consumption When there are benefits to society when individuals consume a good or service

precedent A legal principle that allows earlier actions, events or decisions to be used as a guide in future legal cases. Precedent is used to make sure that the law, and the punishments for crimes, remain consistent

preferential trade agreement A trade agreement that reduces barriers to trade for some goods and/or services

price ceilings Maximum allowed prices set below the equilibrium price

price elasticity of demand (PED) A measure of the responsiveness of quantity demanded to changes in price

price elasticity of supply (PES) A measure of the responsiveness of quantity supplied to changes in price

price mechanism A mechanism that helps to allocate scarce resources in a free market by setting a price that only some consumers will be able to afford

primary data Data or information collected yourself, or a first-hand account from a period of time being studied

producer surplus Any producer willing and able to sell below the market price enjoys a producer surplus. This is represented by the distance between the supply curve and the market price, up to the market quantity

productivity The efficiency with which inputs to the production process are being used to produce output

progressive tax system When the burden of income tax falls more heavily on people with higher incomes

propaganda Information that is written, released or spread in order to promote a particular view, cause or opinion in a way that is often biased or skewed

protectionist policies Policies that are used to restrict trade

public goods Goods that would not be provided by the free market because they are non-excludable and non-rivalrous. We cannot prevent people who do not pay taxes from using street lights, for example

punitive war A war conducted by a state or empire in order to punish another region, state or empire for an offence they have committed

puppet head of state A person who holds a title that suggests they are in a position of political power but, in reality, their power and ability to make decisions is controlled by external or foreign forces (the puppet master)

push factors These refer to the conditions that lead to people leaving their homes. These can be forced or voluntary and examples include unemployment, war, natural disasters and climate

qualitative data Non-numerical data that describes the quality of something, e.g. businesses might want to collect qualitative data about whether customers like their products

quantitative data Numerical data that describes quantities, such as financial information

radiocarbon dating The science of dating organic objects by determining the amount of carbon left in the object. This is done by calculating the rate at which the carbon decays after the object, such as wood, stops growing

ration Trying to distribute a shortage of resources between many people. Setting a price helps to ration a good between people who can afford to pay and those who cannot

recession When there is a fall in national output or GDP (Gross Domestic Product) for at least six months

relief The height and shape of the land

remittances Transfers of money, often by foreign workers to individuals in their home country

retrofit Add (a component or accessory) to something that did not have it when manufactured, such as using technology to make buildings and cities more sustainable and environmentally friendly

Romansch A Romance language descended from Latin that is primarily spoken in eastern Switzerland, and holds 'official language' status in the area, along with Italian and German

savings Money that consumers earn that is not spent on domestic or imported goods and services, or paid in taxes. This money is put aside in a bank and can be used to buy a house or pay university, or other important family costs

scribe A person whose job it is to write or copy out documents, especially before the invention of mass printing

secondary data Information or research data that has been gathered by someone else

semi-arid Dry but having slightly more rain than an arid region or climate

semi-autonomous region An area that operates more or less independently but remains as part of a larger state or empire

silt Mineral-rich soil or mud deposited by a river

slavery A system of organized production in which certain groups in society obtain and retain ownership over labourers

social media influencers People who have a large following online through social media channels, who are able to influence buyers' shopping choices. These people can earn significant amounts of money from companies seeking to exploit the influence they have

social movement A group of like-minded individuals who want to implement changes in society

sociologist Someone who studies the development and structures of societies

staple food A food type that is relied on as a main source of sustenance in a region or country, e.g. rice is a staple food in Asia

subsidies Payments to producers by the government to lower production costs and increase supply

successor state A new, typically smaller, state that is formed when a larger state or empire breaks up. An example of this is Ptolemaic Egypt, which was a successor state of Alexander the Great's empire

sultan The equivalent of a king, sovereign or emperor in some Muslim-majority states or empires, like the Mamluk Sultanate

superpower A state or empire with a dominant position in world politics, that is characterized by its ability to exert influence or project power through economic, technological, military, cultural and diplomatic strength, e.g. the Soviet Union and the USA during the Cold War

supply The willingness and ability of producers to sell goods and services at any given price

supra-national organization An international group or union where the influence and power of member states exist beyond national boundaries, and decision-making affects all member states of the organization, group or union, e.g. the European Union (EU) and the World Trade Organization (WTO)

sustainability Practices that prevent the permanent and irreparable decline of resources, and that do not deprive future generations of their use

tariffs Taxes on imported goods and services

total fertility rate The number of children who would be born per woman (or per 1,000 women) if she/they were to pass through the childbearing years bearing children according to a current schedule of age-specific fertility rates

trade bloc An agreement between countries to reduce or remove barriers to trade

trebuchet A type of catapult that uses a swinging arm to throw a projectile using either traction or a counterweight to increase the distance

trend A change in situation, behaviour or direction

typhoid A bacterial infection due to a specific type of *Salmonella* that is thought to have existed at least since the fifth century BCE

tyrant an absolute ruler who is not controlled by any laws

unemployment Occurs when members of the labour force, who are actively seeking work, cannot find a job

urban stress A term used to describe the tensions that can build up from a fast-paced urban lifestyle. Contributing factors include congestion, overcrowding, high crime rates and pollution, amongst others

vizier Head of the government bureaucracy in a sultanate or caliphate, like a prime minister or president in modern times

war of attrition A lengthy period of conflict during which both sides seek to wear each other down by continued and repeated actions (such as bombing, shelling or sustained gunfire)

warrior class A classification of a segment of society whose only occupation is to engage in war and act as experienced soldiers for the state or empire where they live

way station A stopping point on a journey, usually equipped to allow travellers to eat, drink or rest

welfare loss A loss of community surplus when there is a tax or an externality present in a market

Acknowledgements

The Publishers would like to thank the following for permission to reproduce copyright material. Every effort has been made to trace all copyright holders, but if any have been inadvertently overlooked the Publishers will be pleased to make the necessary arrangements at the first opportunity.

Photo credits

p.2 © Christian SAPPA/Gamma-Rapho/Getty Images; **pp.2–3** © Antiquarian Images/Alamy Stock Photo; **p.3** © Grandfailure/stock.adobe.com; **p.5** © Korrakit Pinsrisook/Shutterstock.com; **p.7** *t* © Daniel Brandt/123RF; *b* © Library of Congress Prints and Photographs Division Washington, D.C. 20540 USA [LC-DIG-ppmsca-04324]; **p.17** *t* © Lee Snider Photo Images/Shutterstock.com; *m* © Ritu Manoj Jethani/Shutterstock.com; *b* © Jointstar/Shutterstock.com; **p.21** © 008melisa/stock.adobe.com; **p.27** *l* and *r* © Cholpan/Shutterstock.com; **p.30** © Pixelchrome Inc/DigitalVision/Getty Images; **p.32** © Hisham/stock.adobe.com; **p.34** © Benoitb/DigitalVision Vectors/Getty Images; **p.35** © Skaman306/Moment/Getty Images; **p.37** © Design Pics / Christine Giles/Getty Images; **p.46** *l* © Alessandro dyd/stock.adobe.com; *r* © Boggy/stock.adobe.com; **p.47** *t* © Viacheslav Lopatin/stock.adobe.com; *b* © Kamira/Shutterstock.com; **p.48** © Glevalex/stock.adobe.com; **p.49** Hongwu © Granger/Shutterstock.com; **p.52** https://commons.wikimedia.org/wiki/File:Ur_Nammu_code_Istanbul.jpg; https://creativecommons.org/publicdomain/zero/1.0/deed.en; **p.64** © Luisapuccini/stock.adobe.com; **p.66** © Jodiecoston/E+/Getty Images; **p.74** © Dinosmichail/stock.adobe.com; **p.80** © Dina/stock.adobe.com; **pp.80–1** *l* © THIERRY/stock.adobe.com; *r* © Patrick Foto/stock.adobe.com; **p.83** © Rafael/stock.adobe.com; **p.85** © Ekaterina Pokrovsky/stock.adobe.com; **p.87** © WitR/stock.adobe.com; **p.89** © Ira Block/National Geographic Image Collection/Alamy Stock Photo; **p.91** © Lynn Abercrombie/National Geographic Image Collection/Alamy Stock Photo; **p.94** *t* © The Art Archive/Shutterstock.com; *b* © Granger/Shutterstock.com; **p.96** © Paulos1/stock.adobe.com; **p.102** © Gianni Dagli Orti/Shutterstock.com; **p.110** © Przemyslaw Iciak/stock.adobe.com; **pp.110–111** © Goldilock Project/stock.adobe.com; **p.111** © Wanchanta/stock.adobe.com; **p.114** © Mikael Damkier/Shutterstock.com; **p.115** *t* © Silken Photography/Shutterstock.com; *b* © Robert Leßmann/stock.adobe.com; **p.116** © Tinseltown/Shutterstock.com; **p.117** *t* © Steve Bower/Shutterstock.com; *l* © Anton Foltin/Shutterstock.com; *r* © Anton Foltin/Shutterstock.com; *b* © Philipus/stock.adobe.com; **p.119** *tl* © Hannes Thirion/Shutterstock.com; *bl* © Oleg Znamenskiy/Shutterstock.com; *tr* © Ignatius Tan/Shutterstock.com; **p.120** © NicoElNino/Shutterstock.com; **p.121** *l* © Silver/stock.adobe.com; *c* © Jim Cumming/Shutterstock.com; *r* © Jim Cumming/Shutterstock.com; **p.122** © Choksawatdikorn/Shutterstock.com; **p.123** *tl* © Vlad61/Shutterstock.com; *bl* © Alexey Belyaev/Shutterstock.com; *r* © Chase Dekker/Shutterstock.com; **p.124** *l* © Mark Green/Shutterstock.com; *c* © Parinya/stock.adobe.com; *r* © Juan Carlos Munoz/stock.adobe.com; **p.127** *l* © Mrfotos_fotolia/stock.adobe.com; *tc* © ESB Professional/Shutterstock.com; *bc* © T photography/Shutterstock.com; *r* © Bruno ismael alves/stock.adobe.com; **p.128** © Charcompix/Shutterstock.com; **p.130** *tl* © Michael Robbins/Shutterstock.com; *bl* © Svetlana Foote/Shutterstock.com; *r* © Anita Warren-Hampson/Shutterstock.com; **p.132** © Sauletas/Shutterstock.com; **p.133** *t* © Jejim/Shutterstock.com; *b* © Wxj651208/Shutterstock.com; **p.135** *t* © Steven May/Alamy Stock Photo; *b* © Acro_phuket/Shutterstock.com; **p.136** © Roundtable on Sustainable Palm Oil; **p.137** *t* © United Nations; *b* © United Nations Convention to Combat Desertification (UNCCD); **p.141** © Marine Stewardship Council; **p.144** © Blue Island/Shutterstock.com; **p.145** © Tomlamela/Getty Images/iStockphoto/Thinkstock; **p.146** © Cozyta/stock.adobe.com; *r* © a2l/stock.adobe.com; **p.149** © PETER PARKS/AFP/Getty Images; **p.154** © Roger tillberg/Alamy Stock Photo; **p.156** © 2017 United Nations. Reprinted with the permission of the United Nations; **p.157** *t* © Oxford Science Archive/Heritage Images/The Print Collector/Alamy Stock Photo; *b* © Historic Collection/Alamy Stock Photo; **p.162** *l* © Adrian Bradshaw/EPA/Shutterstock; *r* © Bettmann/Getty Images; **p.163** *t* © Tupungato/stock.adobe.com; *b* © Jordi C/Shutterstock.com; **p.164** © Vijaifoon13/Shutterstock.com; **p.165** *t* © Bodom/Shutterstock.com; *b* © Dirk Ott/Shutterstock.com; **p.169** © eyetronic/Fotolia; **p.172** © United Nations; **p.177** *l* © Brian Minkoff/Shutterstock.com; *r* © Dinodia/age fotostock/Alamy Stock Photo; **p.179** *t–b* © Trevor Mogg/Alamy Stock Photo; © Zuma/Shutterstock; © Iain Masterton/Alamy Stock Photo; © Iain Masterton/Alamy Stock Photo; **p.180** *t* © Kiev.Victor/Shutterstock.com; *c* © LongJon/Shutterstock.com; *b* © Mario Hagen/stock.adobe.com; **p.181** © Marcio Jose Bastos Silva/Shutterstock.com; **p.182** *l* © Cesar/stock.adobe.com; *r* © Marcelo Rudini/Alamy Stock Photo; **p.183** *l* © ThomasDeco/Shutterstock.com; *tr* © Lev radin/Shutterstock.com; *br* © Pe3k/Shutterstock.com; **p.184** © Fairfax Media/Getty Images; **p.188** © Spanish_ikebana/stock.adobe.com; **pp.188–9** © Elcovalana/stock.adobe.com; **p.189** *r* © Marius Dobilas/Shutterstock.com; **p.193** © Blue Sky Studio/Shutterstock.com; **p.194** © Pictorial Press Ltd/Alamy Stock Photo; **p.197** © Tupungato/Shutterstock.com; **p.198** © Christopher Halloran/Shutterstock.com; **p.202** © Travelpeter/stock.adobe.com; **p.210** © Enchanted_fairy/stock.adobe.com; **p.213** *l* © Granger/Shutterstock; *r* https://commons.wikimedia.org/wiki/File:Ludwig_von_Mises.jpg, https://creativecommons.org/licenses/by-sa/3.0/; **p.214** © Bettmann/Getty Images; **p.218** © Tcly/Shutterstock.com; **pp.218–19** *l* © Neil Mitchell/Shutterstock.com; *r* © Travelview/Shutterstock.com; **p.220** *l* © PRISMA ARCHIVO/Alamy Stock Photo; *r* © Ivelin Radkov/stock.adobe.com; **p.223** *l* © The Picture Art Collection/Alamy Stock Photo; *r* © Pictorial Press Ltd/Alamy Stock Photo; **p.227** *l* © Travel Wild/stock.adobe.com; *r* © GigiPeis/stock.adobe.com; **p.228** © Rick Gershon/Getty Images News/Getty Images; **p.229** *t* © Maksim Shebeko/stock.adobe.com; *b* © GoncharukMaks/Shutterstock.com; **p.234** *l* © Mkos83/stock.adobe.com; *r* © Eyetronic/stock.adobe.com; **p.235** *l* © Photocreo Bednarek/stock.adobe.com; *r* © Kostas Koutsaftikis/Shutterstock.com; **p.237** © Sujit Mahapatra/Fotolia; **p.239** © Bankoo/Shutterstock.com; **p.241** © Eric Fougere/Corbis Entertainment/Getty Images; **p.244** © Africa/stock.adobe.com; **pp.244–5** © Jane McIlroy/Shutterstock.com; **p.245** *r* © Imagenet/Shutterstock.com; **p.247** © Library of Congress Prints and Photographs Division, Washington, DC 20540 USA[LOC_LC-USZ62-23754]; **p.250** *t* © B Christopher/Alamy Stock Photo; *c* © Red ivory/Shutterstock.com; *b* © Asnidamarwani/stock.adobe.com; **p.253** *l* © David Pearson/Shutterstock; *r* https://en.wikipedia.org/wiki/Mahbub_ul_Haq#/media/File:Mahbub-ul-Haq.jpg, https://commons.wikimedia.org/wiki/File:Mahbub-ul-Haq.jpg; **p.258** © The Oxford Union/Shutterstock; **p.259** *t* © Sergii Figurnyi/stock.adobe.com; *b* © Andreykr/stock.adobe.com; **p.264** *l* © Imago Photo/stock.adobe.com; *r* © Mountaintreks/stock.adobe.com; **p.265** *l* © Dtatiana/stock.adobe.com; *r* © Rusty elliott/stock.adobe.com; **p.268** *l* © Namning/stock.adobe.com; *tr* © Donny Ash/Shutterstock.com; *br* © Jens Lambert/Shutterstock.com; **p.270** *t* © Print Collector/Hulton Archive/Getty Images; *b* © Lordprice Collection/Alamy Stock Photo; **p.272** *l* © INTERFOTO/History/Alamy Stock Photo; *r* © Photo Researchers/Science History Images/Alamy Stock Photo; **p.275** *t* © David Low/Solo Syndication; *b* © World History Archive/Alamy Stock Photo; **p.279** *l* © David Low/Solo Syndication; *r* © TASS/ITAR-TASS News Agency/Alamy Stock Photo; **p.281** © PF-(aircraft)/Alamy Stock Photo; **p.282** © Hulton Deutsch/Corbis Historical/Getty Images;

p.283 © Carabay/stock.adobe.com; **p.284** © Four Horsemen of the Drillocalypse COLOR by Monte Wolverton, Cagle Cartoons; **p.287** *t–b* © Chris Ware/Hulton Archive/Getty Images; © Philipus/stock.adobe.com; © Mirrorpix/Getty Images; © Luciano Mortula/123RF; © Paul Popper/Popperfoto/Getty Images; © Neiezhmakov/stock.adobe.com; **p.290** *t* © Konstantin Stepanenko/123RF; *c* © Ilona Ignatova/Shutterstock.com; *b* © GagliardiPhotography/Shutterstock.com; **p.292** *t–b* © Diyana Dimitrova/Shutterstock.com; © Majeczka/stock.adobe.com; © Alexandr Mitiuc/stock.adobe.com; © Maxim Burkovskiy/Shutterstock.com; **p.294** *t* © Igal Shkolnik/Shutterstock.com; *b* © Kittiphan/stock.adobe.com; **p.295** *l* © Tinnakorn/stock.adobe.com; *r* © Catalinlazar/stock.adobe.com

t = top; *b* = bottom; *l* = left; *r* = right; *c* = centre

Text credits

p.7 Quotation from www.adamsmith.org/adam-smith-quotes. **p.8** Karl Marx, *The Economic and Philosophic Manuscripts* p. 110; *Utopia for Realists: And how can we get there* (2017), by Rutger Bregman. Used with permission from Bloomsbury Publishing. **p.10** From All About Dan, http://danariely.com/. Used with permission from Dan Ariely. **p.13** An excerpt from *The Economic Possibilities for our Grandchildren* by John Maynard Keynes, 1930. Used with the permission from W. W. Norton & Co. **p.14** Excerpt from 'Basic income could work – if you do it Canada-style' in *MIT Technology Review*, 20 June 2018. Used with permission via CCC; Excerpt from 'Universal basic income wouldn't guarantee that work pays, finds study' from *Helsinki Times* on 12 August 2019 www.helsinkitimes.fi/finland/finland-news/domestic/16640-universal-basic-income-wouldn-t-guarantee-that-work-pays-finds-study.html. **p.16** Edward Burnett Tylor, 1920 [1871]. *Primitive Culture*. New York: J.P. Putnam & Sons. **p.18** From 'The importance of social media for a company's operational functions (Aichner & Jacob, 2015) Used with permissions via CCC. **p.31** From the Quotation in 'Retaining the Mandate of Heaven: Sovereign Accountability in Ancient China' by Luke Glanville, *Millennium Journal of International Studies*, 8 November 2010. Used with permission via CCC. **p.33** Pour, Ali Bahrani, 2017. 'A Study of an Unknown Primary Document on the Fall of Abbasid Baghdad to the Mongols (written by the defeated side)' *Acta Via Serica* 2(2): 7-27. Used with permission. **p.35** From Robert Drews, *Militarism and the Indo-Europeanizing of Europe*, 2017, p. 109. Used with permission via CCC. **p.50** From Funeral Inscription for The Augustus, the first emperor of Rome. Used with permission from Oxford University Press via CCC. **p.58** Account of the Silk Road by Florentine merchant [from Florence in today's Italy] Pegolotti, 1340, from 'The Romans and their Roads,' J Knapton www.sept.org/techpapers/826.pdf. **p.86** Letter by Pliny the Younger about the eruption of Mount Vesuvius, written to the historian Tacitus believed to be from: A, Scarth and J.-C. Tanguy, *Volcanoes of Europe*, 2001, Oxford University Press; ISBN: 0-19-521754-3. Reproduced with permission of the Licensor through PLSclear. Excerpt from the article 'The Eruption of Vesuvius of 79 CE and its Impact of Human Environment in Pompeii,' by Lisetta Giacomelli, Annamaria Perrotta, Roberto Scandone, Claudio Scarpati, published September 2003, *Episodes*, Vol. 26 no 3. Reproduced with the permission from the Journal Episodes. **p.89** 'Early European Encounters' The Source for Georgia History, Georgia Historical Society, 31 July 2013, www.georgiahistory.com/education-outreach/online-exhibits/online-exhibits/encounter-and-exchange/early-georgia/early-european-encounters/. Used with permission. **p.129** Carl Haub and Toshiko Kaneda, 2014 World Population Data Sheet (Washington, DC: Population Reference Bureau, 2014). www.prb.org/Publications/Datasheets/2014/2014-world-population-data-sheet/data-sheet.aspx. **p.148** Mao Q, Long Y, & Wu K. (2015). 'Spatio-Temporal Changes of Population Density and Exploration on Urbanization Pattern in China: 2000-2010'. *City Planning Review*, 39(2): 38-43. Used with permission. **p.153** http://reliefweb.int/report/syrian-arab-republic/2016-syrian-arab-republic-humanitarian-response-plan-january-december; this page quotes data as being supplied by UN Office for the Coordination of Humanitarian Affairs. **p.156** 2016 UN fertility data from www.un.org/development/desa/publications/graphic/wpp2017-global-fertility-rate. **p.158** Population data for various countries. https://unstats.un.org/unsd/demographic-social/products/dyb/dybsets/2017.pdf. **p.160, 161** Data from populationPyramid.net. **p.163** United Nations, Department of Economic and Social Affairs, Population Division (2018). *World Urbanization Prospects: The 2018 Revision*. Excerpt from 'How the rise of the megacity is changing the way we live by Paul Webster and Jason Burke in Delhi, published on Sat 21 Jan 2012. www.theguardian.com/society/2012/jan/21/rise-megacity-live. Reproduced with the permission from Guardian News & Media Limited. **p.170** ASC (2006) *Making Places: creating sustainable communities. A teacher's guide to sustainable communities*, Leeds: Academy for Sustainable Communities. Contains public sector information licensed under the Open Government Licence v3.0. **p.173** From Facts and figures about SDG goal 11 from www.undp.org/content/undp/en/home/sustainable-development-goals/goal-11-sustainable-cities-and-communities/targets/. An extract on Urban life by the UN. www.undp.org/content/undp/en/home/sustainable-development-goals/goal-11-sustainable-cities-and-communities.html. **p.174** Data from 'The city as a system' by Richard Rogers (from *Cities for a Small Planet*, 1997). **p.175** Data from Climate Watch. 2018. Washington, DC: World Resources Institute. Available online at www.climatewatchdata.org. Original data source: PIK data: Gtschow, Johannes; Jeffery, Louise; Gieseke, Robert; Gebel, Ronja (2017): *The PRIMAP-hist national historical emissions time series (1850-2014)*. V. 1.1. GFZ Data Services. http://doi.org/10.5880/PIK.2017.001. and UNFCCC data: UNFCCC. 2017. Greenhouse Gas Inventory Data - Detailed data by party. Available online at http://di.unfccc.int/detailed_data_by_party. **p.177** WHO report: *Ambient Air Pollution: A Global assessment of exposure and the burden of disease*. Data from 'Top 20 countries with most and least polluted urban areas' www.telegraph.co.uk/travel/maps-and-graphics/most-polluted-countries/. Used with permission of Telegraph Media Group Limited. **p.182** Architect and Urbanist, Jaime Lerner, © Jaime Lerner Arquitetos Associados. Retrieved from: http://jaimelerner.com.br/en/jaime-lerner-2/. Used with permission. **p.199** Marketed natural gas production in the US (2000-2015): US Energy Information Administration, based on US Global Insight and Drillinginfo Inc. **p.208** Data from Kate Raworth – doughnut economics (www.kateraworth.com). **p.215** From Essays in Persuasion by John Maynard Keynes. **p.221** Quotation and data from Peter Dicken, Global Shift: Mapping the changing contours of world economy, © 2015 Guildford Press. **p.222** Quotation by Marine Le Pen: www.express.co.uk/news/world/775740/Marine-Le-Pen-immigration-threat-French-values. Quotation by Anna Lindh. Quotation by Tony Blair, 2001. **p.240** Quotation by Jean-Baptiste Say (1767-1832). **p.241** Copyright American Economic Association; reproduced with permission of the American Economic Journal: Applied Economics. **p.254** Data from Global Footprint Network 2008 report (2005 data) UN Human Development Index 2007/08. Used with permission. **p.255** Progress towards Millennium Development Goals. Published by: UNDG. **p.266** Oil production by country, 2016 – CIA World Factbook. **p.267** Countries by population density in 2015, Ali Zifan, 19 September 2015. **p.269, 283** Daniel Yergin, *The Prize* (Simon & Schuster, Inc.). **p.273** Carnegie Endowment for International Peace (Deborah Gordon, Yevgen Sautin, and Wang Tao), "China's Oil Future", May 6, 2014. Used with permission. **p.276** George Morgenstern, 'The Actual Road to Pearl Harbor', in *Perpetual War for Perpetual Peace*, pp. 322–23, 327–28. **p.281** R. Cargill Hall. *Case Studies in Strategic Bombardment*. University Press of the Pacific, 1998. ISBN 1-4102-2480-5 p. 158. the British Bombing Survey Unit. **p.284** Excerpt from 'Official: US Oil at the Heart of Iraq Crisis' by Neil Mackay. Published on Sunday, October 6, 2002 by The Sunday Herald (Scotland). Used with permission. Excerpt from 'Is this war all about oil?' by Anthony Sampson. www.standard.co.uk/news/is-this-war-all-about-oil-6351624.html. Excerpt from Muhammad Idrees Ahmad, *The Road to Iraq: The Making of a Neoconservative War*. Edinburgh University Press 2014. **p.285** Data of world crude oil prices: US Energy Information Administration. **p.307** Quotation about fake news by James Titcomb and James Carson, Daily Telegraph, April 2018. **p.308** Data from populationPyramid.net

Index

Abbasid Caliphate 33, 65, 83, 96, 105

age-specific fertility rates (ASFRs) 155–6

agriculture 76, 84, 131–2

agro-industrialization 132

aid 241, 258

Akkadian empire 87

alliances 71–2

aquatic environments
    freshwater 121–4, 131–3
    marine 125, 132, 134–5, 140–1

Ariely, Dan 10

asylum seekers 151

Ayyubid Sultanate 96, 97

Aztec empire 88–90, 102, 103

banking industry 209, 257

bureaucracy: record keeping 49–51

birth rates 154, 155, 158, 164, 251

Boserup, Ester 157

Byzantine empire 40, 74, 75

capitalism 7, 8, 190–1, 247

carbon footprints 139, 174, 175

Carthaginian empire 38

chariot warfare 34–6, 101

China 31, 49, 60, 66, 76, 102, 104
    Manchurian crisis 274–5, 277
    Ming revolt 94–5
    one child policy 162
    population density 148–9
    smallpox outbreak 88
    Three Gorges Dam 133
    trade 224

choropleth maps 267

Churchill, Winston 270–1

city-states 29, 73: *see also* Venice, Republic of

civil wars 82, 91–4, 99, 152–3

climate change 40–1, 82, 87, 127, 288

climate graphs 113

Columbian Exchange 69

command economies 190–1

common markets 233

communication systems 61–3

communism 7–8, 190, 216, 247, 274

comparative advantage theory 223

composite bows 32, 34, 36

Constantinople city walls 74–5

coral reefs 125, 132, 134–5, 140

corruption 82, 100, 257, 258

cultural diffusion 16

cultural exchange 64–9

cultural homogenization 16

culture 16, 229

Curitiba, Brazil 181–2

currency 48, 220, 234–9

customs unions 233

cycle of deprivation 178

data gathering 296–7

death rates 154, 155, 158, 164, 178

deforestation 126, 131, 136

Delian (Athenian) League 72

demographic transition model 159

dendrochronology 85

dependency ratio 150, 154

desertification 127–9, 137, 138

deserts 116–18, 126–7, 137

de Soto, Hernando 89

developing countries 131, 158, 164, 173, 177, 178
    challenges facing 257–9
    characteristics 251–4
    and economic growth/ development 247–50
    and living standards 245–63
    and trade 228, 240

disease 82, 84, 87, 88–90, 95
    smallpox 88, 89, 90, 94
    see also public health issues

Dreyfus Affair 6

Dubai 287–8, 290–1

Duflo, Esther 241

Durkheim, Émile 5, 6, 16

earthquakes 83

economic growth 239, 246–50

economic integration 236–7

economics
    empires and 37–9, 209, 213, 260–2
    governments and economy 87
    markets and economy 208–11

education 251, 261

Egan Wheel 170–1

Egyptian–Hittite (Eternal) Treaty 72

empires 27–41, 48–76, 82–107
    aftermath of fall of 106
    central authority 30–1
    characteristics of 28–31
    climate in 40–1
    communication systems 61–3
    defence of 70–6
    definition of 29
    economics in 37–9, 209, 213, 260–2
    environment and fall of 83–90
    external factors for fall of 101–5
    food storage 60–1
    global interactions 64–9
    government and bureaucracy 48–51
    imperial systems, breakdown of 98–100
    infrastructure 56–8, 59
    innovation and technology in development of 34–6
    internal factors for fall of 91–100
    law and law enforcement 52–4
    military in development of 32–3
    and peace 107
    reasons for fall of 82

employment 239

equality 8, 10–14

equity 8

essay writing 44, 51

Eternal (Egyptian–Hittite) Treaty 72

eutrophication 132, 140

exam question answer techniques 308–9

externalities 200–3, 249

factors of production 190

Fatimid Caliphate 96, 97

fertility rates 155–6

feudalism 7, 190

First World War 274, 280

fishing industry 134, 141, 202

forced migration 151–3

foreign markets 210

Fortress of Mirgissa 73–4

4.2 Kiloyear Event 87

fracking (hydraulic fracturing) 198, 199, 268

fractional distillation 270

free trade areas (FTAs) 232

Friedman, Milton 14

Genghis Khan 30, 32, 56, 99

German expansionism 279–81

globalization 18, 142, 221–2

global warming 130–1, 174

glocalization 16–17

Goodall, Jane 116

governments 48–51
    and economy 209, 213
    and intervention in markets 204–6, 260–2

Grand Canal, China 60

grasslands 118–19, 129–30, 138

Great Depression 214–15, 274

Great Wall of China 76

gunpowder 66, 102

ul Haq, Mahbub 253

Hayek, Friedrich von 213

Hittite empire 35, 72, 101

HIV/AIDS 257

Hongwu, Emperor of China 49, 94

Human Development Index (HDI) 252–4

hyper-globalism 222

imperialism 29

Inca empire 57, 61, 94, 103

income inequality 247–8

incomes 14, 246–8, 251
    circular flow of 208–9, 210

independence movements 96–7

Indus Valley civilization 87

inequality 178

infant mortality rates 154, 155, 158, 178, 251

inflation 239

information assessment 307

infrastructure 262

canals   59–60
dams   59–60, 132–3
reservoirs   132–3
roads and bridges   56–8

internal displacement   151–3

international migration   150

investigation framing   298–9

Iraq war   284

Islamic Caliphate   40, 92

Islamic State (IS)   152

Japan   164
expansionism   271–8
Tripartite Pact   276

Justinian Law Code (*Corpus Juris Civilis*)   54

Keynes, John Maynard   13, 214–15

Kublai Khan   41, 65, 94, 99, 100, 104

languages   65

legal systems   15, 52–4

Lerner, Jaime   181, 182

life expectancy   154, 155, 251

Lincoln/Douglas debate format   43

living standards   245–62
challenges facing developing countries   257–9
characteristics of developing countries   251–4
economic growth and development and   247–50

government intervention in markets and   260–2
international development goals   255–6

Malthus, Thomas   157

Mamluk Sultanate   61–2, 105

Manchurian crisis   274–5, 277

Mandate of Heaven   95

market economies   191

markets   190–216
changes in   194
economy and   208–11
externalities   200–3
government intervention   204–6, 260–2
laws and regulations   206
market systems   190–1
supply and demand   192–9

Marx, Karl   7–8, 190–1

Masdar City, Abu Dhabi   179–80

Maslow's hierarchy of needs   4

maternal mortality rates   251

mechanical solidarity   5

Medes–Babylon Alliance   71

megacities   163–5, 173

microfinance   241

Middle Kingdom Egypt   59

migrant workers   291

military
defence constructions   73–4
in development of empires   32–3
naval arms race   270–1
standing armies   70–1
technology   32, 36, 66, 102–3, 104

Millennium Development Goals (MDGs)   255

Ming revolt   94–5

minimum wages   206

Mises, Ludwig von   213

monetary unions   234–5

money, see currency

Mongke Khan   65, 99

Mongol empire   28, 29, 30, 32–3, 40–1, 62–3, 65–8, 104
imperial systems, breakdown of   99–100
military   70–1
Pax Mongolica   71, 107

Mongol law code (*Yassa*)   56

moral density   5

Moyo, Dambisa   258

Narmer Palette   27

natural disasters   83–6

natural environments   111–41
characteristics   114–25
human impact on   126–35
location   112–13
sustainability   136–41

natural increase   154, 155, 158

Nazi–Soviet Non-aggression Pact   279

Neo-Assyrian empire   49, 71

New Kingdom Egypt   28, 29, 30–1, 36, 72, 74

New World   102–3

Nigeria   289–90

oil 198, 266–71
 alternatives to 292
 extraction of 268, 287–8
 producers 266–7
 reliance on 269–84
 sustainability of resource-extraction industries 288–91
 volatility of prices 285–6

Old Kingdom Egypt 87

Operation Barbarossa 279–80

organic solidarity 5

Ottoman empire 51, 75, 105

Parthian empire 92

Pax Mongolica (Mongol Peace) 71, 107

Perez, Carlota 11

Petra, Jordan 227

Plague of Justinian 40

poaching 129

pollution 131, 140, 177, 289

Pompeii 86

population changes
 forced migration 151–3
 internal displacement 151–3
 management of 162
 measurement of 154–61
 megacities 163–5

population density 5, 147, 148–9, 267

population growth 127, 128, 146–65
 in different locations 146–7
 variation within countries 148–50

population pyramids 160–1

poverty cycle 246, 248

preferential trade agreements 232

price ceilings 205

price elasticity of demand (PED) 285

price elasticity of supply (PES) 286

price floors 206

price mechanism 192, 194

protectionism 220, 228–9, 231

public goods 262

public health issues 88, 158, 165, 251, 257, 259, 261: *see also* disease

radiocarbon dating 85

rainforests 114–16, 126, 136–7

Ramses the Great 34, 72

Raworth, Kate 208

rebellions 82, 88, 91, 94–5

recessions 212

recycling 182

Red Turban Rebellion 95

refugees 151, 152

religion 15, 65

replacement level fertility 156

research development 300–2

resources 189–91
 allocation of 190–1
 exploitation as development 287–8
 sustainability of exploitation 265–92
 unsustainable use of 249–50

Ricardo, David 223

Roman empire 28, 29, 30, 31, 37–9, 49, 56, 58, 60, 64–5, 70
 imperial systems, breakdown of 98
 smallpox outbreak 88

Roman law 53–4

Rosling, Hans 154

rural-to-urban migration 148, 164, 173, 251

Russo-Japanese war 272–3

Sahajwalla, Veena 184

Saladin (Salah-ad-Din) 97

Sasanian empire 84, 92

sceptical internationalism 222

Second World War 276, 279–81

Sen, Amartya 253

Silk Road 56, 58, 66, 67–8, 76, 105, 227

slavery 6–7, 190

Smith, Adam 7, 191, 194, 223

social groups 4–24
 behaviour 15–17
 equality 8, 10–14
 reasons for 4
 social media and 18–19
 structure of 5–7
 study of 22–4
 and sustainability 20–1

social media 18–19

subject methodology 303–6

subsidies 204–5

Suez crisis 282–3

superpowers 54, 107

supply and demand 192–5,

197–9, 224
  AS/AD model   210–11, 212, 213
  currency   238–9
supra-national organizations   54
sustainability
  natural environments   136–41
  of resource-extraction industries   288–91
  social groups and   20–1
sustainable development   170–84
  cities as systems   174–5
  innovation and sustainability   183–5
  sustainable cities   179–82
  urban problems   176–8
Sustainable Development Goals (SDGs)   137, 138, 172–3, 177, 256
Syria   152–3

tariffs   230
taxes   10, 14, 48–9, 95, 204
technology   66–7, 252
  in economics and development   11
  empires   34–6, 101–3
  environmental adaptation of cities   181–2
  and isolation   164
  military technology   32, 36, 66, 102–3, 104
  purpose-built eco-cities   179–80
Teotihuacan empire   84
Three Gorges Dam, China   133
total fertility rate (TFR)   156, 158
tourism   129–30, 135
trade   67, 69, 220–41
  currency   239
  economic weakness   104–5

  geographical barriers   259
  globalization   221–2
  impact of   225–6
  importance of   227
  reasons for trading   223–6
  spice trade   105
trade agreements   232–7
trade balance   239
trade restrictions   220, 228–31
Trans-Alaska Pipeline   130
tsunamis   83
tundra   120–1, 130–1, 138
Twelve Tables   53–4

Uber   183–4
Umayyad Caliphate   28, 29, 30, 32, 40, 75, 83, 91
United Arab Emirates (UAE)   180, 287–8, 291
urban congestion   176, 177
Ur-Nammu law code   52
USA   150, 236–7

Venice, Republic of   29, 51, 105
volcanic eruptions   83–4, 86
voluntary migration   148, 150

Waze   183
welfare systems   262
wetlands   123–4, 132

Xi Xia   104

Yam system   62–3
Yellow Turban Rebellion   88, 91